GENERATIONS APART

GENERATIONS APART: Adult Hostility to Youth

by
Leon Shaskolsky Sheleff

McGraw-Hill Book Company

New York   St. Louis   San Francisco   Sydney
Paris   Hamburg   Auckland   Bogotá   São Paulo
London   New Delhi   Mexico   Tokyo   Johannesburg
Panama   Singapore   Montreal   Madrid

Library of Congress Cataloging in Publication Data

Sheleff, Leon Shaskolsky.
  Generations apart.

  Includes index.
  1. Children and adults.   2.   Conflict of generations—Social aspects.   3.   Hostility (Psychology)
4. Children's rights.   5.   Youth.   I. Title.
HQ772.5.S53   305.2'3   80-21766

ISBN 0-07-056540-6

Permission was granted by the following for use of materials:

from *The Interpretation of Dreams* by Sigmund Freud, translated and edited by James Strachey. Published in the U.S.A. by Basic Books, Inc., by arrangement with The Hogarth Press and George Allen & Unwin, Ltd., London, from *Studies in Hysteria*, by Josef Breuer and Sigmund Freud, translated from the German and edited by James Strachey, published in the U.S.A. by Basic Books, Inc., by arrangement with The Hogarth Press, Ltd., London, from *The Standard Edition of the Complete Psychological Works of Sigmund Freud* translated and edited by James Strachey. By permission of Sigmund Freud Copyrights Ltd., The Institute of Psycho-Analysis, and The Hogarth Press Ltd. from *Generative Man: Psychoanalytic Perspectives*, by Don S. Browning. Copyright © MCMLXXIII The Westminster Press. Used by permission, from *Kafka Versus Kafka*, by Michel Carrouges, English translation. Reprinted by permission of The University of Alabama Press, © 1968, pp. 10, 13, 17, 24, 28, 32. from *Dostoevsky. His Life and Work*, by Konstantin Mochulsky, translated by Michael A. Minihan (copyright © 1967 by Princeton University Press): excerpts from pp. 565-646. Reprinted by permission of Princeton University Press. from *Sophocles: The Oedipus Cycle*, translated by Dudley Fitts and Robert Fitzgerald, © 1949. By permission of Harcourt Brace Jovanovich, Inc. from Bruce Mazlish: *The Revolutionary Ascetic: Evolution of a Political Type*, © 1976, by permission of Basic Books, Inc, from Lewis S. Feuer, *The Conflict of Generations: The Character and Significance of Student Movements*, © 1969, by permission of Basic Books, Inc, from Norman O. Brown, *Life Against Death*, copyright © 1959 by Wesleyan University, by permission of Wesleyan University Press, from Thomas J. Cottle, *Time's Children: Impressions of Youth*, published by Little, Brown and Company © 1967, by permission of the author, from Jean Renvoize, *Children in Danger*, published by Routledge & Kegan Paul, © 1974, by permission of Routledge & Kegan Paul, from Ian D. Suttie, *The Origins of Love and Hate*, published by Kegan Paul, Trench, Trubner and Company, © 1935, by permission of the publisher, from Richard H. Solomon, *Mao's Revolution and the Chinese Political Culture*, © 1971, published by the University of California Press, Berkeley, by permission of the University of California Press, from Leon Sheleff, "Beyond the Oedipus Complex," in *Theory and Society*, Vol. 3, 1976, pp. 1–44, published by Elsevier Scientific Co., © 1976, from William A. Madden, *Matthew Arnold: A Study of the Aesthetic Temperament in Victorian England*, © 1967, by permission of Indiana University Press, from Lewis S. Feuer, *Ideology and the Ideologists*, © 1975, by permission of Harper Torchbooks, Harper & Row.

1234567890   DODO   8987654321

The editors for this book were Robert A. Rosenbaum and Carolyn Nagy, the designer was Mark E. Safran, and the production supervisor was Teresa F. Leaden. It was set in Garamond by The Heffernan Press Inc.

Printed and bound by R. R. Donnelley & Sons Company.

For my three generations:
Ruby, of blessed memory, and Jane
Rinah
Kinor and Ariel

CONTENTS

PREFACE

Many people have helped me on this long journey from the inkling of an idea a decade ago, through the gradual formulation of the theoretical framework, to the finishing touches of the final version of this book. To many I owe thanks—for helpful criticism and for needed encouragement, for suggestions of avenues to be explored and for warnings of dead-end paths to be avoided, for listening as I tentatively tried out parts of my thesis, and for telling me of their own experiences that served to bolster my own intuitions.

I shall name as many of these as I can, but one of those to whom I am indebted must remain anonymous—for I do not know her name. She was a young American student at a family party to which I, an outsider, had been invited. It was at one of those periods of peak tension in the Vietnam War, and inevitably the discussion veered in that direction. She was opposed to the war, and was drawn into an argument about it with several of her uncles and aunts. She presented her ideas with clarity and knowledge, with tolerance and respect—only to be met by an unbridled attack, the essence of which was that she was too young to know and understand, and that it was her duty to concentrate on her studies at the university and not to waste her parents' money on extraneous matters beyond her ken. I took no part in that debate, but was impressed with the manner in which the student conducted herself and presented her case. I realized also that something deeper underlay that debate—not just the facts about the particular issue of the war, but the right of young people to express themselves and to evoke respect for their views from those older than they.

Two other events occurred about the same time that acted as catalytic agents for the ideas that formed into the thesis of this book. One was the tragic incident at Kent State University, when four students were shot to death by the Ohio National Guard during demonstrations on the campus against the Vietnam War. I was lecturing at that time at the University of Dayton, also in Ohio. In discussing the incident with students, I was informed by several of them that there had been instances of parents reacting to the tragedy by saying that the students had got what they were asking for, and that if their own children had been involved in the demonstrations, they, too, would have deserved whatever would have happened to them. The information was shocking and forced me to do some hard thinking about generational conflict. Similar facts were given wider publicity when James Michener published his book on the incident, based on extensive interviews with people in Kent, which documented how wide-spread such feelings of hostility were in the town where the tragedy had occurred.

The third event was a lecture by a social science professor who explained that student protest was merely an expression of oedipal problems by students who, having failed to resolve the complex at the appropriate age at home, were now taking out their frustrations on father-figures, represented by presidents of universities and even the President of the United States. I do not remember who the lecturer was, since I did not pay much attention to his ideas at the time. It was only some time later that, in reading a book of Asian poetry, I came across the Persian myth of Sohrab and Rustum, recalling the poem of that same name by the British poet, Matthew Arnold, which I had read as a schoolboy. The climax of this epic poem is when the father, Rustum, unwittingly kills his son in a duel. I realized that here was a story that was a counterpoint to the Oedipus story, and I sensed that a larger truth lay embedded in this tragic ending to the poem.

So began my quest to search out and understand the disturbing phenomenon of parental and adult hostility toward the young. At the beginning of the quest I had the good fortune to be able to test my ideas with colleagues and friends who, in general, were supportive of the idea and offered suggestions of their own as to how my theme could be expanded. Thank you, Francine Landau, Robert and Sheila Conard, Harriet Davidorf-Greenberg, Gideon Levitas, Nurit Schechter, Ruth Rasnic, Bea Goslin and Elaine and John Frank.

Of particular importance were several early discussions with Dr. Jack Weinberg, former president of the American Psychiatric Association, who, though of a different generation, professional background and theoretical persuasion, showed a rare openness in listening to my thesis and assuring me that there was validity in what I was trying to do. I appreciated the opportunity of several talks with my father-in-law, the late Rabbi Philip Lipis, who helped particularly with several insights into aspects of generational conflict in religious themes. A long discussion with my colleague and friend, the late Yaakov Kelner, was of great help.

The manuscript was read at an advanced stage by Simon Dinitz and Gilbert Geis, two wonderful colleagues who still believe that a university should be a community of scholars and know how to help make it so. Their critical questions helped me clarify many of the issues. On several occasions, in long talks, I have received intellectual stimulation and moral support from Rifka and Yehuda Hanegbi, and Elaine and Eliezer Krumbein.

Peter Scharf showed a professional interest in the book at a key stage and has earned my boundless appreciation for his help. Others who have taken the time and effort to read parts of the manuscript that dealt particularly with their own area of expertise were Yona Teichman, Judith Hill, Eva

Simmons, Bernard Susser, Leonard Atkins, Henry Near, Vivien Marcow, Daniel Pekarsky, Yonatan Shapiro and Moshe Shokeid. I am deeply appreciative of their comments. In some cases I have accepted their criticisms and made changes; in other cases I have tried only to tighten my arguments so as to refute their criticisms. I leave each to judge in which category he or she belongs.

The theme of this book was originally presented in an article published in *Theory and Society*. My thanks to the editor, Alvin Gouldner, for the prompt and positive response to my work, and to the publishers for their permission to incorporate passages from that article in the book. The ideas were also presented orally on two occasions: at a round table discussion at the annual meeting of the American Sociological Association in San Francisco in 1975, and at a departmental seminar of the Sociology department at Tel Aviv University. My thanks to colleagues who responded positively on these occasions, in particular Yochanan Peres and Shlomo Deshen, as also to students who have discussed some of these ideas in seminars and classes in the past few years. In this category, particular mention to Dan Sharon, who utilized the theoretical framework in his master's thesis, and has tried out some of the ideas in therapeutic work. Both he and I have been given great assistance by Israel Charny, who has, in this and in some other areas, been independently working along parallel lines. Other colleagues and friends who have discussed the ideas on numerous occasions are Meir Teichman, David Shichor and Menachem Amir.

On one occasion I corresponded with Dr. Arnoldo Rascovsky of Argentina who is working on similar themes, and he was gracious in sending me some of his own material. Thanks for help in translations of the Spanish parts to my cousins, Nili Shelef and Michael Rogozen.

Doreen Schein was around at a crucial time with the kind of help that an author needs from a close friend. Thanks for help along the way also to Margaret Zusky, Caroline Macaulay, Ed Vernoff, Mike Markowitz and Lesley Hazelton.

This book has gone through several versions, and a number of typists have worked on it. Particular thanks to Jane Binet, Rachel Sandler, Joan Gordon and Lillian White, not just for their efficient work but for their encouraging response to what they were typing.

The basic idea for this book was formulated before my children were born. I recall wondering then how I personally would match up to the test of parenthood. I hope that Ariel and Kinor, as they grow older, will read this book with understanding and approval; and will agree that the ideas are important enough to justify the soccer games postponed and the family outings missed.

My wife, Rinah, has been a constant source of encouragement and help. It was she who first heard some of my initial musings on the subject and who prodded me into developing them into a full-scale study; then she critically reviewed earlier drafts and helped edit the later versions. It is customary for authors to absolve all those whom they acknowledge from any blame for any errors in the finished product. I observe this ritual and accordingly release from responsibility all the above-mentioned—with one exception. If there are any errors or faults, Rinah shares a little of the blame, for her criticism all along has been so perceptive that I have come to respect her judgment both in suggestions for changes that should be made, and in approval that the manuscript was finally ready. By the same token, for whatever merits the book has, she is entitled to some of the credit as well.

LEON SHELEFF

GENERATIONS APART

PART ONE
OEDIPUS AT THE CROSSROADS

CHAPTER ONE
WHO SPEAKS FOR THE YOUNG?

There are two central themes to this book, neither of them particularly pleasant. The first—and the main—theme deals with parental and adult hostility toward the young: the hostility of a dominant group in society to one of its most vulnerable groups, the hostility of those entrusted with the care of infants, children, and youth toward the purported beneficiaries of that care.

In the past two decades there has been an increased awareness of the evidence of some aspects of this hostility, ranging from infanticide in earlier times to widespread child abuse today. Too often it is assumed that these more extreme acts of the older generation against the younger are primarily the consequence of individual weaknesses of those directly responsible or of a defective cultural milieu. In contrast, I shall argue that they are often symptomatic of a hostility that runs far deeper and is generally given more subtle, and sometimes more insidious, expression and is itself deeply embedded in the essential nature of generational differentiation.

The secondary theme is a critical analysis of the work and the influence of one of the major thinkers of the modern era, Sigmund Freud, in which one of his key concepts, the Oedipus complex, is challenged insofar as it touches on generational conflict. My concern with Freud has posed some problems in the writing of this book. For some, Freud's work carries an aura of impregnability, having aspects of both the sanctity of an article of faith and the authority of scientific research. For others, his work is dismissed as of little value, having been either rejected outright or subsequently replaced by later thinkers.

My approach to Freud will probably satisfy neither of these groups. On the one hand, it acknowledges the tremendous impact that Freud has had on the modern world while, on the other hand, it suggests that a major aspect of Freud's work has gained acceptance partly because it answers to the biases that many adults have against the young.

The book has not been written in a social vacuum. Some of the theoretical ideas were first tentatively formulated in the 1960s as generational conflict peaked, and some of the empirical data have come from the wide-ranging research carried out in the 1970s into harmful practices against the young. In the sixties generational tensions found much of their expression in violent clashes on university campuses, while in the seventies the focus of attention has been on problems within the home, such as child abuse. In both decades there has also been strong criticism of social institutions, such as juvenile courts and schools, ostensibly intended to serve the special needs of the young. There has also been a growing awareness of the need to protect the rights of the young in various areas of social policy, ranging from the rights of children in divorce proceedings to their rights of access to decent housing and medical facilities.

Much of this activity provides indications of an incipient movement toward children's rights and youth liberation, echoing other social movements concerning deprived or minority groups. But whatever advances have been recorded, this movement of the young has remained, for the most part, inchoate; in fact there seems to be less awareness of youth age-groups nowadays than there was in the 1960s. The youth movement seems to have become almost moribund, compared to the ongoing and expanding operations of other social groups that had their inception at the same time, such as women, ethnic minorities, and several deviant groups.

It is interesting to note, with the hindsight of only a decade, some of the apocalyptic pronouncements made in the late 1960s, according to which there had never before been a generation so imbued with a spirit of change and so destined to bring about a deep-seated transformation in society. The Age of Aquarius had dawned; the millennium was upon us.

Characteristic of much of this writing was a studious avoidance of historical precedents, which in itself was part of the overall ethos stressing the uniqueness of what was then transpiring. This was unfortunate, since the generation of the sixties was by no means unique. Throughout human history, generational conflict has waxed and waned. Militant movements of the young have appeared, seeking a larger share in political power or an acceleration of social change; new religions and new nations have developed out of the creativity of talented young people. Had the youth generation of the sixties, and those adults who identified with them, not shown such a disdain for the past, they might have noted and pondered the many mythical accounts of young gods, as well as the long-haired, disheveled youth of ancient Rome demonstrating against established institutions; the Narodniks in nineteenth-century Russia, or the Wandervögel in twentieth-century Germany, whom they so closely resembled in attitude and actions; and the young in other periods of history who were once in the forefront of social change.[1]

Had the youth of the 1960s been prepared to confront the past instead of merely castigating the present, they might have been more humbly appreciative not just of the excitement of change but also of the power of inertia, not just of the unique aspects of their own generation but also of the ongoing aspects of generational conflict in all societies and at all times. As it is, the sweeping ideas contained in books such as *The Greening of America*[2] have faded long before the pages themselves have yellowed.

I stress the 1960s because the genesis of this book was in that period. I found myself ambivalently watching the clash of generations as it was played out, sometimes vocally, sometimes violently, on campuses and streets in many parts of the world. Although sympathetic to many of the issues espoused by the young—educational reform, peace, civil and minority rights, ecology—I felt that the indifference with which the youth contemplated historical precedents bespoke a fundamental weakness, not just in the movement itself, but in the whole manner in which social reality was perceived.

It is, of course, true that certain aspects of modern society have created experiences never before encountered: instant mass involvement through the media, forays into space, the destructive power of nuclear weapons, the fragility of our environment, readily available means of population control.

Yet, however significant these factors have been in shaping the nature of the modern world, they do not in themselves cause generational conflict. They may influence the form it takes and the intensity with which it is expressed, but this has been true in all times. Specific cultural variables always determine the shape of generational conflict. But the underlying causes go far deeper. They are a consequence of factors closely bound up with the very nature of generational differentation. They lie in the different perceptions that different generations simultaneously inhabiting the earth bring to bear on social reality: the old in terms of their accumulated personal experiences of the past, the young in terms of their hopes and plans for the future.

Generational conflict is a structural fact, affected by cultural factors only in its forms. It is an eternal theme of human history; its manifestations have plagued human relations in all periods. Any attempt to understand the nature of generational contacts and conflicts, in the society and in the family, must probe beyond the passing variables and seek out its underlying base. Much of it revolves around the inevitability of social change, which the young tend to accept eagerly because of its enticing promises of new vistas, and which the old tend to distrust because it marks the end of the world they have known and opens the prospect of a future in which they cannot fully share. While most pronounced—and therefore most clearly perceived—in times of rapid social change, such conflict also occurs in static societies and in tranquil periods.[3]

My original purpose in writing this book was to suggest that we would do well to look beyond the specific cultural, social, and political factors that spawned the generational clashes of the 1960s or, for that matter, those of any other time, and that we should seek the underlying structural factors. As the work developed, as the empirical data accumulated and as the ideas began to crystallize, it became apparent that a wealth of information bearing on my theme already existed in loose form but that little effort had been made to integrate it into a coherent theoretical framework. There seemed often to be a reluctance to give due recognition to the evidence of adult hostility; in many cases, the hostility of parents and adults was blamed on the young, who were seen to have provoked a reactive force.

There emerged also an additional fact, to which I attach major importance and which has become an additional theme of this book. In modern times, many explanations of generational conflict are subsumed within the theoretical perspective of Sigmund Freud's work on the Oedipus complex. With its twin themes of children's incestuous feelings toward the parent of the opposite sex, and consequent parricidal tendencies toward the parent of the same sex for frustrating the consummation of that desire, a powerful theory is available by means of which a wide range of phenomena can be described in terms of a negative innate drive said to be possessed by all children. It seemed to me that the willingness to employ this theory went beyond the validity that it might have or the fit that the data had with the theory. There appeared to be particular eagerness to embrace the idea of the evil intentions of the young.

Not only Freudians were utilizing this theoretical perspective; critics of Freud, too, tended to leave the parricidal aspect untouched by their strictures. Alternatively, where criticisms were made of the parricidal idea, an alternative would be sought, most often in the form of sibling rivalry. Rarely would the alternative theme of parental and adult hostility be suggested, even when the data and the criticism seemed to lead in that direction. Finally, on the few occasions where the work actually suggested the possibility of parental and adult hostility, the idea had almost no impact. In several works, going back to the 1930s, writers had even suggested the possibility of a Laius complex (based on the hostility of Oedipus's father toward him), but these writers had a minimal impact on the scientific community and the public and seemed themselves to be unaware of each other's work.[4]

Why is all this so? It seems to me that it is the biases of the older generation that underlie these selective interpretations. It is my contention that analysis of generational conflict cannot be treated in a purely neutral and objective manner. Perhaps more than any other social variable, generational contacts are too closely bound up with our own personal histories. There are memories of distant childhood, of physical, intellectual, and sexual development in puberty and adolescence, of the struggle to break free of parental controls and restraints in order to attain independence, of the transition to adulthood and then parenthood. Parenting itself involves encountering these earlier processes by watching one's children move through the same stages. Then come the last stages of life and the confrontation with death.

Alone of all the social categories, and in sharp contrast to race, class, ethnicity, religion, and sex, a person, in the course of a normal lifetime, will belong to all the different age groups from infancy through childhood, adolescence, youth, and adulthood to old age. At first glance, this might seem likely to produce greater understanding across the age barriers, since the older generation in particular might be expected to empathize with the younger, having itself experienced many of the same problems. Since we have all been young, we might presume that we are conversant with the feelings, sentiments, needs, and aspirations of the young. We conveniently forget, however, that our memories of infancy, childhood, adolescence, and youth become easily blurred and selective; that the memories are probably more operative, as Freud so clearly showed, at the unconscious, not the conscious, level; and that identification with succeeding generations is not inherent in the nature of things but requires a positive effort on the part of the older generation. Moreover, the very fact of the progression from one age category to another means that, in the normal course of events, power must ultimately be handed over to the younger generation, and it is this inevitability that sometimes gives an extra intensity to generational struggles.

Age, in fact, has a further unique quality that tends to undermine the possibility of a balanced and objective perspective. Of all social conflicts, it alone involves a clash between parties, one of whom is handicapped in putting its own case at an intellectually relevant level. This is absolutely the case for infants and partially so in the case of children, adolescents and youth. Furthermore, while youth is the period when intellectual capacities and social resources may enable a confrontation on equal terms with the adults, the youths themselves are in the process of moving into adulthood, and in doing this they often relinquish their attachment to the interests of the younger generation. Leaders of youth groups require constant replacement, and succeeding cohorts are not always capable of maintaining the impetus of those who preceded them. This, more than any other factor, may be the reason why in the Western world, for instance, the fledgling youth movement of the 1960s has almost disappeared, while the modern women's movement, which had its inception at the same time, has increased its strength.

Throughout history, it is adults who have recorded the facts, expressed their feelings, and interpreted events. The young are generally mute. As if all this were not enough modern society has superimposed on this historical phenomenon a further fact whose significance is immeasurable but has been all but ignored: the existence of a scientific theory, the Oedipus complex, which, whatever validity it might have, provides a basis for interpreting only one aspect of generational conflict—the parricidal hostilities of the young. There is no similar alternative theoretical perspective regarding filicidal tendencies of parents toward their children and infanticidal tendencies of adults toward the young.

Thus, while generational hostility is in reality bidirectional, too often it is presented as flowing only from the young to the old, buttressed by the pervasive influence of the oedipal perspective. From case studies in psychoanalysis to theories of crime, from approaches to child-raising to explanations of youth revolt, from analyses of literature to anthropological studies of myths and legends, from academic research to everyday thinking, the Oedipus theme has become a part of social reality, of the way the world is perceived. Freud's writings provide a scientific explanation by a leading modern figure for understanding problems such as tension within the family, the stresses of adolescence, and the political struggles of youth. It becomes assumed that the troublesome young boy is caught up in the guilt of his love for the woman who bore, nursed, and reared him and of his hatred for the father who rivals him for that love. Similarly, the revolt of youth against an existing status quo is seen as a result of an earlier collective inability to resolve the oedipal dilemma at the critical age of their lives, between the ages of four and six. The tragedy of an ancient Greek myth has become part of today's social reality. As W. I. Thomas wrote, "If men define situations as real, they are real in their consequences."[5] Whatever the role of the Oedipus complex in the *unconscious,* there can be little doubt as to its significance in the *consciousness* of the modern world.

While myths undoubtedly help us to understand social reality, the overriding popularity of any one myth may lead to a biased picture of reality. This, it seems to me, is what has happened with the Oedipus myth.

Mythology is an intricate and complex mosaic of diverse and often conflicting stories. No one myth can give expression to any overriding impulse, instinctive in all people, common to all societies. Myths are useful for establishing a framework for understanding and for pointing to the possibility of hidden or unnoticed impulses. But no one myth can definitively determine the key to human emotions nor provide the basis for understanding even a limited aspect of social life, such as parent-child relations.

Here is one of the major paradoxes of Freud's work. He was one of the first modern thinkers to be aware of how important myths are in expressing hidden aspects and subtle nuances of social life. The more recent work of anthropologists and folklorists in probing the meanings of myths and legends has brought ample retrospective justification for the validity of Freud's insight that myths do affect our perceptions of social reality.[6] Myths may be seen as the societal equivalent of the unconscious in the individual, as the accumulation of historical memories, as the expression of forbidden or unpopular ideas. Unfortunately, the myth that Freud emphasized more than any other, that of Oedipus, seems to have been misinterpreted by him, to have been given a status beyond its intrinsic validity, and to have blocked out the possibility of recognizing and acknowledging alternative and contrasting themes in other myths.

Thus, in challenging the Oedipus complex it is necessary to look at the Oedipus myth; and in trying to understand the complexities of generational contacts it may be useful to examine the meaning of other myths.

For what has often been ignored is the fact that generational conflict is a two-way process: filial hostility is matched by parental hostility, parricide by instances of infanticide. In fact, both in mythical accounts and in the annals of human history, it is quite possible that hostility, homicidal impulses, and incestuous tendencies on the part of the older generation are the more prevalent. Adults certainly have both the opportunity and the physical power to express their hostility.

A fundamental issue arises: what are the reasons for the acceptance of the Oedipus complex as a dominant theme, and the embellishments of it as an explanation for a wide range of social phenomena? Whatever criticisms may have been advanced against the theory and whatever questioning of Freud's ideas there has been over the years, the incontrovertible fact remains that both the Oedipus story and the complex still retain their influence and popularity. Of course, Freud claimed that this was so because they spoke to emotions lurking deep in all of us. Can it not be, however, that the popularity stems from the fact that *the theme accords with what adults wish to hear: namely, that it is the evil inherent in the psychic makeup of the young that is primarily responsible for generational conflict?*

The problem, then, goes far beyond the mere investigation of empirical data and the comparing of instances of child/youth hostility toward their elders with adult/parent hostility toward the young. What is crucial for any analysis of generational conflict is not the facts alone but the manner in which they are interpreted. Indeed, the possibility of even having a theory of adult/parent hostility accepted may be predicated on first examining the strong tendency to resist and reject such an approach and to prefer theories that center on child/youth hostility.

Sociologists, particularly those writing from the perspective of the sociology of knowledge, have long challenged the possibility of value-free research and theories in the social sciences and have argued that researchers and writers are constrained by such personal and social variables as class, race, ethnicity, sex, or religion. But even those who have argued that critical analyses of work in social sciences should not spare an investigation of the personal and social factors influencing the researcher have rarely felt the need to apply such rules to studies in the field of generational conflict. Although one of the main contributors to the sociology of knowledge, Karl

Mannheim, suggested that age differentiation was similar to class in many respects and that work on age structure was clearly amenable to the principles of the sociology of knowledge,[7] only a few attempts have been made to utilize such considerations in analyses of work on generational contacts.

Writing many years later, Howard Becker, in discussing the need for social scientists to "choose sides" when dealing with deviance, drew on the example of age to clarify his point:

> A few sociologists may be sufficiently biased in favor of youth to grant them credibility to their account of how the adult world treats them. But why do we not accuse other sociologists who study youth of being biased in favor of adults? Most research on youth, after all, is clearly designed to find out why youth are so troublesome for adults, rather than asking the equally interesting sociological question: Why do adults make so much trouble for youth?[8]

Becker himself does not pursue this theme, though it touches on a critical issue for all analyses of generational conflict. It is the purpose of this book to try to answer the question why "adults make so much trouble for youth"; to examine the degree, extent, and manner in which the hostility of the older generation toward the young exists as an important factor in social life. I shall try to show that the variable of age is a relevant social factor influencing, consciously or unconsciously, the thought processes of the researcher and the reader, just as is the case for the variables of class, ethnicity, race, sex, or religion. Indeed, the very fact that so many writers who deal with generational conflict do so from the perspective of adulthood and parenthood often gives rise to a bias that is as significant as, and may even transcend, these other social categories and the ideological beliefs linked to them.

One of the goals of the sociology of knowledge is to heighten our consciousness of hidden influences. When age is the variable, this task becomes all the more difficult—and therefore all the more important—because of the many unique aspects of age differentiation.

A sociology of knowledge approach to generational conflict necessitates a direct confrontation with Freudian thinking because of the pervasiveness of the oedipal orientation. It is necessary to show how deeply ingrained and subtly influential the oedipal perspective is. It is necessary to look at Freudian modes of thinking in order to discover the biases—and the errors, misinterpretations, and occasional distortions to which they lead. It is necessary to show why clear evidence of parental/adult hostility is so often disregarded or misunderstood. In many respects, then, this book represents a sociology of knowledge critique of Freudian oedipal modes of thinking. It shows the history of an idea and its influence on society.

In the first part of the book I specifically examine the thinking behind Freud's gradual formulation of the oedipal thesis and show several transparent errors, of fact and of interpretation, in some of his classic case studies, as well as revealing "Freudian slips," which seem to indicate a bias against the young.

In section two I discuss the ways in which Freudian thought has led to selective interpretations of literature, history and politics—interpretations that stem partly from the oedipal theme, partly from the biases of the writers concerned.

Part three deals with the evidence of parental and adult hostility at various historical periods, in modern institutions, in the family, and. in society. Explanations linked mainly to the structural factors of intergenerational contact are advanced. The motif underlying the discussion is a Persian myth that I have chosen to pose as a counterbalance to the Oedipus story. The myth of Rustum and Sohrab, outlined in detail in the next chapter, was selected because, as the tale of a father who unwittingly kills his son, it is the mirror image of the Oedipus myth. Its universality is also seen in the fact that, while an Oriental myth, it has been used as a theme for a well-known epic poem by Matthew Arnold, the nineteenth-century British poet.[9]

If the story of the unwitting killing of a father by a son is the theoretical basis for the Oedipus complex as a description of the hostility of the young to their parents and adults, then the story of the unwitting killing of a son by a father raises the possibility of a Rustum complex as a description of the hostility of the old to the young. I shall adduce evidence attesting to the existence of a Rustum complex as a very real factor in social life.

Finally, in section four, I examine the possibility of coping with parental/adult hostility and of moving toward more harmonious relations between the generations.

In presenting the material in this book, I make no claims for pure, value-free objectivity. I have "chosen sides": I have tried to speak for the young. In doing so, however, I have tried to adhere to the standards of scholarly inquiry—to be thorough in the collection of data, accurate in their presentation, and fair in their interpretation.

I do not deny the existence of the Oedipus complex as such, although its manifestations seem to me more cultural than innate. I question mainly the lavish use that has been made of it and the dominance that it has acquired. I do not deny the fact of child and youth hostility toward parents and adults. I challenge only the one-sidedness of many analyses. I do not deny the many manifestations of parents' love for their children. I ask only that we not allow such positive aspects of parenthood to cause us to lose sight of negative aspects. I do not suggest that parental and adult hostility is inevitable. I do argue that there are many structural factors that make it possible, and even likely.

Much of the evidence of parental and adult hostility is already available. Yet it exists in an amorphous form. Often attempts to describe certain aspects of this hostility treat them in isolation. It is as though the women's issues of rape, lack of political power, job discrimination, and the drudgery of housework were all being dealt with separately without an overall view of what has come to be called the women's movement. It is as though the struggles of oppressed or deprived groups—race, class, religion, nation— were being discussed purely in terms of their specific and isolated problems, without any reference to the overall meaning of race, class, religion, and ethnicity as key variables in social life.

Indeed, as these other minority groups, formerly ignored, deprived, or oppressed, achieve greater status, power, and influence, often backed by explicit legal rules, so the prejudices of many tend to focus increasingly on the young. It is now they who are discriminated against—for instance, in housing and in jobs. It is they who are referred to in derogatory and offensive terms—"dirty," "noisy," "difficult to live with," "irresponsible." It is they who may be left as the final minority, the ultimate deprived group.

As life-styles change, as children become less of an economic necessity and more of an economic burden—not just on the family, but on society as a whole—so it is becoming more fashionable and acceptable to openly verbalize the prejudices and to practice the discrimination.

There is clearly a need to recognize age as a key variable in social life, no less than other, more recognized social variables. There is a need to recognize the existence of the ongoing, well-nigh universal nature of generational conflict. There is a need to recognize the pervasive nature of parent and adult hostility.

For only through honesty in acknowledging these facts of social life, however unpleasant some of them may be, do we have a chance of acquiring the wisdom and determination to cope with them.

References

1.   Details of the historical evidence will be given in chapter 7, "Children of All Ages," and chapter 10, "Faithful to Our Youth." For specific references to the youth of ancient Rome, see A. W. Lintott, *Violence in Republican Rome* (London: Oxford University Press, 1978). On the Wandervögel, see Walter Z. Laqueur, *Young Germany: A History of the German Youth Movement* (New York: Basic Books, 1962).

2.   Charles A. Reich, *The Greening of America* (New York: Random House, 1970).

3.   See, for example, Anne Foner and David Kertzer, "Transitions over the Life-Course: Lessons from Age-Set Societies," *American Sociological Review* 83 (1978): 108.

4.   See Ian D. Suttie, *The Origins of Love and Hate* (London: Kegan Paul, Trench, Trubner, 1935); G. H. Graber, "Der Sohn-Komplex des Vaters," *Der Psychologe* 4

(1952): 250–258; G. J. Dalma, "Nota Sobre el Complejo de Layo," *Presna Med-Argent* 40 (1953): 1806–1809; George Devereux, "Why Oedipus Killed Laius," *International Journal of Psychoanalysis* 34 (1953): 1–10; Erich Wellisch, *Isaac and Oedipus: A Study in Biblical Psychology of the Sacrifice of Isaac—the Akedah* (London: Routledge & Kegan Paul, 1954): 44; Thomas S. Vernon, "The Laius Complex," *The Humanist* 32 (November–December 1972): 27–28. All of these suggestions were apparently made independently of each other. See Note: "More on the Laius Complex," *Journal of Individual Psychology* 29 (1973): 88–91; also, R. Klausen, "Laius Complex and Mother–Child Symbiosis," *Journal of Individual Psychology* 28 (1972): 33–37. All of these writers draw attention to the hostile behavior displayed by Laius, the father, to his son, Oedipus. A more recent use of the term is by Robert Michels, whose explanation, however, is based on "the father's fear of aggression from his son." See his "Student Dissent," *Journal of American Psychoanalytic Association* 19 (1971): 429.

5. W. I. Thomas, *The Child in America* (New York: Knopf, 1928), p. 572.

6. See, for instance, the work of Joseph Campbell, *The Masks of God* (New York: Viking, 1954–1968), 4 vols. See also leading journals such as the *Journal of American Folklore*.

7. For his major work on the sociology of knowledge, see Karl Mannheim, *Ideology and Utopia: An Introduction to the Sociology of Knowledge* (New York: Harcourt, Brace & World, 1936). For his work on generations, see Karl Mannheim, "The Social Problems of Generations" in *Essays on the Sociology of Knowledge* (London: Routledge & Kegan Paul, 1959), and "The Problem of Youth in Modern Society" in *Diagnosis of Our Time: Wartime Essays of a Sociologist* (London: Routledge & Kegan Paul, 1962: first published in 1943). Mannheim's work is discussed in chapter 10.

8. Howard S. Becker, "Whose Side are We On?," *Social Problems* 14 (1967): 239–241.

9. See Kenneth Allott, ed., *The Poems of Matthew Arnold* (London: Longmans, 1965) pp. 302–330.

CHAPTER TWO
THE MYTHS OF
GENERATIONAL
CONFLICT

Few myths have had such a profound effect on people as the Oedipus myth. The drama of Oedipus's inadvertent killing of his father, Laius, and subsequent marriage to his mother, Jocasta, has attracted writers throughout the ages, and several dramatic versions of the myth exist, in addition to the original Greek play by Sophocles.[1]

Sigmund Freud used the Oedipus story to substantiate his contention that children bear incestuous feelings of love for the parent of the opposite sex and, as a consequence of the ensuing rivalry for that parent's love, develop feelings of hostility toward the parent of the same sex, a hostility that reaches its peak expression in parricidal impulses toward that parent.

The popularity of the Oedipus myth and its ability to excite people far removed in time and place from the events recounted is, according to Freud, a result of each individual's capacity to relate personally to the message. Spectators watching Sophocles's play identify with the drama of the royal personages because all, in their own lives, have known love for the parent of the opposite sex and hatred for the rival parent of the same sex.

Freud incorporated references to the Oedipus myth in many of his major writings. Even where no specific reference is made to the Oedipus complex, its underlying premises are tacitly embraced. In his classic work, *The Interpretation of Dreams,* Freud tried to set out publicly, for the first time, the reasoning behind his fascination with the theme and the importance he attached to it, even though he did not, as yet, specifically use the concept of an Oedipus complex:

> If *Oedipus Rex* moves a modern audience no less than it did the contemporary Greek one, the explanation can only be that its effect does not lie in the contrast between destiny and human will, but is to be looked for in the particular nature of the material on which the contrast is exemplified. There must be something which makes a voice within us ready to recognize the compelling force of destiny in the Oedipus fate of all of us. A factor of this kind is involved in the story of King Oedipus. His destiny moves us only because it might have been ours—because the oracle laid the same curse upon

15

us before our birth as upon him. It is the fate of all of us, perhaps, to direct our
first sexual impulse towards our mother and our first hatred and our first
murderous wish against our father. . . . While the poet, as he unravels the past,
brings to light the guilt of Oedipus, he is at the same time compelling us to
recognize our own inner minds, in which these same impulses, though suppressed, are still to be found.[2]

Freud insisted that any theme as universal in legend and literature as
parricide must reflect a deep human emotion: "It can scarcely be owing to
chance that three of the masterpieces of the literature of all time—the
Oedipus Rex of Sophocles, Shakespeare's *Hamlet,* and Dostoevsky's *The
Brothers Karamozov*—should all deal with the same subject, parricide. In all
three, moreover, the motive for the deed, sexual rivalry for a woman, is laid
bare."[3]

In subsequent years, many of Freud's followers attempted to show that
the twin themes of incestuous feelings for the mother and parricidal impulses for the father could be discerned in many works of literature, even
though the ideas were not so apparent as in *Oedipus Rex.* In one of the most
extreme instances, Ernest Jones, Freud's biographer, devoted a full study to
the attempt to substantiate Freud's casual comment that *Hamlet* was based
on the same impulses of incest and parricide as *Oedipus Rex.*[4] The major
theme of the play—Hamlet's desire to avenge the death of his father the
king—is presented by Jones as being basically a repression of his actual
desires:

. . . the true meaning of the story is concealed by the identical mechanism that
in real life conceals "repressed" hostility and jealousy in so many families,
namely the exact opposite attitude of exaggerated solicitude, care and respect.[5]

In more extensive treatments both Geza Roheim and Otto Rank tried to
show that the Oedipus theme could be found in a series of myths from
different parts of the world.[6] These and related works helped supply much
credence to Freud's basic contention that the Oedipus theme is universal
and speaks to people of the most diverse social and cultural backgrounds.

Much anthropological work in the study of folklore has sought out
oedipal themes in the stories of preliterate and simple societies; slowly, over
the years, evidence has accumulated that seems, at first glance, to bear out
Freud's theory, though it should be noted that the incest aspect is more
prevalent than that of filial hostility.[7] The idea of universality is crucial for
Freud, not only in terms of understanding primary relations between parents and children within the family, but also for its relevance in understanding the way society functions. Freud claimed that the theme is the basis in
prehistoric times for man's earliest concepts of society, religion, law, moral-

ity, and justice, for it is social life which enables the individual to master the Oedipus complex by offering an acceptable outlet for infantile libidinal attachments.[8]

Followers of Freud have similarly explored the sociological possibilities contained in the Oedipus theme and have utilized it to provide psychoanalytical explanations for phenomena ranging from crime and juvenile delinquency to youth protest. Thus, Franz Alexander and Hugo Staub write:

> The human being enters the world as a criminal, i.e., not socially adjusted. . . . His actual social adjustment begins only at the time after the Oedipus complex is overcome. This happens during the so-called latency period which was described by Freud. This period begins between the ages of four and six and ends at puberty. It is at this period that the development of the criminal begins to differentiate itself from that of the normal.[9]

Equally significant are the attempts to apply oedipal reasoning to explain social movements. Jones, for example, discusses the deep-seated psychological motivations underlying revolutionary movements and suggests: "The natural resentment against the father may be more or less openly manifested later on, a rebellion which occurs commonly enough, though the true meaning of it is not recognized. To this source many social revolutionaries—perhaps all—owe the original impetus of their rebelliousness against authority."[10] Lewis Feuer, a political scientist, adopts a similar oedipal perspective in his comparative study of student protest movements, explaining that, despite the altruism and idealism characteristic of most of these movements, the young are basically acting out the rejection of their fathers and the older generation."[11] More specifically, Morton Levitt and Ben Rubinstein, discussing student revolt and attempting "to try to make psychoanalytic sense out of student behavior," claim that "we must return to familiar grounds, to Oedipus and Laius, to the shaky relations between the child and his parents."[12]

For all the support the oedipal concept receives in academic work and in popular thinking, it has also been criticized from a number of different perspectives. Indeed, some of Freud's closest disciples broke with him partly over this very issue. Thus the break with Otto Rank was occasioned by the latter's emphasis on the trauma of birth,[13] which stressed the importance of that trauma for subsequent socialization, thereby challenging the overriding impact of the oedipal stage upon such socialization. In a letter to Rank, Freud suggested that some people might be supporting Rank's approach because of a "strong desire to get away from the Oedipus complex whenever there is a chance."[14]

Freud acknowledged that the break with Carl Jung was caused partly because Jung had proposed different interpretations of the oedipal problem "and thus hoped to escape the need for recognizing the importance of infantile sexuality and of the Oedipus complex. . . ."[15] Alfred Adler, taking issue with Freud over the emphasis he placed on sexuality, argued that the problems of the oedipal stage were far more related to feelings of inferiority and powerlessness than to sexual desires and consequent murderous drives, and that the existence of such inferiority feelings was a result of errors in upbringing and not of inescapable drives. Adler also differed with Freud as to the meaning of the Oedipus story within the historical context of Greek society: "The Oedipus story means many different things. Socrates used it to warn people not to abandon crippled children, as was the custom in those days."[16]

A major assault on the thesis of the Oedipus complex as a universal phenomenon was Bronislaw Malinowski's anthropological study of the Trobriand Islanders.[17] Describing how fathers played a negligible role in bringing up their children, who were mainly under the control of their maternal uncles, Malinowski claimed that this demonstrated that there was no universal Oedipus complex involving child and parents. If such a complex should be found to exist, Malinowski maintained that it would arise not from automatic and instinctive feelings but from the social structure in which the children were brought up.

When William Lessa examined several thousand folk stories from Oceania, he found that only twenty-three resembled the Oedipus myth, and not all of these related to the specific theme of parricide.[18] Other writers have suggested that, while the killing of the father is the central theme of the Oedipus myth, its meaning need not necessarily be parricide. Lord Raglan claimed that the real theme was regicide, and he made a comparative analysis of some forty-eight well-known myths of generational conflict to substantiate his argument.[19]

Several writers have argued that Freud misinterpreted the Oedipus myth and that a more careful reading of the story would lead to conclusions vastly different, indeed diametrically opposed, to those he proposed. After all, although it was Oedipus who slew his father, the hostility between the two was really initiated by the parents, Laius and Jocasta, who attempted to rid themselves of their newborn child by abandoning him in order to forestall a prophecy that their son would one day kill his father. Furthermore, in their chance meeting at a crossroads, it was Laius who instigated the altercation by ordering his charioteer to force Oedipus off the road. After the latter lunged in retaliation at the charioteer, Laius attacked him. Only after this did Oedipus turn on Laius directly and deal him a fatal blow.

The story takes on a poignant dimension when one remembers that Oedipus met Laius because he was on his way to Thebes to avoid the oracular prophecy telling that he was foredoomed to kill his father. Not knowing his true parentage, Oedipus had hoped to thwart the prophecy by leaving the home of the man who found him as an abandoned infant and whom he presumed to be his father. It was while he was on the road that he met his real father, whose identity remained unknown to him, and unwittingly fulfilled the prophecy.

Laius's hostility toward Oedipus has prompted several writers to suggest independently the concept of a "Laius complex."[20] They raise questions as to the true direction of generational hostility and the nature of the socialization process. There seems, however, to be an inherent weakness in the concept as a counterpoint to the Oedipus theme. Dramatically speaking, the hostility of Laius is only a peripheral aspect of the story, not its central focus. It therefore fails to appeal to the emotions of the spectator and to seize the imagination of behavioral scientists.

In any case the parental and adult hostilities underlying the Oedipus story emerge far more clearly in the second and third plays of Sophocles's trilogy. Erich Fromm has suggested that Freud misinterpreted the meaning of the myth by concentrating only on the first play rather than considering all three as a unit:

> The theme running through the three tragedies is the conflict between father and son. In *King Oedipus,* Oedipus kills his father, who has intended to take the infant's life. In *Oedipus at Colonnus,* Oedipus gives vent to his intense hate against his son, and in *Antigone* we find the same hate again between Creon and Haemon. . . . If we interpret *King Oedipus* in the light of the whole trilogy, the assumption seems plausible that the real issue in *King Oedipus,* too, is the conflict between father and son and not the problem of incest.[21]

Fromm, however, goes beyond the specific theme of father-son conflict and argues that

> the struggle against paternal authority is its main theme [and that] the roots of this struggle go far back into the ancient fight between the patriarchal and matriarchal systems of society; Oedipus as well as Haemon and Antigone are representative of the matriarchal principle, they all attack a social and religious order based on powers and privileges of the father, represented by Laius and Creon.[22]

This is an intriguing argument, which is carefully developed by Fromm with much reliance on J. J. Bachofen's controversial nineteenth-century study of mother-right.[23] Yet it tends to take Fromm away from the more obvious and more relevant theme of intergenerational hostility. Instead of addressing himself directly to the theme of paternal hostility toward the son, or of adult hostility toward youth, Fromm sees the various actors as playing the symbolic roles of the matriarchal and patriarchal orders. Ironically, while this theme is noticeable in the last two plays, it is almost completely lacking in the first play of the trilogy. Furthermore, it is not clear why, of the three people purported to be representatives of the matriarchal system, two, Oedipus and Haemon, should be males.

It would seem that an analysis of the Oedipus trilogy as a whole shows not only a struggle between matriarchal and patriarchal social orders but also a struggle for power between the old and the young, in which the fears and hostilities of the parental generation are strikingly apparent, while the younger generation generally seeks a compromise or a way out of the impasse.

In the second play, *Oedipus at Colonnus,* Oedipus is cast in the role of the father—almost as if to stress the timeless, recurring nature of the father-son conflict. His hatred for his two sons knows no bounds, and despite the efforts of one of them, Polyneices, to seek a reconciliation, Oedipus remains adamant. At a climactic moment in the play, Polyneices pleads with his father: "Speak to me, father! Don't turn away from me! Will you not answer me at all? Will you send me away without a word?" Yet Oedipus remains implacable; no sentiment of paternal love sways him as he calls down a final curse on his son: "Now go! For I abominate you and disown you; You utter scoundrel! Go with the malediction I have pronounced for you . . . you should die by your own brother's hand and you should kill the brother who banished you. For this I pray!"[24]

(The vehemence of Oedipus's reaction takes on added meaning when it is remembered that the play was written when Sophocles himself was involved in judicial litigation against his son. Sophocles won the case, but it is interesting to speculate how this conflict influenced him in his choice of theme, plot, and words.)

Rollo May concurs in Fromm's assessment that Freud erred in confining his attention to the first play in the trilogy, and comments that the fact that *Oedipus at Colonnus* "is never mentioned in psychoanalytic literature at all [is] an amazing fact in itself."[25]

The conflict between the generations reaches its peak in the third and final play, *Antigone,* portraying the naked hostility and cruelty of the parental generation. The plot revolves around the attempt of Creon, the newly instated king of Thebes, to have his niece, Antigone, daughter of Oedipus, put to death. Antigone has defied Creon's decree that her brother, who, in fulfillment of Oedipus's curse, had been killed in fraternal strife, should be buried outside the gates of the city, thereby stigmatizing his memory forever. Creon turns a deaf ear to the entreaties of Haemon, his son, to spare the life of Antigone, to whom he is betrothed. Indeed, Haemon's pleading provides Creon with an ideal opportunity to set forth his view of father-son relations, as he forces Haemon to choose between unquestioning obedience to his father and love for his cousin. Haemon's initial stance is one of meek filial submission: "I am your son, father. You are my guide.

You make things clear for me, and I obey you. No marriage means more to me than your continuing wisdom."[26] Having elicited this declaration of submission, Creon then expounds upon his belief about what a son should be:

Good. That is the way to behave:
Subordinate everything else, my son, to your father's will.
This is what a man prays for, that he may get
Sons attentive and dutiful in his house,
Each one hating his father's enemies,
Honoring his father's friends.
But if his sons
Fail him, if they turn out unprofitable,
What has he fathered but trouble for himself.[27]

After hearing these admonitions, Haemon tries to warn his father that the populace has reacted angrily against the harshness of his decree against Antigone, and once again begs his father to retract it. When a witness to the discussion suggests that Haemon's attitude is sensible, Creon replies in language that has echoed down the ages: "You consider it right for a man of my years and experience to go to school to a boy?"[28]

Creon's implacability produces an inevitable escalation of the quarrel, which ends with Creon flaunting the full power of his status as king and father to issue a final command in as humiliating terms as possible: "Bring the woman out! Let her die before his eyes! Here, this instant, with her groom beside her!" Shocked by the depth of his father's hatred, Haemon tries to kill Creon. Failing, he then commits suicide, "driven mad by the murder his father has done." Too late, Creon confesses to his dead son: "I was the fool, not you, and you died for me."[29]

It is easy to understand Freud's enthusiasm for the first play in the Oedipus trilogy. The themes of incest and parricide in *Oedipus Rex* illuminated Freud's own developing beliefs about the nature of parent-child relations. They confirmed his intuition of childhood sexuality and parricidal impulses and reinforced his ideas on the importance of the unconscious in human behavior. Neither the brilliance of Freud's insight nor the aptness of the Oedipus story can be gainsaid. Nor can their importance for understanding some aspects of human nature be ignored. The problems of the Oedipus complex are not whether it contains some measure of truth but the degree of that truth and the extent of its influence. This insight, at first presented with hesitation and trepidation, and accepted only gradually and reluctantly, has attained over the course of time an importance and impact far beyond its true value.

The one-sided focus in Freud's statement of the Oedipus complex has been attacked in the past, but often its challengers tried to avoid the full implications of parental hostility. Even when the oedipal perspective is questioned, its residual influence often determines the direction the new analysis takes.

An example of this form of reasoning can be found in the critical analysis made of the Oedipus theme by Melville and Frances Herskovits. Extensive field research in West Africa led them to conclude that the Oedipus theme was only "infrequently" encountered in folklore. They note further: "When we turn to the Dahomean tales, we find that the classical Oedipus formulation can be reached only by distorting the intent of the myths, whereas the factor of the father's anxiety in the face of the challenge of the son, or of rivalry between brothers, stands out in bold relief."[30]

Faced with an abundance of myths dealing with parental hostility, the Herskovitses argue that only by taking into account both generational and sibling rivalry can a true perspective be obtained. Yet their conclusion changes the intent of the myths they discuss, for they submerge the hostility of parent *qua* parent by explaining it in terms of sibling rivalry. According to them, sibling rivalry

> sets up patterns of reaction that throughout life give rise to attitudes held toward the sibling substitutes with whom the individual was in competition during infancy, and it is our hypothesis that these attitudes are later projected by the father upon his offspring. . . . [W]e must point out that the threat to the father or father-surrogate is to be seen as a projection of the infantile experience of sibling hostility upon the son.[31]

While sibling rivalry is undoubtedly an important theme in both myth and human behavior, it seems less able to provide a satisfactory explanation of parental hostility than would a direct examination of the relationship between parents and children.

The Herskovitses are not alone in trying to explain parental hostility in terms of earlier sibling rivalry. In a critical discussion of the theme of parricide in Freud's writings, Philip Rieff notes the existence of other mythological themes and takes Freud to task for not giving sufficient weight to the motif of fratricide. The primal crime in the Bible is fratricide, while in *Hamlet* (perceived in oedipal terms by both Freud and Jones), "the killing of the brother is the demi-urge of the plot."[32]

Rieff stresses that in Hamlet the first corpse in the play is that of the brother; the curse comes from the usurpation of the throne by fratricide; and Hamlet kills Laertes, his prospective brother-in-law. "Fratricide is what makes life rotten in Denmark! Freud seems to have been deaf to the importance of both sororicide and fratricide, though it fairly shouted at him in his analysis of King Lear. . . ."[33] Yet, for all his stress on the role of fratricide as an alternative to the theme of parricide, Rieff is also marginally aware of the possibility of a third theme, filicide, where it "is the father who would kill the son, not the son who would kill the father."[34] Quoting Kierkegaard, he refers to this as the "Abraham myth."[35] But, having stated this point, Rieff allows it to lapse.

Rieff may be as "deaf" to the theme of filicide "fairly shouting" at him as he accuses Freud of being to the themes of fratricide and sororicide in *King Lear.* The key to the tragedy of King Lear is not fratricide nor sororicide but Lear's rejection of Cordelia, the daughter who bore him true love. While Lear undoubtedly is the victim of the false and greedy protestations of love from his other daughters, his attitude toward Cordelia is completely negative. Like Creon, Lear too insists that his child put love for him above marital love. If there are nuances of incest in the story, they emanate from the father, not from the daughter.

Some of the most striking examples of the impact of the oedipal perspective on the manner in which interpretations of generational conflict are made occur when distinct instances of parental hostility are seen as illustrating the working of the Oedipus fixation. Roheim has argued that even among the Trobriand Islanders, who, according to Malinowski, manifest no Oedipus complex, there are myths with oedipal themes. Roheim's examples, however, are unconvincing. The father in one story "has intercourse with his daughter, the girl commits suicide by inducing a shark to eat her up, then he kills his wife by coitus, finally he cuts off his own penis and dies." Roheim comments: "If this is not an Oedipus story I don't know what is."[36] Rather than an Oedipus story, we have here an example of the gross distortions that allow Oedipus themes to be read into stories where essential elements are lacking and where, in fact, the real meaning may be in direct contrast to the Oedipus myth. In this Trobriand story there is no parricide (there is not even a son!); the incestuous relations are initiated by the father; the first deaths are those of the daughter and the wife. The self-castration and suicide at the end are, no doubt, symbolic, but not readily associated with any element in the Oedipus story.

Roheim's tendency to force stories into an oedipal mold can also be noted in his study of those elements common to the disciplines of psychoanalysis and anthropology.[37] Clyde Kluckhohn, in a critical response to this work, points out that

> Roheim's contention that certain Navaho myths are oedipal myths strikes many as strained. The main emphasis is on the father killing his own children . . . in only 4 of the 48 myths does the hero cause the death of his father . . . [N]either parricide nor Raglan's regicide motifs will stand up literally, without a great deal of far-fetched interpretation.[38]

Similarly, the Herskovitses, discussing Rank's work on myth, state:

> It is clear . . . that the dominance of this hypothesis [the Oedipus complex] over the data made for the manipulation of these motifs to the neglect of [other] possible conclusions.[39]

They note that, while myths contain instances of "an unconscious wish to kill the father or father surrogate. . . ," when attempts are made "to inquire into the problem of other possible motivations, it becomes apparent that invariably it is the father who initiates the hostility."[40]

When a balanced view is taken of the accumulated evidence of myths it seems possible that, within the context of family rivalry, filicidal themes may very well be in the majority. Certainly, a perusal of Stith Thompson's authoritative analyses and coding of myth motifs suggests that those bearing indications of parental hostility (varying from cruelty to actual filicide) may be more numerous than those involving children's hostility toward parents.[41]

In fact, the very mythical tradition from which Freud took his parricidal theme contains ample key examples of parental hostility and filicidal tendencies. A. J. Levin notes that the Oedipus story itself expressed the Greeks' "fear of their own cruel impulses arising from their own infantile experience and accentuated by the prevailing attitude toward children."[42] He notes that, in addition to Oedipus, two of the most famous Greek plays, *Agamemnon* and *Medea,* are about filicide. In the former, Agamemnon, the leader of the Greek army, agrees to sacrifice his daughter in order to appease one of the gods, Artemis, so that he might be successful in battle; in the latter, Medea kills her two children to gain revenge at the expense of her erstwhile lover.

In addition, the primal story of Greek mythology deals with the attempt of Cronus to be rid of his children. While it is true that Cronus, together with his Titan followers, was killed in battle against his son Zeus, the latter had, as Edith Hamilton observes, "good cause for going against his father":

> Cronus had learnt that one of his children was destined some day to dethrone him and he thought to go against his fate by swallowing them as soon as they were born. But when Rhea bore Zeus, her sixth child, she succeeded in having him secretly carried off to Crete, while she gave her husband a great stone wrapped in swaddling clothes which he supposed was the baby and swallowed them accordingly.[43]

For Freud the primal crime is of major significance, for through it he sees a close relation both to the earliest origins of society and the socialization processes which every child must undergo.

In his classic study, *Totem and Taboo,* Freud adapted his concept of mankind's original crime to the key features of the Oedipus story as he understood it. He hypothesized a prehistoric event in which parricide was committed by a group of sons joining together to kill their father. He writes: "All that we find is a violent and jealous father who keeps all the females for himself and drives away his sons as they grow up." He then adds:

> One day the brothers who had been driven out came together, killed and devoured their father and so made an end of the patriarchal horde. United they had the courage to do and succeed in doing what would have been impossible

for them individually. . . . Cannibal savages as they were, it goes without saying that they devoured their victim as well as killing him. The violent primal father had doubtless been the feared and envied model of each one of the company of brothers; and in the act of devouring him they accomplished their identification with him, and each one of them acquired a portion of his strength. The totem meal, which is perhaps mankind's earliest festival, would thus be a repetition and a commemoration of this memorable and criminal deed, which was the beginning of so many things—of social organization, of moral restrictions and of religion.[44]

Freud's explanation, then, is based directly on oedipal principles: the struggle of a child with his own Oedipus complex is a reflection and a repetition of humanity's own earliest history. In the aftermath of this deed, the sons, overcome with guilt and regret, attempted to sublimate the impulses that led to the act and to prevent its repetition by creating religious rituals, such as taboos and ceremonial meals, all recalling the horrendous deed.

Further, it was in reaction to this crime that the framework was provided for the origins of religion, society, morality, and law. The enormity of the act led the conspirators-culprits to search out both symbolic and concrete measures—in the form of principles of morals and rules of law—to prevent future repetitions of the heinous act, thereby, according to Freud, laying down the basis for human society:

Totemic religion arose from the filial sense of guilt in an attempt to allay that feeling and to appease the father by deferred obedience to him. All later religions are seen to be attempts at solving the same problem . . . and our reactions to the same great event with which civilization began and which, since it occurred, has not allowed mankind a moment's rest.[45]

Since Freud admits that his description is hypothetical, what he calls "a wishful fantasy of killing and devouring," it provides, more than most of his other writings, an insight into his thought processes. If mythology is so important, then certain questions cry out for answers. Why was the father violent? Why was he jealous? Why did he keep all the females to himself? Did this include his own daughters, with the clear implications of incest? Why did he drive away his sons as they grew up? And if he was violent, jealous, possessive, and vindictive, was it not inevitable that his sons would rise up against him? According to Freud's own speculative account of the primal crime, it seems clear that it was the father who bore major responsibility for the outbreak of generational conflict.

In the Greek tradition—so important for Freud because there he found his powerful Oedipus myth—the killing and devouring were carried out by Cronus against his very own children. Freud, in fact, refers several times to this myth, adding that it is a common theme in children's fairy tales, such as "Little Red Riding Hood." But instead of finding creative possibilities in this sort of story, Freud is puzzled and states that "the idea of being devoured by the father . . . is so strange to us that we can hardly credit its existence in a child. Nor do we really know if it means what it seems to say."[46] Thus, while Freud is more than willing to credit the existence in a child's mind of a desire to kill his father, he is unable to conceive that the same child may have fears that his far more powerful father wishes to kill him.[47]

Similarly, the biblical tradition provides not even the slightest hint of a primal event to parallel Freud's description, despite his assertion that it was the primal father, killed by his sons, who subsequently became the "prototype of God, the model after which later generations have formed their figure of God."[48]

In the Bible, however, the primal sin was eating the forbidden fruit; the primal murder was the fratricidal killing of Abel; the primal step toward organized society was Cain's query, "Am I my brother's keeper?"; the primal symbol of law, order, and morality was the mark of Cain. These are all tremendous themes and have been extensively used in literature and social research.

Since the biblical tradition of the Western world contains no record of an event that comes even close to paralleling Freud's speculative description, Freud attempted on various occasions either to reinterpret key biblical events or to suggest different historical circumstances for well-known, widely accepted stories. In his last work, *Moses and Monotheism,* Freud makes Moses into both the founder and the father-figure of the Jewish people, ignoring the earlier patriarchs, Abraham, Isaac, and Jacob.

Although many people are inclined to dismiss this work as an irrelevant and unimportant addendum to the total corpus of Freud's writing, there is ample evidence to show the significance Freud himself attached to this work. It is, in many ways, the climax to which he was constantly working, involving even a close ongoing personal identification with the figure of Moses.

According to Freud's thesis, Moses, born an Egyptian, formed and used the Jewish people as an instrument through which an earlier monotheism originally propounded by the pharaoh Ikhnaton was to be preserved. The Jews, reluctant to accept Moses's difficult message, rebelled against him and put him to death. According to Freud, "fate had brought the great deed and misdeed of primaeval days, the killing of the father, closer to the Jewish people by causing them to repeat it on the person of Moses, an outstanding father figure."[49]

This parricidal act evoked feelings of remorse among subsequent generations of the Jewish people. These guilt feelings had long-term implications in that "remorse for the murder of Moses provided the stimulus for the wishful fantasy of the Messiah." For Freud it is no coincidence that "the violent killing of another great man became the starting point for the Christian religion."[50]

While this reference to the crucifixion of Jesus clearly indicates that his death is to be seen, just as that of Moses in Freud's version, as a reenactment of the primal killing of the father, elsewhere Freud describes it as a killing of the son of God. His explanation of its symbolic meaning retains, however, the essence of the oedipal framework:

> There can be no doubt that in the Christian myth the original sin was against God, the Father. If, however, Christ redeemed mankind from the burden of original sin by the sacrifice of his own life, we are driven to conclude that the sin was a murder. The law of talion, which is so deeply rooted in human feelings, lays it down that a murder can only be expiated by guilt. And if this sacrifice of a life brought about atonement with God, the Father, the crime to be expiated can only have been the murder of the father.
>
> In the Christian doctrine, therefore, men were acknowledging in the most undisguised manner the guilty primeval deed, since they formed the fullest atonement for it in the sacrifice of this one son.[51]

The Bible, of course, abounds in stories involving intrafamilial hostilities: fratricide and/or sibling rivalry (Cain and Abel, Jacob and Esau, Joseph and his brothers, Absalom against Amnon); filial hostility (Absalom's rebellion against his father with an attempted parricide); parental hostility (Abraham's expulsion of Ishmael, Laban's treachery toward Rachel and Jacob, even Saul's attitude to his son-in-law, David); and outright filicide (Jephthah's sacrifice of his daughter).

In searching for a model to understand the religious fount of society and the deeper messages about society contained in religion, Freud ignored all the alternative possibilities within his own religious tradition. Although he was not an observant Jew, and although he was severely critical of organized religion in *The Future of an Illusion,* there is little doubt that his Jewish background and the overall Jewish-Christian tradition within which he lived had a tremendous impact on his work. Freud himself referred to the love he had for the Bible and even named one of his daughters after the daughter of his childhood Bible teacher.

Why then did Freud fail to notice these generational themes in the Bible, not one of which, with the dubious exception of Absalom's struggle against David, parallels his own thesis? Why did he deliberately forge his own version of the primal crime and his own version of Moses's life-history?

In a book warmly supportive of Freud's achievements, Rieff has expressed surprise that, of the three possible generational homicidal themes, Freud failed to notice the themes of fratricide and filicide in his analyses of religion.[52] Yet, again, Rieff has failed to deal adequately with the latter theme, for while he expands on the theme of fratricide and sibling rivalry, his only reference to filicide is a marginal comment, tentative and guarded.

He acknowledges the crucifixion as an example of filicide but with the rider that the killing of the son may be seen basically in fratricidal terms, with God, the Father, sanctioning the act, thereby providing a solution for the fratricidal dilemma. As for the sacrifice of Isaac, Rieff casts doubt on the real meaning of what he terms the Abraham myth:

> A third myth complicates the Freudian selection: the Abraham myth. . . . Unless dismissed as "manifest content," in the Abraham myth it is the father who would kill the son and not the son who would kill the father.[53]

The brevity of Rieff's handling of this story indicates that he himself is reluctant to attempt to unravel the "complication." Freud, too, avoided any significant reference to this most powerful and popular of Bible stories, except in side references, as in his work on the Wolf-man, where he quotes, without comment, his patient's difficulty in believing in a God who could demand of a father the sacrifice of his son.[54] Freud's avoidance of this theme stands out even more in the light of the creative efforts made by other writers to probe the symbolic meaning of the act. Some have developed theories of filicide around Abraham's intention to kill his son; others see the last-minute grace given to Isaac as signaling a momentous message against the filicide that had been prevalent in the early stages of human society and that had flourished widely during Abraham's time.

Erich Wellisch uses the stories of both Oedipus and Isaac to draw a broad picture of the sweep of human history, which he divides into three phases.[55]

The first is that of parental aggression, including particularly its most extreme form, infanticide. The second stage, based on the Oedipus complex, or rather what he calls the *complete* Oedipus complex, involves not only the hostility of the sons to the father (the Oedipus subcomplex) but all the other intrafamilial generational confrontations—the hostility of the father (the Laius subcomplex), the hostility of the mother (the Jocasta subcomplex), and the hostility of the daughter (the Electra subcomplex). Wellisch sees the complete Oedipus complex as referring to the guilt feelings associated with the ambivalence felt by the generations toward each other. Compromise would be sought for the hostility but there would be no complete solution.

This stage is the prelude to the third and final stage of Wellisch's thesis, when the infanticidal tendencies are completely overcome and replaced by a covenant of love between parent and child. While this stage is really a resolution of the Oedipus complex, the full import must be found in the symbolism not of Greek mythology but of biblical teaching, particularly the story of the *Akedah,* the binding of Isaac for a sacrifice.

Using the same reasoning process that Freud had used for Greek mythology, Wellisch claims that ". . . phenomena which were described in the Bible occur in every person and provide a unique source for psychological research and insight."[56]

For Wellisch the true meaning of the Akedah is not Abraham's willingness to sacrifice his son, but the last-minute withdrawal of his raised hand, the last-minute reprieve that he, at God's behest, granted. The long-standing problem of infanticidal impulses was thereby resolved:

> The tendencies of thousands of years had reached fulfillment. A fundamental change had taken place in Abraham, *a turning of mind* which divided the history of the world into two parts: one before and one after the Akedah.[57]

This positive interpretation of the story of the Akedah is in line with much standard biblical commentary:

> The story of the Binding of Isaac opens the age-long warfare of Israel against the abominations of child-sacrifice which was rife among the Semitic peoples. ... In that age, it was astounding that Abraham's God should have interposed to *prevent* the sacrifice, not that he should have asked for it.[58]

Wellisch sees the importance of the story not only in its historical context, but as an ongoing aspect of family life. In essence the Akedah story provides a final resolution of the complete Oedipus complex in all its manifestations as Wellisch had described it. Wellisch uses the term "Akedah motif" to designate "an unconscious constellation of religious-psychological experiences which aim at a complete resolution of parent-child conflicts."[59]

Other writers have also used the tremendous theme of the sacrifice of Isaac as a basis for better understanding the complexities of generational relations.

One Freudian writer has used the story to provide an oedipal explanation of the incident. R. Money-Kyrle writes that

> to the sacrificing father the meaning is both parricidal and suicidal. Parricidal because the son is to the unconscious a reincarnation of the father. Suicidal because the son is also a part of the self.[60]

No suggestion here that the act being contemplated is a filicidal one!

Erich Neumann suggests an Isaac complex to describe the submissive and obedient role of a son. Neumann is critical of such obedience, which he sees as a "sterile conservatism and a reactionary identification with the father, which lacks the living, dialectical struggle between the generations."[61]

Israel Charny has adopted a broader approach to the Akedah by examining the roles played by each member of the family. He, like Neumann, is critical of Isaac and suggests that Isaac should have sensed his imminent danger and, instead of meekly submitting, should have attempted to evade the decree.[62]

In contrast, S. Giora Shoham, building on some of the filicidal aspects of the story, has proposed the concept of an Isaac syndrome to signify the "pressures to expel the growing child from the family . . . initiated by covert dynamics within the family which stem from the father."[63] The use of the Isaac syndrome in this context is questionable, as it is intended to be the opposite of the Oedipus complex and similar to the Laius and Medea complexes. The description thus seems more akin to the idea of an Abraham complex or myth as used by Rieff and Kierkegaard.[64]

One of the most significant and perhaps best-known attempts to probe the deeper meaning of the sacrifice is found in Kierkegaard's *Fear and Trembling*. Ignoring any potential message against child sacrifice, Kierkegaard concentrates instead on the test of faith imposed on Abraham and insists that any indication of the slightest wavering on the part of Abraham, or even of any hope that there might be a last-minute reprieve, would undermine the meaning of the test.[65]

Kierkegaard's intention is brought out even more clearly in the comparison he makes between Abraham's willingness to sacrifice his son and three other instances of sacrifices by parents of their children—Agamemnon's sacrifice of his daughter, Iphigenia, in order to ensure victory in warfare; Jephthah's sacrifice of his daughter in fulfillment of a prior pledge to give thanks for a victory; and the action of Brutus, the first consul of Rome, who had two of his sons put to death for joining a conspiracy against him. Kierkegaard argues that Abraham's test is more difficult and his proof of faith superior to these three acts, since in Abraham's case there was no rational reason for the action. Unlike the three cases mentioned, Abraham stood to gain no earthly material benefit as a result of his act. Yet Kierkegaard, in trying to show how much easier it is to understand the actions of Agamemnon, Jephthah, and Brutus, nevertheless waxes perhaps overenthusiastic in discussing the fathers' actions in these cases:

> When Agamemnon, Jephthah, Brutus at the decisive moment heroically overcame their pain, have heroically lost the beloved and have merely to accomplish the outward sacrifice, then there never will be a noble soul in the world who will not shed tears of compassion for their pain and of admiration for their exploit.[66]

Now, while it is true that both Agamemnon and Jephthah were responding to a divine entity, this is not true of the case of Brutus, whose action against his sons was dictated by pragmatic, political considerations. Here, indeed, was the primal crime of the Roman consulate—vengeful filicide. Yet Kierkegaard is particularly approving of this latter act:

> When a son is forgetful of his duty, when the state entrusts the father with the sword of justice, when the laws require punishment at the hand of the father, then will the father heroically forget that the guilty one is his son, he will magnanimously conceal his pain, but there will not be a single one among the

people, not even the son, who will not admire the father, and whenever the law of Rome is interpreted, it will be remembered that many interpreted it more learnedly, but none so gloriously as Brutus.[67]

It is doubtful if Brutus's act could be considered in such a singular manner, mainly because it was by no means unique. If anything, it may have served as no more than a precedent, which became firmly entrenched in the law, the ethics, the religious principles, and the practice of the Romans. Fustel de Coulanges refers to the judicial power, including the power of life and death, that the father in ancient Rome had over all the members of his family:

> Justice for wife and son . . . was in the house. The chief of the family was the judge. This judicial authority which the chief of the family exercised in his house was complete and without appeal. He could condemn to death like the magistrate in the city, and no authority could modify his sentence.[68]

In contrast, David Bakan has adopted an interesting and novel approach to generational conflict depicted in the Bible, arguing that one of the major contributions of the two major Western religions, Judaism and Christianity, was their abjuration of child sacrifice in any form.[69]

While he acknowledges that the exigencies of population problems in primitive societies might be partly responsible for such practices, Bakan also discusses some of the more subjective reasons for infanticidal practices, including the burdens of raising children, the fear of their behavior when they are no longer dependent on their parents, and—for fathers—the problems of proving paternity:

> The essence of Judaism and Christianity is the management of the infanticidal impulse . . . and a binding of the father against acting out the impulse. One of the main historical functions of the Judeo-Christian tradition has been to counteract the infanticidal impulses which arise as a dialectical antithesis to the assumption of paternal responsibility on the part of men.[70]

Unfortunately, despite many allusions to this problem in the Bible, Bakan feels that "one of the most serious limitations of the contemporary versions of the Judeo-Christian tradition is the failure to bring out the significance of the paternity question in modern times."[71]

Bakan's work involves complicated reasoning about the symbolic meaning of many of the rituals of both religions—for example, the Passover commemoration of the sparing of the first-born of the Israelites and the ceremony of circumcision in Judaism, or of the death of the son of God on the cross in Christianity. In fact, according to Bakan, Jesus's crucifixion at the time of Passover was not fortuitous, but shows a clear link between the infanticidal themes that both the Old and the New Testaments stress.

Bakan has touched on an extremely important issue. For both Judaism and Christianity are replete with symbols of and references to generational themes. The story of the sacrifice of Isaac is intricately woven into the prayer ritual of the two holiest days of the Jewish calender. On the New Year, the story is read in the synagogue service; several times during the service a *shofar* is sounded, a shofar being a ram's horn in remembrance of the sacrificial animal that was placed on the altar instead of Isaac. The Day of Atonement services are also climaxed by the blowing of a shofar at the end of the day's fasting. In Christianity, the primary symbol is the cross on which Jesus was crucified, and the two major holidays, Christmas and Easter, revolve around the birth and death of Jesus, with all the generational tensions embedded in those events. In Islam, too, one of the major holidays is the Festival of the Sacrifice, commemorating, according to Moslem tradition, Ishmael on the altar.

In addition, it should be noted that the ultimate message appearing in the final passage of the concluding Book of the Prophets is of generational contacts, a message that contains both a great vision and a dire warning:

> Behold, I will send you Elijah the prophet before the coming of the great and terrible day of the Lord.
> And he shall turn the heart of the fathers to the children, and the hearts of the children to their fathers; lest I come and smite the land with utter destruction.[72]

Bakan seems right then in arguing the importance of generational considerations for an understanding of a deep message in the religious traditions of the Western world. He may, however, have overlooked the fact that these considerations are by no means unique to the Western world.

The lives of religious leaders from the East—Zoroaster, Buddha, Krishna—contain parallels with the vicissitudes of Moses and Jesus, including references to infanticide. Young gods—Dionysius, Mithra, Tammuz, Adonis—have been put to death. The message, whether symbolic or direct, warning against infanticidal practices is widespread; stories as to their prevalence abound.[73] Why then has the message not been accorded sufficient attention?

In the modern world, why has the opposite message, of parricidal tendencies, as set forth by Freud in the Oedipus complex, gained so much support? Is it because we have been vouchsafed insights and wisdom denied former periods? Or is it because social reality has undergone a change in recent times? Alternatively, is the message of infanticide too unpleasant to accept? Could it be that the idea of an Oedipus complex holds certain attractions for adults?

Whatever the position, there is a further factor that makes the Oedipus story qualitatively different from the myths, legends, and life-stories mentioned—the role of the unconscious, itself so important for a total understanding of Freud's theoretical framework. For all the above-mentioned actions taken against the young were done deliberately. Part of the impact of the Oedipus story lies in the fact that the parricidal act was done unwittingly, as a result of a fortuitous meeting at the crossroads, when the identities of father and son were unknown to each other. Herein lies part of the power and attraction of the Oedipus story.

Yet, there are alternative stories in which the filicidal act is also carried out unwittingly, through a similar chance encounter, where the identities of father and son are unknown. In fact, a true counterweight to the Oedipus story would be a myth in which the son is killed inadvertently, in which the true identities of the opposing parties are unknown to each other, and in which the expression of hostility is made unconsciously. Myths of this type exist; perhaps the best known is the Persian tale of Rustum and Sohrab.[74] In this story, Rustum, a redoubtable warrior, famous in Persian literature for his exploits, unwittingly kills his son, Sohrab, in face-to-face combat, and to his grief discovers their kinship only as the son's life is ebbing away. The story was introduced to the Western world in an epic poem by Matthew Arnold.[75]

The roots of this fateful and ultimately fatal conflict between father and son had been planted many years prior to the combat. Before Sohrab's birth, Rustum sets out for conquests in far-off places, leaving his pregnant wife a charm bracelet and instructions that, if a son is born, the bracelet should be placed on his arm to inspire him to great deeds. On the birth of a son, the wife, fearful that Rustum wishes to make him a warrior in his own image, determines to conceal from Rustum that he has a male heir. She accordingly sends him a message that she has given birth to a daughter.

Over the years, unaware that he has a male heir, Rustum remains absent from home. As he grows up, Sohrab develops his physical prowess and himself becomes a warrior. Despite her reluctance to see her son follow in his father's footsteps and leave home for battle, Sohrab's mother finally relents. Before Sohrab's departure, she informs him that he is the son of the illustrious Rustum and tells him that his father had left a charm for him and requested that he wear it on his arm.

In the course of time, the armies to which the father and son respectively belong meet on the field of battle. Neither Rustum nor Sohrab knows of the presence of the other. To avoid the carnage of a full-scale battle, the armies agree that the leading warriors of each side should meet in single combat to determine the victor. Thus Rustum and Sohrab, father and son, are brought together. Sohrab, sensing a mysterious bond with his adversary, suggests that they forego battle and then asks his foe outright whether he is not the famous Rustum. But Rustum prefers to hide his identity, taunts his opponent for being afraid to do battle, and insists on immediate combat. A fierce struggle is waged in which Sohrab gains the upper hand; yet, instead of thrusting home his advantage, he offers a truce. This Rustum rejects. When the battle is resumed, Rustum finally overpowers his younger foe and, fearful lest he should not be able to maintain his advantage, hastens to deliver the death blow.

Realizing that his end is near, Sohrab cries out that his father, Rustum, will avenge his death. Rustum refuses to believe that the stricken warrior could be his own son, and declares that no son was ever born to the illustrious warrior. However, Sohrab proves his true identity by revealing the bracelet on his arm. At this Rustum acknowledges the relationship, and Sohrab laments their fate, crying out:

> If thou art Rustum, cruel is thy part;
> No warmth paternal seems to fill thy heart.

A prose version reads: "If you are indeed my father then you have stained your sword in the life-blood of your son! And you did it out of your own stubbornness. For I tried to turn to you in love, and begged you to tell me your name. But I appealed to your heart in vain, and now the time for meeting is gone."[76] Rustum can do no more than give vent to his anguish: "I that am old have killed my son; I that am strong have uprooted this mighty body. I have torn the heart of my child."

The climax of the story is the killing of the son by the father, yet there are biographers and critics of Arnold who interpret the story in oedipal terms, further illustrating the all-pervasive nature of the oedipal approach and the reluctance to face the existence of parental hostility. This becomes particularly pertinent when the story is examined in the context of the personal relations between Matthew Arnold and his famous father, Dr. Thomas Arnold, one of England's leading nineteenth-century educators.

Biographers of Arnold suggest that his attraction to the Rustum story was based on his own feelings of impotence in relation to his renowned father. Lionel Trilling writes:

> It is almost impossible not to find throughout "Sohrab and Rustum" at least a shadowy personal significance. The strong son is slain by the mightier father, and in the end Sohrab draws his father's spear from his own side to let out his life and end the anguish. We watch Arnold in his later youth and we must wonder if he is not, in a psychical sense, doing the same thing.[77]

John D. Yohannan echoes this approach, noting further that "the myth has recoiled upon Matthew Arnold, who has been charged with projecting his own suppressed desire to do battle with a stronger father, the renowned Thomas Arnold of Rugby."[78] Kenneth Burke claims that the theme of the poem is a suicidal one, in which "[t]he poet . . . imagines that the figure with whom he identifies is being killed."[79] Bruce Mazlish, comparing the story to the Oedipus myth, suggests that when the identities of both parties are revealed at the end, the "son offers grateful submission to the now tender father."[80]

A more far-reaching oedipal interpretation is that of A. Dwight Culler, who, noting that "Sohrab and Rustum is often interpreted as an expression of the Oedipus conflict," centers his discussion on the presumed sexual overtones in the story:

> The redoubtable masculinity of Rustum, as witnessed by the vast club he wields, the tower and pillar by which he is symbolized, together with the presumed effeminacy of the son, make it a conflict between the masculine and the feminine principles, and in the end, when the virility of the son has been established by planting a far-seen pillar over his grave, replacing the fallen pillar of his father, he is clearly the sexual victor. At the level of the Super-Ego he has been conquered, and of course, it is his joy to be so conquered.[81]

This analysis may have some interest, and even perhaps some validity, but surely it pales into insignificance compared to the powerful emotional effect of a father inadvertently killing his own son. But Culler remains completely silent about this aspect of the story. If the oedipal perspective causes critics to search for marginal sexual meanings and blinds them to the significant theme of filicide, then the value of the perspective is surely undermined by the irrelevant, trivial purposes for which it is used.

While Culler is aware that father-son tensions were a constant background to Arnold's life, for the senior and junior Arnold were vastly different in temperament, interests, and philosophy of life, he believes that in *Sohrab and Rustum,* written some years after his father's death, Matthew Arnold finally resolved the tensions, gaining at last a feeling of empathy for his father. After noting that Arnold's first two books of poetry had been published anonymously, and only in the third volume, where the poem of Sohrab and Rustum appears, does Arnold use his own name, Culler claims that at this stage Arnold's "true self had come to the fore . . . the name of Arnold could be allowed to appear on the title-page, where it stands, a far-seen pillar over all, identifying the poet as his father's son."[82]

Yet, if Arnold had found his "true self," it was more likely to be a product of breaking away from the pull of his father rather than identifying with him. The theme of Rustum and Sohrab had greatly excited him and he noted that the poem was "by far the best thing I have yet done."[83] He certainly seems to have seen parallels with his own situation, not, however, in terms of oedipal ideas of sexual rivalry, as Culler suggests, nor in terms of the impotence of youth, as Trilling proposes, but rather in terms of the oppressive environment of an authoritarian home and society, in which his poetic soul had found little understanding and less encouragement.

From this perspective, William Madden's biographical analysis of

Matthew Arnold is far closer to portraying the relationship between father and son, and the true meaning of *Sohrab and Rustum*.[84] He warns against underestimating the differences between Matthew Arnold and his father and notes that the latter's personality was bound to affect the son's life.

Dealing specifically with the poem, Madden argues that it was here that Arnold expressed his attitude toward his father:

> Arnold's deepest response to his father's personality was too obscure, instinctive, and unsettling, and too mixed up with filial love and respect, to permit explicit formulation beyond apologetic and evasive remarks in letters to his mother, but it did find oblique expression, on one occasion at least, in his poetry. In *Sohrab and Rustum* the threatening forces which Arnold is indirectly resisting . . . find successful embodiment in the figure of Rustum; like all viable poetic personae, the figures of both Sohrab and Rustum had their roots beyond the reaches of the poet's discursive awareness in his most deeply felt experience, and thus gives to the poem a pathos and power. . . . We can only speculate in such matters, but it seems probable that the tragedy in which an unrecognized son is unwittingly killed by a famous father found a responsive chord in the lonely poet-son of the famous "Arnold of Rugby."[85]

Madden sums up the poem at both the immediate familial and the general societal level:

> It seems clear enough that the poem gives symbolic statements to Arnold's feeling as a poet toward his father and, beyond this, to his sense of his predicament in an uncongenial age. Energetic, successful, and famous though he is, Rustum is devoid of precisely those qualities that Arnold saw as characteristic of the poetic temperament and which he embodies in the gentle Sohrab. It is not too much to say that in the poem Arnold portrays his father as unwittingly instrumental in his own "death" as a poet. . . . According to the poem, Sohrab, had he wished, might have slain his father with the father's own weapons of war, but restrained himself out of filial piety.[86]

The theme of Sohrab and Rustum—of a father unwittingly killing his son—touched a deep chord in Arnold, as the Oedipus story was later to touch a similar chord in Freud. While Arnold presumably found sufficient expression for his emotions and the reality he attempted to portray in the framework of an epic poem, Freud devoted years to developing and embellishing his oedipal theme into an extensive theoretical framework, one that was to become one of the dominant social theories of modern times.

A question inevitably arises: what would have been the impact on people's perceptions of society if there had been a theoretical perspective based not on Oedipus's killing of Laius but on the reverse situation, Laius's attempt to be rid of Oedipus or, more directly, Rustum's killing of Sohrab? This is not merely an academic issue, for the Rustum-Sohrab theme is pregnant with meaning for both the nature of familial relations and the historical analysis of intergenerational relations. The Persian tale offers a theoretical framework for interpreting the problem of generational contacts. Conflicts between the generations—in both myth and reality—are bidirectional; hostilities flow both ways, tensions emanate from both sides.

The Rustum-Sohrab confrontation suggests that parents have a built-in antagonism toward their progeny, that their attitude toward them may range from ignorance and indifference, through denial and contempt, to open attack and ultimate destruction. The Rustum theme is too common in myth and literature to be ignored, too much part of everyday life to be dismissed, and too meaningful and direct to be distorted. A theoretical framework is needed for comprehending parental and adult hostility. Such hostility could well be called the Rustum complex.[87]

This theoretical position offers a framework that might offset the influence of the Oedipus complex and the biased perspective it has fostered. It might open us to new meanings and insights to be gleaned from myth, literature, and reality. Instead of awkward attempts to find oedipal themes in folklore, anthropologists could become more sensitive to contrasting and opposing themes, and prepared to locate indications of parental hostility, varying from cruelty to actual filicide.

In choosing this theme I have taken into account two facts: first, that the story is found in both an Eastern and a Western culture, in the former as a Persian legend, in the latter as a well-known poem by a British poet; second, that the act of killing is carried out unwittingly. While outright accounts of filicide are prevalent in many cultures, much of the special nature and powerful impact of the Rustum story arises from the coincidence that brought father and son into confrontation in a manner similar to the fateful encounter of Oedipus and Laius.

Despite this unusual aspect of the story, it is not unique; a number of close parallels do exist. Thus, in Celtic culture, a third-century bard, Ossian, related the tale of Clessamor, who killed his son Carthon in single combat. The story was popularized by James MacPherson in the eighteenth century.[88]

In Chinese culture, there is a story of an army officer, Hsueh Jen-Kichei, who is sent away to battle when his wife is pregnant. On his return home, eighteen years later, he encounters a youth displaying his skills of marksmanship while shooting at wild geese. Hsueh challenges the youth to a test of marksmanship, boasting of his own prowess. When the challenge is accepted, Hsueh shoots his arrow at his young rival, fearful that the youth might prove to be a superior archer. Hsueh then travels on to his home, where he accuses his wife of infidelity when he discovers a pair of man's shoes under the family sleeping platform. The wife explains that they belong to their son, upon which they discover, to their horror, that the youth whom Hsueh had met, challenged, and killed was their son.

For those who seek oedipal overtones in myth, the suspicion as to the presence of a man's shoes under the family bed neatly covers the sexual and incestuous aspect, but the climax of the story is clearly the filicidal aspect.

This story is used by Richard Solomon in an important analysis of modern Chinese politics to suggest the differing ways in which Chinese and Western cultures deal with family relations.[89] Solomon contrasts the story with the Oedipus story. He does not deal with hostility as such but suggests that the theme is a "father's reluctance to let the son grow to maturity; his unwillingness to be challenged by him."[90] In Chinese culture, according to Solomon, there is a "tie between the dependent son and the powerful and disciplining father" that leads the son to "realize his social identity in a life-long prolongation of his original state of dependency. . . ."

In contrast, Solomon argues that since, in Western culture, the parents

> perceive the potential for conflict born of childhood dependency and its concomitant process of disciplining . . . [t]hey thus set the matured child on his own to seek in adult life alternative social contexts and behavioral forms for the gratification of his hostile and pleasure-seeking impulses.[91]

There can be little doubt that Western and Chinese cultures contain many differences, including their child-rearing practices and generational attitudes. What is of interest, however, is the use that Solomon makes of the two contrasting mythical themes, the Chinese story and the Oedipus myth. At one level, it might be noted that the submissiveness of the son in Chinese culture resembles the submissiveness that Neumann terms the Isaac complex.

More relevant is Solomon's use of the Oedipus story. Here at least it is clear that the parents did not set the matured child out to seek alternative social contexts and behavioral forms; on the contrary, they attempted to destroy the helpless child in infancy in order to prevent any possible future challenges from him. Further, insofar as Solomon discusses alternative social contexts, he sees them in negative terms as a gratification of hostile and pleasure-seeking impulses, instead of appreciating their potential importance in precipitating needed social change.

Finally, Solomon carries his strictures against Oedipus a stage further, suggesting that

> Oedipus . . . by Confucian standards was a most unfilial son; not only because he unknowingly murdered his father and loved his mother, but also in that he mutilated himself. In tearing out his eyes . . . he was violating that rule which Confucius tells us is the beginning of filial piety, the inviolability of life which parents give the child. For, by mutilating himself Oedipus was threatening to break the cyclical life pattern, through which life is given to the group and to its future generations rather than to the individual alone.[92]

It is rather strange that Solomon should see in Oedipus's blinding of himself a threat to the cyclical life-pattern. Surely the continuation of future generations was less threatened by this act than by Oedipus's curse that his sons kill each other, for it was the consummation of this curse that ended Oedipus's prospects for a male continuation of the patrilineal line. Even stranger is Solomon's failure to note Hsueh's filicidal act, which constitutes an even greater threat to familial continuity, and might have led him to probe further into the true nature of generational contacts in Chinese culture.[93]

The ultimate test of the accuracy and value of theoretical presentations is, of course, not the extent to which they are substantiated by myths but the extent to which they reflect empirical reality. It is by this standard that the direction of generational hostility must be measured.

Recent studies have accentuated the need for a Rustum perspective. Thomas Vernon, in his references to youth protest, has noted the harsh response of the adult generation. He suggests that the Kent State killings and the approval with which they were greeted indicate the "depth and intensity of hatred that is to be found among the older generation for members of the younger."[94] Research in the last decade has focused on the cruelty shown toward children by their parents in what is now known as the "battered-child syndrome." Incest, too, so heavily emphasized by Freud, seems to be the result of parental seduction rather than the sexual yearnings of children.

There is scope for reassessment of many phenomena that, for the most part, have been looked upon as mere idiosyncrasies, or explained in ways that obscure parental/adult hostility. Such phenomena include infanticide, child sacrifice, exploitation of children in the labor market (still very prevalent, according to the International Labor Organization), and the authoritarian legal powers accorded to parents.[95]

Other phenomena requiring more attention include the crisis of parenthood, the sociological—as contrasted to the biological and psychological—factors involved in postpartum depression, and marital frictions often engendered by the arrival of children. It must also be appreciated that problems of adolescence are not confined to the adolescent, but that this stage of life creates difficulties for parents as well. These involve coming to terms with a young person's new identity and increased intellectual, physical, and sexual capacities as they reflect on the position and relative strength of the parents. As Helm Stierlin has noted, a youth's problems may largely reflect his parents' concerns.[96]

In his study of fathers in preliterate societies, Malinowski points out the inescapable dilemma of parenthood, particularly paternity:

The father sees in the son his successor, the one who is to replace him in the family lineage and in the household. He becomes, therefore, the more critical, and this influences his feelings in two directions; if the boy is not up to the type of ideal in which the father believes, he will be a source of bitter disappointment and hostility. On the other hand . . . a certain amount of rivalry . . . lead[s] again to hostility. Repressed in both cases, this hostility hardens the father against the son and provokes by reaction a response in hostile feelings.[97]

These ideas are echoed by Erich Fromm in terms of modern societies:

Even in our nonauthoritarian culture, it happens that parents want their child to be "serviceable" in order to make up for what the parents missed in life. If the parents are not successful, the children should attain success so as to give them a vicarious satisfaction. If they do not feel loved (particularly if the parents do not love each other) the children are to make up for it; if they feel powerless in their social life, they want to have the satisfaction of controlling and dominating their children.[98]

In recent years, there seems to be a groping toward a new theoretical framework that will provide an explanation for the phenomena bound up with parental/adult hostility.

Gerard Mendel has argued for the "decolonization" of the young, contending that this age group is becoming a politically defiant class and that a true social revolution must be accompanied by a pedagogical revolution.[99] Arnoldo Rascovsky has established an association for the study of filicide, arguing that its findings may, among other things, help us understand war, where the young are sacrificed by the politically powerful older generation.[100] In a similar vein, Rollo May claims that modern civilization has not advanced much beyond the human sacrifices of primitive societies, since it offers thousands of its youth in war to Moloch because of the elders' envy and fear of the innocence of youth.[101]

In the course of their work on the nature of childhood in history, psychohistorians have accumulated a mass of data regarding cruelties meted out to the young through all historical periods. Lloyd deMause, a leading figure in this effort, has developed an evolutionary theoretical framework suggesting that the farther back into history one goes, the greater the cruelty. Other writers suggest that deMause's approach may be too sanguine and that mankind may not have progressed in its treatment of children as much as he maintains.[102]

There is ample evidence that hostility and cruelty persist into the modern age, though perhaps they take refined forms. David Rothman claims that in the middle class, parental authority may have maintained itself through a change in tactics. He believes that manipulation of the child, rather than outright coercion, has become more prevalent.[103] Anthony Platt points out that actions and institutions that appear to be for the benefit of the young actually may have the ulterior purpose of serving adult needs. Reviewing the history of the juvenile court, Platt notes that the true motivation for this social reform was the desire of the "child-savers" to establish an acceptable framework for controlling the troublesome young, as opposed to their stated concern for the needs of the young themselves.[104]

Israel Charny, attacking the myth of happy family life, states that "over and over again we see mothers who reject, hate, and persecute their children . . . fathers who abandon, resent, ignore, and impatiently assign their children and wives to each other while pretending loyalty to both." After giving examples of marital friction, sibling rivalry, and child hostility toward parents, Charny concludes, "We need to have data about what really happens in family life."[105]

My contention is that such data would show the existence of parental hostility unsuspected by those who think and work in an oedipal mode. I doubt whether there has been a significant diminution of such hostility through the ages, though its expression has obviously taken different forms. There is something happening between parents and children, and between adults and youth, that requires the development of an independent theoretical framework to aid in understanding, researching, and explaining the roots of generational conflict.

The Rustum complex provides such a theoretical framework. Within the family setting, it touches on the most intimate and intricate of human relations—the only ones from which physiologically, and probably psychologically, there can be no escape. On a societal level, it has far-reaching implications for understanding social change. Although generational conflict may be bidirectional, it seems likely that much of the initial manifestations of hostility emanate from parents and from adults and that some of the hostility felt by children and youth is a reaction. If we wish to minimize and control hostility by parents and adults, we would do well to begin by recognizing and acknowledging it. Ignoring it may well ensure its perpetuation.

Whether or not the concept of a Rustum complex is acceptable, or whether it is more apt than the Laius complex, what must certainly be acknowledged is the biased approach of the Oedipus complex with all the inaccuracies it leads to in analyzing reality, mythology, and literature; with all the impact it has had on the modes of thinking in modern times; with all the prejudices about the young it has sanctioned and encouraged. The insights of the oedipal approach, for what it is worth, have been considered, accepted, and applied in full measure in therapy, in academic research and theory, and in popular lay thinking.

What is needed now is an awareness of the weakness of the Oedipus perspective and of the prejudices that often lie behind it. Only then will it be possible to perceive hidden, latent, and open parental and adult hostility. Only then will it be possible to move beyond the Oedipus complex.

To do so means to work toward an understanding of the many structural factors making for parental and adult hostility. It means an awareness that instances of callousness or indifference in the upbringing of children cannot be seen only as mere idiosyncratic aberrations from a universal norm, the consequence of specific defects within the personality of the errant parent, or, where such instances are more numerous, of defects within the subculture to which the parents belong. Rather they must be seen as the overt pathological expressions of deep-seated feelings that are more widely held. One of the contributions of the Oedipus complex was the insight it provided that children might harbor sentiments of hatred or hostility toward their parents. Only by spelling out such hostility was it possible to be forewarned and to take the steps necessary to minimize such feelings.

A similar perspective is needed to explain parental hostility: a realization that the biological nexus of parenthood provides no instinctive capacity to love one's offspring. Neither the sexual ecstasy preceding conception nor the wondrous mystery of birth nine months later carries any inherent guarantees that the physical progenitors of a newborn will be willing or capable of subsequently bestowing the love, care, and affection that the infant needs. Unlike other mammals, human mothers and babies are incapable of knowing each other without artificial means of identification. If a true rapport is to develop it must be worked at, sought out, strived for. If not, the relationship can easily degenerate into one of rivalry, mutual distrust, and hostility. These simple facts of life are too often denied in an ideology of the idyllic nature of family life flowing out of presumed innate maternal instincts, paternal pride, and parental joy.

In truth, most parent-child relationships are characterized at best by an underlying ambivalence. Mixed with the love that a child may show his parents is the frustration they engender in him as he seeks his own independent way of life, his growing awareness of a distaste for various aspects of their behavior, his resentment over the controls they impose upon him. Mixed with the love of a parent for his offspring is the burden that their upbringing will place on him, the anxiety that each stage of their development arouses in him, the fear that they will reject his guidance and abandon him in his old age.

For the child, the parent constitutes not just the fount of his being but a shadow from the past impinging on his actions, inhibiting his growth; for the parent, children not only represent the assurance of the continuity of name and memory but also are a reminder that theirs is a future in which he cannot share. The symbiotic attraction of mutual need is offset by the centrifugal forces of diverging, often opposing, interests. In the words of

James Joyce, "The son unborn mars beauty; born he brings pain, divides affection, increases care . . . [H]is growth is his father's decline, his youth his father's envy."[106]

The true message of the Delphic oracle in *Oedipus Rex* could well have been intended to warn Laius that his son would surpass him in the future. The core of the tragedy, in such terms, would involve the futility of trying to escape the inevitable. The solution was not to attempt to be rid of the son, nor to ignore the warning, but to realize that the message was speaking of the difficulties of parenthood and of a future when the parents would be obliged to make way for the growing powers of their child.

The message of the oracle posed a challenge—the challenge of parenthood, of learning to cope with the problems posed by the young. The message was misunderstood by Laius, who tried to defy it; it was misinterpreted by Freud, who build a theoretical model of universal child hostility around it; it has been misused by those who attempt to offer one-sided explanations for generational tensions within the family and in society.

The Rustum complex might well help us to understand the overall meaning of the Oedipus story. For the importance of the Rustum complex lies not merely in its indication of parental/adult hostility but also in the possibility that awareness of the several factors inducing such hostility may facilitate efforts to ameliorate it. Rustum, after all, felt genuine grief at the death of his son. He was as misguided as Laius. Laius had abandoned his son to die. Rustum had abandoned his son by ignoring him through the years of his growth in the mistaken notion that it was "only" a daughter who had been born.[107] The tragedies of both stories result from the physical separation over the years.

Both myths, by pointing out the dangers of separation, emphasize thereby the need for a bridge between the generations. Both myths, by pointing out the difficulties of living together, emphasize the need for mutual efforts at understanding. Both myths address the dilemmas of generational conflict—and warn of the dire consequences of failing to resolve it.

References

1. See Martin Kallich, Andrew MacLeish, and Gertrude Schoenbohm, eds., *Oedipus: Myth and Drama* (New York: Odyssey Press, 1968). The book contains the versions by Sophocles (*Oedipus the King*), John Dryden and Nathaniel Lee (*Oedipus*), and Hugo von Hofmannstahl (*Oedipus and the Sphinx*). Other versions include those by Seneca, Pierre Corneille, and Voltaire. The story has also been given several cinematic presentations.

2. Sigmund Freud, *The Interpretation of Dreams* (1900), in *The Standard Edition of*

the Complete Psychological Works, edited by James Strachey, 24 vols. (London: Hogarth Press, 1953–66), 4: 262–263.

3.   Sigmund Freud, "Dostoevsky and Parricide" (1928), in *The Standard Edition,* 21: 188.

4.   Ernest Jones, *Hamlet and Oedipus* (Garden City, N.Y.: Doubleday Anchor, 1949).

5.   Ibid., p. 152.

6.   See Geza Roheim, *Psychoanalysis and Anthropology* (New York: International Universities Press, 1950); and "Society and the Individual," *The Psychoanalytical Quarterly* 9 (1940): 526–545; Otto Rank, *The Myth of the Birth of the Hero* (New York: Robert Brunner, 1952; the first edition of the book was published in German in 1909).

7.   See, for instance, W. N. Stephens, *The Oedipus Complex: Cross-Cultural Evidence* (Glencoe, Ill.: Free Press, 1962), which concentrates almost solely on incest.

8.   See Sigmund Freud, *Totem and Taboo* (1913), in *The Standard Edition,* 13: 156. See also "A Short Account of Psychoanalysis" (1924), in *The Standard Edition,* 19: 208.

9.   Franz Alexander and Hugo Staub, *The Criminal, the Judge and the Public—A Psychological Analysis,* (Glencoe, Ill.: Free Press, 1956), p. 30. See also Kate Friedlander, *The Psychoanalytical Approach to Juvenile Delinquency* (London: Routledge & Kegan Paul, 1951). For a general analysis of the impact of the Oedipus complex on a number of non-Freudian or neo-Freudian psychoanalysts, see Patrick Mullahy, *Oedipus: Myth and Complex—A Review of Psychoanalytic Theory* (New York: Hermitage Press, 1948). Mullahy discusses the work of Adler, Jung, Rank, Horney, Fromm, and Sullivan.

10.   Jones, *Hamlet and Oedipus,* p. 89.

11.   Lewis S. Feuer, *The Conflict of Generations: The Character and Significance of Student Movements* (New York, Basic Books, 1969). Feuer picks up these themes at several places—see especially chapter 1, "The Sources and Traits of Student Movements." I discuss this work at length in chapter 6.

12.   Morton Levitt and Ben Rubenstein, "The Student Revolt: *Totem and Taboo* Revisited," *Psychiatry* 34 (1971): 160. See also Gerald H. Pearson, *Adolescence and the Conflict of Generations* (New York: Norton, 1958).

13.   Otto Rank, *The Trauma of Birth* (New York: Harcourt, Brace, 1929). It should be noted, however, that although Freud's relations with many of his disciples were stormy, in this case Freud did do his best to adopt a conciliatory attitude toward Rank; it was the more orthodox among his followers who pressed for a break with Rank (see Marthe Robert, *The Psychological Revolution—Sigmund Freud's Life and Achievement* [New York: Avon Books, 1966, pp. 336–339.] See discussion on the book in "Editor's Introduction" to Sigmund Freud, *Inhibitions, Symptoms and Anxiety* (1926), in *The Standard Edition,* 20: 85–86.)

14.   Letter No. 210 in Ernst L. Freud, ed., *Letters of Sigmund Freud* (New York: Basic Books, 1960).

15. Sigmund Freud, "An Autobiographical Study" (1925), in *The Standard Edition*, 20: 53.

16. Alfred Adler, *Superiority and Social Interest* (London: Routledge & Kegan Paul, 1965), pp. 207ff. See also the discussion of the Oedipus complex in Heinz and Rowena Ansbacher, *The Individual Psychology of Alfred Adler* (New York: Basic Books, 1956), pp. 375–376.

17. Bronislaw Malinowski, *Sex and Repression in Savage Society* (New York: Harcourt, Brace, 1927). See response to Malinowski by Ernest Jones, "Mother-Right and Sexual Ignorance of Savages" in *Essays in Applied Psychoanalysis* (New York: International Universities Press, 1964), pp. 145–173. See also Anne Parsons, "Is the Oedipus Complex Universal?: The Jones–Malinowski Debate Revisited and a South Italian 'Nuclear Complex,' " *The Psychoanalytic Study of Society* 3 (1964): 278–328.

18. William Lessa, "Oedipus-Type Tales in Oceania," *Journal of American Folklore* 69 (1956): 63–73.

19. FitzRoy R. Somerset, Baron Raglan, *The Hero: A Study in Tradition, Myth and Drama* (London: Methuen, 1963). For a criticism of this analysis see William Bascom, "The Myth-Ritual Theory," *Journal of American Folklore* 70 (1957): 103.

20. For list of writers see footnote 4 in chapter 1.

21. Erich Fromm, "The Oedipus Complex and the Oedipus Myth," in Ruth Nanda Anshen (ed.), *The Family: Its Function and Destiny*, rev. ed. (New York: Harper and Row, 1959), p. 426.

22. Ibid., p. 427.

23. See Johann J. Bachofen, *Myth, Religion and Mother Right: Selected Writings*, trans. by Ralph Manheim (Princeton: Princeton University Press, 1967).

24. Sophocles, *Oedipus at Colonnus*, in *The Oedipus Cycle*, trans. by Robert Fitzgerald [New York: Harcourt Brace Jovanovich, Inc. (a Harvest book), 1949], Scene 6, pp. 147–151.

25. Rollo May, "The Meaning of the Oedipus Myth," in Roger W. Smith (ed.), *Guilt: Man and Society* (Garden City, N.Y.: Doubleday Anchor, 1971), pp. 171–183, reprinted from *Review of Existential Psychology and Psychiatry* 1 (1961). For a further analysis of the play, see Donald C. Hodges, "Fratricide and Fraternity," in Smith, ed., ibid., pp. 198–216, reprinted from the *Journal of Religion* 38 (1958). Hodges argues that the concept of brotherhood is a reaction to fratricidal strife.

26. Sophocles, *Antigone*, in *The Oedipus Cycle*, trans. by Dudley Fitts and Robert Fitzgerald, New York: Harcourt Brace Jovanovich, Inc., Scene 3, p. 211.

27. Ibid., p. 211.

28. Ibid., p. 214.

29. Ibid., p. 217.

30. Melville J. and Frances S. Herskovits, *Dahomean Narrative* (Evanston: Northwestern University Press, 1958), p. 90; also in "Sibling Rivalry, the Oedipus Complex and Myth," *Journal of American Folklore* 71 (1958): 1–15.

31. Herskovits and Herskovits, *Dahomean Narrative*, pp. 94–95. For an interesting

comparison between Oedipus and a leading myth from Benin in West Africa, see Peter P. Ekeh, "Benin and Thebes: Elementary Forms of Civilization," *The Psychoanalytic Study of Society* 7 (1976): 68–69.

32.   Philip Rieff, *Freud: The Mind of the Moralist* (London: University Paperbacks, 1965), p. 195.

33.   Ibid., p. 196.

34.   Ibid., p. 195.

35.   See Søren Kierkegaard, *Fear and Trembling* (Garden City, N.Y.: Doubleday Anchor, 1954). Kierkegaard deals with the agonizing of Abraham as he responds to God's test to sacrifice his son. The idea of the sacrifice of Isaac has often been used as a symbol of generational conflict. This topic is discussed further on in this chapter.

36.   Roheim, "Society and the Individual," p. 542.

37.   Roheim, *Psychoanalysis and Anthropology.*

38.   Clyde Kluckhohn, "Recurrent Themes in Myths and Mythmaking," *Daedalus* 88 (1959): 273.

39.   Herskovits and Herskovits, "Sibling Rivalry," p. 11.

40.   Ibid., p. 11.

41.   Stith Thompson, *Motif Index of Folk Literature* (Copenhagen: Rosenkilde and Bagger, 1957); and Stith Thompson, *The Folktale* (New York: Holt, Rinehart & Winston, 1946).

42.   A. J. Levin, "The Oedipus Myth in History and Psychiatry," *Psychiatry* 2 (1948): 287.

43.   Edith Hamilton, *Mythology* (New York: Mentor, 1942), pp. 65–66. See also G. S. Kirk, *The Nature of Greek Myths* (Harmondsworth, England: Pelican, 1974), pp. 113–118. Kirk also points out that Zeus continues the pattern of his father's behavior as "in his turn [he] is threatened by the problem of a powerful son destined to overthrow him, and he meets it . . . by swallowing the mother and so preventing the child from even being born" (p. 120). Kirk also draws attention to the close parallel between the Cronus-Zeus myth and another neo-Eastern myth of Kumawbi and Anu (p. 117).

44.   Sigmund Freud, *Totem and Taboo* (1913), in *The Standard Edition,* 13: 141–142.

45.   Ibid., p. 145.

46.   Freud, "Inhibition, Symptoms and Anxiety," 20:105. Greek tradition also has the story of Tantalus serving the flesh of his own son, Pelops; see Henry A. Bunker, "The Feast of Tantalus," *Psychoanalytic Quarterly* 21 (1952): 355.

47.   Freud was also puzzled by another Greek myth where the young god Dionysius is torn to pieces and killed by the older Titans. Freud uses this incident to substantiate the importance of the totemic feast but adds: ". . . there is a disturbing difference in the fact of the murder having been committed on a *youthful* god" (see *Totem and Taboo,* p. 154).

48. Sigmund Freud, *The Future of an Illusion* (1927), in *The Standard Edition,* 21: 42.

49. Sigmund Freud, *Moses and Monotheism* (1939), in *The Standard Edition,* 23: 88–89.

50. Ibid., p. 89. See also similar oedipal analysis by J. C. Flugel, *Man, Morals and Society: A Psycho-analytical Study* (London: Backworth, 1945), p. 273; and Erich Fromm, *The Dogma of Christ* (New York: Holt, Rinehart & Winston, 1955), p. 46. See also Robert Bank, "A Neo-Freudian Critique of Religion: Erich Fromm on the Judeo-Christian Tradition," *Religion* 5 (1975): 125.

51. Freud, *Totem and Taboo,* p. 154.

52. Philip Rieff, *Freud: The Mind of the Moralist,* p. 195.

53. Ibid., p. 195.

54. Sigmund Freud, *From the History of an Infantile Neurosis* (1918), in *The Standard Edition,* 17: 66.

55. Erich Wellisch, *Isaac and Oedipus: A Study in Biblical Psychology of the Sacrifice of Isaac—the Akedah* (London: Routledge & Kegan Paul, 1954).

56. Ibid., p. 5.

57. Ibid., p. 88.

58. J. H. Hertz, *The Pentateuch* (London: Soncino Press, 1950), p. 201.

59. Wellisch, *Isaac and Oedipus,* p. 78.

60. Roger Money-Kyrle, *The Meaning of Sacrifice* (London: Hogarth Press, 1930), p. 234.

61. Erich Neumann, *The Origins and History of Consciousness* (New York: Torchbooks, 1962), vol. 1, p. 190.

62. Israel Charny, "And Abraham Went to Slay Isaac: a Parable of Killer, Victim, and Bystander in the Family," *Journal of Ecumenical Studies* 10 (1973): 304–318. For other references to the sacrifice of Isaac see Shalom Spiegel, *The Last Trial* (Philadelphia: Jewish Publication Society, 1967); Ignaz Maybaum, *Creation and Guilt: A Theological Assessment of Freud's Father-Son Conflict* (London: Valentine, Mitchell, 1969); Arnoldo Rascovsky, *El Filicido* (Buenos Aires: Ediciones Orion, n.d.); Gustav Dreiffuss, "Isaac, the Sacrificial Lamb: A Study of Some Jewish Legends," *Journal of Analytic Psychology* 16 (1971): 69–78, and "The Binding of Isaac (Genesis 22—the Akedah)," *Journal of Analytic Psychology* 20 (1975): 50–56; H. Westmann, "The Akedah," *Journal of Existential Psychiatry* (1961): 512–518.

63. S. Giora Shoham, "The Isaac Syndrome," *American Imago* 33 (1976): 232.

64. Shoham takes note of the fact that Wellisch and others had earlier suggested a Laius complex, but Shoham claims that an Isaac syndrome is "more forceful, explicit and dramatic." However, it is not clear that the use of Isaac embraces Shoham's intention, for the opposite of Oedipus the son should be a father—in this case Abraham. Thus Shoham notes that the Medea complex, suggested by E. S. Stern (see *Journal of Mental Science* 94 (1948): 329) is "the maternal counterpart of the

Isaac syndrome insofar as it expresses the infanticidal urges of the mother"—Medea being the mother who killed her children. Here, too, it seems that the Abraham complex or syndrome would be the proper counterpart to a Medea complex. In a Hebrew version of his article, Shoham uses the term "Akedah complex." (See chapter 8 in S. Giora Shoham, *Halichei Tantalus* (Tel Aviv: Tcherikover, 1977).

65.   Kierkegaard, *Fear and Trembling.*

66.   Ibid., p. 69.

67.   Ibid., pp. 68–69.

68.   Fustel de Coulanges, *The Ancient City: A Study on the Religion, Laws and Institutions of Greece and Rome* (Garden City, N.Y.: Doubleday Anchor, 1956), p. 93.

69.   David Bakan, "Paternity in the Judeo-Christian Tradition," *The Human Context* 4 (1972): 354.

70.   Ibid., p. 354.

71.   Ibid., p. 358. Bakan deals with the theme of Biblical references to the question of infanticidal impulses in two further books, *Disease, Pain and Suffering: Toward a Psychology of Suffering* (Chicago: University of Chicago Press, 1968); and *The Duality of Human Existence: An Essay on Psychology and Religion* (Chicago: Rand McNally, 1966). Bakan also has a fascinating analysis of the underlying meaning of many nursery tales and other stories and poems for children in his book *Slaughter of the Innocents* (San Francisco: Jossey-Bass, 1967). He sees many of these stories as being subtle warnings to children of covert hostile feelings felt by parents. For a totally different approach to nursery tales, based on an oedipal perspective, see Bruno Bettelheim, *The Uses of Enchantment* (New York: Knopf, 1976).

72.   Malachi, chapter 3, verses 23–24.

73.   See, for example, Charles S. T. White, "Krsna as Divine Child," *History of Religion* 10 (1970): 159; J. G. Frazer, *The Golden Bough: A Study in Magic and Religion,* abridged ed. (London: Macmillan, 1963), p. 359.

74.   From the *Shahnamah* by Firdausi (932–1020). See John D. Yohannan, *A Treasury of Asian Literature* (New York: Mentor, 1956), pp. 108–130. For further references to the exploits of Rustum, see E. G. Browne, *Literary History of Persia* (Cambridge: Cambridge University Press, 1956), 4 vols., and Jan Rypka, *History of Iranian Literature* (Dordrecht, Holland: D. Reidel, 1968). Both Browne and Rypka discuss Firdausi's achievements as one of Persia's greatest national poets.

75.   Kenneth Allott, ed., *The Poems of Matthew Arnold* (London: Longmans, 1965), pp. 302–330. In the introduction to the poem, Allott notes the circumstances in which the poem was written, the poet's pleasure with the poem, and the version of the story Arnold had originally read in Sir John Malcolm's *History of Persia.*

76.   Anne Terry White, ed., *Myths and Legends* (London: Paul Hamlyn, 1964), p. 131.

77.   Lionel Trilling, *Matthew Arnold* (New York: Meridian Books, 1955), p. 124.

78.   Yohannan, *A Treasury of Asian Literature,* p. 108.

79. Kenneth Burke, *A Rhetoric of Motives* (Berkeley: University of California Press, 1969), p. 8.

80. Bruce Mazlish, *James and John Stuart Mill: Father and Son in the Nineteenth Century* (New York: Basic Books, 1975), p. 33. Mazlish bases this interpretation on Howard R. Wolf, "British Fathers and Sons, 1773–1913: From Filial Submissiveness to Creativity," *The Psychoanalytic Review* 52 (1965): 53–70.

81. A. Dwight Culler, *Imaginative Reason: The Poetry of Matthew Arnold* (New Haven: Yale University Press, 1966), p. 229.

82. Ibid., p. 230.

83. Allott, *The Poems of Matthew Arnold,* p. 302.

84. William A. Madden, *Matthew Arnold: A Study of the Aesthetic Temperament in Victorian England* (Bloomington: Indiana University Press, 1967).

85. Ibid., pp. 27–28.

86. Ibid., p. 32.

87. I am hesitant to add another complex to the many that have been suggested over the years, but I feel that there is a great need to offset the influence of the Oedipus complex. Among the complexes that have been put forward, apart from the Laius complex, are: the Medea complex (E. S. Stern, "The Medea Complex: The Mother's Homicidal Wishes to her Child," *Journal of Mental Science* 94 [1948]: 329); the Isaac complex (see Neumann, *The Origins and History of Consciousness*); the Joseph complex (M. Sperber, "Misère de la psychologie," *Preuves* 4 [1954]: 9–26), the Lear complex (Richard J. Tuarrma, "The 'Lear Complex' in *The Two Gentlemen of Verona,*" Literature and Psychology 27 [1972]: 199–202); the Orestes complex (Frederic Wertham, "The Matricidal Impulse," *Journal of Criminal Psychopathology* [1944]: 455, and *Dark Legend* [Garden City, N.Y.: Doubleday, 1949]); the catastrophic death complex (Joseph Rheingold, *The Mother, Anxiety and Death: Catastrophic Death Complex* [Boston: Little, Brown, 1967]); the Ulysses complex (Luciano Santiago, "The Ulysses Complex," *American Imago* 28 [1971]: 158–185); the Polyneices complex (Donald C. Hodges, "Fratricide and Fraternity," in Smith, *Guilt: Man and Society,* and in *The Journal of Religion* 38 [1958]); the Griselda complex (J. J. Putnam, "Bemerkungen über einen Krankheitsfall mit Griselda-Phantasien," *Internationale Zeitschrift für Psychoanalyse* 1 [1913]).

88. William Rose Benét, *The Reader's Encyclopedia* (New York: Thomas Crowell, 1948), p. 184.

89. Richard H. Solomon, *Mao's Revolution and the Chinese Political Culture* (Berkeley: University of California Press, 1971).

90. Ibid., p. 35.

91. Ibid., pp. 35–37.

92. Ibid., p. 35.

93. Solomon's work, inasmuch as it touches on generational conflict in China, is dealt with further in chapter 5.

94. Thomas S. Vernon, "The Laius Complex," *The Humanist* (November–December 1972): 27.

95.   These phenomena (child abuse, infanticide, exploitation of children) will be examined in chapter 7, "Children of All Ages," and incest in chapter 3, "Beyond Incest and Parricide."

96.   See Helm Stierlin, J. David Levi, and Robert J. Savard, "Parental Perception of Separating Children," *Family Process* 10 (1971): 411; and J. David Levi, Helm Stierlin, and Robert J. Savard, "Fathers and Sons: The Interlocking Crises of Integrity and Identity," *Psychiatry* 35 (1972): 48–57.

97.   Malinowski, *Sex and Repression in Savage Society,* pp. 37–38.

98.   Erich Fromm, *Man for Himself: Inquiry into the Psychology of Ethics* (New York: Rinehart, 1947), pp. 153–154.

99.   Gerard Mendel, *Pour décolonier l'enfant: Sociopsychoanalyse de l'autorité* (Paris: Petite Bibliothèque Payot, 1971).

100.   Arnoldo Rascovsky, "Filicide and Its Relation to War," paper at a conference on "The Role and Relevance of Psychology in World Politics," held in New York in 1970. For references to Rascovsky's work see Emanuel K. Schwartz, "Child Murder Today," *The Human Context* 4 (1972): 360, and the column by Schwartz, "Facts, Fancies and Reflections," *The Human Context* 1 (1968): 346, and 4 (1972): 192 and 376.

101.   Rollo May, *Power and Innocence* (New York: W. W. Norton, 1972). See especially the extract from this book, "The Innocent Murderers," *Psychology Today* 6 (December 1972): 52.

102.   Lloyd deMause (ed.), *The History of Childhood* (New York: The Psychohistory Press, 1974). See also *The History of Childhood Quarterly: The Journal of Psychohistory* 1 (1973) for deMause's introductory article to his book and the responses to it by several writers, especially Rudolph Binion (pp. 576–577), Helm Stierlin (p. 583), John F. Benton (pp. 584–585), Herbert Moller (pp. 590–591) and Michael B. Katz (pp. 601–602).

103.   David J. Rothman, "Documents in Search of a Historian: Toward a History of Childhood and Youth in America," *Journal of Interdisciplinary History* 2 (1971): 376.

104.   Anthony Platt, *The Child Savers: The Invention of Delinquency* (Chicago: University of Chicago Press, 1969).

105.   Israel W. Charny, "Injustice and Betrayal as Natural Experiences in Family Life," *Psychotherapy: Theory, Research and Practice* 9 (1972): 86.

106.   James Joyce, *Ulysses* (New York: Modern Library, 1940), pp. 207–208.

107.   The fact that Rustum ignored his child under the incorrect impression that a daughter had been born is, of course, a further indication of parental deficiency, though as a manifestation of hostility it lacks the two primary qualities of the ultimate Rustum-Sohrab confrontation: namely, that, as in the Oedipus story, the hostility both is unconsciously expressed and has fatal consequences. Although the book is based on the story of a father-son confrontation, my discussion, for the most part, centers on parents as parents, and children as children. Inasmuch as gender comes into consideration, it is primarily because of social and cultural arrangements, where men and women are assigned different roles. In any event, the hostility

arises not so much from the specific roles of mother and father but from the broader factors of parenthood as such. Much of the discussion, particularly of mythology, literature, and historical facts, centers on father-son relations; but this is because the nature of the evidence in patriarchal society is male-oriented. While I came across stories similar to that of Sohrab and Rustum (a single confrontation ending in filicide with identities unknown) in Celtic and Chinese mythology (see footnotes 88 and 89) I did not come across any similar stories of clashes between a father and his daughter or a mother and her child (whether son or daughter). There are other stories in which mothers do destroy their children, and Stern has used one of these stories as the basis for a Medea complex (see footnote 87), but here, as also in other stories of fathers destroying their daughters (Agamemnon and Iphigenia, Jephthah and his daughter), the act is done intentionally.

Freud himself used the concept of the Oedipus complex initially to refer to both male and female and claimed, at the beginning, that the processes—of incestuous and homicidal feelings—were similar for boys and for girls. Later, when he modified his ideas and explained that male and female went through different socialization experiences (see footnote 30 in chapter 11), he continued to use oedipal terminology, e.g., "preoedipal" for the stage where the difference originated because of children of both sexes being exposed to similar nurturant, and therefore erotic, sensations by the mother. He never used the phrase Electra complex, which is sometimes used by other writers, and in common parlance, to denote the girl's hostility to the mother. In any case, Electra's matricide also lacked the element of the unconscious. Neither Laius nor Rustum had a daughter. It should also be mentioned that Tanima, the mother of Sohrab, did not show any clear hostile feelings, though it was, of course, her original untruth as to the gender of the child that contributed to the later tragedy. Her own role can also be seen as generally overprotective of her son, but again this is of minimal import compared to the act of Rustum, or even compared to Jocasta's role in abandoning Oedipus. In some versions of the story Rustum and Tanima are presented not as a married couple but as lovers.

My intention when dealing with the story of Sohrab and Rustum, or in using the term Rustum complex, is to stress the hostility of parents of either sex toward their children of either sex. In this context I might add that I have used the male form—"he, his, him"—when referring to child, parent, adult, or person . This seems to me less awkward than alternating between "he" and "she," or using simultaneously "he and she," or "he/she." I do so on the basis of an approach that I offer for general consideration, as a means of resolving the problem of which gender to use grammatically when dealing factually with both genders: that writers should use their own gender—males to use "he, his, him," and females to use "she, hers, her." Such a solution would resolve the added problem that exists in many languages other than English, where the form of the verb and adjective also changes according to the gender, often in both the singular and the plural, so that the solutions available in English become technically impossible in other languages. In addition many languages also lack a neuter form of nouns and pronouns so that even using a plural form—"they, their, them"—(as many writers are now wont to do) does not solve the problem, since in such languages one is still obliged to choose between masculine and feminine forms in the plural.

CHAPTER THREE
BEYOND INCEST AND PARRICIDE

In the previous chapters I have argued that we will be able to come to terms with the full impact of parental and adult hostility only after we have shorn ourselves of many of the premises of Freudian thinking. I have suggested that we need to move beyond the Oedipus complex, with the constraints that it imposes on our thought processes.

How to do this will form the essence of this chapter. Since empirical evidence of parental and adult hostility is in itself apparently insufficient to break through the theoretical premises and the ongoing prejudices that adults bring to bear on this topic, it seems necessary to mount a frontal attack on the Oedipus complex itself. Later chapters will adduce empirical evidence of, and suggest further theoretical explanations for, parental/adult hostility. Here I shall try to show how both the general biases of adulthood and the specific biases of Freud himself are reflected in the development of the oedipal theory.

The sociology of knowledge[1] asserts that a healthy skepticism is an essential ingredient for a critical analysis of themes of human behavior and social life. A writer's background should be subjected to close scrutiny in order to determine the extent to which social and personal factors have intruded on his thinking and influenced his findings.

In few cases has scientific theory been so closely linked to personal background as in the case of Sigmund Freud, who based much of his theoretical framework on his own experiences, both personal and clinical. In no aspect of his theory is the personal aspect of his writing more fully integrated and expressed than in the Oedipus complex. Its twin themes of incest and parricide were agonizingly developed in the course of Freud's attempts, through self-analysis, to understand himself, particularly in relation to his father.[2]

In this pioneering and momentous attempt at self-analysis Freud also claimed to have discovered the truth of filial hostility, which he saw as a universal phenomenon providing a key to the understanding of human relations, and which he later developed into a broad theory embracing all aspects of life and society. His own ambivalence toward his father, the slaying of Laius by Oedipus, and the "primal crime" of parricide—all sprang, according to Freud, from the same source of filial envy and hostility.

It was as a reaction to the sentiments that engulfed him after his father's death that Freud gained an insight into his ambivalence toward his father and came to understand the source of his negative feelings. Freud's followers have heaped praise on him not only for the originality of his insight but also for the courage and honesty that he displayed in openly acknowledging his own Oedipus complex and his negative feelings toward his father.

While Freud has been criticized for misinterpreting the Oedipus story and for trying to extrapolate from his own personal feelings to a universal theory of human behavior, there has, however, been little challenge to the validity of Freud's self-analysis, or questioning of the underlying assumptions that form the basis of the thought-processes that he employed in the course of his analysis.[3]

I shall try to show that Freud's conceptualization of the Oedipus complex was not only a reflection of the honesty with which he grappled with the problem of his relation with his father but also a reflection of a biased approach to the young—and, specifically, a consequence of his attempt to concentrate on the personal meaning of generational conflict in terms of his own problems *as a son,* while avoiding a confrontation with the personal meaning of generational conflict in terms of his own problems *as a father.*

Thus, within the constellation of his own family, Freud was trying to solve only one problem, that of his relationship toward his recently deceased father, whereas a no less significant problem for him at that particular time concerned his relations with his recently born children.

Prior to any attempt to penetrate into Freud's private and inner world, however, it is necessary to judge him on the basis of his open and presumably objective scientific writings, particularly as expressed in his attempts to probe into the private and inner worlds of those of his patients whose personal problems became the basis for Freud's presentation of his theories. A persistent pattern can be discovered in many of Freud's major clinical works that indicate partiality to the parental and adult generation. As Freud absorbed the details of his patient's problems so he constantly selected out and interpreted the data in such a way as to allow for presentations and explanations favorable to the parents and critical of the children.

This attitude can be seen at all stages of his career—during the very formulation of the idea of the Oedipus complex; subsequently, as the Oedipus complex tended to overshadow much of his work; and, even prior to the conceptualization of the Oedipus complex, when Freud should have been most free of any of the constraints that the theory may later have placed upon his perception and his perceptiveness. I shall analyze some of Freud's classic studies, pointing out errors that stem, it seems to me, from his selective perspective. I do this in all awareness of the greatness of Freud's work, of his dominance in the modern world, and of the deep change in our understanding of ourselves and our world that he fostered. It is precisely this greatness that obligates us to come to terms with Freud, even at the most personal level.

Frederick Hacker has posed the question, "What is the real Freud—and where do we find him—in his clinical papers, in *Beyond the Pleasure Principle*, in his *Moses and Monotheism?*"[4] I argue, in all of them, and in his other works. What is to be found, however, is not always favorable. Hacker has warned against the dangers of a vulgar, crude approach in which a great man such as Freud is shown to have "his foibles, his prejudices, his irrationalities, and his symptoms."[5] I hope to avoid these dangers; my intent is to expose his errors and prejudices in the realm of generational relations only insofar as they are relevant and essential for a fuller understanding of his work. Hacker himself concedes that he "cannot think of any more timely task than to try to re-discover Freud, or some aspect of him for ourselves as a personal, living, present experience, before he has completely ossified into the remote monument of 'the great man.' "[6]

There can indeed be no avoidance of a confrontation with Freud, the man, in all his capacities—as scientist and as citizen, as son and as father. For, in order to move *beyond* the Oedipus complex, we have to first look *behind* the Oedipus complex, and include in our gaze even some of the foibles, the prejudices, the irrationalities, and the symptoms of the man who discovered and formulated the complex.

In discussing Freud's work on the Oedipus complex, one must make a clear distinction between the two aspects of his theory—incest and parricide. Although neatly integrated into the Oedipus complex, they were developed separately. There is, for instance, no major recorded case in Freud's writing in which a parricidal act flowed directly out of incestuous rivalry. His view of incest was based on clinical work with female patients, that of parricide based on his own musings as to his relations with his father and on his interpretations of the meaning of dreams.

Although Freud's clinical work during the critical stage in his career at the end of the 19th century revolved mainly around the presumed fantasies of his patients as to incestuous relations with their parents, his first written reference to the Oedipus complex was made in a completely different context, that of the parricidal element, as expressed in dreams. Freud claimed that there were many cases of such tendencies, but specific examples to back up his contention are conspicuously lacking. In his major work, *The Interpretation of Dreams,*[7] published in 1900, Freud gives public expression for the first time to his new and revolutionary idea. The term Oedipus complex has not yet been used, but the importance of parricide is clearly brought out.

In the section entitled "Dreams of death of persons, of whom the dreamer is fond," Freud climaxes the twenty-page discussion by a four-page reference to the Oedipus story, in which, at this early stage, he is already seeing possible universal implications. After noting that we all share a common fate with Oedipus of feeling sexual impulses to our mother and hatred and murderous wishes to our father he adds "our dreams convince us that this is so."[8]

But what dreams? One would expect that in presenting so revolutionary and so controversial an idea, Freud would have made every effort to buttress his argument with irrefutable clinical evidence. Yet, of the ten dreams discussed in this section, none deal with incest and only two are by children dreaming of their parents' death.

In both these latter cases the dreamers are girls dreaming of the deaths of their mothers. Although Freud's prototype for the Oedipus complex is that of a son desiring the death of his father, *he does not present even one example* of a dream that fits this model.

The sum total of the evidence initially presented by Freud to support a new idea that he considered a key to one of the riddles of human life consists then of two matricidal dreams, one by a neurotic adult patient who recalled a dream from her childhood when she was four; the other by a mentally ill young woman who, according to Freud, displayed a "quite special aversion to her mother"[9] during her waking hours as well, so that her dreams were hardly supplying any new information about repressed, unconscious hostility. The only other example given of child hostility, in this section, is that of a man suffering from an obsessional neurosis that Freud traces to "an impulse to murder his somewhat over-severe father,"[10] impulses, however, that were not dreamt but were openly expressed. While perhaps consistent with Freud's thesis of filial hostility, this example does not really seem appropriate for a book on dreams, especially when it is the *only* example given of the "typical" Oedipus situation, e.g., of a son *vis-à-vis* his father.

Did Freud have no further examples on which he could draw; no other patients who had recounted their parricidal dreams; no such dreams related to him by colleagues or friends; none of his own dreams, considering the fact that it was during this period, while he was at work on *The Interpretation of Dreams,* that he was struggling to understand the nature of his relations with his father? (Although, interestingly, elsewhere in the book Freud does refer to his own dreams.[11])

How representative of humankind were these three examples? Was Freud really justified in using them as an entree into the tremendous oedipal theme? Could, for example, the recollection by a woman of a dream at the age of four be considered reliable, particularly given Freud's general reluctance to rely on the childhood memories of adults (and especially when they dealt with seduction by parents)? Could the dreams of a woman who openly hated her mother be considered relevant, given the fact that part of the profundity of the Oedipus story lay in the unconscious nature of filial hostility? And what about the neurotic son's "rather over-severe father"? Were the son's murderous impulses—again very much at the forefront of his consciousness—entirely unidirectional and based only on sexual rivalry, or were they perhaps a response to his father's "over-severe" behavior?

The paucity of sufficient data in respect of a crucial thesis that Freud was presenting is highlighted by the fact that, in making other merely marginal points, Freud often presented a surfeit of examples. Thus, at the end of this section, dealing with death-dreams against loved ones, Freud makes passing reference to the fact, not at all relevant to the section, that all dreams are egoistic, i.e., related directly to the dreamer even when he himself does not appear in the dream. In proof of this point, he provides as many as four examples, three of them from his own dreams.

Furthermore, according to his own presentation of the data at his disposal, the logical consequences of Freud's analysis of dreams should have led him in directions different from the Oedipus story. Thus, at one point in this section Freud states that "in none of my woman patients . . . have I failed to come upon this dream of the death of a brother or sister."[12] If the parricidal feeling was universal, as he claimed, why, then, was there not a similar prevalence of death wishes against parents? On the basis of these dreams, so significant by Freud's own contention, he should obviously have been seeing sibling rivalry as the universal phenomenon, which would also have been in line with the primal crime in the Bible. Some writers have taken issue with Freud on this very point and argued for a Cain complex or Cain jealousy.[13]

It is also interesting to note that in this section the first two dreams that Freud deals with in the opening paragraphs are *filicidal* dreams by mothers against their children.[14] Yet, Freud uses them only as examples of dreams that do *not* have to be analyzed in detail since they are *not* typical dreams; in the one case Freud claims that the dream has a meaning different from its apparent one; in the other, Freud explains that the dream of the death of a child was no more than a repetition of a dream from fifteen years earlier. While Freud makes only passing reference to them in this section, he discusses them at some length in another part of the book, in the chapter on "Distortion in Dreams."[15] Here his analysis is extremely revealing both for the brilliance of the manner in which he probes beyond the bare facts and for the selective approach that underlies his innovative manner of interpretation.

In the one case Freud explains that an aunt dreaming of the death of her nephew was really wishing for something else, the opportunity to be near a man whom she loved. This young woman had lived with an older sister; at the time of the treatment, the sister had one surviving son, after another son had died. While living with the sister she had developed a strong affection for a man who was a family friend of the sister. After some time, the man had broken off the relation with the woman, who, obsessed by her love for him, had sought various means to be near him, including attending public meetings and concerts where he was likely to be.

On the day before she was due to attend a concert at which the object of her affection was likely to be present, she dreamed of the death of her surviving nephew. Freud builds on these facts in masterly fashion to draw out of his patient the fact that, on the death of her other nephew, this man had come to her sister's house to express his condolences. Freud, having creatively pieced together the loose ends, shows the patient that she had, in her dream, wished for the death of the second nephew in the hope that the man might once again visit the sister's house, so that she could be near him. In essence, the thought of the nephew's death was in anticipation of the fact that she might be seeing the man the following day, just as she had seen him, on the last occasion, at the funeral of the other nephew.

This is in many respects a beautifully constructed analysis, of the sort that earned Freud his fame and that shows the power of insightful interpretation. But an uncomfortable question arises: was Freud's analysis, beautiful and brilliant as it was, correct? Before embarking on this involved analysis, Freud had been told by the woman herself of her own rather negative interpretation of the dream:

> As you will remember my sister has only one boy left now—Karl. She lost his elder brother, Otto, while I was still living with her. Otto was my favorite; I more or less brought him up. I'm fond of the little one too, but, of course, not nearly so fond as I was of the one who died. Last night, then, I dreamt that *I saw Karl lying dead before me. He was lying in his little coffin with his hands folded, and with candles all around;* in fact, *just like little Otto whose death was such a blow to me.* Now tell me, what can that mean? You know me. Am I such a wicked person that I can wish my sister to lose the one child she still has? Or does the dream mean that I would rather that Karl were dead than Otto, whom I was so much fonder of?[16]

Freud's reaction to the patient's musings is, "I assured her that this last interpretation was out of the question."[17] Note, not "unlikely" or "doubtful," but a categorical rejection. Freud gives no reasons for dismissing so peremptorily her interpretation, even though it fits in so ideally with Freud's own work on the role of dreams in expressing the unconscious.

Freud not only dismisses her interpretation, but links the dream directly to his own work. Thus, he goes on to suggest that the dream is an example of a dream being offered by a patient specifically in order to contradict his theory of the wish-dream, i.e., that the patient was trying to show him a dream, which since it could not be true, would undermine his theory of the role of dreams in expressing the unconscious. But the woman herself thought that the dream might be a true wish—it was Freud who denied its possibility. Perhaps that is why he was so abrupt and definite about rejecting her explanation; it seemed to have upset him more than her. For her explanation is a logical one—and possibly correct. She herself clearly had preferred the dead nephew; might she not be wishing that the favorite nephew were still alive, that if one of the nephews had to die it could have been the other one? The dream itself may well have been occasioned by the prospect of seeing the man she loved—but in contradistinction to Freud's argument, it could be that the association between seeing the man the following day and the last occasion she had seen him, at the nephew's funeral, might have touched off the normally suppressed wish that the less favored nephew could have been the one to die. Further could it not be that the filicidal overtones in the dream caused Freud not just to deny her interpretation but to do so in a categorical and final manner?

In the second case Freud discusses the meaning of a mother's death-wish against a child by explaining that it was merely a repetition of an earlier dream, dreamt fifteen years earlier. This, of course, doesn't negate the issue of maternal hostility. If anything, it accentuates it by showing the longevity of the sentiment. Freud's explanation is that this is an example of a screen memory, where a dream may relate to an earlier sentiment. His patient had dreamed that her fifteen-year-old daughter was lying dead before her in a box. By drawing a parallel between the box and a child in a mother's womb, Freud was able to elicit from the patient that she had had death-wishes against her child fifteen years before, when she was still pregnant. Freud explains:

> Like so many young married women, she had been far from pleased when she became pregnant, and, more than once, she had allowed herself to wish that the child in her womb might die. Indeed, in a fit of rage, after a violent scene with her husband, she had beaten with her fists on her body so as to hit the child inside it. Thus, the dead child was in fact the fulfillment of a wish, but a wish that had been put aside fifteen years earlier. It is scarcely to be wondered at, if a wish that was fulfilled after such a long delay, was not recognized; too much had changed in the interval.[18]

Once again there are gnawing questions that have to be put. Although Freud states that much had changed in the fifteen years since the birth of the child, intimating that there was no further reason for her to resent the daughter, can he—or we—be sure? Was the conscious wish of fifteen years ago the cause of her dream, as Freud would have it, or was it perhaps the result of a death-wish that had persisted over the years but that had been repressed, as the very logic of pure Freudian thinking based on the unconscious would sustain?

If Freud is convinced that her reluctance to have a child is shared with "so many young married women," surely this is a factor requiring further investigation, not necessarily in a work on dreams, but in a separate work.

For, after all, what happens to all these once-unwanted children? Do their mothers always accept their later appearance willingly and joyfully, when the initial reaction was so negative? Perhaps, in this insight that so many young women are unhappy to be pregnant, may be found the germ of an idea that could be pursued so as to enquire into such other phenomena as abortion, neonaticide, infanticide, and the postpartum depression.

In addition, Freud notes that, in wishing for the death of the child in her womb, the woman was only repeating the experience of her own mother, who had had such death-wishes against her when she was in her mother's womb. An interesting analysis, one that again shows the perceptive manner of Freud's probing but that obviously begs the question as far as parental hostility is concerned. For we are now left totally without an explanation for the hostility of the mother toward the patient and the reason for the mother's death-wish against her while she was still in the womb. Was it perhaps because of the death-wish by the patient's grandmother against the mother when the latter had been in the former's womb—perhaps tracing back such feelings through the generations *ad infinitum?*

Other indications of Freud's biased position may be noted in the manner in which he deals, in general terms, with the theme of death-wishes against close relatives. At one point Freud stresses that

> If anyone dreams with every sign of pain that his father or mother, his brother or sister has died, I should never use the dream as evidence that he wishes for that person's death *at the present time* [italics in original]. The theory of dreams does not require as much as that; it is satisfied with the inference that this death has been wished for some time or other during the dreamer's child-hood.[19]

So, even when dealing directly with the theme of parricide (together with matricide, fratricide, and sororicide) Freud stresses that it is only a reflection and repetition of a childhood-wish. In other words, a child might have meaningful parricidal or fratricidal dreams; but an adult, having similar dreams, is not likely to intend such negative wishes.

On two other occasions, in later works, Freud discusses death-wish dreams toward the immediate members of the family, yet leaves out the example of death-wishes toward sons and daughters. On one occasion he writes: "Whenever anyone in the course of one's life gets in one's way . . . a dream is promptly resorted to to kill that person, even if it be the father or mother, brother or sister, husband or wife."[20] What about son or daughter—do they never get in one's way? And if they do, is a dream never resorted to? What makes this slip even more strange, and perhaps more significant, is the fact that it follows immediately after Freud had actually related two dreams in which parents had wished for the death of their children—which Freud, in any case, had tried to explain by stating that they were not real wishes.

In another work, Freud repeats the slip: "Anyone who investigates the origin and significance of dreams of death of loved relatives (of parents or brothers or sisters) will be able to convince himself that dreamers, children and savages are at one in their attitude towards the dead."[21] Once again the examples given in parenthesis omit the possibility of sons and daughters (as well as husbands and wives). What is the reason for twice leaving out the examples of death-wishes against children? Are the omissions accidental, deliberate, unconscious? Were these mere oversights on Freud's part? Can they be seen as *mere* oversights, given Freud's own writings on the *Psychopathology of Everyday Life,*[22] and the importance he himself attached to "accidental slips"? Is it not possible that lurking behind these apparently minor lapses is a reluctance on the part of Freud to allow even the most innocent of alternative references to upset the original and creative model of human behavior built around child hostility that he had so assiduously carved out?

Exactly how oblivious Freud was to possible parental hostility may be noted by a footnote quotation in a major work. After stating that "the evidence of psycho-analysis shows that almost every emotional relation between two people which lasts for some time—marriage, friendship, the relations between parents and children—contains a sediment of feelings of aversion and hostility. . . ." Freud adds in a footnote: "perhaps with the solitary exception of the relation of a mother to her son. . . ."[23]

In discussing Freud's work on dreams it must be conceded that some, at least, of the critique is speculative. After all, despite Freud's own original ideas on the psychopathology of everyday life, his lapses in discussing dreams may be genuine oversights without any covert meaning behind them. Also, his examples in the *Interpretation of Dreams* may be only random choices taken from a far larger sample at his disposal, and the possible alternative explanations are admittedly open to debate, with the actual information provided by Freud rather limited.

However, a clearer picture of Freud's selective approach emerges from his classical case studies—Schreber, Little Hans, Dora[24]—in which Freud sets out in detail the facts on which he based his analysis. Here we may move beyond surmise to examine far more precisely the thought processes that Freud employed.

These cases have attracted intense interest over the years, for the mastery of Freud's analysis, for the clarity and beauty of his language, and for the importance of his theoretical presentation, expecially in the area of psychopathology. Despite their continuing popularity, however, these studies have also been subjected to harsh criticism for basic errors of methodology in collecting the data and of logic in interpreting them. In some instances Freud has been accused even of distortion and bias.

Morton Schatzman[25] has reappraised the case of Schreber, in which

Freud set out a theory of paranoia: Schatzman's contention is that the basis for Schreber's "paranoid delusions" was the prior persecution by the father. The case of Little Hans has been subjected to criticism by Erich Fromm[26] and by Joseph Wolpe and Stanley Rachman;[27] Freud's claim that he had found direct proof of oedipal tendencies in the young five-year-old is challenged as the critics point out clear instances of sexual abuse by the parents. L. J. Simon[28] and Steven Marcus[29] have both strongly disputed Freud's handling of the case of Dora. To refute Freud's description of his young patient's behavior as hysterical, they accuse Freud of lack of sympathy for the girl and point out how Freud ignored the negative role played by her father in causing her mental distress.

All of these critiques were made independently; all of them relate directly to the empirical data of each case, as related by Freud, and seem to have no clear unifying theoretical perspective. Yet, there is a definite connection between the three cases. All three contain errors and distortions in Freud's analysis that can be traced partly to his commitment to the Oedipus complex and related ideas, with his concomitant disregard for any alternative explanation that might involve disapproval of parental conduct.

The full range of Freud's creative mind can be seen at work in his case studies; indeed, much of his towering status in the world of psychology rests upon the convincing tone of these presentations. Sometimes, however, the sheer virtuosity of Freud's reasoning process tends to overshadow the paucity of his data, the inconsistencies in his argument, or the fact that he usually concentrated his analyses on his patient alone, with little or no consideration of the impact of the latter's interaction with significant others, particularly parents.

The study of Schreber is a case in point. Schreber was a prominent German jurist who, during a remission between nervous breakdowns, wrote a book about his mental illness,[30] much of it consisting of fantasies of persecution drawn from his childhood and of delusions concerning a fearful, omnipotent God-figure. Although he never met Schreber personally, Freud used Schreber's book to analyze his illness and to evolve a theory of paranoia. According to Freud, Schreber had harbored a forbidden homosexual love for his father, which he overcame by turning his love into hate and then rationalizing this hatred as a reaction to his father's prior hatred and persecution of him. Since, according to Freud, no parental hatred had in fact existed, Schreber's mental illness could be attributed to his fantasies and delusions of persecution, hence the basis for his paranoia.

When considering most of the case studies, the reader is forced to rely solely on the information provided by Freud, which, naturally, is selective. In the case of Schreber, however, there is an independent source that can serve as a measure of Freud's analysis. In his illuminating and incisive book, Schatzman shows how an examination of this independent source exposes both the fallacy of Freud's reasoning and his biased perspective.

The independent source is the writings of Schreber's father,[31] one of Germany's leading educators in the nineteenth century who wrote a great many books on child training. Freud was well aware of the senior Schreber's stature and influence in the realm of education, yet he did not avail himself of the latter's writings in order to gain a fuller understanding of the son, even though he had traced the younger Schreber's illness to his problematic relationship with his father. Ironically, Freud did concede that a more precise knowledge of Schreber's life would be valuable in deciding whether his or Schreber's account more closely tallied with the true situation:

> Anyone who was more daring than I am in making interpretations, or who was in touch with Schreber's family and consequently better acquainted with the society in which he moved and the small events of his life, would find it an easy matter to trace back innumerable details of his delusions to their sources and so discover their meaning.[32]

This is precisely what Schatzman has done—and with a vengeance. Reviewing the senior Schreber's educational theories, Schatzman concludes that if the father had faithfully adhered to these theories, there would have been ample reason for his son to feel persecuted, for his books abound with advice on gaining strict control over children by measures that often border on sheer brutality.[33] Indeed, some historians have suggested that Schreber's theories helped lay the foundation for the development of the authoritarian personality in Germany that later was to prove so amenable to the political program of the Nazi regime.[34]

Schatzman notes that some of the son's fantasies bore close resemblance to physical exercises recommended by his father. For example, when the son, presumably in a "paranoid delusion," raves on about a painful head-compressing machine, he may actually be remembering the Kopfhalter (headholder) devised by his father—a strap affixed to the child's underwear and head that "served as a 'reminder' to keep the head straight," by pulling on the child's hair whenever he bent his head.[35]

More significant than the many parallels between the father's educational practices and the son's subsequent delusions is the educational philosophy propounded by the senior Schreber. To him, the ideal situation is when the parent gains absolute control over the child in "a wonderful relationship where the child is nearly always ruled merely by parental eye movement."[36]

Basing himself on the father's philosophy and recommended practices, Schatzman arrives at the conclusion that young Schreber was not paranoid: he was persecuted, and by his father. Noting that another son actually committed suicide, Schatzman suggests that Schreber's mental illness was probably a result of his constant battle to avoid hating his father for all the harm that he had inflicted on him. The sheer paradox of the case, with its implications for psychiatry, for education, and perhaps even for modern history, is succinctly expressed by Schatzman:

Irony is everywhere. An eminent pedagogue has a psychotic son; it does not hurt his reputation. Freud, an avid reader, neglects—as do his followers— books on child-rearing by a man whose son's childhood experiences he is trying to infer. German parents rear their children by the ideas of a man whom many people now would see as sadistic or mentally ill.[37]

There seems little doubt that Schatzman has made a strong case for his argument that there is as much substance in Schreber's sometimes incoherent ramblings as in Freud's supposedly objective analysis. Schatzman was able to discover more meaning in this case, not because, in Freud's words, he was more daring or better acquainted with the Schreber family, but because he was open to alternative interpretations of the data at his disposal—and this openness led him to the right hunches and the right methodological approach. The moment one admits the possibility of parental hostility as the cause of the son's problems and fears, the rest falls into place, including the systematic verification of the father's attitudes and behavior.

The second case study by Freud, that of Little Hans, concerns a five-year-old boy who had an intense phobia of horses. His parents, firm adherents of Freud and praised by him for avoiding "the usual educational sins," played an active role in the child's psychoanalysis. The father, a physician, was delegated by Freud to probe his son's fears and to relay his responses to questioning back to Freud for interpretation. Apparently oblivious to the inevitably biased nature of the information provided him by an interested and involved party, Freud justified this unorthodox procedure by claiming that

the special knowledge by means of which (the father) was able to interpret the remarks made by his five-year-old son was indispensable, and without it the technical difficulties in the way of conducting a psychoanalysis upon so young a child would have been insuperable. It was only because the authority of a father and of a physician were united in a single person, and because in him both affectionate care and scientific interest were combined that it was possible in this one instance to apply the method to a use to which it would otherwise not have lent itself.[38]

This contention has been challenged by critics and supporters alike. Fromm and Wolpe and Rachman have questioned the scientific objectivity of a father whose partiality to Freud's ideas and whose eagerness to have the child respond to leading questions in a manner consistent with Freudian ideas emerges so clearly from the verbatim conversations with Little Hans, as reported in the case study.

Freud's supporters lament over, rather than criticize, his failure to realize the possibilities for the further development of psychoanalysis opened up by the Little Hans case. Marthe Robert writes:

The extraordinary development of child analysis and all the psychotherapeutic techniques inspired by it has shown that, for once at least, Freud's perspicacity was at fault on an important matter. Must we think that after carrying the exploration of child psychism further than it had ever been taken before, for inner reasons, remnants of scruples and inhibitions, he refused to go further himself? The fact is that in this field of research . . . Freud showed a singular reserve throughout his life.[39]

What were these "scruples and inhibitions" that kept Freud from coming into direct contact with his young subject? Surely it is strange that a man who had displayed such courage in venturing into the uncharted territory of the unconscious, who clung steadfastly to his convictions in the face of derision and desertion and at the risk of his professional reputation, should have shrunk timidly from the rare opportunity to validate some of his most controversial ideas by directly exploring the mind of a child.

Apart from the questionable methods employed in this case, Freud's interpretation of the actual data supplied him has also come under attack. Thus, Fromm[40] wonders if Little Hans's parents were really as exemplary as Freud believed, since there are a number of instances of far-from-commendable behavior on their part, ranging from threats to lying. Freud used this case to test some of his ideas on child sexuality, incestuous impulses, and castration fears. While he seems to have felt that the existence of such feelings in Little Hans confirmed his theories, Fromm takes him to task for failing to realize that they may have been instilled in the child by his mother, who clearly behaved seductively when taking him, as was her habit, into her bed and bath and who reportedly threatened to have his penis cut off. In the words of Schatzman, Freud "disregarded at least certain behavior of Hans' parents that could frighten and confuse a little boy."[41]

Hans did apparently recover from his phobia, but it is not clear whether this recovery was spontaneous or a result of Freud's indirect therapeutic influence. In any case, according to Wolpe and Rachman:

> The chief conclusion to be derived from our survey of the case of Little Hans is that it does not provide anything resembling direct proof of psychoanalytic theorems. We have combed Freud's account for evidence that would be acceptable in the court of science and found none . . . Freud fully believed that he had obtained in Little Hans a direct confirmation of his theories but infantile complexes were not revealed . . . behind Hans' phobia; they were merely hypothesized.[42]

Fromm tries to explain Freud's errors: "It seems that Freud, influenced by his bias in favor of parental authority and of male superiority, interpreted the clinical material in a one-sided way, and failed to take account of a number of data which contradict his interpretation."[43]

Both these factors of parental authority and male superiority occur in the case of 18-year-old Dora. Dora had been caught up in a strange sexual network. Her father, who was involved in a liaison with the wife of a friend, had, to offset his own behavior, encouraged the same friend's sexual interest in Dora. When she was 14, the friend duped her into a meeting with him, enticed her into an office building, and suddenly grabbed her and kissed her. "This," says Freud, "was surely just the situation to call up a distinct feeling of sexual excitement in a girl of fourteen who had never before been approached. But Dora had at that moment a violent feeling of disgust, tore herself free from the man,"[44] and in future meetings avoided being alone with him. Basing himself on Dora's reaction to the man's sexual advances, Freud pronounces his diagnosis:

> The behavior of this child of fourteen was already entirely and completely hysterical. I should without question consider a person hysterical in whom an occasion for sexual excitement elicited feelings that were preponderantly or exclusively unpleasurable.[45]

This case, used by proponents of the women's movement[46] as an example of Freud's sexist attitudes, also highlights his proparent, antiyouth bias. In his interpretation of Dora's behavior, he showed a lack of sensitivity or sympathy for the plight of a young adolescent girl, inveigled into a sexual encounter with a man she disliked by her father, who, even Freud admitted, "was partly responsible for her present danger, for he had handed her over to this strange man in the interests of his own love-affair."[47] On the contrary, as Simon points out, "despite Freud's knowledge of her father's predilections, he ignored the manner in which her father was using her," and denied that "her accurate perception of the situation was germane."[48]

It is no wonder that Dora terminated her psychoanalysis after only three months, without having her problems resolved. That they continued to plague her may be seen from the fact that, many years later, she was to seek further psychiatric advice.[49]

Given the revelations of Schatzman's analysis of the Schreber case; given the biased approach seemingly adopted by Freud in the case studies of Little Hans and Dora; given his reluctance to probe death-wishes toward children; given his Freudian slip of twice leaving out the possibility of parents having death-wish dreams toward children when dealing with all the other examples of death-wish dreams to loved ones—is it not fair, is it not obligatory, to question both the original basis of the Oedipus complex and Freud's regular use of oedipal ideas?

Of course, it could be argued that, once Freud had actually set up the complex, it would only be natural for him to do his subsequent work within the boundaries of its theoretical framework.

The Oedipus complex undoubtedly made Freud less amenable to ideas of parental hostility; it could be argued even that the very intellectual effort involved in formulating the radically innovative idea of an Oedipus complex could have blunted the edge of Freud's sensitive understanding of social phenomena and that allowance must accordingly be made for Freud's errors. There is merit in such argument, but the problem of Freud's biases at the personal level is more complicated, for evidence of these biases appear in his earliest works, which *preceded* his conception of the Oedipus complex.

The joint study in hysteria, published as Volume II of Freud's *Collected Works,* which Freud carried out with his mentor, Josef Breuer, in the 1880s is considered as showing Freud's preliminary gropings toward psychoanalysis at a stage when he was still using mainly the technique of hypnosis to delve into the patient's past. The two authors presented their findings on their own patients separately; in several of the cases discussed by Freud and in the summary there are significant revelations, both as to the nature of parental seduction and hostility and to the manner in which Freud interpreted and presented the material.

The major case study presented by Freud in his book concerns Frau Emmy von N., who was a patient in an asylum when Freud was a young beginning doctor, using, at that stage, the technique of hypnosis in treatment. According to Freud,

> Under hypnosis I asked her what event in her life had produced the most lasting effect on her and came up most often in her memory. Her husband's death, she said. I got her to describe this event to me in full detail, and this she did with every sign of deepest emotion.[50]

Freud then relates in a few sentences two occasions on which her husband had collapsed, the second time proving fatal. Having related this, Freud then carries straight on:

> And, she then went on to say, how the baby, which was then a few weeks old, had been seized with a serious illness which had lasted for six months, during which she herself had been in bed with a high fever. And there now followed in chronological order her grievances against this child, which she threw out rapidly with an angry look on her face, in the way one would speak of someone who had become a nuisance. This child, she said, had been very queer for a long time; it had screamed all the time and did not sleep, and it had developed a paralysis of the left leg which there had seemed very little hope of curing. When it was four it had visions; it had been late in learning to walk and to talk, so that for a long time it had been believed to be imbecile. According to the doctors it had had encephalitis and inflammation of the spinal cord and she did not know what else besides. I interrupted her here and pointed out to her that this same child was today a normal girl and in the bloom of health, and I *made it impossible for her to see any of these melancholy things again, not only by wiping out her memories of them in their plastic form but by removing her whole*

recollection of them, as though they had never been present in her mind [My italics].
I promised her that this would lead to her being freed from the expectation of
misfortune which perpetually tormented her and from the pains all over her
body, of which she had been complaining precisely during her narrative, after
we had heard nothing of them for several days.[51]

Despite Freud's casual approach to the memories of the daughter's
childhood problems, it seems quite clear that the death of the patient's
husband was only part of the most significant event in her life—perhaps it
was remembered also for having ushered in the years of agony that the
patient had suffered in relation to her child. Yet, instead of attempting to
come to terms with this deep problem, Freud casually points out to his
patient that the child was now normal, and then exploits his power of
hypnosis to erase all memory of the former difficult period. How successful
he was, even superficially, may be judged from his footnote comment that

On this occasion my energy seems to have carried me too far. When, as much
as eighteen months later, I saw Frau Emmy again in a relatively good state of
health, she complained that there were a number of most important moments
in her life of which she had only the vaguest memory. She regarded this as
evidence of weakening of her memory, and I had to be careful not to tell the
cause of this particular instance of amnesia.[52]

So Freud, encountering what was obviously a deep experience in the life
of his patient, proceeded to block it completely from her memory instead of
helping her empathetically to cope with these difficult recollections. A
perusal of the rest of Freud's report indicates that he never again returned
to the subject of the mother's problems with her child, except this once,
eighteen months later, and then only to indicate the success of the treatment (his only reservation being that he might have blocked out other
memories as well). In notable contrast to this rapid treatment of troublesome memories of the patient's child, Freud records the extensive treatment given the patient for other memories that disturbed her. Further,
despite the apparent success of Freud's rapid treatment, from Freud's own
account there are clear indications of the failure of his use of amnesia to
solve real and deep human problems. Thus, in his diary account of this case,
he opens his report of the day immediately following the amnesia treatment
by stating that

Contrary to my expectation she had slept badly and only for a short time. I
found her in a state of great anxiety, though, incidentally, without showing her
usual physical signs of it. She would not say what the matter was, but only that
she had had bad dreams, and kept seeing the same things.[53]

Freud recounts some of these dreams, dealing mainly with snakes, monsters, and wild animals. When Freud tried to elicit from her the reasons for these animal hallucinations,

> Her answer, which she gave rather grudgingly, was that she did not know. I requested her to remember by tomorrow. She then said in a definitely grumbling tone that I was not to keep on asking here where this and that came from, but to let her tell me what she had to say. I fell in with this, and she went on without preface: "When they carried him out, I could not believe he was dead." (So she was talking of her husband again, and I saw now that the cause of her ill-humour was that she had been suffering from the residues of this story which had been kept back.) After this, she said, she had hated her child for three years, because she always told herself that she might have been able to nurse her husband back to health if she had not been in bed on account of the child.[54]

What is intriguing is the manner in which Freud calmly disposes of her acknowledgement that for three years she had hated her child. He does not even consider that the cause for her ill-humor might be related not merely to the thoughts of her husband's death but also to the residual impact of her hostility to the child, particularly since she was now incapable of recalling the details, because of the amnesia induced by Freud on the previous day. In fact, contrary to Freud's contention, it would seem that the amnesia was not quite as complete or successful as he had claimed.

The real tragedy of this case, however, and the full enormity of Freud's failure to solve the very real problem of the relations between his patient and her children, are brought out not in the case study itself but in a footnote, added in the 1924 edition. Acknowledging that "I am aware that no analyst can read this case history today without a smile of pity,"[55] Freud indicates that he does not wish to defend himself against criticism that could be made of it in retrospect. One doubts, however, whether the criticisms relate to the points I have attempted to deal with, in terms specifically of maternal hostility; they more likely relate to the use of hypnosis, which he later rejected for free association.

In any event, Freud goes on to state that more than twenty-five years later he had had further news of this patient:

> Her elder daughter . . . approached me with a request for a report on her mother's mental condition on the strength of my former treatment of her. She was intending to take legal proceedings against her mother, whom she presented as a cruel and ruthless tyrant. It seems that she had broken off relations with both her children and refused to assist them in their financial difficulties.[56]

So, years later, well into adulthood, the earlier hostility of the mother was apparently being repeated. Freud had blocked out—partially—some of the specific memories of this earlier hostility but had not got to the roots of it, the underlying emotions and motivations relating to it. Years later, they were to find expression in newer forms. Freud, the analyst, who had discovered this hostility, chose to block the memories connected with it instead of treating it directly. Thereby he had missed seizing the opportunity for a deeper investigation—both of the real problems of his patient toward her daughter and of the total concept of parental hostility.

Was this an error that could be adduced to his inexperience in the profession, a one-time aberration—or was it the harbinger of a whole pattern of treatment, analysis, and attitudes that was to overshadow his mature work in all its aspects? Was the attempt to induce amnesia a technical error on Freud's part—or was it somehow symbolic of the "amnesia" that was to accompany Freud in his subsequent work, a blocking out of the very real human and social problem of parental hostility?

Let us assume that the evidence presented thus far in this chapter is accepted as being proof positive of a biased approach shown by Freud. For the historical record this would be important—but, in and of itself, it would not directly affect the validity of the Oedipus complex. For in Freud's thinking, parricidal tendencies were not an independent factor—they arose only as a result of prior incestuous tendencies. The parricidal tendencies, for all their importance, are chronologically an epiphenomenon, an outcome of an earlier stage in the child's development. In contrast, the first stage of the complex—the incestuous feelings—are predetermined and inescapable, embedded in our very phylogenetic makeup. Thus, for instance, it is possible that Freud in his eagerness to prove his theory overextended himself in attributing child hostility where none existed, or ignored parental hostility where such did exist. However, if he is wrong in the specific instances of dealing with generational tensions, this would be no more than proof of his own prejudices or errors; it would not necessarily disprove the theory in toto, especially since the incestuous aspects are both an independent factor and an essential catalyctic agent for the subsequent parricidal feelings. What evidence is there then in Freud's work and elsewhere for the existence of incestuous feelings in children?

In the closing years of the nineteenth century, parallel with Freud's agonizing reflections on the nature of his relations with his father, he was also engrossed in trying to fathom the meaning of a consistent pattern of stories that he had encountered in the course of treating his patients. Constantly worried by the recurrent accounts of acts of seduction perpetrated against them by their parents, when they were young, Freud found it increasingly difficult to accept these stories at face value.

After much deliberating within himself, Freud finally resolved the issue by opting to deny the truth of the statements made by his patients—the younger generation—as to what had happened and by attributing these stories to the residual memories of fantasies that they had had during early childhood, based on a strong desire for their parent of the opposite sex.

This was a major breakthrough in Freud's intellectual development, a benchmark moment in his career. Together with his own musings as to his relationship with his father, it provided the incisive insight that led to the development of the Oedipus complex.

Slowly the realization emerged that the patients had not been seduced at all but had desired to be seduced because of their attraction to the parent of the opposite sex. The stories were no more than figments of the child's own sexual imaginations, the consequences of desires felt so strongly that these imaginations were preserved into adulthood by those, such as his patients, who had been unable to resolve such pressures when young.

The moment that these accounts of parental seduction were seen by Freud to be fantasies, produced originally in the mind of the child and subsequently retained into adult life, the basis was laid for developing the idea of infantile sexuality, incestuous feelings for the parent of the opposite sex, then the hostile and ultimately parricidal impulses of the child toward his rival—the parent of the same sex—and finally, the full-blown concept of the Oedipus complex, as a universal, instinctive problem, which every child is obliged to resolve on the long road to mature adulthood.

For Freud, this momentous line of reasoning occasioned a great deal of mental torment, in which he wrestled with the idea that the child was not as innocent as he, and most people, presumed but harbored both incestuous and parricidal wishes. It was the sheer multitude of stories of parental seduction that finally caused him to become skeptical as to their truth.

In a contemporaneous letter to Wilhelm Fliess, his confidant of that time, Freud described his thought processes. After recording his "surprise at the fact that in every case the father, not excluding my own, had to be blamed as a pervert," Freud concludes that "such a widespread extent of perversity towards children is, after all, not probable."[57] It is interesting to note that Freud here includes his own father, and not his mother, in the role of seducer—yet, in Freud's personal case, the seducer should obviously have related to his mother, an indication perhaps of the confusion existing in his own mind as he struggled simultaneously with the problems of treating his patients, almost all of them female, and his own problems of coming to terms with his father.

How deeply Freud was affected altogether by the momentous meaning of the new theory he was working on is indicated later in his autobiographical account where he wrote:

> When, however, I was at last obliged to recognize that those scenes of seduction had never taken place, and that they were only phantasies which my

patients had only made up or which I myself had perhaps forced on them, I was for some time completely at a loss. . . . When I had pulled myself together, I was able to draw the right conclusions from my discovery, namely that the neurotic symptoms were not related directly to actual events but to wishful phantasies. . . . I had in fact stumbled for the first time upon the Oedipus complex, which was later to assume such an overwhelming importance, but which I did not recognize as yet in its disguise of phantasies.[58]

Almost all commentators of Freud's work, and biographers of his life, are in agreement about the overwhelming significance of this line of reasoning. There has been almost no questioning as to the accuracy of Freud's statement that he was able to "draw the right conclusions" about these stories being a consequence of collective, though independent, fantasizing on the part of his patients. Yet, can we trust Freud's analysis? Where is the actual evidence by which Freud's reasoning and conclusions may be judged?

The truth of the matter is that this significant aspect of Freud's work has been accepted largely on the basis of Freud's simple announcements. There is no detailed account of these cases; they have never been submitted for investigation to the scientific community; there are no indications that Freud ever attempted to ascertain the veracity of these stories. Given the paucity of Freud's direct evidence, it is surely legitimate to ask whether he was correct in rejecting so completely the truth of the stories of his patients and in interpreting them as mere repetitions of childhood fantasies. Are Freud's assertions in this regard impeccable? How can we be sure that the similar stories of so many of his patients were no more than collective, yet independent, fantasizing? Did Freud attempt to reconstruct their childhood? Did he attempt to check what kind of people their parents were? Is it not possible that these stories were true accounts, and that it was Freud who read into them the element of fantasy? Questions of this nature take on an added importance, given the accumulation of data in recent times as to the prevalence of all forms of abuse, including sexual abuse, against children.

In addition, it should be noted that, many years later, in one of his most famous case studies (of the Wolf-Man, written in 1914–1915),[59] Freud was prepared to accept the stories of seduction told him by his male patient, in which the seducer was a sister, older than he by two years (and when he himself was only three-and-a-quarter-years of age). According to Freud, "his seduction by his elder sister was certainly not a phantasy."[60] Further, Freud was also willing to give credence to the patient's memory that at the age of about one and a half, he had witnessed acts of sexual intercourse between his parents, which fact became of crucial importance in Freud's search for the causes of his patient's illness. Why should the evidence of Freud's patients some twenty years earlier as to seduction and childhood memories be considered less reliable than the evidence of the Wolf-Man?[61]

Not only are there legitimate doubts as to the evidence to support

Freud's thesis of fantasized seduction, but there is also a record of Freud's vehemence to any challenge of these ideas. Erich Fromm notes[62] that when one of Freud's disciples, Sandor Ferenczi, argued that Freud might have been right in his original thesis that parents seduced children and that he might have erred in attributing memories of such seductions to childhood fantasies, Freud reacted strongly and passionately.

Fromm uses the intensity of Freud's reaction as part of his reasoning to raise doubts as to the validity of Freud's work. He notes that, at this moment, Freud changed from being "the accuser against parental exploitation" (in which the parent would seduce the child) to the person who presented the picture of the "sinful child" and proclaimed the slogan that the "child is guilty." Fromm suggests that this change was not based purely on an objective analysis of scientifically collected data. On the contrary he opines that "I cannot help suspecting that Freud was motivated in this change of opinion not so much by his clinical findings, but by his faith in the existing social order and its authorities."[63]

Fromm's suspicions rest on three factors: in addition to the vehemence of Freud's reaction to Ferenczi, Fromm notes Freud's categorical denial of parental seduction despite the fact that "adult incestuous interest in their children is by no means rare,"[64] and the errors in interpreting the evidence in the case history of Little Hans.

After noting these three factors, Fromm repeats rhetorically, "Was it a matter of something more important than a clinical problem?" He then goes on to suggest that, "It is not too far-fetched to suppose that the main point was not the correctness of the clinical theory, but the attitude towards authority."[65] I would partly agree with Fromm's contention, but I feel that the reasons for any biased interpretation go much further, relating to Freud's overall general biases as an adult, and more specifically to his obsessive struggle at that time to understand the full nature of his relations with his father, while ignoring his relations with his children.

Thus, in the course of his own self-analysis Freud confided to Fliess the problems that he was encountering and linked them to his parallel work with his own patients. In 1897 he wrote:

> My self-analysis is still interrupted and I have realized the reason. I can only analyse myself with the help of knowledge obtained objectively (like an outsider). Genuine self-analysis is impossible; otherwise there would be no illness. Since I still find some puzzles in my patients, they are bound to hold me up in my self-analysis as well.[66]

These puzzles were apparently the recurrent stories of seduction that he was hearing.

Despite the momentousness of his discovery of incestuous feelings by children and their subsequent negative feelings against the rival parent, despite the overwhelming impact that these ideas were to have on all his subsequent work, both practical therapy and speculative theorizing, *Freud never, in any of his works, set out a full-scale presentation of the theory.* Slowly it just grew, increasingly pervading Freud's writings. Sometimes there are references to Sophocle's drama, sometimes there are descriptions of individual case studies or of historical events within the framework of the Oedipus story. Finally, unheralded by any specific announcement of a fully formulated idea, the use of the term Oedipus complex creeps into the writings, the first time in a minor article written in 1910, and then only *en passant.*[67] It is only later that Freud makes an attempt to describe what the basic concept involves and how it developed. (Even then, much of what we know of the process by which the idea was formulated became known only after the publication of the Fliess letters, letters that were fortunately saved for posterity by Marie Bonaparte, who bought them and saved them, much against Freud's wishes.)[68]

Even in these later discussions, Freud acknowledges that the issue of parental seduction has not yet been finally resolved. He continues to be aware of sexual feelings emanating from adults to their children—yet he continues to discount their importance. Thus he writes:

> We must not omit to add that the parents themselves often exercise a determining influence on the awakening of a child's Oedipus attitude by themselves obeying the pull of sexual attraction, and that where there are several children the father will give the plainest evidence of his greater affection for his little daughter and the mother for her son.

But having posed the issue, Freud goes on immediately to assure the reader that "the spontaneous nature of the Oedipus complex in children cannot be seriously shaken even by this factor."[69]

Yet, the question still persists, with even more pertinence: what was the basis for Freud's interpreting *all* of the stories of his patients as fantasies? Even assuming that there is such a process as spontaneous oedipal feelings, can that alone entitle the therapist to discount the tales of seduction practiced by parents? What if there was actual seduction? Was Freud capable of giving his patients the therapeutic help they needed after he had categorized such stories as fantasies? Was he entitled to build up his theory on such a flimsy basis?

Freud's work on the group of female patients who claimed to have been seduced presents certain problems because of the lack of a full published account of their cases. Whether Freud's perception and interpretation of these cases is correct, or whether adult (and male) biases were present, is thus a matter of conjecture. Simply put, was there incestuous seduction, was it real or imagined—and, by whom: the father or the daughter?

In recent years, there have been several publications on incest, out of which emerges a composite picture indicating a far higher incidence than official figures would suggest and a fairly constant pattern in which the initiative for sexual relations stems from the parents, more particularly from the father toward his daughter, often through coercive means.

The nature of this evidence is clearly inconsistent with Freud's claim that all of the stories he heard were fantasies. In fact, Florence Rush[70] actually argues that it was the persuasive power of Freud's writings on incest that was partly responsible for the full extent of this practice being ignored for so long. She writes that Freud's "theories, surrounded by scientific aura, allowed for the . . . concealment of the sexual exploitation of the female child." As a result "the sexual abuse of the child is the best-kept secret in the world."[71]

In discussing sexual abuse in general, David Walters[72] has remarked on the misinformation and myths that surround the subject, and he tries to set aside some of these myths. He states, for instance, that, contrary to popular thought, the abuser is generally a father or other close relative, or a family friend or neighbor. Walters also stresses the problem of correctly interpreting behavior that is ambiguous. Even so, one example he provides to suggest the ambiguity involved seems to be actually a clear-cut case of abuse, the misunderstanding as to the nature of the action being chiefly in the subjective appraisal of the father, who saw nothing wrong in his own behavior toward his daughter but felt that *her* attitude was the real problem. A father had approached Walters seeking help for his eleven-year-old daughter "because of her problem." When pressed for details the father complained "she no longer likes to take baths with me."

Walters asks, "who has the problem, the maturing daughter aware of her sexuality, or the father? Then, we might ask, if he insists that she continue to bathe with him, is he sexually abusing her . . . ?"

He adds, "Another father installed a one-way mirror in the bathroom, so he could observe his daughters taking showers. Was he sexually abusive?"[73]

Often incest or sexual abuse is presumed to be a lower-class phenomenon, but when Walters conducted a pilot project on 412 university students, 17% of his interviewees reported some type of sexual conduct in the period prior to puberty, with most sexual advances being made by relatives. Of course, Freudians could argue that these students might have been fantasizing as well, but then, it must be remembered that the students—unlike Freud's group—were not patients suffering from emotional problems.

Herbert Maisch, in a basic survey,[74] also provides ample evidence of widespread sexual abuse and incestuous practices, in which the general pattern is of father-daughter, with the former being the instigator, and with little evidence of the pure oedipal pattern of son-mother.

It should also be noted that even when acknowledgment is made of the existence of incestuous practices, there is a tendency to minimize the exploitation by the father and to suggest the willingness of the child to be a party to the sexual advances. Joseph Rheingold finds justification even for incestuous relationships between father and daughter (but not mother and son), seeing it as a supreme example of the father's love, providing the daughter with positive proof of her own worth. Rheingold writes: "The girl receives the sexual act indifferently or as a demonstration of affection. It may even have therapeutic effects."[75]

Similarly, Kate Friedlander, a Freudian psychoanalyst, suggests that since there is an ". . . unconscious preparedness for incestuous relationships in every human being . . . [this] explains why girls give in easily to their father's or brother's desires, and why they are likely to keep it as secret as the male partner."[76] Thus, according to Friedlander, on those occasions when the incest is reported it is only after the sex relation has ended and because of the girl's jealousy. In contrast to this approach, Karin Meiselman shows that where the girl does acquiesce in the act it is because of "her perception of the father's authority and because of all her past experience with failures to obey him,"[77] especially since the incestuous father is generally dominant in the family, and even tyrannical. In many instances where the daughter is unwilling to continue the liaison she will still not report the relationship, preferring to leave home.

Sandra Butler[78] sees the predicament of the daughter as even more complex. Since often the incestuous behavior is initiated by an adult when the family is in a state of disintegration, her acquiescence in the relationship is a desperate attempt to save the family from total breakup. "In such families children sense, at a surprisingly early age, what is required of them to keep the family together and they will do so, even at the price of their own victimization."[79] Butler quotes one incest victim, now serving as a group facilitator for other incest victims, as suggesting that the victims will even deny that there was incest in order to protect the family.

In the light of this accumulating evidence, can we continue to accept the validity of Freud's assertion that the stories he was told of seduction by his patients were all fantasies? Is it not possible that some at least of these stories might have been true? What would be the impact of an error in Freud's interpretation on the theory of the Oedipus complex?

Freud's own handling of cases of incest is highly questionable. As noted, we have only minimum data on the cases that served as the basis for Freud's claim of incestuous fantasies. However, once again, Freud's earliest work, the joint effort with Breuer, may provide us with some help. In two of the cases that Freud presents he refers to claims of seduction. Case No. 4 in the book—the case of Katherina, an 18-year-old girl[80]—deals with a neurosis that Freud traces back four years, when her father had made sexual advances to her. After giving a detailed description of the first occasion when this happened, Freud adds that "she went on to tell me of yet other experiences of somewhat later date; how she had once again had to defend herself against him in an inn, when he was completely drunk and other stories."[81] At least in this case the patient was not referring to fantasies from the oedipal period.

Freud recounts also the case of Fräulein Rosalie H., who had also had particularly bad relations with her father, who was a "manifestly pathological person, brutally ill-treated his wife and children [and] . . . wounded their feelings more particularly by the way in which he showed open sexual preference for the servants and nursemaids in the house."[82] One hysterical symptom of the patient Freud traced back to a childhood incident in which the father

> who was suffering from rheumatism had asked her to massage his back, and she did not dare to refuse. He was lying in bed at the time, and suddenly threw off the bed-clothes, sprang up and tried to catch hold of her and throw her down . . . a moment later she had escaped and locked herself in her room.[83]

Here there is a possibility that the patient was fantasizing the massage incident, but the fact is that, by Freud's own account, the father was pathological, brutal to his wife, and sexually exploitative of his servants. Could he not have been similarly derelict in his relations with his daugher?

The question that must be posed is whether Freud was referring to cases such as these two when he later wrote of his reluctance to accept such stories at their face value. However, there is no indication in later editions as to whether or not Freud considered these stories also to be only fantasies.

Although Freud found it so difficult to accept the large number of cases of presumed parental seduction, if these two cases from an earlier period were not fantasies, then surely such examples of seduction by fathers of their daughters would prove the possibility, or even the likelihood, that other children may have been seduced by their fathers—possibly at an even earlier age, including during the oedipal years. But for some time at least, Freud was unable to relate to this question at all, for in presenting these cases he referred to the fathers as *uncles!*

It is only some thirty years later—in the 1924 edition of the book—that Freud makes known the distortion in footnote form without changing the text itself. In the footnote Freud writes of Katherina's case:

> I venture after the lapse of so many years to lift the veil of discretion and reveal the fact that Katherina was not the niece but the daughter. . . . The girl fell ill, therefore, as a result of sexual attempts on the part of her own father. Distortions like the one which I introduced in the present instance should be altogether avoided in reporting a case-history.[84]

Why, then, did Freud commit the distortion? It could hardly have been to camouflage the identity of the patient. On the contrary, without contributing anything to preserving the hidden identity of the patient, Freud has changed a material fact in the case. In the footnote he himself concedes that "From the point of view of understanding the case, a distortion of this kind is not, of course, a matter of such indifference. . . ."[85] This seems to be a slight understatement. The question of whether the seduction was carried out by the father or by the uncle is a material fact. It subsequently became absolutely decisive for the Oedipus complex on the question as to whether or not fathers seduced their daughters, a fact that Freud himself found so difficult to accept. Yet, difficult as it was to accept, it had apparently been true in at least these two cases. But having referred publicly to the seductive adults as uncles Freud was undoubtedly in an easier position to present the sexual aspects of the child's Oedipus complex. One could ask whether the reaction to his first references to the Oedipus complex would not have been undermined had the true situation in these examples been known. By the time Freud casually acknowledged the distortion thirty years later, the Oedipus complex had been, to a certain extent, accepted. It certainly was not going to be undermined at that stage by reference to a book written so many years before.

Several questions arise. Why did Freud commit the distortion and then wait so long to admit it? Why did he then not change the facts in the body of the text, as he was wont to do in many of his other works,[86] instead of only in a footnote reference? Finally, why does he not indicate clearly whether retrospectively he considers these reports of seduction (committed in at least one case after the oedipal years) to have really happened, and what impact they had had on his thinking when he was in the process of totally rejecting the possibility of parental seduction.

Mark Poster argues, referring to these cases, that "Freud had great difficulty simply discussing incest," and that "we are dealing with experiences about which the scientist himself cannot offer objectively the simple facts of the case."[87] Poster in fact accuses Freud of allowing the "science of psychoanalysis" to become the "ideology of parentism."[88] There is a recurrent systematic way in which Freud distorts the exchanges that occur in the family, while "pretending to represent the child, pretending to give us insight into the family through the eyes of the child."[89]

It is also worth noting that the joint work with Breuer contains an account of a case of hysteria being solved by Freud's actually basing his treatment on information, supplied to him by the family doctor, of seduction practiced by a governess against his patient when she had been a young girl.[90] According to the doctor, the stuporose condition to which the patient was prone had started when she was a girl, and had been traced to the fact that the governess was in the habit of visiting the child in bed at night. After discovering this, the family had dismissed the governess, without telling the girl of the reason for the dismissal. According to Freud, "My therapy, which was immediately successful, consisted in giving the young woman the information I had received."[91] So here is a case where the seduction by a governess was not a fantasy of the patient, but a fact supplied by an independent and reliable source, the knowledge of which proved to be essential for Freud's therapy. The fact that the seduction was committed by a female to a girl means that there is no connection here with classic oedipal factors, but what is of prime importance is the fact that seduction by adults of children is a possibility that cannot be dismissed out of hand, as Freud did when it involved the father, and that honesty about the seduction is of therapeutic value.

There is a simple basic point that must be stressed. Working backward: the parricidal tendencies to the parent of the same sex arise from the incestuous tendencies to the parent of the opposite sex. Whereas the fact of parricidal tendencies receives confirmation from Freud's own feelings toward his father, the incestuous tendencies are based on his interpretation of tales of seduction provided by his female patients. Freud saw these tales as being fantasies—based on the incestuous yearnings. We now know, from recent research, that incest and seductive practices are quite prevalent at all ages and generally instigated by the parent, particularly the father. This recent research was obviously not available to Freud. But his own clinical experiences could have served to provide him with similar information. Yet he chose to reject the truth of these stories. Is it not possible that however creative his analysis, he was wrong?

However strong the evidence as to the prevalence of incest instigated by fathers it must be conceded immediately that the actual practice of incest is not the ultimate test, or even the best test of the existence of oedipal tendencies. Where it does occur at the instigation of the parent it certainly hints at the possibility of Freud's patients having, indeed, been seduced. But where it occurs it is still no more than a minority phenomenon, a pathological expression of sexual attraction within the family.

The proof of the existence of oedipal feelings (as well as the test of Freud's ideas) is not in actual incest (as occurred in the Oedipus story) but in sexual yearnings and ensuing sexual rivalry, in the everyday patterns of affection and rejection. What are these patterns? Seymour Fisher and Roger Greenberg[92] recently made a comprehensive analysis of research projects based on Freud's ideas. Only one small section of their book is devoted to an examination of research projects aimed at testing some parts of the basic Oedipus thesis, and they make little effort to probe the evidence on the existence or not of the child's hostility to the parent of the same gender. But they do examine research projects aimed at testing whether children are more attracted to the parent of the opposite sex and conversely more resentful of the parent of the same sex. Where the intrafamilial sexual rivalry does not take pathological forms this should be the pattern at least during the oedipal stages. The results of their examination are inconclusive. While there is some support for the oedipal thesis in some projects, in others the thesis is not borne out. In fact, it is sometimes at ages outside of the traditional oedipal stage that the oedipal pattern is followed, while during the oedipal period itself other patterns of attraction and rejection are observed.

However, even where patterns of attraction exist, should this be interpreted as an expression of incestuous yearnings, or of inevitable sexuality? Why can it not be seen as legitimate affection, part of the young child's quest to be accepted, to belong, to be loved?

Just such an approach characterizes the work of Ian Suttie,[93] a British psychoanalyst, who in the 1930s published one of the earliest full-range critiques of Freud's work. Unfortunately, his work has received only minimal recognition, even though much of what he wrote is similar to and preceded the neo-Freudianism of popular American writers such as Herbert Marcuse, Norman Brown, and others.[94] In Britain his work has had some influence but mainly in the field of education and not so much in psychological theory or practice.[95]

In his wide-ranging analysis of Freud's work, Suttie faults Freud for being "preoccupied with sexual struggles,"[96] involving only Oedipus jealousies of sons and penis envy of women, for being antifeminist, and for being unable to recognize that his own society was the most patriarchal of all societies. Suttie explains his break with Freudian thought:

> Formally, the tentative theory I have formed belongs to the group of psychologies that originate from the work of Freud. It differs fundamentally from psycho-analysis in introducing the conception of an innate need-for-companionship which is the infant's only way of self-preservation. This need, giving rise to parental and fellowship "love," I put in the place of the Freudian Libido, and regard it as genetically independent of genital appetite.[97]

Suttie claims that society is suffering from "a *taboo on tenderness* every bit as spontaneous and masterful as the taboo on sex itself."[98] In fact, it is not the denial of sexuality and the repression of sex that is at the core of human problems but the taboo on tenderness. For Suttie, "tenderness is a primal independent reality,"[99] present from the earliest moment of life. The infant craves tenderness and love both for self-preservation and for the creation of a social bond with others.

One of Freud's major errors, says Suttie, was to negatively interpret the yearnings of infants and young children as sexual drives and to seek to control them. On the contrary, the positive response to the desire for tenderness is what provides a healthy basis for both the socialization of the child and the development of culture; it is the denial of tenderness that is the source of such negative impulses as hate, aggression, and anxiety. The latter are not innate to the human psyche but develop out of unhappy personal experiences.

Suttie argues that

> the germ of goodness or of love is in the individual (of every species which has evolved a nurtured infancy) from the very beginning and . . . our traditional method of upbringing frustrates this spontaneous benevolence and substitutes a "guilt-anxiety" morality for natural goodness.[100]

The consequences of the taboo on tenderness is to create artificial barriers between the sexes and between the generations:

> [I]ts worst effects lie in separating parent from child. The former, unconsciously resisting and defending himself from regressive longings, is impatient with childishness and forces the child to grow up and to abandon its naive, unguarded, emotional relationship to social environment.[101]

In such circumstances, the child is denied the "right to childhood," while simultaneously adult life is not made especially attractive. The ultimate consequences are

> a puritan intolerance of tenderness [which] increases the unconscious regressiveness it hates, and interposes unnecessary moral obstacles in the way of the maturation it designs to accelerate. It forces development to proceed by a violent change with repression instead of by gradual process. It does not produce really mature minds, but merely a hardness and cynicism with a core of anxious, angry, infantility. It loses the generosity of the child without acquiring the stability and integration which should belong to the adult.[102]

The implications that flow from Suttie's analysis are far-reaching. They affect not only the way in which adults might perceive the needs of young children but also the way they might perceive themselves. In particular, the taboo on tenderness inhibits adults, especially males, from spontaneously expressing affection or from fulfilling a nurturant role within the family.

Suttie takes direct issue with Freud over the Oedipus complex, seeing the constellation of family relations as involving more interactions than Freud had considered. Whereas Freud devoted major attention to the son's jealousy of the father (the Oedipus complex) and the "penis envy of women for the supposedly superior male,"[103] Suttie adds three more interactions. In no case are any of the complexes or jealousies inevitable—these are possibilities that might emerge, depending upon cultural conditions and personal qualities. The major one is sibling rivalry, which Suttie terms the Cain Jealousy. Then, in contrast to the wife's penis envy, he argues that the father has a "jealousy of the women's power of producing and suckling the baby,"[104] which he terms the Zeus Jealousy, based on the myth that Zeus had swallowed his pregnant wife so that he could bear the child himself. Finally, in contrast to the Oedipus complex, there is a Laius Jealousy, which is the "father's regressive jealousy of the child's nurturant possession of the mother."[105] Suttie's concept of the Laius Jealousy involves mainly jealousy revolving around access to wife/mother. He does not, however, elaborate on this idea, nor does he examine the hostilities and the jealousies of the father at later stages of the child's growth. Even so, there are obvious parallels with the Rustum complex.

The difference between tenderness, as discussed by Suttie, and sexuality, as discussed by Freud, is not merely semantic. It goes to the very heart of the manner in which the child's need for tactile contact with adults will be interpreted and responded to. Is the child's desire to touch and be touched, to hug and be hugged, an overt expression of inner sexual drives, to be suspiciously regarded and strictly controlled as an essential aspect of the normal socialization process, as Freud holds? Or is the need for tender interaction to be seen as an important component of social life, as affirmation of acceptance, as an expression of a healthy bonding relationship, as the basis for trust and the learning of values, as Suttie argues?

Karen Horney[106] also faults Freud for failing to make the distinction between sexuality and tenderness. It is on this failure that Freud built his theory of the Oedipus complex. Like Suttie, Horney does not see the Oedipus complex as universal, nor sexuality as a primary need, nor the child's jealousy of the father as the major factor in determining family relations.

Where symptoms of the Oedipus complex do exist, they are generally a direct reaction to the parents' behavior. It is the neurotic parents who forced the child into these passionate attachments with all the implications of possessiveness and jealousy described by Freud.[107] Overt displays of genital sexuality by children arise either out of erotic stimulation by the parents or as a reaction by the child to a lack of desired tenderness and a search for reassurance and acceptance. Inasmuch as child hostility arises, Horney sees its antecedents in the prior behavior of the parents,

> by the parents' lack of respect for him; by unreasonable demands and prohibitions; by injustice; by unreliability; by suppression of criticism; by the parents dominating him and ascribing these tendencies to love; by misusing children for the sake of prestige or ambitious goals.[108]

Horney concludes that the Oedipus complex is not "the origin of the neurosis, but is itself a neurotic formation."[109]

What are the implications for Freud's theory of parricidal urges if it appears that there are no universal incestuous urges? Within the framework of the Oedipus complex it must be remembered that while for Freud the first stage of the Oedipus complex—the incestuous feelings for the parent of the opposite sex—are physiologically predetermined and inescapable, the second stage—of hostile feelings for the parent of the same sex—arise only out of the first stage. Thus, if there is no first stage, then, according to the theory, there is no consequent second stage; if there are no incestuous desires, there are no subsequent parricidal tendencies.

However, even if it can be shown that there is no oedipal basis for hostile feelings by children for their parents, the problem of children's hostility to their parents is by no means resolved. For it may well exist for other reasons, reasons that have nothing to do with prior incestuous desires. In fact, the very structural differences between the generations are likely to lead to such hostilities, just as the structural factors of class, religion, ethnicity, and sex often lead to hostility.

The problem of the Oedipus complex is not that it draws attention to the hostility of children (which doubtless exists), but that it presents such hostility as arising largely from prior predetermined incestuous feelings (which all the evidence seems to contradict) and of its being basically a unidirectional theory (which ignores the evidence of parental hostility). If childhood hostility does exist there may be many and diverse reasons for it, including the simple fact of its being a reaction to the prior hostility or the damaging behavior of the parents.

Kate Friedlander's classic psychoanalytic study of juvenile delinquency[110] provides a good example of the manner in which the automatic presumption of incestuous feelings, and the denial of parental fault, lead to selective utilization of empirical data and an inability to perceive the contribution of the parent's behavior to the child's pathological condition, including hostility to his father.

In a chapter on "Anti-social Character Formation,"[111] she presents a lengthy case study of a young boy, Billy, showing how his oedipal problems were a fundamental cause of his subsequent antisocial behavior and of his hatred for his father. But the facts that she provides suggest that the problems were not a consequence of the boy's failure to cope with predetermined and genetic oedipal yearnings but rather were induced by the parents' behavior.

She presents Billy as a child of normal intelligence, splendid physique, and fair general abilities. The source of his problem, according to Friedlander, was to be found in the boy's early relationship with his mother. This is possibly so, but, far from the child's incestuous yearnings for her, there is abundant evidence of the mother's failure, particularly in the sensitive area of the child's gender identity. According to the evidence of Friedlander, the mother had wanted a girl and disdained every sign of masculinity in the boy. She forbade him to play with other boys, she frightened him by threats of leaving him and his father, and she refused to allow the father to have anything to do with his upbringing. Relations between father and mother were strained, there were many quarrels, the father was often drunk, and he left the home when Billy was eight. Even when the father was in the home the mother used to share a room, and sometimes a bed, with her son, while the father slept in a separate small room. We learn that Billy hated his father, which might fit in superficially with the parricidal tendencies of the Oedipus complex, but surely, given the evidence in this case, it is straining incredulity to its extremes—or surrendering creative thinking to a theoretical commitment—to believe that the Oedipus complex was the cause of the child's problems rather than the faulty child-rearing practices imposed on Billy. Yet, there is no criticism of the parents' behavior, no hint that they had caused their son's problems; there is only an eager use of a simplistic oedipal mode.

Billy's is an isolated case; though given the most extensive coverage by Friedlander, some of the facts may well be open to alternative interpretations. More revealing as to the manner in which a Freudian theoretical framework affects the manner of interpretation is Dorothy Bloch's recent study in this area.[112] Her work relates not to incest or child hostility but to children's perceptions of the existence of parental hostility.

Bloch explains that, in the course of a long career, spanning twenty-five years and involving about six hundred patients, she had constantly encountered stories of fears of infanticide told her by both her child and her adult patients. While at the beginning Bloch had rejected outright any basis for such fears, the sheer accumulation of such tales had forced her to reassess the meaning of these constantly repeated tales and finally, despite the deviation from standard Freudian thinking, to acknowledge the validity of such fears. In doing so, she takes specific issue with one of the most prominent Freudian child psychoanalysts, Melanie Klein,[113] who had also been given ample similar evidence of children's fears and had rejected any rational basis for them. Bloch argues that Melanie Klein was unable to move out of the confining structure of oedipal thought in order to fully perceive the real feelings and the fear of the child. When Klein denies the legitimate fears of the children, Bloch sees this as being a

> measure of the persistent reluctance to challenge the idealized parental image which derived from the oedipal theory. To have conceded not only that children were afraid of being killed by their parents but that in reality their parents might have a wish to kill them would have violated a rigidly defended taboo.[114]

It should be noted that Bloch, claiming to be in the tradition of Freud, argues that her ideas are only an elaboration of his ideas. Bloch is, in fact, understanding of Freud's problem in recognizing infanticide after the struggle he had had in announcing parricide. But whatever the validity of

Bloch's tolerance toward Freud's position, there can be no doubt that her own research, stemming from a pure Freudian perspective, is a clear departure from Freudian thought.

It may well be that in the realm of Freudian child therapy a serious reassessment of the nature of children's fears is called for. Eric Lustig, himself a Freudian psychoanalyst, suggests that the fears of children may have been misunderstood by psychoanalysts. "The fears of children have been ascribed to castration anxiety. Can it be that castration anxiety should be renamed infanticide anxiety?"[115] Is there, in fact, any basis for these fears? Is Bloch's reassessment of the meaning of these reported cases accurate? Or are we dealing with more of the fantasy life of children as claimed by Freud in the case of seduction?

In recent years, irrefutable evidence as to the existence of parental hostility has become available with the use of sophisticated radiological techniques and pioneering research to prove the prevalence of the "battered child syndrome."[116] In the last few years, in fact, it has emerged from being a little-known concept in professional circles to become the subject of regular coverage in the mass media.

Whether or not Freud or his followers could have been expected to be aware of the widespread nature of this phenomenon, there is no doubt that the recent evidence necessitates the reconsideration of their theoretical presentation, based only on parricide.

However, it is also possible that Freud, even without modern technological help, came across this problem. It seems most likely, for instance, that if Freud had probed into the family background of Schreber, as Schatzman did, he might well have discovered that during the lifetime of Schreber, he had been physically abused by his father—which could have been the case if his father had actually carried out his child-rearing techniques. On one occasion Freud actually related to the problem of child-beating.[117] Here he discusses it purely in the context of fantasies of child-beating. Freud himself claimed that this phenomenon of fantasies of child-beating was common; his actual article is based on six cases, but unfortunately he provides no details of their actual childhood experiences, beyond a laconic statement that "the individuals from whom the data for these analyses were derived were very seldom beaten in their childhood, or were at all events not brought up by the help of the rod."[118] Freud's actual explanation for his patients' fantasies is an involved one, including sexual perversions based on masochistic and sadistic tendencies linked to the Oedipus complex and incestuous feelings. Is it not possible, though, that there might have been more direct reasons for these "fantasies"—dim memories of the patients' own childhood, repressed desires that they felt as adults toward children, or an actual beating disguised as a fantasy? Some of these possibilities Freud considers but dismisses.

It is not possible to investigate today the backgrounds of Freud's patients and to use our present-day knowledge as to the widespread incidence of the battered child syndrome. There is a recent research project, however, based on replicating Freud's work and carried out by a group of psychoanalysts, that provides a glimpse of Freudian analysis. Edward Joseph and his co-workers,[119] after looking into the possibility that the beating fantasies of a number of patients may have been related to actual experiences, concluded that "the occurrence of physical beating seemed to have played a minor part in the lives of most of these patients."[120] However, of the eight cases in the study for which detailed information is provided, three contain clear instances of patients with beating fantasies who had actually been beaten in their childhood. One such study is of "a patient with beating fantasies whose father had spanked her every morning until she stopped wetting her bed at the age of thirteen."[121]

Thus, in a study purporting to replicate Freud's work on beating fantasies, a number of cases contain evidence of prior childhood beatings that might well have touched off the later reports. No less significantly, the researchers themselves fail to recognize the import of their evidence. Is it not possible that Freud himself had made similar errors of interpretation and inference? Is it not possible that Freud had encountered a hint of a social problem of immense proportions—the battering of children—but had failed to probe deeper and to pursue this possibility? It was to be over a half century before the irrefutable evidence of widespread child abuse became available.

It might be argued that, overall, the errors in Freud's work are being slowly corrected, the lacunae filled, the necessary additions made. Why, then, must a book on parental and adult hostility focus so much on Freud's possible errors—made in another era, with nearly all his patients long since dead and the society and culture in which he worked much transformed? Further, even within the field of therapy, newer ideas have been advanced—existentialist approaches, family therapy, considerable neo-Freudian work—that are no longer bound by the rules of Freudian orthodoxy.

There are two key answers to such queries: first, despite the fact that Freud's dominance in therapy and psychology has long been challenged, his work retains an evergreen appeal and even an increasing popularity in many areas, whereas little attention has been paid to the doubts, reservations, and retractions of therapists and psychologists. My own concern in this book is not with therapy and deviant or problematic cases but with the way in which social life is played out each day in normal settings by normal people, and with the political implications of Freud's ideas. Here, an increasing number of historians, sociologists, anthropologists, psychologists, political scientists, psychohistorians, theologians, and literary critics are turning to Freud, and in many cases specifically to the Oedipus complex, for a theoretical framework within which to understand social reality. As Freud's own base of support from therapists is slowly being whittled away, so, phoenix-like, his ideas are gaining greater credence in areas where he had little expertise and where his ideas are little more than passing comment (as in literature), speculative theories (as in religion), or tentative probings (as in political science and psychohistory).[122]

Second, Freud's errors are not a consequence of any extreme antichild or antiyouth bias, nor a consequence of the specific impact of his own times or culture on his work. They are, for the most part, no more than an expression of the biases that adults often bring to bear in discussing generational contacts. If the oversights and the errors appear more glaring and numerous in the case of Freud it is because he devoted so much of his work to this issue and because much of the work was so closely bound up with personal factors. I have devoted so much space to these oversights and errors because of Freud's impact and importance.

From a sociology of knowledge approach, Freud's middle-class background or his patriarchal culture may have affected his work in one way or another. But above all, what must be constantly borne in mind, and with particular pertinence for the Oedipus complex, is that Freud wrote as an *adult* and as a *parent*. His work undoubtedly yielded many insights into the life of the child. But as a totality it represents the perspective of an adult and a parent.

This is not Freud's bias alone. It is shared by many who write—and read—without an awareness of the very real influence that adulthood and parenthood can have on their perceptions. One of the consequences of the Oedipus complex—perhaps unforeseen and unintended—is that it has facilitated the perpetuation of this bias, as will be shown in the next section.

References

1. See Gunter W. Remmling, *The Road to Suspicion: A Study of Modern Mentality and the Sociology of Knowledge* (New York: Appleton-Century-Crofts, 1967). Interestingly, Remmling notes Freud's contribution to the sociology of knowledge by virtue of his work on the role of the unconscious in human behavior (pp. 181–198).

2. For the background to Freud's self-analysis, see his correspondence with Wilhelm Fliess in which he revealed some of his intellectual and emotional development at this time. Sigmund Freud, *The Origins of Psychoanalysis, Letters to Wilhelm Fliess, Drafts and Notes: 1887–1902,* Marie Bonaparte, Anna Freud, and Ernst Kris, eds., (New York: Basic Books, 1954).

3. For a partial example of such criticism see Erich Fromm, *Sigmund Freud's Mission* (New York: Harper and Brothers, 1959).

4. Frederick J. Hacker, "The Living Image of Freud" in Hendrick Ruitenbeek, ed., *Freud as We Knew Him* (Detroit: Wayne State University, 1973), p. 323.

5.   Ibid., p. 325.

6.   Ibid.

7.   Sigmund Freud, *The Interpretation of Dreams* (1900), in *The Standard Edition of the Complete Psychological Works,* edited by James Strachey, 24 vols. (London: Hogarth Press, 1953–66), vol. 4.

8.   Ibid., p. 263.

9.   Ibid., p. 259.

10.   Ibid., p. 260.

11.   For a full list of Freud's dreams, see ibid., pp. 715–716.

12.   Ibid., p. 253.

13.   See Matityahu Timor, *The Ultimate Book about Jesus and Freud* (Tel Aviv: Academy Books, 1965); and Ian D. Suttie, *The Origins of Love and Hate* (London: Kegan Paul, Trench, Trubner, 1935).

14.   Freud, *The Interpretation of Dreams,* pp. 248–249.

15.   Ibid., pp. 152–155.

16.   Ibid., p. 152.

17.   Ibid. In another translation the word used is "impossible."

18.   Ibid., pp. 154–155.

19.   Ibid., p. 249.

20.   Sigmund Freud, *Dreams* (1916), in *The Standard Edition,* 15: 203–204.

21.   Sigmund Freud, *Totem and Taboo* (1913), in *The Standard Edition,* 13: 62.

22.   Sigmund Freud, *The Psychopathology of Everyday Life* (1901), in *The Standard Edition,* vol. 6. For a critical analysis of this book, see Sebastiano Timpanaro, *The Freudian Slip: Psychoanalysis and Textual Criticism* (London: NLB, 1976).

23.   Sigmund Freud, *Group Psychology and the Analysis of the Ego* (1920), in *The Standard Edition,* 18: 33; see footnote 2.

24.   For the Schreber case, see Sigmund Freud, *Psycho-Analytic Notes on an Autobiographical Account of a Case of Paranoia (Dementia Paranoides)* (1911), in *The Standard Edition,* vol. 12. For the case of Little Hans, see *Analysis of a Phobia in a Five Year Old Boy* (1909), in *The Standard Edition,* vol. 10. For the case of Dora, see *Fragment of an Analysis of a Case of Hysteria* (1905), in *The Standard Edition,* vol. 7.

25.   Morton Schatzman, *Soul Murder: Persecution in the Family* (New York: Signet, 1974); see also "Paranoia or Persecution: The Case of Schreber," in *Family Process* 10 (1971): 171–212, and in *History of Childhood Quarterly: The Journal of Psychohistory* 1 (1974): 62–89.

26.   Erich Fromm, "The Oedipus Complex: Comments on the Case of Little Hans," *The Crisis of Psychoanalysis: Essays on Freud, Marx and Social Psychology* (London: Pelican, 1973), pp. 98–110.

27.   Joseph Wolpe and Stanley Rachman, "Psychoanalytic Evidence: A Critique Based on Freud's Case of Little Hans," *Journal of Nervous and Mental Diseases* 131 (1960): 130–148.

28. L. J. Simon, "The Political Unconscious of Psychology: Clinical Psychology and Social Change," 1970, as quoted by Phyllis Chesler "Patient and Patriarch: Women in the Psychotherapeutic Relationship," in Vivian Gornick and Barbara K. Moran, eds., *Women in Sexist Society* (New York: Signet, 1972), pp. 382-392.

29. Steven Marcus, "Freud and Dora," *Partisan Review* 61 (1974): 12-23, 89-108. Marcus deals in detail with Freud's hesitation in publishing the work on Dora.

30. See D. P. Schreber, *Memoirs of My Nervous Illness* (London: Dawson, 1955), originally published in 1903 in German.

31. For a list of some of the father's books, see Schatzman, *Soul Murder,* p. 155.

32. Freud, *Psycho-Analytic Notes,* p. 47.

33. For another attempt to trace back the family details, see William G. Niederland, *The Schreber Case: Psychoanalytic Profile of a Paranoid Personality* (New York: Quadrangle, 1974). Schatzman has reviewed this book very critically, pointing out that, although Niederland has divulged much interesting data on the father-son relationship (and Schatzman's book has footnote references to Niederland's earlier articles on the topic), Niederland himself has failed to draw the necessary conclusions that Schreber, the son, was not paranoid. (See Morton Schatzman, "Book review," *History of Childhood Quarterly: The Journal of Psychohistory* 2 [1975]: 453-456). Even so, in another review of the book, the reviewer has succinctly summed up the key factors in the father's personality, writing that the father was ". . . by all accounts an autocratic, harsh and controlling person. He used orthopedic devices to terrify children into submission and thus generated excessive fear and guilt in them." (Henry Z. Shelton, "Book Review," *Journal of the History of the Behavioral Sciences* 2 [1975]: 4).

34. See, for example, Elias Canetti, *Crowds and Power,* trans. by Carol Stewart (London: Gollancz, 1962).

35. Schatzman, *Soul Murder,* p. 41. In general, for parallels between the son's writings and the father's educational techniques, see chapter 4, "Memories and Hallucinations," pp. 32-52.

36. Ibid., p. 27. For further examples of the father's philosophy, see especially chapter 5, "Nature and Unnature," pp. 53-67.

37. Ibid., p. 8. For a good analysis of Schatzman's book see Robert Boyers, "The Laingian Family," *Partisan Review* 41 no. 1 (1974): 109.

38. Freud, *Analysis of a Phobia,* p. 5.

39. Marthe Robert, *The Psychoanalytic Revolution: Sigmund Freud's Life and Achievement* (New York: Avon, 1968), p. 195. See also Ernest Jones, *The Life and Work of Sigmund Freud,* 3 vols. (New York: Basic Books, 1953-1957).

40. Fromm, *The Crisis of Psychoanalysis,* pp. 100-101.

41. Schatzman, *Soul Murder,* p. 107.

42. Wolpe and Rachman, "Psychoanalytic Evidence," pp. 146-147. Wolpe and Rachman suggest that the evidence in the case could be far better presented in terms of the approach of the Hullian school of psychology (p. 145).

43. Fromm, *The Crisis of Psychoanalysis,* p. 110.

44. Freud, *Fragment of an Analysis,* p. 28.

45. Ibid.

46. See especially Chesler, "Patient and Patriarch."

47. Freud, *Fragment of an Analysis,* p. 86. Freud repeats several times that Dora often reproached her father for his behavior.

48. Simon, 1970. See quote in Chesler, "Patient and Patriarch." Marcus, "Freud and Dora," also notes how Dora was exploited by all three adults—her father, his mistress, and the latter's husband. Yet Freud, according to Marcus, sided with them and in fact seems to have been frustrated at his inability to convince Dora that her perception was incorrect.

49. See Felix Deutsch, "A Footnote to Freud's 'Fragment of an Analysis of a Case of Hysteria,'" *The Psychoanalytic Quarterly* 26 (1957): 159–167. For further interesting comments on the case, see Robert Lang, "The Misalliance Dimension in Freud's Case Histories: The Case of Dora," *International Journal of Psychoanalytic Psychotherapy* 5 (1976): 301–318. Lang notes that Freud knew personally both Dora's father and the male friend, and that this fact contributed to "a very early and intense erotization of her relationship with Freud" (p. 307).

50. Sigmund Freud, *Studies in Hysteria* (1893–1895), in *The Standard Edition,* 2: 60.

51. Ibid., pp. 60–61.

52. Ibid., footnote, p. 61.

53. Ibid., p. 62.

54. Ibid., p. 63.

55. Ibid., p. 105.

56. Ibid.

57. Sigmund Freud, Letter No. 69 to Fliess, Sept. 21, 1897, "Extracts from the Fliess Papers, 1892–1899," in *The Standard Edition,* vol. 1. See also Sigmund Freud, *The Origins of Psychoanalysis.*

58. Sigmund Freud, *An Autobiographical Study* (1925), in *The Standard Edition,* 20: 73.

59. Sigmund Freud, *From the History of an Infantile Neurosis* (1918), in *The Standard Edition,* vol. 17. For a fascinating follow-up to this study, in which the Wolf-Man writes of his own recollections of Freud, see *The Wolf-Man* by the Wolf-Man (New York: Basic Books, 1971). The book also contains a "Supplement" to Freud's case study in the report of subsequent treatment given to the Wolf-Man by Ruth Mack Brunswick, a follower of Freud.

60. Freud, *From the History of an Infantile Neurosis,* p. 21.

61. Freud's vacillation as to whether to accept that the patient remembered seeing the sexual act or had only fantasized it (as he argued in the case of alleged memories of seduction) is seen by the fact that he discusses at some length the possibility of the Wolf-Man's memory being correct.

62. Erich Fromm, *The Crisis of Psychoanalysis: Essays on Freud, Marx and Social Psychology,* pp. 42–43.

63. Ibid., p. 42.

64. Ibid., p. 43.

65. Ibid.

66. Freud, "Extracts from the Fliess Papers" (Letter No. 75, Nov. 14, 1897), in *The Standard Edition*, 1: 271.

67. See Sigmund Freud, "A Special Type of Choice of Object Made by Men (Contributions to the Psychology of Love)" (1910), in *The Standard Edition*, 11: 171. A fuller description of the meaning of the Oedipus complex appears in Sigmund Freud, *Introductory Lectures on Psycho-Analysis* (1917), in *The Standard Edition*, 16: 329–338.

68. See Walter A. Stewart, *Psychoanalysis: The First Ten Years, 1888–1898* (London: George Allen & Unwin, 1969), p. 27.

69. Freud, *Introductory Lectures on Psycho-Analysis*, p. 333.

70. Florence Rush, "The Freudian Cover-Up: The Sexual Abuse of Children," *Chrysalis* 1 (1977): 44.

71. Ibid., p. 45. See also Judith Herman and Lisa Hirschman, "Father-Daughter Incest," *Signs: Journal of Women in Culture and Society* 2 (1977): 735–757. Both these articles see Freud's approach as being sexist.

72. David R. Walters, *Physical and Sexual Abuse of Children: Causes and Treatment* (Bloomington, Indiana University Press, 1975).

73. Ibid., p. 116.

74. Herbert Maisch, *Incest* (London: Andre Deutsch, 1973), pp. 36–37. See also Blair and Rita Justice, *The Broken Taboo: Sex in the Family* (New York: Human Sciences Press, 1979).

75. Joseph C. Rheingold, *The Fear of Being a Woman: A Theory of Maternal Destructiveness* (New York: Grune & Stratton, 1964), p. 91. Rheingold suggests that incestuous acts by fathers toward their daughters should be accepted and not condemned, for "if we set aside moral considerations and think only of the effect on the girl, we must say that such rejection and stigmatization of the daughter's femininity do her more harm than seduction. The frank appreciation of her femininity, courting behavior, and a certain amount of physical intimacy have positive value in her psychosexual development" (p. 89).

76. Kate Friedlander, *The Psycho-Analytical Approach to Juvenile Delinquency: Theory; Case-Studies; Treatment* (London: Routledge & Kegan Paul, 1947), p. 174.

77. Karin C. Meiselman, *Incest: A Psychological Study of Causes and Effects with Treatment Recommendations* (San Francisco: Jossey-Bass, 1978), p. 149.

78. Sandra Butler, *Conspiracy of Silence: The Trauma of Incest* (New York: Bantam, 1979).

79. Ibid., p. 128.

80. Freud, *Studies in Hysteria*, pp. 125–134.

81. Ibid., p. 130.

82. Ibid., p. 170.

83. Ibid., p. 172.

84. Ibid., p. 134. See also the footnote on p. 170, referring to the other case.

85. Ibid., p. 134.

86. See, for instance, references to Adler reflecting Freud's changing attitudes to him.

87. Mark Poster, *Critical Theory of the Family* (New York: Seabury Press, 1968), p. 10.

88. Ibid., p. 4.

89. Ibid.

90. Freud, *Studies in Hysteria,* p. 275.

91. Ibid.

92. Seymour Fisher and Roger P. Greenberg, *The Scientific Credibility of Freud's Theories and Therapy* (New York: Basic Books, 1977).

93. Ian D. Suttie, *The Origins of Love and Hate* (London: Kegan Paul, Trench, Trubner, 1935).

94. Herbert Marcuse, *Eros and Civilization* (Boston: Beacon Press, 1955); Norman O. Brown, *Life Against Death* (Middletown, Conn.: Wesleyan University Press, 1959). Their work will be discussed in chapter 11.

95. See comment by the British writer David Holbrook, *Human Hope and the Death Instinct* (Oxford: Pergamon Press, 1971), p. 49.

96. Suttie, *The Origins of Love and Hate,* p. 107.

97. Ibid., p. 6.

98. Ibid., p. 78. There is extensive discussion of the taboo on tenderness throughout the book; see especially chapter 6, pp. 80–96.

99. Ibid., pp. 80–81.

100. Ibid., p. 52.

101. Ibid., p. 95.

102. Ibid., p. 96.

103. Ibid., p. 107.

104. Ibid., p. 110.

105. Ibid.

106. Karen Horney, *The Neurotic Personality of Our Time* (New York: W. W. Norton, 1937); and *New Ways in Psychoanalysis* (New York: W. W. Norton, 1939), especially chapter 4, "The Oedipus Complex," pp. 78–87.

107. Horney, *Neurotic Personality of Our Time,* p. 84.

108. Horney, *New Ways in Psychoanalysis,* pp. 82–83.

109. Horney, *Neurotic Personality of Our Time,* p. 161.

110. Kate Friedlander, *The Psycho-Analytical Approach to Juvenile Delinquency.*

111.   Ibid., part II, chapter 2, pp. 78–94.

112.   Dorothy Bloch, "Fantasy and the Fear of Infanticide," *Psychoanalytic Review,* 61 (1974): 5; and *So the Witch Won't Eat Me: Fantasy and the Child's Fear of Infanticide* (Boston: Houghton Mifflin, 1978).

113.   For examples of the work by Melanie Klein, see her collection of articles, *Contributions to Psycho-Analysis, 1921–1945,* (London: Hogarth Press, 1950). In the article "On Criminality" (1934), she writes, "Children would show asocial and criminal tendencies and act them out (of course in their childish way) over and over again, the more they were dreading a cruel retaliation from their parents as a punishment for their aggressive phantasies directed against those parents. Children who, unconsciously, were expecting to be cut to pieces, beheaded, devoured and so on, would feel compelled to be naughty and yet punished, because the real punishment, however severe, was reassuring in comparison with the murderous attacks which they were continuously expecting from fantastically cruel parents. . . . The small child first harbours against its parents aggressive impulses and phantasies, it then projects these on to them, and thus it came about that it develops a phantastic and distorted picture of the people around it" (p. 278).

114.   Bloch, "Fantasy and the Fear of Infanticide," p. 7. For a similar approach, see George Devereux, "The Cannibalistic Impulses of Parents," *Psychoanalytic Forum* 1 (1966): 114. Devereux also criticizes the narrow approach of Melanie Klein and other psychoanalysts. He concludes: "The near-complete bypassing of parental cannibalism impulses in psychoanalytic literature suggests the presence of massive resistances against this insight."

115.   Eric Lustig, "On the Origin of Judaism: 'A Psychoanalytic Approach," *The Psychoanalytic Study of Society* 7 (1976): 366.

116.   See R. E. Helfer and C. H. Kempe, eds., *The Battered Child* (Chicago: University of Chicago Press, 1968).

117.   Sigmund Freud, "A Child Is Being Beaten," in *The Standard Edition,* 17: 175–206.

118.   Ibid., p. 180. But Freud does concede that beating was practiced in the schools, at least in the lower classes.

119.   Edward D. Joseph, ed., *Beating Fantasies,* monograph no. 1, Study Group of the New York Psychoanalytic Institute (New York: International Universities Press, 1965).

120.   Ibid., p. 57.

121.   Ibid.

122.   See discussion in later chapters; especially chapters 4, 5, and 6.

PART TWO
THE USES OF
THE OEDIPUS
COMPLEX

CHAPTER FOUR
FICTIONAL WORLDS
OF CHILDHOOD

Although Freud's occasional ventures into analysis of literature have provided a fertile ground for a host of critiques in literature that interpret an author's intended message through the focused prism of the Oedipus complex, his own work consists of little more than marginal commentaries.

Freud never fully deals with the Oedipus theme itself; references to the story are scattered in several places; the Sophoclean trilogy as a whole is ignored. Other works of literature are given passing reference, with provocative insights that are not always subsequently pursued. Freud never developed his own oedipal interpretations of *Hamlet,* which he referred to on several occasions; it was left to one of his followers to expand the idea into a full-fledged analysis. This work, by Ernest Jones,[1] has served as a model for using the Freudian perspective to develop original and challenging interpretations of literary works. Such a perspective may also be seen in the works of writers such as Jack Spektor, Frederick Hoffman, Louis Fraiberg, Claudia Morrison, F. L. Lucas, Norman Holland, J. I. M. Stewart, E. Freeman Sharpe, and Daniel Schneider.[2]

There can be no gainsaying the fact that Freud's thinking on human nature has affected our capacity to understand hidden and subtle meanings set out by sensitive writers who are able to perceive and express qualities of human nature and social life that are beyond the ken of the average person. Freud opened up new vistas for understanding and for enhancing communication between the artist and his audience, thereby significantly enriching the culture of the modern world.

While much Freudian interpretation has centered on the role of the unconscious, depth psychology, sexuality, basic drives, and the impact of childhood experiences in later life, there has also been considerable reliance on the Oedipus complex, which is constantly resorted to as the theoretical framework for understanding instances of generational conflict, itself a prevalent theme in much of literature.

Freud's own statement in this regard is that

It can scarcely be owing to chance that three of the masterpieces of the literature of all time—the *Oedipus Rex* of Sophocles, Shakespeare's *Hamlet* and

Dostoevsky's *The Brothers Karamazov*—should all deal with the same subject, parricide. In all three, moreover, the motive for the deed, sexual rivalry for a woman, is laid bare.[3]

I have already offered my own view of the Oedipus story: even though Oedipus did kill his father, parricide was not the only, or even the major, theme of the story; inasmuch as the story deals with generational conflict (particularly in the total trilogy), what emerges most clearly is parental hostility.

Similar considerations, I believe, apply to *Hamlet* and *The Brothers Karamazov*, although the parallels between the works are not complete. Particularly in *Hamlet*, there is no direct parricide, a fact that has sponsored intricate, yet fascinating, interpretations that cast the story in an Oedipus mold. In *The Brothers Karamazov*, the parricide is committed by an illegitimate son who is treated throughout the book far more like a serf than a son. Whatever the worth and the degree of truth in the various oedipal explanations that have been essayed in an extension of Freud's ideas, they cannot be accepted as sole explanations of the author's intentions, nor can they negate other interpretations.

Some psychoanalytic analyses are stimulating and deserving of close study. Often, however, their useful insights into hidden themes, into the role of the subconscious, or into sexual factors are undermined by too great and too narrow a commitment to the Oedipus theme. A more open and flexible mode of thinking would allow for alternative explanations, including those of an opposite nature.

We have seen how even the filicidal story of Rustum and Sohrab—and particularly the meaning assigned to it by Matthew Arnold—has been incorrectly seen in oedipal terms. Just as Arnold, who intended to call witness to his own father's hostility toward him, has been misunderstood and misinterpreted, so have Shakespeare and Dostoevsky. Their respective works—not just *Hamlet* and *The Brothers Karamazov*, but others as well— certainly revolve around generational conflict, but the oedipal interpretation is not necessarily the correct one nor, certainly, the only one. On the contrary, the perspective afforded by a Rustum complex may help illuminate their meaning.

My analysis will be based on the actual content of the works, as well as certain personal and social aspects of the authors' life histories. As in the case of Arnold there are critics who have sensed the import of parental hostility, but have lacked a suitable theoretical framework that might have sharpened their insights.

In almost any work of literature that deals with generational conflict, several options exist for its interpretation. Except in the most extreme instances, the hostility is not one-sided. The key question often is to determine which character—parent or child—bears major responsibility for the hostility and its consequences; which one initiated the hostility, and which one tried to compromise and obtain a reconciliation.

In the story of Oedipus itself it seems that not only is the hostility bidirectional but also that major responsibility for initiating, intensifying, and perpetuating the hostility rests with the father. This is even more pronounced in the subsequent development of the story: Oedipus's relations with his own sons, and Creon's with his son, nephews, and niece. While not denying aspects of filial hostility (in fact, more openly expressed by Oedipus's sons toward him than by Oedipus himself toward his father), the overriding motif seems to be far more attuned to parental hostility.

Similar considerations apply to other works that have been presented in the classical oedipal mold. Freud may have been correct in seeing oedipal overtones in both *Hamlet* and *The Brothers Karamazov*. In the former, this meaning is embedded deep in the interstices of the plot, and it was only Jones's ingenious argumentation that made possible an interpretation of Hamlet's indecision over the time and means of exacting revenge for his father's death as springing from his own repressed wish for that death. In *The Brothers Karamazov*, the theme of parricide certainly runs as a constant thread through the book. Some of Karamazov's sons talk of their desire to have him killed; he is verbally and physically abused by them; he is actually killed by an illegitimate son; and the word parricide itself appears on several occasions throughout the book. Indeed, if parricide is Dostoevsky's major theme, he resorts to little subtlety in putting over this message and is even heavy-handed in belaboring the theme. Yet is this really the message? With *Hamlet*, where the son does not kill the father but is bent ostensibly on avenging his death, the Freudians have resorted to imaginative and convoluted reasoning in order to point out the latent meaning of filial hostility and parricidal wishes; with *The Brothers Karamazov*, on the other hand, they have willingly accepted the manifest content of actual parricide without any attempt to search for alternative, disguised messages. M. Sperber's clear-cut terms echo the normal approach to the book: "*The Brothers Karamazov* is a novel of parricide."[4]

A renewed look at these works will reveal that alternative explanations are available and seem more likely, both within the confines of the text and in the larger context of the authors' backgrounds and the personal and social influences that, directly or unconsciously, influenced their writing.

The willing Freudian acceptance of the manifest theme in the account of the Karamazov family becomes all the more perplexing when it is remembered that, more than almost any other modern writer, Dostoevsky is credited with having preceded Freud in his insight into the human psyche and in his realization that much of social behavior is a reflection of unconscious impulses.

I do not propose to suggest any definitive treatment of Dostoevsky's work;[5] I wish only to offer examples of how a Rustum complex perspective is capable of divulging some of the inner essence of the story that has been lost, for the most part, in the world of oedipal literary criticism. The intention is not so much to inquire into Dostoevsky as to examine the premises of Freudian thinking.

In *The Brothers Karamazov*, while it is admittedly the father who dies at the hands of a son, the essence of the plot is the father's own hostility toward all four of his legitimate and illegitimate offspring. This emerges in the opening chapters of the book, as Dostoevsky lays down the framework of the family background for the succeeding events. Chapter 2, entitled "He Gets Rid of His Oldest Son," describes the vicissitudes of the early years of Dimitri, the son who, though innocent of the charge, is, at the end of the book, found guilty of the murder of his father. After he had been abandoned at the age of three by his mother, who absconded with a lover, his father completely ignored him, "not from malice, nor because of his matrimonial grievance, but simply because he forgot him."[6] As a child Dimitri lived in a servant's cottage until a cousin agreed to take the child and bring him up. The cousin himself related that "when he began to speak of Dimitri the father looked for some time as though he did not understand what child he was talking about, and even as though he was surprised to hear that he had a little son in the house."[7] Years later, when the contact between the two is renewed, the father cheats his son out of his rightful share of the family estate and becomes the son's rival in a love affair, which Freud sees as confirming the incestuous aspect of the Oedipus story.

The son who actually commits the murder, Smyerdyakov (who, though not accused of the crime, pays the penalty through suicide on the eve of the judgment against his half-brother), is the product of his father's sexual exploitation of an illiterate peasant woman. His role in the Karamazov home is that of a servant, denied any filial rights, deprived of any parental affection.

The father, Fyodor, is presented throughout the book in the most negative terms. His life is one long bout of lustful and drunken debauchery, his appearance repulsive, his concern for his sons nonexistent.

The book is replete with oblique references to Dostoevsky's own life. Many of the scenes, the characters, and the events were drawn from his personal experiences.[8] His father resembled Fyodor Karamazov in many ways. In William Hadden's words, "His father, who was an erratic and irritable alcoholic, acquired a small farm in the Tula region [where the events in the book take place], where he treated his few serfs so badly that they murdered him when Fyodor was sixteen years of age."[9]

Dostoevsky himself suffered from epilepsy, which either started or became intensified after his father's death. In *The Brothers Karamazov* it is the illegitimate son who has this affliction and commits the murder during a fit—whether real or feigned is not clear. Here there are what seem to be oedipal symbols. The father is killed by an epileptic, part son, part serf, as if Dostoevsky is indicating his own identification with the dozen or so of his father's serfs who, frustrated into aggression, killed his father. Yet what kind of father is portrayed; what are Dostoevsky's own memories of his father? Is he not trying to describe the provocative behavior of the father that might have precipitated the parricide? Dostoevsky is in fact posing the deep moral question of the right of a son to take revenge for the harm his father has caused him. As Edward Wasiolek notes, the "defense attorney at Dimitri's trial will argue that a child has the right to demand that a father prove his love, and that a child has the right to look upon a bad father as an enemy."[10]

Yet that right does not come without a heavy price, as three of the sons discover. Smyerdyakov commits suicide; Ivan, beset by his guilt feelings at having wished his father's death, goes insane; Dimitri is accused, indicted, convicted, and punished for a parricidal crime that he did not commit. The irony is that even though he had wished to commit the crime, had spoken and written about his intention, had planned a similar crime, and had even, on one occasion, embarked on it, the fact is that at the last moment he was unable to consummate the crime and withdrew from the scene.

Dimitri, then, not only bears the suffering of having been abandoned by his parents, deprived of his birthright by his father, and challenged by his father for the love of a young woman, but is also unjustly convicted and condemned to serve a twenty-year sentence in Siberia. From a Freudian perspective this may be seen as a necessary expiation for the criminal thoughts and plan, one which Dimitri needs in order to overcome his guilt feelings at his father's death. Such a fate may be preferable to going insane as did his brother Ivan.

Dimitri's *unjust* punishment for parricide, however, takes on new meaning when it is related to a similar real-life incident, ignored in most analyses of the book. The model for Dimitri's unjust punishment was a similar unjust punishment of a person called Ilyinsky, whom Dostoevsky had personally met during his own banishment to Siberia; this had greatly disturbed him. In the first chapter of his autobiographical *Notes from the House of Death*, originally published in serial form in a magazine, Dostoevsky writes:

> I especially cannot forget a certain parricide [who] . . . had killed [his father], through greed for his inheritance . . . . He did not confess, was deprived of his nobility, rank and exiled to hard labor for twenty years. All the time that I lived with him, he was in the most excellent, in the most cheerful frame of mind. . . . I never noticed any particular cruelty in him . . . . It goes without

saying, I did not believe in this crime. But people from his town, who must have known all the details of his history, related the whole affair to me. The facts were so clear that it was impossible not to believe them.[11]

Nevertheless, as Dostoevsky's biographer, Konstantin Mochulsky, notes:

[I]ntuition did not deceive the writer. In the seventh chapter of *House of Death* which was printed . . . a year and a half after the first chapter, the author tells how he had received information from Siberia. "The criminal was, in fact, innocent and for ten years had suffered in penal servitude—for no reason; his innocence has been established by the court officially; the real criminal was found and has confessed; the unfortunate man has already been released from prison." And Dostoevsky concludes: "There is nothing to say or add regarding all the tragic depths in this fact, regarding the life that was already ruined in the time of its youth, under such a terrible charge."[12]

But Dostoevsky did apparently have much to say and add—and used the medium of *The Brothers Karamazov* to do so:

[Dostoevsky] was shaken by the *tragic* fate of this innocent convict who had borne the accusation of parricide. For sixteen years this terrible recollection lived in his memory, and determined the plot of his last novel. Flighty and light-headed Dimitri is placed in the same relation toward his father . . . as Ilyinsky. Like the hero of the novel, the alleged murderer was a healthy and strong individual, lived in a small provincial city . . . came from a noble family, and had the rank of sub-lieutenant in a line battalion. Ilyinsky's father was sixty years old, Fyodor Pavlovich Karamazov fifty-five. Ilyinsky was exiled to penal servitude by Imperial decision. Dimitri "will smell the mines for twenty years."[13]

The clear connection between the two characters is underscored by the fact that in the rough drafts of the book Dimitri bears the name Ilyinsky.[14]

Thus, while parricide was one of the themes of *The Brothers Karamazov*, the actual motivation for the plot was the injustice caused by false accusation of parricide. Was Dostoevsky suggesting, perhaps, that children are too often incorrectly blamed? Was he drawing attention not to the parricide itself but to its incorrect and unfair attribution? If so, nothing could be more tragically unfair than the constant attempts to see the book in pure parricidal terms. Dostoevsky's own regular use of the word "parricide" in the novel may have been part of the technique he used for stressing the need to look *beyond* the most obvious theme; after all, it is the Freudians who first praised Dostoevsky's understanding of hidden meanings and of the unconscious.

Dostoevsky is not especially subtle about handling some of these suggested hidden meanings; he provides ample hints that there was, in fact, no parricide. After all, whatever his thoughts, Dimitri did *not* commit parricide, yet was punished for it, while Symerdyakov, the actual murderer, was more serf than son. Inasmuch as Dostoevsky is dealing with parricide in the book, it is the plight of the falsely accused son that is uppermost in his mind.

Dostoevsky's concern for the plight of the young in general runs as a constant theme throughout the book; as Wasiolek states, "Children are the moral touchstone of the novel."[15] This aim finds its expression in the epilogue to the book, where a young child, Ilyusha, is buried in the presence of the youngest Karamazov brother, Alyosha, the only one to emerge unscathed from his father's death.

One Freudian critic's explanation of this episode at the end of the book is the need for the young boy, Ilyusha, to die as the only expiation possible for an earlier death in the book of a monk, Father Zossima, who had been Alyosha's mentor. While some literary writers have criticized Dostoevsky's excursion into the subplot revolving around Alyosha, Gilbert Chaitin claims that this aspect of the book is a "well-integrated subplot." He notes that there are four deaths in the novel: "Just as the rebellious son, Symerdyakov, must die for the murder of Fyodor . . . so Ilyusha must die as a punishment for the death of Father Zossima."[16] Rarely has the Oedipus complex been used in such an illogical, in fact heartless, manner, for there is no direct connection whatsoever between Father Zossima and Ilyusha. (Their only connection is through their separate contacts with Alyosha.)

Chaitin himself is aware of this gap in his chain of thinking but hastens to justify his interpretation by stressing the need for an oedipal symmetry:

> Of course Ilyusha was not the cause of Zossima's death, not even in thought, but I am looking at this event in terms of the total fantasy, according to which the death of a Father must be paid for by the death of a Son. Only thus can order and normalcy be restored. . . . Ilyusha's disease and subsequent death can be understood only as a result of the conflict caused by his repressed death wishes against his own father. . . . Otherwise the boy would not have been so profoundly affected by the unavenged insult to his father. In the last analysis, then, Ilyusha, too, like the Karamazovs is a rebellious son. . . . Once he is dead, the world of the novel has been cleansed of its parricidal taint.[17]

One can but stand aghast at the callousness of this oedipal analysis, which insists, like the infanticidal practices of old, on the sacrifice of a son, and at the perverse manner in which the Oedipus complex may be applied. This analysis becomes all the more ridiculous when it is realized that it is a direct violation of Dostoevsky's intention.

For, despite all the evil and ugliness in the book, Dostoevsky did attempt to end it on an optimistic note. His use of Alyosha and the boys was not merely a subplot for *The Brothers Karamazov* but was intended to serve as an entree into a sequel to the book.

Mochulsky notes that in 1881, at the time of his death, Dostoevsky had intended

> to begin writing the second part of Karamazov; all the former characters would appear in it, but now, twenty years later, almost in the contemporary period. The main hero of the novel would be Alyosha Karamazov.[18]

The epilogue with the boys burying their friend in the presence of Alyosha may thus be seen as the transition to the future novel.

Beyond this, though, it also provides a clue to the underlying theme of the book—not parricide as the fate of the father but the fate of young people. Dostoevsky had been so engrossed by his children's theme that in preparation for the book he had written to a leading pedagogue, Mikhailov:

> I am very interested in the fact that you love children, have lived a great deal with children . . . . I have planned, and soon will begin a big novel in which, among other things children will play a large part, especially young ones from 7 to 15 years, approximately. Many children will be introduced. I am studying and have studied them all my life, love them very much, and have some of my own. But the observations of a man such as yourself . . . will be invaluable to me. And so, write to me what you yourself know about the children. . . . Things that happen, their habits, answers, words and little sayings, traits of character, their relations to their families, faith, misdeeds, and innocence.[19]

Mochulsky goes on to point out that both the first notes for the novel and the first rough draft are full of references to the "children's theme." The notes contain cryptic entries—"Inquire about child labor in factories," "about gymnasiums, life in a gymnasium, about Pestalozzi, about Froebel."[20] Wasiolek, too, writes that Dostoevsky began *The Brothers Karamazov* as a novel about children; he visited pedagogical institutions; his first notes on the novel had to do with children.[21]

These notes found their outlet in the book, with its myriad references to the unfortunate plight of children.[22] Some of this involvement with children is found in the "biographical notes" of the monk, Father Zossima, where there are many references to the world of childhood. More particularly, in the fifth book (Pro and Contra) which is "ideologically central we have Ivan's confession and his legend of the Grand Inquisitor,"[23] and here Dostoevsky sets out clearly his own views about the unkind fate of children. Indeed, in trying to present his own *Weltanschauung*, Ivan resorts mainly to using examples drawn from the world of childhood. He ponders over their fate, recounting instances of torture practiced on children; of children suffering for the sins of their fathers; of an illegitimate son, given to peasants, who was forced to work for them and was treated like a wild beast; of how a "well-educated, cultured gentleman and his wife beat their own child with a birch-rod, a girl of seven."[24] They are brought to court, the jury, convinced by the defense counsel's rhetoric ("It's such a simple thing . . . an everyday domestic event. A father corrects his child"),[25] finds the parents innocent, and the public roars with delight that the torturer is acquitted.

Ivan continues:

> I've still better things about children. I've collected a great, great deal about Russian children. . . . There was a little girl of five who was hated by her father and mother, "most worthy and respectable people, of good education and breeding" . . . it is a peculiar characteristic of many people, the love of torturing children, and children only. To all other types of humanity these torturers behave mildly and benevolently, like cultured and humane Europeans; but they are very fond of tormenting children. . . . It's just their defenselessness that tempts the tormentor, just the angelic confidence of the child who has no refuge and no appeal, that sets his vile blood on fire. In every man, of course, a demon lies hidden.[26]

A demon that breaks out, in the final story in this section, of a landowner who, in retaliation for the act of an eight-year-old serf boy in harming his favorite dog, has the child stripped naked and sets his pack of dogs on him, to tear him to pieces before his mother's eyes.[27]

Ivan Karamazov's rage at the world, his lack of faith in God, and his rebellion against religion relate directly to his awareness of the suffering of innocent children: "If it is really true that they must share responsibility for all their fathers' crimes, such a truth is not of this world and is beyond my comprehension."[28]

This is the essence of Ivan's soul-searching for a meaningful philosophy of life. Dostoevsky, who researched many of the factual details related in the book—including the instances of child abuse—doubtless shared Ivan's anguish.

Further, the subplot of Alyosha and the boys is probably not so much a minor dimension of the book as the essential message toward which Dostoevsky was working—a message of hatred between the generations being replaced by harmonious understanding.

On a personal level, it should be mentioned that during the writing of this novel, Dostoevsky's three-year-old son, Alyosha, died. It was after his death that Dostoevsky decided to give this name to the most honorable of the Karamazov brothers, the one around whom he intended developing his theme of generational harmony in the sequel to *The Brothers Karamazov*. Mochulsky suggests that Dostoevsky expressed the depth of his grief in the lament of a peasant woman weeping over her dead son:

> He was three years old, just two more months and he would have been three years. For my little son I'm tormented. . . . If only I could look at him one little time . . . so often, I remember how he used to run to me, shout, and laugh; if only I might hear, might hear his two feet, I would know him.[29]

Mochulsky concludes that

> the father's anguish caused by the death of his favorite son intensifies the emotional tone of the story regarding the children; the description of Ilyusha's death and the father's grief will forever pierce the heart with an unforgettable pain.[30]

Ilyusha's death, then, is neither an attempt to gain oedipal symmetry, nor an irrelevant closing scene, but constitutes at least part of the essence of Dostoevsky's theme. As Wasiolek notes,

> The novel begins with the hand of a child raised against the father; it ends with the cheers of children for another Karamazov. . . . With Alyosha the boys are confident in the beauty of life, the reality of immortality, and the hope in the future.[31]

To ignore this aspect or to distort or misinterpret it through oedipal blindness is to miss the thrust of Dostoevsky's work and to block out the message that his own death, within weeks of publication of the book, prevented him from completing.

The third major literary work that Freud claimed bore testimony to his dual theme of parricide and incest was Shakespeare's *Hamlet*. Freud alluded to the story several times and was obviously intrigued by the possibility of an oedipal interpretation. In *The Interpretation of Dreams* he suggests that the death of Shakespeare's father in 1601 may have been the motivating force behind the writing of the play, since the death may have revived "his own childish feelings in respect of his father."[32] Freud sees parallels between the feelings that had possessed him after the death of his own father and that had directly influenced *The Interpretation of Dreams* and the reactions of the author of *Hamlet* to his father's death.

Jones attempts to buttress Freud's argument by proving that *Hamlet* was written shortly after the death of Shakespeare's father.[33] Yet he admits that determining the actual date of writing and publication presents "one of the knottiest problems in the history of English literature."[34] The play was published some time in the early years of the seventeenth century but on several occasions and in different versions. Furthermore, it had been preceded by an earlier version by Thomas Kyd, which had been widely performed but of which there are no existing copies.

Jones discusses the various theories, then opts for Dover Wilson's contention[35] that the play was written in the summer or autumn of 1601, a period that he links to two key events in Shakespeare's life: the Essex uprising, which resulted in the imprisonment of his patron, the Earl of Southampton, and the death of his father in September 1601. But surely, if *Hamlet* was written in the summer or autumn of the same year, it would have been all but completed by September; certainly the plot would have been thought out long beforehand, though Shakespeare might have made some changes in the dialogue or the sequence of scenes.

Jones himself seems aware of the weakness of his and Freud's case and notes, almost as an aside, that, "Unfortunately, we have no data about the cause of his father's death or how long he had been known to be suffering from a fatal illness."[36] The latter statement is simply wishful thinking, for Jones has no evidence of a lingering illness that may have preyed on Shakespeare's mind.

Shakespeare did, however, suffer another family loss prior to his father's death: the death of his eleven-year-old son, Hamnet. It is likely that this loss had at least some impact on Shakespeare, possibly compounded by the guilty knowledge that he had abandoned this son shortly after his birth. Jones ignores both the symbolic connection between the names of the child and of the dramatic hero, and the fact that the five years that elapsed between the death of Hamnet and publication of the play were identical to the time span between the death of Freud's father and publication of *The Interpretation of Dreams*. The irrelevance of the son's death for Jones may be noted from the casual way in which he refers to it:

> The name Hamlet itself, or some modification of it, was common in the Stratford district. . . . As is well known, Shakespeare in 1585 christened his only son, Hamnet, a frequent variant of the name; the boy died in 1596.[37]

One further point of major significance should be noted. While some authorities consider that Shakespeare based his play on an earlier version by Thomas Kyd, there is another play by Kyd, *The Spanish Tragedy*, which also contains many parallels with *Hamlet* and which some authorities see as having influenced Shakespeare, except that in this instance it is the son who is murdered and the father who ponders whether or not to seek revenge and who feigns madness. The interconnection between the parricidal and filicidal themes is stressed by Geoffrey Bullough, who suggests that Kyd wrote the two plays, *The Spanish Tragedy* and his version of *Hamlet*, as companion pieces, and that Shakespeare himself uses many ideas from *The Spanish Tragedy* in his *Hamlet* (Bullough lists over a score of parallels).[38]

As for the play itself, its greatness, of course, lies in the fact that it has no one overriding theme but is open to a multiplicity of interpretations. While psychoanalysis provides a new dimension to *Hamlet*, nevertheless, as Lionel Trilling argues, "Shakespeare did not intend the Oedipus motive or anything less than *Hamlet*; if meaning is effect then it is *Hamlet* which affects us, not the Oedipus motive."[39]

Alternative interpretations of *Hamlet* include those by Frederic Wertham and by Natalie Shainess, both of whom argue that the play expresses matricidal as opposed to parricidal tendencies.[40] Wertham suggests an

Orestes complex, while Shainess sees Hamlet not as vacillating but as waiting for the right moment to take revenge upon his mother. Though she rejects the typical oedipal explanation of Hamlet's behavior, Shainess is nevertheless critical of the young man who has been deprived of his birthright. She brands him "an alienated, destructive man who cannot tolerate . . . his loss of the throne and all that goes with such a position."[41] It may be asked why an heir apparent should be expected to tolerate his loss of the throne, especially when he has lost it through foul play.

Neil Friedman and Richard Jones offer a different perspective, which, though grounded in the tradition of psychoanalytic interpretation, nevertheless points to the possibility of an analysis based on the Rustum complex.[42] For them the key to *Hamlet* is the societal context: there was indeed something rotten in the state of Denmark. "What," they ask, "had set the time so out of joint? What social excesses existed that only the psychological excesses which rankled Hamlet sufficed to set them right?" Their solution is a psychological approach which would enquire into

> the child-rearing practices typical of the times. The reply is definite; the prevailing educational assumptions supported a system of tacit intrigue and unabashed spying by the elder generation into the private affairs of the younger generation. The adults of the play are paternal rather than parental; children are to be watched over, seen into, and so controlled.[43]

While I do not necessarily agree with all the examples and conclusions offered by Friedman and Jones to support their thesis, their reasoning seems no less sound than that of Ernest Jones. It is grounded in Eriksonian psychological theory,[44] in the text of the play, and in the social circumstances. Their conclusions point to what they call the "mutuality" of the Oedipus complex:

> Adult intimacy was precluded in Denmark by forces of social inertia. Therefore (1) children became increasingly threatening, (2) infanticidal wishes became increasingly pressing. . . . The cultural super ego . . . then settled on an enduring missolution: It is as if it said to the parents: "Now hear this, the thing to do is to spy on your children. See how it works: (1) you get to be in on matters intimate, (2) you control the little devils, and (3) you get to kill your children.[45]

I have many misgivings about the factual and theoretical basis for this argument. But Friedman and Jones do show that, just as a perspective of filial hostility (the Oedipus model) may illuminate aspects of *Hamlet,* so may a perspective of parental hostility (the Rustum model). What appears particularly interesting—and deserving of further analysis—is their contention that children may very well need what Virginia Woolf calls "a room of one's own," a sanctuary or privacy beyond the prying eyes of adults.[46]

Another Shakespearean tragedy dealing with generational conflict and referred to by Freud is *King Lear*. This play, too, has been submitted to oedipal interpretation by Freudians and, once again, the more likely meaning seems to be just the opposite of their conclusions.

For F. L. Lucas, "The primitive clash between generations is the theme of Shakespeare's most primitive tragedy—Lear."[47] Although he begins his analysis in typical oedipal terms, calling *King Lear* "the story of two fathers ruined by their children,"[48] Lucas actually deals more with the fathers' faults and errors. He asks: "Can psychological experience justify this old father's quarrel with his favorite daughter over the mere wording of her affection?"[49] Lucas sees the Lear-Cordelia conflict as akin to a lovers' quarrel, in which it is Lear who is jealous. He takes note of

> the hidden pitfalls which civilization has introduced into the human family. Parents too fond may tangle their children in emotional leading-strings; parents not fond enough can breed in their children a rankling resentment.[50]

In spite of his original oedipal bias, Lucas concludes that "Lear . . . is a concentrated tragedy of the jealousy between parents and children, between sisters and brothers."[51] In a *volte face* he concludes that the tragedy is "above all, of a father's morbid possessiveness towards a favorite daughter."[52]

In contrast to Lucas, Mark Kanzer insists on seeing even the two innocents of *King Lear*—Cordelia and Edgar, both victims of their respective fathers' actions, both loyal to them to the end—as hostile ingrates.[53] "Under close scrutiny," he argues, "Edgar scarcely emerges before the bar of justice as a helpless innocent."[54] In a highly forced manner he criticizes a whole list of Edgar's qualities and actions, only reluctantly acknowledging: "True, he . . . saves the father from suicide and from Oswald."[55]

This negative appraisal may be compared with an analysis by Lawrence Berns, who tries to come to terms with the very real problem of a child's eternal gratitude to his parents for the gift of life and with the objective inability to repay them.[56] Berns sees Edgar coming as close as humanly possible to repaying one's parent—neither exploiting his potential power over his blind, helpless father nor seeking revenge for the latter's previous cruelty to him, but loyally helping, guarding, and guiding his father, finally even saving him from death.

Of Cordelia, one of Shakespeare's most attractive characters, Kanzer has little to say, except to find a parallel between the hanging of Cordelia and the hanging of Jocasta,[57] though Jocasta had been guilty of abandoning her son, Oedipus, then subsequently marrying him, while Cordelia's only sin was her devotion to the truth and her refusal to compromise it, despite her genuine love for her obstinate father.

In contrast, Arpad Pauncz postulates a "Lear complex," which endeavors to account for the specific erotic attachment of the father for his daughter. In establishing these concepts, an attempt is made to supplement the one-sidedness of the infantile libido and Oedipus complex, which are concerned exclusively with the child or the infantile aspect of the adult, while completely disregarding the characteristics of adulthood as such.[58]

Lucas, whose account of Lear seems to confirm Pauncz's thesis, also notes numerous cases in world literature wherein

parent is tied to child, though less prominent in psychological literature than their converse, where child is tied to parent. . . . In story after story we have a king who imposes dire penalties on the suitors of his daughters.[59]

Why, one may ask, is this theme "less prominent in psychological literature"? If it is so widespread in literature, why has it been ignored by the adherents of psychoanalysis?

Only occasionally does a writer who is steeped in the Freudian tradition succeed in breaking free from the narrow constrictions of the Oedipus complex. Such an achievement is seen in M. D. Faber's work on *Romeo and Juliet,* in which he draws attention to parental/adult hostility not just within the family setting but also in the larger societal context.[60] Within the family Faber sees the suicides of Romeo and Juliet as consequences of the blocking of adolescent attempts to transfer the libidinal energies to nonincestuous objects, thereby achieving one of life's major separations, that of the sexually mature child from the parents.

If the play indeed deals with generational separation, then it is the children who are prepared for such a break, while the adults cannot accept their maturing children's newly acquired powers and demands for rights. Like Lear and Creon, the adult figures in *Romeo and Juliet* are not prepared to let their children make their break and choose their own partners and futures, untrammeled by traditional parental prejudices and power. The separation anxieties of adolescents may be a less serious problem than those of their parents. As Lucas notes:

There are only too many mothers that find no girl good enough to marry their sons; and every now and then we read of some father who has unaccountably committed suicide just at the period of his daughter's wedding.[61]

At the societal level, Faber is even more precise and even more in line with the Rustum perspective:

Romeo and Juliet presents us with the breakdown of an entire social order, a breakdown that engenders problems of growth and separation in its adolescent young. The narcissistically diseased city of Verona is actually destroying its children, driving them to carry the seeds of renewal, the promise of growth and non-incestuous involvement, into the very tomb that contains the children's forebears.[62]

Faber's flexible and open approach reminds us that Shakespeare's plays do not allow themselves to be easily categorized, either in the individual analysis of any one play or by means of a constant theme running through all of them. If the Oedipus theme is picked up in one play, it will not necessarily appear in another; if a Rustum meaning is noted in one play, this will not necessarily be Shakespeare's only motif. Shakespeare tried to encompass an entire range of human emotions and intentions. He was a student of the human psyche and soul in all its manifestations. No one idea captured him; no one theoretical mold can contain him.

The oedipal interpretations are welcome additions to the feast of Shakespeare interpretation; it is their exclusive, imperialistic contentions and their recurrent illogical conclusions that are to be deplored, more particularly since this often leads to misinterpretation of the writer's intent. This was earlier noted in the oedipal interpretations of Matthew Arnold's poem, *Sohrab and Rustum*. Arnold, however, limited his desire to express his awareness of parental hostility to this one poem. It was a necessary cathartic experience; once said and done, it released him from childhood tensions and left him free to develop his talents. It has not been so easy for other writers to find release from similar tensions and to escape their childhood past.

For Franz Kafka, for example, the scars went much deeper. His work is, in many respects, an ongoing dialogue with his father, a dialogue with a man in whose physical presence neither had much to say. Kafka himself expressed unequivocally his own feelings about his work, which he saw as an "attempt to escape from father," a theme he once considered using as the overall title for his collected works.[63] Lest the message be missed by his father, who, as far as one can judge, gave his son's work only minimum passing acknowledgment, Kafka also put his indictment in the form of a letter to his father.[64] At his mother's discretion, the latter was never delivered and was published only posthumously as a unique literary document. As Michel Carrouges notes:

> We have only begun to explore the immense labyrinth of Kafka's life and works. The keys that he would provide would not be sufficient if he had not given us that very first, most important key, the one that permits us to open the main gate into the labyrinth: the "Letter to His Father."[65]

There is almost no dispute as to the impact of Kafka's father on the literature of his son. It is clear both that there was little communication across the generations in real life and that domineering father figures predominate in Kafka's works. But what was Kafka actually trying to say: was it that he regretted and felt guilt-laden for his oedipal sentiments, or was it that he sensed the unfairness in his father's attitude toward him and wished to challenge him for the inequities that had caused him so much pain?

The typical Freudian approach is most succinctly stated by Bernard Hecht, who, in his discussion of Kafka's two major novels, *The Trial* and *The Castle,* writes: "We know that in both novels the Oedipus theme is a paramount one. Both deal with attempted propitiation of the higher authorities or father surrogates."[66] Since there is no parricide in these novels, Hecht stresses the sexual aspects of the Oedipus complex; but then, since there is no mother, he sees the sexual liaisons of the heroes, K. and Joseph K., as representing "really their wish to possess the mother representatives that lead to the fruitless struggles with the omnipotent restrictive father."[67]

In contrast, Frederick Hoffman notes the constant conflict of father and son and its echo in Kafka's work, yet claims that the work has a depth that transcends the limiting bidimensional relationship of father and son:

> Kafka's *life* may be a simple, open and shut case for a psychoanalytic biography; his *art* is far too complex, much too richly rewarding in several areas of aesthetic and intellectual contemplation, to be dismissed as an imperfect sublimation or an "anxiety neurosis."[68]

Hoffman then goes on to give a description of what "Freud might have said about Kafka's life," revolving around typical oedipal concepts and conceptualizations, and concludes:

> Psychoanalysis might thus have explained Kafka's affairs and should certainly have had little difficulty adjusting each of his writings to that explanation. Kafka's ambivalent attitude toward his father, and the power which his father apparently had over him, affected the development of conscience, or superego, on his personality. Kafka's God, therefore, bore strange but undoubted resemblance to the writer's father. . . . Most of Kafka's shorter stories deal symbolically with the strange figure of the father and his family position. *The Trial, The Castle,* and "The Penal Colony" treat of the father-position transformed into the image of an inaccessible and incomprehensible God, the whimsical God of the Book of Job, or the stern and demanding God of Kierkegaard's *Fear and Trembling.*[69]

According to Max Brod, Kafka's friend, literary executor, and biographer, Kafka himself had been well aware of Freud's ideas. His diary of the night of September 22–23, 1912, when, in one long tumultuous session, he wrote "The Judgment," the story of a father condemning his son to break his engagement by killing himself, contains the cryptic reference, "thoughts about Freud, of course. . . ."[70] However, Brod also claims that Freudian interpretations were considered by Kafka himself as "too facile"; in Brod's opinion, "they didn't do justice to detail, or rather to the real heartbeat of the conflict."[71]

Hoffman himself notes this reservation on the part of Brod and finds it "curiously ambiguous."[72] According to Hoffman, while Brod "admits the opportunity for psychoanalysis, he insists that psychoanalysis can never search deeply enough for essential causes."[73] This is hardly ambiguous; rather, Brod realized the limitations of Freudian analysis, even as he acknowledged its value. Carrouges shares these reservations. After noting that "on every side, Kafka came up against the prodigious power of his father, a dark Prometheus blocking all exits,"[74] he asks:

> Oedipus complex? No doubt. But let us please avoid reducing the numberless varied experiences of Oedipus' tragedy to mechanical variants of an explanatory gimmick that is never any more than the beginning of an explanation. For the further one goes the more one sees that one is entering into a labyrinth of explanations. The true power of psychoanalysis is that it explains the myth a good deal less by way of the complex than the complex by way of the myth; the very nature of myth is to be inexhaustible and fathomless.
>
> This too, Kafka was aware of. He had Freud in mind when he wrote *The Judgment,* but he objected to the claims of psychoanalysts of having arrived at definitive explanations. Kafka knew how to probe ever deeper and further.[75]

Unlike Hoffman, Carrouges has little doubt that Kafka's life is of the essence of his art, furnishing material and motivation for his writing, providing the very basis for understanding:

> The unbreathable atmosphere of Kafka's tales is not . . . a gratuitous invention of his imagination; his art flows out of the conflict with his father, it manifests that conflict and re-creates it all over again.[76]

Carrouges gives the clearest expression to that conflict in the title of his book, *Kafka Versus Kafka,* which he explains was chosen "because *The Trial* of Kafka, the writer and lawyer, is the trial of the son by the father, of the father by the son and even of the son by the son. Woman, society, the human condition, and God Himself are also placed on trial."[77]

For Carrouges "Everything in Kafka's life is bound up together. Between what he did, what he dreamed, and what he wrote there are innumerable relationships."[78] Carrouges then devotes most of the book to pointing out the parallels between Kafka's work and events in his life, some recorded in this diary, others related by his friends and confidants.

Both Hoffman and Carrouges, from their different perspectives, see some relevance in Freud's work for an understanding of Kafka, both acknowledge Kafka's own awareness of Freud's impact, yet neither is able to embrace the total message of Kafka's work within the Freudian orbit. Hoffman finds parallels between Freud and Kafka, especially as regards their common interest in religion and the role of the god-figure for social life. Kafka was particularly interested in Kierkegaard's involvement with the biblical figure of Abraham. The theme of the sacrifice of Isaac intrigued Kafka and became "a key to his philosophy."[79] Inasmuch as religion aroused Kafka's interest, it was then, to a large degree, in terms of generational considerations.

Carrouges's interpretation is devoted to exploring in detail the theme of generational conflict and the relationship between Kafka and his father. Having pinpointed the core of Kafka's writings in his conflict with his father, Carrouges bypasses Freud and the Oedipus complex and sets out to prove the direct, mostly negative impact of Kafka's father and the prevalence of this impact in Kafka's writing.

Carrouges sees Kafka's work as a constant yet futile attempt at communication, a subtle means of expressing the suffering that his father's negative, repressive attitude toward him had caused:

> How can one not be aware of all the emanations of that terrible paternal influence in the figures of the Emperor in *The Great Wall of China,* of the former commandant in *The Penal Colony* and of the civil servants in *The Castle* and *The Trial?* Are not the inaccessibility in which they all entrench themselves, the impossibility of truly communicating with them, an exact reflection of Franz's situation with regard to Hermann [his father]?[80]

In much of his writing Kafka was intent on recreating the world of childhood, especially the sense of powerlessness it evoked, the awareness of arbitrary rule it engendered, the feeling of injustice it aroused. Kafka, of course, was dealing with more than just the world of childhood; he was concerned with many social issues of the day, with the nature of the society in which he lived, and with the future development of incipient social processes. His portrayal of an anonymous, insensitive, all-embracing, incomprehensible bureaucratic world is correctly seen as the situation *in extremis* of the modern world, which, in its cold cruelty, presaged the horrors that were subsequently enacted in the dictatorial regimes of Europe.

Yet this portrait has another dimension. It is also an attempt to present the world through the eyes of a child. In Kafka's personal case, this was a child who never grew up, the son who never escaped the clutches of an authoritarian father, remaining a bachelor, breaking off engagements, living mainly with his parents, constantly under their solicitous and often gratuitous surveillance, dreaming of a distant Utopia that he was never to see, regretting his inability to break the ties of familial respect.[81]

Kafka's work is not an apology or expression of regret or guilt for all the evil thoughts that he had harbored toward his parents, as oedipal interpretations suggest. It is a direct indictment of the manifold repressions visited on him by the dominant and powerful being who begot him and raised him. His writing reflects not only his own personal experiences but also his perception of what it means to be a child in an alien world.

Paradoxically, Kafka came from a background almost identical to that of Freud—middle class, Central European, Jewish. The work of both was critically influenced by their attempts to understand the nature of their relations with their fathers. Yet they came to opposite conclusions, Freud trying to interpret the meaning of child hostility, Kafka launching a devastating attack upon adult hostility. Because of the impact of Freud, Kafka's message has often been missed by those, who, obsessed with the universal validity of the Oedipus complex, have turned Kafka upside down. He did indeed carry with him the scars of his childhood, but the wounds were not self-inflicted, the consequence of his failure to resolve an oedipal situation; they were the wounds of the hostile environment in which he grew up, of the stifling of his talents by a domineering father who could not appreciate the potential genius that resided in the person of his own son; they were the wounds of his father's Rustum complex.

Children as such do not play any significant role in Kafka's novels. The generations of sons and fathers meet as adults. But it is the world of children that Kafka is attempting to represent, not just his own unpleasant childhood but childhood in general. His adult characters are confronted by a bureaucracy that rules their lives, that acts capriciously, that sits in judgment. This is the kind of world that children, even under the most ideal conditions, encounter. Kafka was not content to limit his sources to his own experience. Like Dostoevsky, he sought other models to fill out his own concept of childhood, including models of children who had suffered even more than he: not merely emotional deprivation, verbal abuse, and humiliation, but actual physical hardships. And so he turned to Charles Dickens, a writer who had been forced to work at an early age to support his family, which was slowly sinking into a morass of poverty, and who had devoted many of his novels to depicting the lives of deprived children. Mark Spilka has argued incisively that it was Dickens's portrayal of the indignities and injustices meted out to children that served as Kafka's chief model.[82]

Kafka clothed his society in the impersonal bureaucratic forms characteristic of the twentieth century, a presentation that has been incorporated into the language through the adjective "kafkaesque." Dickens, on the other hand, railed against the cruelties inflicted on the young in the burgeoning industrial society of nineteenth-century England, basing many of the incidents in his books on the experiences and encounters of his own childhood.

Spilka notes several references in Kafka's diaries to Dickens, suggests that Kafka had read a biography of Dickens, and then provides detailed references of parallels in the work of the two authors. The essence of Spilka's book is summed up in the title to Part One, "A Child's View of The Universe." According to the author, "It was the child's views of the world, then, which Kafka shared with Dickens. He knew what it was like to be considered something less than a member of the human family, to be considered almost an animal, and he found a strong rendition of this experience in Dickens' life and work."[83] One of the marked features of Dickens's work is his concentration on the sufferings of children. Lionel Trilling claims that, for Dickens, "the perfect image of injustice is the unhappy child," and that he connected "the fate of nations with the treatment of children,"[84] an approach reminiscent of Ivan Karamazov's musings. While few writers have devoted so much of their work to the theme of childhood or have attempted to relive so much of their own experiences through the literature, as did Dickens, the use of the treatment of children as touchstone for delineating and gauging society is more widespread than is commonly realized.

Peter Coveney's *Image of Childhood* bears testimony to the large number of writers who have used the child as a key theme in their works:

> Childhood as a major theme came with the generation of Blake and Wordsworth. . . . Within the course of a few decades the child emerges from comparative unimportance to become the focus of an unprecedented literary interest, and, in time, the central figure of an increasingly significant proportion of our literature.[85]

Coveney raises many interesting issues, which converge into two main themes: one, of children seen in romantic terms as the embodiment of original virtue; the other, of the hardships they are forced to undergo— "Idealization of the child's nature and cruelty toward the children of Satan existed side by side in nineteenth-century society."[86]

While noting that "Dickens is, of course, the focus for any study of the establishment of the child in the nineteenth-century novel," Coveney adds that there were other novelists who "echoed his own intense concern with English childhood."[87] The industrial age had spawned a host of social problems, including many exploitative practices against the young; public consciousness had been aroused by the findings of various governmental and parliamentary commissions that exposed the depths of degradation to which the young were subjected. Thus Benjamin Disraeli's *Sybil* was inspired by the *Report of the Commission on the Employment of Young Persons and Children of 1842,* while other books picked up similar themes: Frances Trollope's *Michael Armstrong* "took the theme of the defenseless orphan," Charles Kingsley's *Alton Locke* deals with "the care of a child and his later development, at the mercy of sweated laboring conditions and the severity of puritan morality," Charlotte Bronte's *Jane Eyre* "portrays the psychic condition of deprived childhood."[88]

In Dickens, the deprivations of childhood is a constant theme. Much of this relates to his own experiences as a child. He had suffered some of the physical hardships that Kafka had been spared; he had been forced to leave home at the age of eleven in order to work (paradoxically, a separation, at an early age, that Kafka had craved in adulthood but never attained). The five months Dickens worked under difficult conditions in a blacking warehouse in order to help the family's finances were to leave an indelible impression on him and would be revived and reenacted throughout the pages of his novels. Coveney notes:

> There is no doubt of the deep psychological wounding which Dickens suffered at the hands of his parents. . . . As a child, Dickens undoubtedly received the wound from which so much of his sentimentality springs. But the experience was not only traumatic; for he gained no less an awareness of society and "experience" which served him throughout his creative life.[89]

No less than Kafka's, then, Dickens's work grew out of his own unhappy childhood memories. Yet, more direct in his approach, less disturbed in his personal life, he has not been subjected to the same Freudian analyses; his father is not seen as a constant brooding presence. But, by virtue of his sensitive perception and accurate presentation of his personal experience, he vouchsafed to his audiences a glimpse into some of the agonies of childhood, an awareness of the hardships that parents and society are capable of inflicting on the young.

To Spilka, Dickens and Kafka are not only directly related to each other but form part of the connection between nineteenth- and twentieth-century fiction, which, despite many differences, are united in their common concern for the fate of children. Dickens's contemporaries—George Eliot in *The Mill on the Floss,* Henry James in *The Turn of the Screw,* Samuel Butler in *The Way of All Flesh,* Ivan Turgenev in *Fathers and Sons,* Mark Twain in *Huckleberry Finn,* Charlotte Bronte in *Jane Eyre*—all deal essentially with the same problem of childhood despoiled and find their echo in Kafka's twentieth-century contemporaries: Joyce, Faulkner, Proust, Lawrence, and Mann.[90] The circumstances might change, but the theme remains the same: "In Faulkner's *Southern Mansions,* which closely approximates the Victorian hothouse, the fusion of childhood damage with the quest for significant life seems most painfully apparent; but other novelists send damaged figures on similar quests."[91]

Among the examples that Spilka gives is James Joyce's Stephen Dedalus, a character caught in the conflict of generations. Edmond Epstein, who devoted a full study to this theme,[92] sees Joyce as unique in the depth with which he handles it, owing most of his inspiration to Henrik Ibsen and to Butler's *The Way of All Flesh,* one of the most extreme examples of outright cruelty visited by a father on a son. To Spilka's list of authors who deal with generational conflict, "one of the characteristic themes of modern literature," Epstein adds more names: Virginia Woolf, Thomas Hardy, William Thackeray, Jane Austen, Joseph Conrad, Thomas Synge, and William Butler Yeats.[93]

These lists are by no means exhaustive. Many other modern writers have touched on the theme—even before the nineteenth century, writers had used the role of children as keys. This is particularly true of the work of Jonathan Swift, who wrote much of his social satire in the form of children's stories. *Gulliver's Travels,* ostensibly about the little people of Lilliput and the big people of Brobdignag, may offer some insights about different perceptions of the world arising from one's size and power.[94] Swift himself had an unhappy and humiliating childhood. Like Dostoevsky, Kafka, and Dickens, he was made acutely conscious of the evils of society by his childhood experiences; like them he carried the scarred memories with him into adulthood; like them he drew on these experiences to present his critique of society through literature. He preceded both Butler and Kafka in posing the possibility of children being separated from their parents, since "parents are the least of all others to be trusted with the education of their children,"[95] particularly because of the power they hold over them. Kafka, building on this idea, suggests that only when children are equal to the parents in body and spiritual strength can a truly "loving adjustment" between them be made.[96]

It is tempting and all too easy to consign the sociological and psychological issues raised by some of these writers to the ash heap of personal problems, the product of unique childhood experiences. It is always possible to draw a distinction between the depth of one's literary genius and the irrelevance of one's theoretical perspective or practical suggestions for reform. But it is doubtful if full justice can be done to an understanding of literary works concerned with the suffering and fate of children without taking cognizance of the childhood experiences of the authors and of their perceptions of children in general.

Spilka poses the dilemma of interpretation neatly:

> We may lump together the fiction of two centuries as mere private spleen, the work of cultural misfits and disguised as plain degenerates; or we may explore that fiction for the severe disruptions it exposes, and for the variety of means by which creative artists mend them. Fortunately, we are beginning to follow the latter course.[97]

Few critics have demonstrated as keenly as Coveney the possibilities of what can be achieved by close and sympathetic scrutiny of children in literature. It is particularly interesting to note that, at the end of his book, after analyzing a wealth of poets and authors, Coveney turns to Freud, and Freud alone among nonnovelists, in order to deepen his readers' understanding of childhood.[98] In a few pages he lays out the essence of those Freudian ideas that are relevant to understanding children: infantile sexuality, the role of the unconscious in preserving repressed childhood memories, the impact of the early years of life on the adult character, the struggle of the child to cope with the demands of the reality principle that society imposes on him, the lack of any idealistic, "childlike" innocence. Of the Oedipus complex, Coveney makes only passing mention, though he calls attention to a statement by Freud that the discovery of the complex was perhaps his most important psychoanalytic contribution. In his brief discussion of the Oedipus complex Coveney ignores completely the parricidal aspects of filial hostility, envy, and guilt, limiting his remarks to the child's sexual attraction to the parent of the opposite sex. His disregard for the parricidal aspects of the Oedipus complex is highly significant. Coveney's immersion in the works of writers such as Dickens and Butler may have blunted any tendencies to see the factor of instinctive filial hostility as a regular concomitant of childhood years. The accumulation of contrary evidence, based on the actual experiences of many of the authors, was too overwhelming. Yet Coveney has shown how relevant Freud can be, particularly when shorn of restrictive thought processes stemming from the Oedipus perspective.

Coveney has provided a model that could be usefully emulated, not merely for the sake of heightening literary appreciation but also for furthering the capacity to deepen the knowledge, awareness, and appreciation of the world of childhood. Children, for all that their lives are interwoven with those of adults, live in a world of their own. The adult's own life experiences as a child do not guarantee his capacity to empathize fully with children with whom he is in contact. The child himself possesses only some of the technical means to articulate his feelings and ideas. We are, to a large extent, dependent on people with heightened sensitivity and expressive capacity to explain to us the world of childhood, some by recreating their own childhoods, others by imaginatively and empathetically studying the childhoods of others.

Living in a constant, symbiotic relationship with children, unable always to penetrate the mysterious world of childhood, adults are in particular need of fictional, yet faithful, representations of that world. It is a world that is close yet alien, ostensibly simple and carefree yet in reality complex, a world with its share of suffering and oppression, of magic and joy.

From Sophocles through Shakespeare to Dostoevsky and a host of modern writers, the theme of generational conflict underlies literature as it does life. Unquestioning acceptance of the universality of the Oedipus complex can only prevent a balanced perspective of this fundamental aspect of the human condition.

Writers who attempt to conjure up the world of childhood have an important contribution to make in helping to bridge the gap between the generations. In many cases they have dug deeply into the recesses of their own memories and experiences in order to unburden themselves of some of their own pain and in order to ensure the accuracy and validity of the fictional account. They have illuminated the many facets of the complex relationship between parents and children. They deserve, and society needs, the most faithful interpretation of their intention.

References

1. Ernest Jones, *Hamlet and Oedipus* (Garden City, N.Y.: Doubleday Anchor, 1954).

2. See Jack Spektor, *The Aesthetics of Freud* (New York: McGraw-Hill, 1972); Frederick J. Hoffman, *Freudianism and the Literary Mind* (Baton Rouge: Louisiana State University Press, 2d ed., 1957); Louis Fraiberg, *Psychoanalysis and American Literary Criticism* (Detroit: Wayne State University Press, 1960); Claudia L. Morrison, *Freud and the Critic: The Early Use of Depth Psychology in Literary Criticism* (Chapel Hill: University of North Carolina, 1968); F. L. Lucas, *Literature and Psychology* (Ann Arbor: University of Michigan Press, 1957); Norman N. Holland, *Psychoanalysis and Shakespeare* (New York: McGraw-Hill, 1966); J. I. M. Stewart, *Character and Motive in Shakespeare* (London: Longmans, Green, 1949); E. Freeman Sharpe, "Papers on Literary Criticism," in *Collected Papers on Psychoanalysis* (London: Hogarth Press, 1950); Daniel E. Schneider, *The Psychoanalyst and the Artist* (New York: International Universities Press, 1950).

See also Norman Kiell, *Psychoanalysis, Psychology and Literature: A Bibliography* (Madison: University of Wisconsin Press, 1963) and articles: William J. Griffin, "The Use and Abuse of Psychoanalysis in the Study of Literature," *Literature and Psychology* 1 (1953): 16; Mabel Collins Donnelly, "Freud and Literary Criticism," *College English* 15 (1953): 158.

3. Sigmund Freud, "Dostoevsky and Parricide" (1928), in *The Standard Edition of the Complete Psychological Works,* edited by James Strachey, 24 vols. (London, Hogarth Press, 1953–66), 21: 188.

4. M. Sperber, "The Daimonic: Freudian, Jungian and Existential Perspectives," *Journal of Analytic Psychology* (1975): 42.

5. My discussion of Dostoevsky is similar to the approach adopted by Arnoldo Rascovsky, a psychoanalyst living in Argentina. I first heard of Rascovsky while researching this book; his work on filicide was reported in Emmanuel K. Schwartz's column, "Facts, Fancies and Reflections," in the now-defunct *The Human Context* (1968): 346; 4 (1972): 192, 316; see same issue for Schwartz's article, "Child Murder Today," p. 360.

I corresponded with Dr. Rascovsky and sent him a copy of my original article on the Rustum complex. He very kindly sent me his book, entitled *El Filicido* (Buenos Aires: Ediciones Orion, n.d.).

The chapter "Dostoievsky y El Filicido" contains parallels to this chapter on literature, in some cases citing identical passages from Dostoevsky's fiction. Since I had already completed this chapter when I received Rascovsky's book I decided to publish it as it stood, as Rascovsky's book has not been translated from Spanish and so the ideas are not available to an English-reading public.

Dr. Rascovsky is conducting extremely important research into filicide and has organized a society in South America for the study of filicide. Some of his articles in English are: "On the Genesis of Acting Out and Psychopathic Behavior in Sophocles' Oedipus: Notes on Filicide" (with Mathilde Rascovsky), *International Journal of Psychoanalysis* 49 (1968): 390; "The Prohibition of Incest, Filicide and the Sociocultural Process," *International Journal of Psychoanalysis* 53 (1972): 271; "Filicide and Its Relation to War," paper presented at a conference on The Role and Relevance of Psychology in World Politics; "Outline on Filicide: Theoretical and Clinical Considerations," and "Filicide and the Unconscious Motivation of War."

6.   Fyodor Dostoevsky, *The Brothers Karamazov,* trans. by Constance Garnett (New York: Random House, 1950) p. 6.

7.   Ibid., p. 7.

8.   See Edward Wasiolek, *Dostoevsky: The Major Fiction* (Cambridge, Mass.: M.I.T. Press), p. 212. Wasiolek writes *inter alia* "other sources for the novel are childhood memories. . . ."

9.   William Hadden, *Dostoevsky, Kierkegaard, Nietzsche, and Kafka: Four Prophets of our Destiny* (New York: Collier, 1962), p. 54.

10.   Wasiolek, *Dostoevsky,* p. 150.

11.   Fyodor Dostoevsky, *Notes from the House of Death,* as quoted in Konstantin Mochulsky, *Dostoevsky: His Life and Work,* trans. by Michael A. Minihan (Princeton: Princeton University Press, 1967).

12.   Ibid., p. 577.

13.   Ibid.

14.   See the several uses of the name in Edward Wasiolek (ed.), *The Notebooks for "The Brothers Karamazov" by Fyodor Dostoevsky* (Chicago: University of Chicago Press, 1971). The first time the name is used Wasiolek explains that it is that of "a nobleman in Dostoevsky's *Memoirs from the House of the Dead* who was—like Dimitri—unjustly accused of killing his father. Dimitri is called Ilinsky from time to time, even after he receives his real name" (p. 30). See also Wasiolek's *Dostoevsky,* where he writes, "One of the sources of the novel is the life of one of the prisoners Dostoevsky met in Omsk. His name was Ilinsky, and he had been condemned for killing his father. Later he was found not to be guilty" (p. 212).

15.   Wasiolek, *Dostoevsky,* p. 150.

16.   Gilbert D. Chaitin, "Religion as Defence: The Structure of the Brothers Karamazov," *Literature and Psychology* 22 (1972): 85.

17.   Ibid., pp. 85–86.

18.   Mochulsky, *Dostoevsky,* p. 646. See also Wasiolek's *Dostoevsky,* where he writes, "The fate of the brothers at the end of the novel are still in the making, pointing to the continuation of *The Brothers Karamazov* Dostoevsky had planned" (pp. 186–187).

19.   Mochulsky, *Dostoevsky,* pp. 565–566. Mochulsky also refers to an earlier work, *The Diary of a Writer,* as being a preparation for "his last, greatest work. The *Diary* is the laboratory of *The Brothers Karamazov.* Observations on children occupy an important place in it" (p. 557).

20. Ibid., pp. 569–570.

21. Wasiolek, *Dostoevsky,* p. 186.

22. Mochulsky, *Dostoevsky,* p. 605. In another context Harry Slochower has noted that in "Dostoevsky's attack on the West in *Winter Notes of Summer Impressions* (New York, 1955) [he] was particularly outraged by child labor in the West" (Harry Slochower, *Mythopoesis: Mythic Patterns in the Literary Classics* [Detroit: Wayne State University Press, 1970]).

23. Mochulsky, *Dostoevsky,* p. 605.

24. Dostoevsky, *The Brothers Karamazov,* p. 286.

25. Ibid.

26. Ibid., pp. 286–287.

27. Ibid., p. 288. Some of the cases mentioned by Dostoevsky were based on actual events that he had recorded.

28. Ibid., p. 290.

29. Mochulsky, *Dostoevsky,* pp. 572–573.

30. Ibid., p. 573.

31. Wasiolek, *Dostoevsky,* pp. 185–186.

32. Sigmund Freud, *The Interpretation of Dreams* (1900), in *The Standard Edition,* 4: 266.

33. Jones, *Hamlet and Oedipus.*

34. Ibid., p. 91.

35. J. Dover Wilson, *The Manuscript of Shakespeare's Hamlet and the Problems of Its Transmission* (Cambridge: Cambridge University Press, 1934).

36. Jones, *Hamlet and Oedipus,* p. 128.

37. Ibid., p. 129.

38. See Geoffrey Bullough, *The Narrative and Dramatic Sources of Shakespeare* (New York: Columbia University Press, 1973), pp. 17–18. I am indebted to Eva Simmons for drawing my attention to this point.

39. Lionel Trilling, *The Liberal Imagination: Essays on Literature and Society* (London: Secker and Warburg, 1955), p. 48.

40. Frederic Wertham, "The Matricidal Impulse: Critique of Freud's Interpretation of Hamlet," *Journal of Criminal Psychopathology* 2 (1941): 455; also in M. D. Faber (ed.), *The Design Within* (New York: Science House, 1970), p. 113; Natalie Shainess, "Hamlet—The Coup that Failed," *Journal of American Academy of Psychoanalysis,* 3 (1975).

41. Shainess, "Hamlet," p. 401.

42. Neil Friedman and Richard M. Jones, "On the Mutuality of the Oedipus Complex," in Faber, ed., *The Design Within,* p. 132; see also *American Imago,* 20 (1963): 107–131.

43. Friedman and Jones, "Oedipus Complex," p. 132.

44. Erik Erikson, *Childhood and Society* (New York: W. W. Norton, 1950).

45. Friedman and Jones, "Oedipus Complex," pp. 143–144.

46. Virginia Woolf, *A Room of One's Own* (London: Hogarth Press, 1959). Woolf, of course, was writing of a woman's need, but the same considerations apply to children.

47. Lucas, *Literature and Psychology,* p. 62.

48. Ibid.

49. Ibid., p. 63.

50. Ibid., p. 66.

51. Ibid.

52. Ibid., p. 71.

53. Mark Kanzer, "Imagery in King Lear," in Faber, *The Design Within*, p. 227; also *American Imago* 22 (1965): 3–13.

54. Kanzer, "Imagery," p. 227.

55. Ibid.

56. Lawrence Berns, "Gratitude, Nature and Piety in King Lear," *Interpretation: Journal of Political Philosophy* 2 (1972): 49. See further comments in chapter 9 on the problems caused by a child's feelings of gratitude to his parents.

57. Kanzer, "Imagery," p. 229.

58. Arpad Pauncz, "Psychopathology of Shakespeare's 'King Lear'," *American Imago* 9 (1952): 58.

59. Lucas, *Literature and Psychology,* p. 64.

60. M. D. Faber, "The Adolescent Suicides of Romeo and Juliet," *The Psychoanalytic Review* 59 (1972): 169–181.

61. Lucas, *Literature and Psychology,* p. 65. Lucas notes that "Charlemagne could not bear to let his daughter marry; nor could Mr. Barrett of Wimpole Street. Mr. Barrett may seem a Victorian monstrosity. But his case is not so rare."

62. Faber, "The Adolescent Suicides," p. 180.

63. Max Brod, *Franz Kafka* (New York: Schocken, 1947), p. 24.

64. Franz Kafka, *Letter to His Father* (New York: Schocken, 1953).

65. Michel Carrouges, *Kafka Versus Kafka* (The University of Alabama Press, 1968), p. 17.

66. M. Bernard Hecht, "Uncanniness, Yearning and Franz Kafka's Works," *American Imago* 9 (1952): 46.

67. Ibid.

68. Frederick J. Hoffman, "Escape from Father," in Angel Flores (ed.), *The Kafka Problem* (New York: New Directions, 1946), p. 225. See also Hoffman, *Freudianism and the Literary Mind.*

69. Hoffman, "Escape from Father," p. 228.

70. Franz Kafka, *Diaries, 1910–1913,* ed. by Max Brod (New York: Schocken, 1948), p. 276.

71. Max Brod, *Franz Kafka,* p. 20.

72. Hoffman, "Escape from Father," p. 224. See the interesting discussion of this item by Ernest Becker, "Kafka on the Oedipus Complex," in *Angel in Armor: A Post-Freudian Perspective on the Nature of Man* (New York: George Braziller, 1969), pp. 41–70.

73. Hoffman, "Escape from Father," p. 224.

74. Carrouges, *Kafka Versus Kafka,* p. 28.

75. Ibid. Carrouges goes on to state that on one occasion Kafka had said that, "The revolt of the son against the father is one of the primeval themes of literature."

76. Ibid., p. 29.

77. Ibid., p. 10.

78. Ibid., p. 13.

79. Hoffman, "Escape from Father," p. 233. Carrouges also notes that, "In speaking of Abraham, Kafka was led to mention Iphigenia"—Agamemnon's daughter (*Kafka Versus Kafka,* p. 101).

80. Carrouges, *Kafka Versus Kafka,* p. 32.

81. Gustav Janouche in *Conversations with Kafka* (New York: Praeger, 1953) provides several examples of encounters between Franz Kafka and his father, in which the latter treated his adult son much as a child. On one occasion, when out walking with Kafka, they came across the father who said loudly, "Franz. Go home. The air is damp." Kafka turned to Janouche and said, "My father. He is anxious about me. Love often wears the face of violence. Come and see me." At that, "Franz Kafka departed without shaking hands" (p. 31).

82. Mark Spilka, *Dickens and Kafka: A Mutual Interpretation* (Bloomington: Indiana University Press, 1963). For a similar attempt to draw parallels between Dickens and Dostoevsky, see N. M. Lary, *Dostoevsky and Dickens: A Study of Literary Influence* (London: Routledge & Kegan Paul, 1973) with several references to their mutual interest in children.

83. Spilka, *Dickens and Kafka,* p. 41.

84. Lionel Trilling, "Little Dorrit," *Kenyon Review* 15 (1953): 585.

85. Peter Coveney, *The Image of Childhood: The Individual and Society—A Study of the Theme in English Literature* (London: Peregrine, 1967), p. 29. F. R. Leavis, in the "Introduction" to the book, refers to the book as "unusual . . . original . . . important." The book was published in an earlier edition as *Poor Monkey.*

86. Coveney, ibid., p. 34.

87. Ibid., p. 92.

88. Ibid., see pp. 93, 94, 107.

89. Ibid., pp. 118–119.

90. Spilka, *Dickens and Kafka,* pp. 264–265.

91. Ibid., p. 265. Spilka's examples of such damaged figures are Joyce's Dedalus, Lawrence's Birkin, Mann's Castrop, Woolf's Mrs. Dalloway, Proust's Marcel.

92. Edmond Epstein, *The Ordeal of Stephen Dedalus: The Conflict of Generations in James Joyce's "A Portrait of the Artist as a Young Man"* (Carbondale: Southern Illinois University Press, 1973).

93. Ibid., p. 2.

94. For perceptive use of this symbolism see Selma Fraiberg, *The Magic Years* (New York: Scribner, 1968).

95. See William Rose Benét, *The Reader's Encyclopedia* (New York: Crowell, 1948), p. 1089.

96. See Brod, *Franz Kafka,* pp. 215–220; Spilka, *Dickens and Kafka,* p. 123.

97. Spilka, *Dickens and Kafka,* p. 265.

98. Coveney, *The Image of Childhood,* chapter 11, "The End of the Victorian Child, Freud's Essay on Infantile Sexuality," pp. 291–302.

CHAPTER FIVE
AN ANALYSIS OF PSYCHOHISTORY

The story of Oedipus takes place on two distinct levels: one, within a family, involving a wide range of human emotions that accompany interactions between parents and children; the other, at the sociopolitical level, involving the succession of rulers in Thebes. Oedipus not only killed his father and married his mother but succeeded to the kingship, thus gaining political control over the kingdom formerly ruled by his father. Similarly, Hamlet's dilemma was not just a personal one—the desire to revenge his father's death—but a political one, the desire to inherit the kingdom that was rightfully his.

One of the earliest critics of Freud's oedipal theme was Lord Raglan, who stressed that the real meaning of the Oedipus myth, as well as of similar myths from other cultures, was not parricide but regicide. Otto Rank's analysis of the myth of the heroes also emphasizes the political and social implications of most of the key myths in which tensions between father and son were described.[1]

The story of Rustum and Sohrab, too, is based not on direct personal animosity between them but on their conflict as representatives of two opposing, warring groups, the one side choosing its renowned and proven hero, the other sending into combat its eager and promising hope of the future.

Freud himself made intensive efforts to explain the origins of political society by means of the oedipal theme. However, while he devoted several books to discussing issues of a broad cultural and social nature, he never dealt directly with the question of generational conflict within modern society.

In fact, despite his great interest in social issues, Freud refrained, for the most part, from political analysis; and, with few exceptions, he avoided any involvement in contemporary political developments. Insofar as he discussed modern society, he did so in general cultural terms, as in *Civilization and its Discontents*; when he dealt with political struggles, he did so in historical or—to be more exact—prehistorical terms, as in *Totem and Taboo*.

The one notable exception is his work on group psychology, where he describes, in oedipal terms, the relationship between a political leader and his followers;[2] but, as will be shown, this book does not really come to grips with the political implications of generational conflict.

A number of historians have tried to discern the reasons for Freud's reluctance to become directly involved in ongoing political issues. Some have seen total involvement in psychoanalysis as a substitute for his deferred interest in politics.

Both Carl Schorske and W. J. McGrath suggest that in his youth and during his student years Freud had been keenly sensitive to social injustices and had desired to participate in political struggles aimed at rectifying these faults.[3] He had even been a member of a number of radical movements and for some time had been greatly influenced by a leading socialist, Heinrich Braun, who had been a childhood friend of his.

Schorske notes that during the crisis period of Freud's life, when he was working out the basic ideas of the Oedipus complex and writing his classic *The Interpretation of Dreams,* he was both professionally frustrated in his work and personally affected by political developments—particularly the crisis in Austria-Hungary and the rise of anti-Semitism in Vienna. Freud belonged to one of the most threatened groups—Viennese middle-class liberal Jewry; his response to these professional and political frustrations was to retreat into intellectual endeavors. Schorske finds proof of this in some of Freud's dreams as recounted in *The Interpretation of Dreams.* He concludes:

> The brilliant, lonely, painful discovery of psychoanalysis . . . was a counterpolitical triumph of the first magnitude. By reducing his own political past and present to an epiphenomenal status in relation to the primal conflict between father and son, Freud gave his fellow liberals an ahistorical theory of man that could make bearable a political world spun out of orbit and beyond control.[4]

McGrath focuses even more specifically on Freud's interest in the life and struggles of Hannibal (which he terms the "Hannibal complex"), interpreting this interest as an expression of Freud's identification with the underdog, due to his own personal background as a Jew (part of a minority group) and as an Austrian (part of a waning empire).

Such speculations have been challenged by other historians who claim that, far from being a sublimation of suppressed radical political activity, psychoanalysis is a radical movement in its own right.[5] They argue that Freud's impact has actually been greater than that of Marx, since Marxism is clearly an ideology and could be easily refuted in the political arena, whereas Freud's writings are scientific and therefore present a far greater challenge to the upholders of the status quo, who are unable to dismiss it out of hand.

This argument is rather facile, as Marx himself claimed that his writings were scientific and scoffed at the utopian socialists who lacked the accuracy and reliability of his scientific analysis. Conversely, one of the major criticisms that have been leveled against Freud's work is its lack of scientific rigor.

This is not to deny, however, the radical overtones in much of psychoanalytic writing. Freud certainly did attack and undermine many of the conventional moralities of his time and of his middle-class environment, and he provided many innovative ways of analyzing social phenomena. Yet, when it came to analyzing one particular phenomenon, intergenerational contact, Freud chose to ignore the radical role of the young in the political and social processes of the time.

The debate initiated by Schorske is of major importance for a full understanding of Freud's work. It relates not only to the personal, professional, and political pressures that were exerted on Freud during those crucial years of crisis at the end of the nineteenth century, when he was turning away from direct political involvement to the tremendous task of laying the basis of his radical theory of psychoanalysis. It also applies to the question of why, with his catholic and wide-ranging interests, he never subsequently tackled the role of youth.

A reason for this omission may stem from a larger lacuna in his work: Freud's failure to discuss the problems of the adolescent years. So intent was he on stressing the impact of the early years of childhood that he made little attempt to understand the specific problems of adolescence. Such an analysis might have raised questions about the political awareness of the young and about the nature of adult-adolescent struggles as an aspect of group conflict.

Although Freud's major essay in political analysis, *Group Psychology and the Analysis of the Ego,* is based on a model of generational conflict, that of the primal family, Freud does not describe society in terms of generations in conflict. Instead he translates the relations of powerful father and dependent sons into the prototype of the relations between leader and followers, based on their separate and often contradictory psychological makeups.

Freud thus becomes a prisoner of his "primal horde" theory, which obliges him to see even modern politics in terms of a single "father" and his follower-sons and renders him incapable of coping with the generations as separate, rival groups.

In *Group Psychology and the Analysis of the Ego,* Freud explains the behavior of people in terms of their group affiliation as an extension of individual psychology. The book's starting point is "the attempt at using the concept of *libido* for the purpose of throwing light upon group psychology."[6] As a corollary, Freud notes the "supposition that love relationships . . . also constitute the essence of the group mind."[7] Then he directly links his work to *Totem and Taboo*: "the group appears to us as a revival of the primal horde."[8] Going beyond this, Freud tries to show that the group psychology grew out of the nature of the relationship between the primal father and the primal sons:

> The primal father had prevented his sons from satisfying their directly sexual impulsions; he forced them into abstinence and consequently into the emotional ties with him, and with one another, which could arise out of those of their impulsions that were inhibited in their sexual aim. He forced them, so to speak, into group psychology. His sexual jealousy and intolerance became in the last resort the causes of group psychology.[9]

These feelings persist into modern life:

> Even today the members of a group stand in need of the illusion that they are equally and justly loved by their leader . . . the leader himself need love no one else, he may be of a masterful nature, absolutely narcissistic, self-confident and independent.[10]

Drawing parallels with the organizational structure of the army and the church, Freud notes that an illusion is built up that the leader of a group "loves all the individuals in the group with an equal love,"[11] the leader thus fulfilling the role of a substitute father. On the other hand, the leader himself has no love dependency; he has "few libidinal ties."[12]

Although lacking in insight with respect to generational conflict as an agent for social change, Freud's book on group psychology merits consideration here because it provides an example of the use of oedipal ideas for interpreting political and social phenomena. It has also served as a framework for other writers, who have applied oedipal ideas directly to generational issues in the political arena. In addition, it is an important book in its own right, providing a prescient description of the type of political leader that was to dominate much of Europe, the father-figure dictator with submissive, dependent, mass followers. As Theodor Adorno says, Freud "clearly foresaw the rise and nature of fascist mass movements in purely psychological categories."[13]

A further interesting attempt to expand on Freud's work is Norman O. Brown's use of *Group Psychology and the Analysis of the Ego,* together with *Totem and Taboo* and *Moses and Monotheism,* to deal with the clash between a patriarchy and a fratriarchy.[14] Criticizing those who speculate that the historic clash was between partriarchy and matriarchy, Brown commends Freud for directing us "to the idea that the true, the only, contrary of patriarchy is not matriarchy but fraternity."[15]

Brown provides historical examples of struggles between patriarchal approaches to government, based on political power and the possession and control of property, and the fraternal principles of liberty and equality. Discussing the constitutional crisis of seventeenth-century England, Brown notes that the primal father is *absolute monarch* of the horde; the females are his *property*. The sons form a *conspiracy* to *overthrow* the despot, and in the end substitute a *social contract* with *equal rights* for all.[16]

The debate at that time between Sir Robert Filmer and John Locke as to the desired form of government revolved, to a large extent, around this theme, the former defending absolute monarchy in terms similar to those that Freud was later to use in describing the primal father's power and the latter putting the case that

all men in the primal state of nature [are] free and equal. To vindicate liberty is to vindicate the children, *liberi,* the sons, against personal despotism. Liberty means equality among the brothers (sons).[17]

Although Brown presents the struggle for liberty as an integral part of the fraternity principle, there is an underlying ambiguity in this struggle. Despite its many positive features, brotherhood is also "always a quarrel over the paternal inheritance. . . . Equals are rivals; and the dear love of comrades is made out of mutual jealousy and hate."[18] Finally, citing the best-known tales of strife between brothers—Romulus and Remus, Cain and Abel, Osiris and Set—Brown declares: "All fraternity is fratricidal."[19]

Brown's view of life is based upon interminable tragedy devoid of any solution; the self-same liberty, gained by overthrowing the despotism of the father, leads to inevitable and endless strife for the spoils of the father's property. Bound by a predetermined fate, humanity as a whole is faced with the terrible paradox that liberty itself must lead to strife. Analyzing fraternal strife in the Roman Republic, a body politic split in two by civil war, Brown juxtaposes the alternatives—freedom with strife or peace with dependence:

In the end, in accordance with the Freudian law of the return of the repressed, the murdered father returned and put an end to the quarrelling brothers; it came as a choice between *liberty* and *pax.*[20]

The inner contradiction in liberty, equality, and fraternity is that, as they are based on sonship and brotherhood, there is a need for a father:

Locke's sons—like Freud's—cannot free themselves from father psychology, and are crucified by the contradictory commands issuing from the Freudian super-ego, which says both "thou shalt be like the father, and thou shalt not be like the father," that is many things are his prerogative. Fraternal organization in the body politic corresponds to ego-organization in the body physical. As fraternal organization covertly assumes a father, ego-organization covertly assumes a super-ego.[21]

Brown's ultimate message for generational conflict is that liberty for the sons is no more than an illusion. Paternal power cannot be destroyed or evaded; it lives on in the patrimony. The need to dispose of the father's property must always lead to a struggle among his sons. This is the terrible legacy that the father bequeaths, and in so doing he ensures his ongoing authority and control.

Bruce Mazlish has also attempted to use Freud's ideas of group psychology to describe what he considers a new phenomenon in history, the revolutionary ascetic.[22] After noting "a persistent affinity between revolution and puritanism,"[23] Mazlish sets out to develop Freud's inchoate ideas on the nature of the leader who has "few libidinal ties."

> The revolutionary ascetic provides an ego-ideal which can serve as an alternative to the dominant values of the society . . . the libido formerly attached to real persons is now displaced into the ego-ideal by the revolutionary ascetic. . . . It is extended to the followers by a chain of libidinal relations to which they are enclosed, but from which the revolutionary ascetic is himself left free.
> It is of such psychological dynamics that revolutionary change is made.[24]

Essential to Mazlish's thesis is the followers' need to love their leader and to be loved by him, and the converse lack of any such need on the part of the leader. Revolutions thus consolidate around the psychological makeup of the actors, not overall social conditions.

Mazlish offers a psychohistorical analysis of a number of such leaders: he deals with Cromwell and Robespierre, then focuses the latter part of his book on extended case studies of Lenin and Mao Tse-tung. Like so many Freudian interpretations, the book is fascinating and raises many thoughtful issues; like them, it suffers however from the often-constricting limits of its theoretical basis. The book also contains its own independent paradoxes: thus, while Mazlish provides some material to indicate the ascetic aspects in the lives of Lenin and Mao, there are at the same time also clear indications of nonasceticism in their personal lives and, indeed, of very strong libidinal drives.

I shall not deal in any detail with his analysis of Lenin, since it contains only mimimal reference to the question of generational contact. A close reading of the material presented by Mazlish does however raise the question as to why he chose Lenin as the prototype of the ascetic leader, since much of the material presented is ambiguous; there are many indications of libido in Lenin's life, most particularly in his extended love affair with Imessa Amand, who, as Mazlish concedes, "awakened the passionate, emotional side of Lenin."[25] To add to the nonascetic elements, his lover was a talented musician, and their common love of music helped deepen the bond between them. One ends the reading of this chapter rather unconvinced that Lenin fulfilled the requirements of an ascetic.

One is also rather surprised to find in a book devoted to proving the psychological need for the followers to love their leader that, in the case of Lenin, "his followers had little love for him."[26]

For Mao the paradox of Mazlish's analysis is even greater, for here Mazlish almost completely deserts his theme, presents almost no examples of ascetic characteristics in Mao's life, and analyzes his personal background mainly in the more general oedipal terms of generational conflict between him and his father, in which what emerges from the facts that Mazlish presents is the cruel treatment of a harsh father. In terms of his thesis Mazlish even concedes: "Unlike Lenin, who is almost a prototype of the revolutionary ascetic, Mao Tse-tung presents a far more difficult case."[27]

Much of the difficulty stems from the fact that Mao seems to have been possessed of a normal share of libidinal drives and ties. The evidence is provided by Mazlish himself, what he calls the "counterevidence." Mazlish notes that Mao married three times and had several children (unlike Lenin, who had no children), that Edgar Snow, a Western biographer of Mao who interviewed him at length, attributes to him depth of feeling,[28] that he wrote poetry, and that he lacked charisma (which would affect his capacity to attract the libidinal feelings of his followers).

And so having presented the convincing counterevidence controverting his theory, Mazlish himself poses the question: "Whence, then, the claim of asceticism and displaced libido?" His answer: "Fundamental to his personal development was Mao's identification with his father, and this meant embracing the virtues of hard work, energetic activity, and frugality,"[29] which, of course, is, as Mazlish himself briefly notes at the beginning of his book, more or less the essence of Weber's Protestant ethic.

Thus, as an answer to the counterevidence of the existence of libido in Mao's life and in order to validate his own theory of revolutionary asceticism based on Freud's concept of group psychology, Mazlish is forced to claim that Mao learned the virtues of the business-oriented Protestant ethic from his Confucianist peasant father as an essential stage in the development of his qualities of becoming a revolutionary Communist leader!

Yet even this complicated scenario is based on the flimsiest of evidence—for the truth is that, far from identifying with his father, Mao hated him and saw in his harsh disciplinary practices within the family a microcosm of the larger ills of the society at large. Once again the evidence is supplied by Mazlish.

Completely forsaking his ascetic theme, Mazlish turns to the typical oedipal approach; this is used to describe conflict situations between father and son, despite the fact that the father's cruelty is clearly the dominant factor in the conflict. Mazlish notes that the account of Mao's conflict with his father ". . . offers what is almost a classic study of, among other things, an oedipal struggle of titanic dimensions."[30]

But what are the facts of this struggle? Mazlish writes: "The father, a 'hot-tempered man,' frequently beat both Mao and his brothers, gave them no money, and provided the most meagre food," apparently even less than was given to laborers.[31] As a consequence of the father's constant cruelty,

Mao states that he learned to hate him. Mazlish also recounts an incident that had a great impact on Mao as a schoolboy. During a famine, a group of peasants attacked a local government headquarters, cut down the flagpole, and drove out the governor. The new governor had the leaders of the revolt beheaded and then displayed the heads in public as a warning. Noting the impact this incident had on Mao, Mazlish interprets his response beyond the actual cruelty involved:

> On the unconscious level, an additional element offers itself. Mao's account cries aloud for "castration" interpretation; the rebels cutting down the flag-pole, "symbol of office," and being "beheaded" for their audacity. Well might Mao understand that it did have a relation to his life, and that the injustice of the treatment was resented because, on the symbolic level, it was treatment meted out to *him*. [32]

Mazlish then concludes that Mao's claim that the incident influenced his whole life is a "relatively inexplicable statement," [33] unless note is taken of its symbolism.

Mazlish maintains this oedipal approach in analyzing Mao's career in learning as a teenager. After leaving home at the age of sixteen, Mao had vacillated between different forms of study—"testing, teasing and taunting his father." [34] A number of changes in his program of studies are described by Mazlish:

> The whole situation is presented by Mao in a straightforward tone, as if his vacillation were the most natural thing in the world. He offers no indication as to how his father reacted to his changes of mind (although we can guess). [35]

Whereas earlier Mazlish is unable to understand the impact that a public beheading might have on a young child, here he presumes to guess at Mao's inner emotions, claiming that Mao, having left home, should have been concerned as to how his father reacted to his changes of study programs.

Finally, Mazlish describes a situation where Mao, as a student, was saved from being killed by soldiers through finding a hiding place in a toilet. Mazlish is at a loss to understand why Mao should subsequently relate such an instance; it doesn't seem to fit in with what should be his heroic revolutionary image, though the question of asceticism has by now been totally forgotten. And so we read of

> ... the image of Mao hiding in the toilet! These are hardly heroic portraits and we must wonder why Mao paints them for us and for his countrymen. Is the conflict of students and soldiers (perhaps symbolic of Mao and his father) so strong that Mao is literally *compelled* to recall the episode? [36]

I have given these few isolated examples to indicate the manner in which oedipal thinking is utilized to provide simplistic psychological and personal explanations for complicated historical data. There can be little doubt that psychohistory has much to offer in expanding understanding of political and social events. But this kind of forced analysis can only do it discredit. A close reading of the chapter on Mao shows that it contains no further evidence of asceticism than those few crumbs I have mentioned. The final question must then be not why Mao was an ascetic, which he seems almost certainly not to have been, but why Mazlish bothered to choose him as an example for his thesis. Ideological considerations seem to have been relevant, not so much those of generational differences but those based on Mazlish's attitude to Communism.

The very use of an oedipal perspective in a non-Western culture raises a number of serious and interesting preliminary questions as to the relevance of such a perspective. Mazlish does not deal with this problem at all, blandly imposing his oedipal model on Mao's personal history. Yet this specific issue had been very fully examined by Richard Solomon several years prior to the publication of Mazlish's work.[37] Mazlish makes only passing reference to the book, and barely touches on this issue.[38]

Unlike Mazlish's rote-like use of oedipal concepts, Solomon conducts a searching examination into the possibility of applying a psychohistorical approach, based on oedipal principles, to an understanding of Mao and his place in the political culture of China. Instead of limiting himself to the Oedipus story, Solomon also examines the sources in Chinese mythology that deal with generational conflict in order to understand the impact of Mao's early years on his subsequent political behavior. His analysis is a valuable comparison of myth, literature, and culture. The work has aroused much interest, though some criticism has been leveled at it for its selective choice of stories and for its inaccurate presentation of Chinese culture. My own critique will relate specifically to Solomon's interpretation of generational rivalry.

Solomon's theoretical framework can be seen in the way he deals with the meaning of the Oedipus story. In his opinion, stress is incorrectly placed on family conflict, while the larger social and political implications are generally ignored. Of Laius and Jocasta he writes:

> In abandoning their "fated" son they are trying to deal with the problem of regicide, as well as patricide and incest. . . .
> In mythical terms, the inexorable working out of Oedipus's fate raises serious community and political problems: How is the ruler (Laius) to deal with a subordinate (Oedipus) who would destroy him and enjoy the pleasures that come with great power?[39]

Note the selective choice of words: the son who wants to "destroy" (not, for instance, "replace" or "succeed"), the "pleasures" of power (not the responsibilities).

In his analysis Solomon ignores the incest aspect of the story. His conceptualization of the Oedipus complex is close to Alfred Adler's appraisal—that it is mainly a question of power:

> In dealing with the oracle's presentation of his son's terrible fate, Laius was facing the paradox that the dependent child must be disciplined if he is to become a participating member of society. But the process of socialization, which is the child's first exposure to "politics"—to the relation of the strong who have and the weak who want—will leave a residue of resentment of authority and a desire to "do in" the one who first forced denial or restrictions of the pleasures of life. The solution to this paradox which Oedipus's parents chose, the casting out of the family of the ill-fated child, is in symbolic terms the solution worked out by Western culture: The potentially disruptive dependent is "abandoned," or more correctly, "sent forth," after a period of disciplining to seek for himself in new social contexts alternative solutions to his life's most original hates and loves.[40]

Having rightfully touched on discipline and power as being at the heart of generational conflict, Solomon, in ignoring the effect of parental hostility, fails to see the oppressive nature of the solution chosen by Oedipus's parents. He therefore misinterprets their behavior, seeing it as a necessary separation for the development of the child's own identity. But Oedipus was not "sent forth" as a young man; he was abandoned as an infant, not to find his way in life but to die. It is precisely this aspect of the story that requires interpretation and that Solomon ignores.

It may well be that the stress on individualism in Western culture has led to a situation in which children are indeed sent forth to make their way in life—in sharp contrast to Chinese concepts of familial piety—but the sending forth is usually not so much a willing release by the parent as a reluctant, often disruptive, break. Helm Stierlin and his coworkers describe the psychological and sociological effect of different patterns of separation between parents and adolescents in the Western world.[41] Stierlin has found different forms, which he calls binding, delegating, and expelling. All three entail problems of parents in coping with and accepting the child's growth to maturity and independence. Solomon's interest is not to reach the deeper meanings of Western culture and its myths but of the nature of Chinese mythology, to compare it with Western mythology and, by noting their differing presentations of generational contact, to deduce larger differences in the cultural patterns of childrearing and socialization. Solomon claims that "the Chinese have since early times been concerned with the same problems of resentment of superior by subordinate and of disruptive social conflict which underlie the Oedipus myth. They have sought their own solution to such problems."[42]

Solomon deals with a framework of stories known as the twenty-four modes of filial piety, attempting to show the degree to which Chinese cultural patterns, unlike those of the West, are oriented toward ensuring the continuing dependence of the son on his parents well into adulthood. Solomon's work has been subjected to some criticism, and I do not wish to enter into the issue of whether his overall interpretation of socialization is a valid reflection of Chinese culture. What does emerge from the stories he quotes is a repetitive pattern of adult hostility, a fact that he fails to recognize and which, incidentally, has also failed to attract the attention of his critics.

According to Solomon,

> the first of the twenty-four modes of filial piety is Yu Shun, who, like Oedipus, was rejected by his family. It is not clear what motivated Yu's father and brother to drop him down a well and throw stones upon him, or set fire to a granary when he was inside; we are only told that his father and brother were "stupid" and "conceited." But unlike Oedipus who rewarded his rejecting parents with an inexorable, fate-driven vengeance of death and violation of social taboo, Yu continued a life of toil on his family land and returned his parents' rejection with reverence for them and sincerity in his life-long social obligation as a son.[43]

Solomon provides evidence to show that parental hostility existed not only in Chinese mythology but also in real life. Most of the adults in one sample recalled having been beaten with boards, whips, or rulers, as corporal punishment was an accepted way of intimidating children into obeying adult commands:

> Such punishments were not given *indiscriminately,* but resulted from disobeying parental orders, from failure to meet their standards of performance (especially in school). Through it all, the child can perceive a rationale and predictability behind parental power . . . through his own behavior he can avoid punishment. Yet because his parents allow him no opportunity to "talk back" or reason with them in the matter of discipline, the child learns that it is safer and less painful to accept parental injunctions in a passive manner. . . . Attempts by the child to question the guidance of authoritative elders, or to reason and develop independent judgments can only invoke parental displeasure.[44]

If Solomon's description is to be accepted—and the critics have not challenged him on this aspect of his work—then here there is a substantial proof of parental cruelty in one of the dominant non-Western cultures. Beyond this it gives us a better perspective of some aspects of Mao's behavior when he was a child. Thus Mazlish stresses the so-called identification between him and his father on the basis of Mao's acceptance of his father's values of hard work and frugality. From Solomon's book it appears that identification with a father was not a unique response of a young future revolutionary ascetic trying to solve his oedipal problems but a pattern of behavior apparently common to large sectors of the Chinese population as a defense mechanism against the cruelties of their physically stronger parents. What made Mao unique was not his identification with his father but his capacity to break away from the traditional submission to parental tyranny, which he did by leaving home at the age of sixteen.

Solomon refers to the submissive nature of the son (comparable to Neumann's concept of the Isaac complex in Western society[45]) as an essential factor in his interpretation of the patterns of Chinese social and political behavior. Both the models of filial piety and the strict socialization techniques described are important elements in understanding Chinese politics:

> Several important patterns in relations between superior and subordinate which find clear manifestation in Chinese political behavior seem to have their roots in the harsh and distant treatment a father accords his growing sons. . . . The father passes judgment regardless of child's will.[46]

It was under these circumstances that Mao, as he subsequently confided to Edgar Snow, learned to hate his father. It was in this context, too, that he drew parallels between the authority patterns of his father and those of society at large. On one occasion, Mao finally stood up to his father and challenged him; only then did his father agree to compromise. Mao learned an important political lesson within the "class" system of his family: "When I defended my rights by open rebellion, my father relented, but when I remained weak and submissive he only cursed and beat me the more."[47]

According to Solomon, Mao's subsequent break with the Confucian order was specifically intended to create, in organized fashion, a political personality type capable of reacting as he had done: "Perhaps Mao's most innovative reaction against tradition has been his effort to liberate in disciplined, politicized fashion the aggressive emotions which were denied legitimate expression in the political culture of dependency."[48]

Solomon's analysis of the cultural background to Mao's later political behavior seems far more relevant than Mazlish's. Unlike Mazlish, Solomon has not become the captive of a narrow Freudian perspective, artificially forced as an explanation for almost any phenomenon, particularly one with the slightest hint of generational conflict. As such, his book provides a more meaningful analysis of the psychological underpinnings of political behavior. Yet it lacks a theoretical perspective offering sufficient recognition of parental/adult hostility. Such a perspective is essential for understanding some of the stories that he quotes and some of the empirical facts that he presents.

No less important, it might even help to provide a larger view of Mao, not only as a son who suffered at the hands of his father, but also as to the manner in which Mao himself related to his own children. Did the revolutionary change that he helped bring about cause any transformation in the nature of generational contacts? According to Harold Isaacs, at least at the personal level, Mao seems to have been as wanting in his relations with his children as his father had been with him.[49] Isaacs suggests that most of Mao's biographers, particularly those who show reverence for him, have been very careful to avoid probing too deeply into this aspect of his life, which seems to involve the rather unflattering facts of "Mao's abandoning and ignoring his children—no one is even sure of how many there are—suggesting a Mao who never wanted to be a father to his sons and daughters, deserting and expending them one after another. . . ."[50]

Mazlish and Solomon, of course, are not at all reverent to Mao, yet they fail to probe this aspect of Mao's life, despite the fact that both take note of generational relations and that both make references to the Rustrum theme. As noted in Chapter 2, Solomon discusses the oedipal theme in contrast to a Rustum-style Chinese story, while Mazlish makes passing reference to the story of Sohrab and Rustum in a book on the generational aspects of the famous nineteenth-century family of James Mill, the father, and his son John Stuart Mill.[51]

In this latter book, interestingly enough, Mazlish does recognize that "generational change, almost necessarily through conflict, is a prime mechanism of social change."[52] He goes on:

> . . . in time of pressing new problems of required rapid social transformation, a new generation is challenged to shake off part of the burden of the past in order to be free to march into a new future. The break is never more than partial, and should not be; but without the "death" of an existing generation, the "birth" of a new society or culture, is unlikely, if not impossible.[53]

Here Mazlish seems to have penetrated to much of the essence of generational conflict.[54] Yet, in discussing modern Chinese culture, Mazlish shows none of the understanding for social change in times of pressing new problems that he showed toward nineteenth-century British society. Of course, Mazlish presumably does not like what emerged in China. That in itself is perfectly legitimate. But surely that is not sufficient reason for using totally different models and explanations of social change.

This inconsistency toward social change and the role of the young, as well as an even greater reliance on an oedipal model, may be seen even more clearly in Lewis Feuer's study on the conflict of generations, which will be discussed in detail in the next chapter.

References

1.   FitzRoy R. Somerset, Baron Raglan, *The Hero: A Study in Tradition, Myth and Drama* (London: Methuen, 1963); Otto Rank, *The Myth of the Birth of the Hero* (New York: Robert Brunner, 1952).

2.   Sigmund Freud, *Group Psychology and the Analysis of the Ego* (1921), in *The Standard Edition of the Complete Psychological Works of Sigmund Freud,* edited by James Strachey, 24 vols. (London: Hogarth Press, 1953–66), 18. Philip Rieff suggests that this book is an implicit rebuttal to the criticisms of *Totem and Taboo.* He notes that "of Freud's various subjects, politics appears . . . the least attended. The word is little used, and *Group Psychology and the Analysis of the Ego,* his most concentrated political essay, is brief even for a writer of such graciously slim books" (Philip Rieff, "The Origins of Freud's Political Psychology," *Journal of History of Ideas* 17 [1956]: 235).

3.   Carl E. Schorske, "Politics and Patricide in Freud's 'Interpretation of Dreams,' " *The American Historical Review* 78 (1973): 328–347; W. J. McGrath, "Freud as Hannibal: The Politics of the Brother Band," *Central European History* 7 (1974): 31–57.

4.   Schorske, "Politics and Patricide," p. 347.

5.   Stanley Rothman and Philip Isenberg, "Sigmund Freud and the Politics of Marginality," *Central European History* 7 (1974): 58–79.

6.   Freud, *Group Psychology,* p. 90.

7.   Ibid., p. 91.

8.   Ibid., p. 123.

9.   Ibid., p. 124.

10.   Ibid., pp. 123–124.

11.   Ibid., p. 94.

12.   Ibid., p. 123.

13.   Theodor W. Adorno, "Freudian Theory and the Pattern of Fascist Propaganda," *Psychoanalysis and the Social Sciences* 3 (1951): 281.

14.   Norman O. Brown, *Love's Body* (New York: Random House, 1966).

15.   Ibid., p. 11.

16.   Ibid., p. 3.

17.   Ibid., p. 4.

18.   Ibid., p. 17.

19.   Ibid., p. 26.

20.   Ibid., pp. 28–29.

21.   Ibid., pp. 5–6.

22.   Bruce Mazlish, *The Revolutionary Ascetic: Evolution of a Political Type* (New York: Basic Books, 1976).

23.   Ibid., p. 4.

24.   Ibid., p. 37. In using Freud's psychoanalytical concepts, Mazlish makes a point of stressing that, as a result of Freud's work, "for the first time in history, deep insight into *human* history was possible in terms of concepts and theories scientifically elaborated and grounded in sustained clinical observation" (p. 21).

25.   Ibid., p. 37.

26. Ibid., p. 124. Mazlish does add, a page later, that some of his followers did love him, and then goes on to note the difficulty, based on Lenin's case, of deciding whether boundless love was a necessary characteristic of the relations of followers to leaders or if its absence in this case arose out of the particular ideological dimensions (see pp. 125–126).

27. Ibid., p. 157. In this quotation and in the text, I have used the old spelling/ transliteration of Mao.

28. Ibid., pp. 206–207. For Snow's biography, see Edgar Snow, *Red Star over China* (New York: Grove Press, 1961).

29. Ibid., p. 207. At the end of the book Mazlish calls into use Freud's concept of repression of impulses to suggest that, despite Mao's libidinal ties, he actually "projected" and "embodied" the image of a leader "with few libidinal ties." Mazlish suggests that this repression was not only unconscious, arising out of personal needs, "but extremely conscious as well, out of stringent political requirements" (p. 208). But this seems to be standing the evidence on its head, for it is precisely the libidinal aspects—of having children, writing poetry, having deep feeling, lacking charisma—that Mao projected.

30. Ibid., p. 22 and p. 29.

31. Ibid., p. 167.

32. Ibid., p. 176. Mazlish goes on to admit the validity of Mao's overt explanation of this act and the strong impression that it made on him as an instance of injustice, but adds that the castration explanation "enriches" Mao's explanation.

33. Ibid., p. 177.

34. Ibid.

35. Ibid., p. 181.

36. Ibid., p. 182.

37. Richard H. Solomon, *Mao's Revolution and the Chinese Political Culture* (Berkeley, University of California Press, 1971).

38. Mazlish, *The Revolutionary Ascetic,* p. 171.

39. Solomon, *Mao's Revolution,* p. 29.

40. Ibid., p. 30.

41. See especially Helm Stierlin, *Separating Parents and Adolescents* (New York: Quadrangle, 1976); see also Helm Stierlin, J. David Levi, and Robert J. Savard, "Parental Perception of Separating Children," *Family Process* vol. 10 (1971): 411, and J. David Levi, Helm Stierlin, and Robert J. Savard, "Father and Sons: The Interlocking Crises of Integrity and Identity," *Psychiatry* 35 (1972): 48. These items will be further discussed in chapter 9. For a similar attempt to deal with the question of separation, see S. Giora Shoham, "The Isaac Syndrome," *American Imago* 33 (1976): 329–349. As far as Chinese culture itself is concerned, Benjamin Schwartz claims that sons were not as passive as Solomon indicates and that they could seek separation from their parents by going away and becoming, for example, successful officials. See the review by Schwartz of Solomon's book. *Journal of Interdisciplinary History* 4 (1973): 569.

42. Solomon, *Mao's Revolution,* p. 31.

43. Ibid.

44. Ibid., p. 51.

45. See Erich Neumann, *The Origins and History of Consciousness* (New York: Harper Torch, 1954), p. 189.

46. Solomon, *Mao's Revolution,* p. 57. This pattern, in which authoritarian fathers in the family lay the basis for authoritarian rule in society, also bears resemblance to Western patterns; see my discussion of this point in chapter 11.

47. Ibid., p. 177, quoted from Snow, *Red Star,* p. 126. Mazlish also refers to this story on p. 170.

48. Solomon, *Mao's Revolution,* p. 513. Solomon thus sees the Red Guard movement as an attempt by Mao to artificially create a rite of passage that would "recreate his own socialization experiences for millions of Chinese youngsters" (p. 525).

49. Harold Isaacs, "Bringing up the Father Question," *Daedalus* 107 (1978): 189.

50. Ibid., p. 190. Isaacs bases his discussion of Mao's abandoning his children on Lucian Pye, *Mao Tse-tung, The Man In the Leader* (New York: Basic Books, 1976). Isaacs claims that Pye is the only writer to deal with this aspect of Mao's life.

51. Bruce Mazlish, *James and John Stuart Mill: Father and Son in the Nineteenth Century* (New York: Basic Books, 1975).

52. Ibid., p. 429.

53. Ibid.

54. This theme of social change is dealt with in chapter 10, "Faithful to Our Youth."

CHAPTER SIX
THE ENDS OF
IDEOLOGY

Lewis Feuer's *The Conflict of Generations* is probably the most ambitious and important attempt to apply basic oedipal concepts to the political struggles of youth.[1] Written as a direct response to the turbulence of the 1960s, particularly in the United States, Feuer's work incorporates a mine of information on youth, mainly student movements, within a broad oedipal framework. The ambivalence so prevalent in much of the writing about generational conflict reaches a peak in this work, as Feuer moves from an initial attraction to and respect for the altruism and idealism behind the students' endeavors to a devastating criticism of the inevitable tendency, in his opinion, for their actions to become irrational and self-destructive. Unfortunately, Feuer's ambivalence leads not to a balanced picture but to exaggerations and distortions aimed, for the most part, at discrediting the young. I shall deal in detail with this work, as it is an outstanding example of how modes of Freudian thinking can be used to present a one-sided, deterministic picture of complex social phenomena. Through reiteration of several key phrases, written in the Freudian idiom—particularly rejection, deauthoritization (to use the author's term), and destruction of the elder generation—the political and social struggles of youth are condemned, and the youth themselves are blamed for many of the ills of the world.

At the broader level, Feuer blames the extremism and irrationality of youth for dissipating much that is positive in their initial motivation, for destroying sanguine hopes for reform, and for perverting inspiring ideas. More specifically, he sees irrational assassination attempts by young men acting out their parricidal hatred as directly responsible for the outbreak of World War I and for snuffing out the possibility of liberal, gradual reform in both Czarist and Soviet Russia; further he claims that it was the youth of Germany that bore major responsibility for the rise of Nazism, while the youth of America bore much responsibility for the failure to combat the rising power of Nazi Germany.

These are just a few of the views expressed by Feuer in his 500-page treatise. His detailed arguments require extended treatment.

There are four major points that I wish to deal with:

1. Feuer's commitment to the Freudian model, despite the lack of any direct acknowledgment of Freud's influence;

2. the fund of empirical data presented to describe student movements of the nineteenth and twentieth centuries, offset by the selective manner in which the data are presented;

3. recognition of the importance of generational conflict in human history, offset by a one-sided emphasis on the negative role of student movements;

4. personal ideological motives underlying the analysis, openly conceded in the preface, and specifically developed in the chapter dealing with the Berkeley student movement,[2] when Feuer was on the Berkeley faculty, and actively involved against the student uprising.

One of the most intriguing aspects of *The Conflict of Generations* is that, although it is deeply and clearly immersed in the Freudian tradition, Feuer, a political scientist, makes no clear acknowledgment of the fact. There are about half-a-dozen references to Freud scattered throughout the book, generally in peripheral contexts (only one of the references appears in the index), but the major references to the key ideas of rejection, deauthoritization and destruction of the fathers, which Feuer liberally intersperses throughout the book, all appear without the slightest indication that these ideas stem directly from the theoretical premises of Freud's work on the Oedipus complex. There are also several references to the Oedipus complex itself, this time without any index reference at all. Only once, at the end of the preface, does Feuer make any direct acknowledgment of the oedipal framework of his book. In setting out the motivation for writing the book, he states that he does not accept any "fateful, Oedipal determinism."[3] He goes on to assure the reader that, having adopted a critical approach to student movements, he does not believe their negative aspects to be inevitable. The accent, then, is on determinism; it is the determinism that Feuer is challenging and so, by implication, conceding the oedipal background.

At no stage does Feuer set out the key ideas of Freud in an attempt to trace the intellectual antecedents of his own thinking. It is not clear whether this omission stems from a reluctance to acknowledge his indebtedness to Freud or from a confidence that Freud's ideas are so widely accepted that they do not require any acknowledgment or elaboration.[4] Thus he casually throws in a reference to Freud in the course of describing the Russian students' assassination of Czar Alexander II, writing that "their dramatic idealism projected on a national political scale the emotional pattern of 'totem and taboo,' the revolt and guilt of the primal sons Freud described."[5] There is no footnote reference to the book *Totem and Taboo,* no brief description of Freud's thesis; the reference is made as though the idea of primal sons killing their father is an accepted theory of modern life, like the theories of gravity or evolution. There is no hint that this is one of Freud's most problematical works, that even some Freudians are skeptical, or embarrassed, about the idea of primal sons killing and devouring their primal father.

Feuer's book is no simple catalogue of events; it is an attempt to provide a theoretical model applicable to all student movements. After dealing extensively with three student movements (Russian, German, and Bosnian), Feuer provides information on dozens of other movements throughout the world to prove the broad applicability of his theory.

The Freudian model chosen by Feuer provides a handy framework for facile explanations of the negative aspects of student movements. Without going deeply into actual causes and issues, Feuer can casually attribute fault to students, every now and then throwing in a reference to rejection of elders or explaining the existence of secret societies in oppressive regimes as being merely the reenactment of children's propensity toward secret groupings to hide things from their parents. Basically, Feuer has used a neat antiyouth theoretical model to make far-reaching accusations against the young. As in the fields of literature and psychohistory, here, too, if one discards the restrictions of the oedipal mode, one can easily arrive at contrary interpretations of many of Feuer's data.

Feuer has delved deeply into student movements in the nineteenth and twentieth centuries. He probes the personal backgrounds of some of the student leaders and activists in order to relate their conflicts with their parents to their subsequent revolutionary activities. He stresses particularly the irrationality, self-destructiveness, and violence of many of these students' activities, the secrecy of their organizations, and specific instances of suicide and assassination.

Feuer's examples are taken from movements that either failed or else, in succeeding, led to the greater failure or perversion of the original pristine aims. He builds his thesis mainly around the student movements of Germany, Bosnia, and Russia. The first are blamed for the rise of Nazism, the second for World War I, the third for having destroyed any hopes that Russia might move gradually to a liberal democratic state. Feuer constantly states or implies that the movements that he discusses are prototypes of all youth activitists.

Feuer's most detailed analysis is devoted to the Russian student movement. Although this movement has been well documented, Feuer feels that most writers have failed to pay sufficient attention to its specific generational aspects. He attempts to rectify this lacuna:

> The Russian student movement, classical exemplar of all modern student movements, concentrated in an almost pure state the characteristics of emo-

tional, generational revolt which have inspired all student movements. Ceasing to respect their elders, the students looked elsewhere for guidance among the most advanced contemporary philosophical prophets. Stirred by an amalgam of emotions—with all the ingredients of self-sacrifice and self-destruction, the desire to identify with the lowliest, along with the contrary desire to rule as the highest—the student movement tragically combined a high idealism with a violent irrationality destructive of its own ideal. The Russian student movement was the historical integument in which the anxieties of the children externalized themselves in political form.[6]

He adds: "Russian students were moved by powerful unconscious forces to sunder their ties with the prevailing, parental culture."[7]

This is the essence of Feuer's message. The young are at war with their elders, rejecting their parents, breaking away from the values and the culture their parents have imparted to them, acting out in politics their personal oedipal conflicts, setting up secret organizations, committing irrational and destructive acts of assassination and/or suicide.

The Russian student movement is an extreme example, but it is also the prototype of all other student movements. Feuer has almost nothing to say about the oppressive nature of the Czarist regime, of the decadent culture that was being rejected, of the accumulation of historical pressures.

When Feuer does make passing reference to the regime, it is generally in order to intensify and expand his accusation against youth. Thus, according to him, if it had not been for the assassination of Alexander II by young radicals, Russia would probably have moved into gradual constitutionalism. Dramatically we are informed: "A half-hour before the Czar set out on his last journey on March 1, 1881, he approved the text of a decree announcing the establishment of a commission likely to lead to the writing of a constitution."[8]

The imponderables here are limitless, some of the big "ifs" of history; Feuer, however, has no hesitation in blaming the youth for Russia's later ills. Instead of progress toward constitutionalism, "the students' acts of Czar-killing and self-killing brought into Russian politics all the psychological overtones of sons destroying their fathers."[9] This was to continue into the present century and would help explain the success of the Communists in gaining power.

To Feuer, both Lenin and Stalin were involved in a generational conflict with their fathers. Ideology, the oppressiveness of Russian society, glaring economic disparity, all pale into insignificance in comparison with the dominant factor of revolt against the fathers. The details he gives of both leaders' family backgrounds are skimpy and hardly worth arguing over. More impressive is Feuer's attempt to describe the familial background of one of the young radicals who had been involved in the conspiracy to assassinate the Czar. After noting that "[t]he revolutionary student activist was, indeed, an invariant, unchanging psychological type from his first appearance in the 1860's to the early 1900's,"[10] Feuer cites Sophia Perovskaya, who "had all the character traits in their purity of the student revolutionist."[11] Feuer quotes from her biography and three other histories of the period to explain succinctly how "[s]he was driven by the compulsions of generational revolt."[12] And so we read, without comment, of how harsh and tyrannical her father was, both in his official role as governor-general of St. Petersburg and toward his own family: "A staunch advocate of serfdom, the father brought its violence into his own home."[13] The oppression within the home included a ban on Sophia being visited by her friends. At this Sophia, then sixteen years old, left home. Without any critical comment on the father's behavior, Feuer concludes: "Such were the ultimate nuclei in the unconscious from which the energies for the student movement were liberated."[14]

While I do not propose to attempt any psychological analysis of Sophia Perovskaya, I would question the role of her oedipal feelings in leading her to revolutionary activity. Surely the cruelty of her father, representative of the Czar, toward his family, his serfs, and the citizens under his control had at least something to do with it.

It is possible, as Feuer maintains, that the daughter carried a load of psychological tension within her, but can an analysis of generational revolt based on the irrationality of the young ignore the prior irrationality and cruelty of the parental generation? What, after all, did Feuer expect the young girl to do: passively to acquiesce in the irrational, tyrannical, and humiliating behavior of her father? Did he expect her to ignore the parallels between the cruel regime he imposed on his own family and the Czarist regime of which he was a noted representative? Of course, too much should not be made of one particular case but, after all, it was Feuer who chose the case as a typical example.

At one point in the book Feuer seems on the threshold of realizing the degree to which the actions of the parental generation influence youth behavior. Speaking of contemporary Soviet youth, Feuer notes that "[t]here is a muted confrontation in the Soviet society between the existentialist student generation and those of middle age who in varying degrees bear the guilt or corruption of Stalinism."[15] Thus the prior faults of what Feuer calls the "fathers" may be a key to understanding the confrontation between generations, even if only muted.

But, making one of his few specific references to Freud, Feuer deftly slips out of the trap that he had inadvertently set for himself. For, according to Feuer, Stalin's generation is not just a fathers' generation to today's youth; it is also, *mirabile dictu,* a sons' generation to the original revolutionaries. Thus, with Feuer's masterly juggling, Stalin's excesses become not those of a father but of a son:

> The characters in the drama of generational conflict in the Soviet Union might most accurately be described as the grandsons and the fathers. For the fathers, the Stalinist generation, destroyed the Leninist grandfathers, the Old Bolsheviks, the Makers of the Revolution. On the executed bodies of Bukharin, Zinoviev, Kamenev, and the exiled Trotsky, the Stalinist generation of bureaucrats climbed the ladder of upward mobility to power and prestige. This intervening generation profited from the purges as a device which ensured it access to vacated high posts, the Soviet generational escalator. The third generation, insofar as it is moved to rebellion, refuses to share the guilt of the second; the grandsons blame the fathers who murdered the grandfathers. Here were consequences of social parricide that Freud never explored.[16]

I do not wish to go into the details of any theoretical possibilities contained in this idea, nor to enquire into the full background of Stalinism. But the statement as it stands is completely devoid of any contact with reality; indeed, if I may be permitted the use of one of Feuer's pet terms, the statement is almost "irrational."

For the simple facts are:

1.   Stalin was not a son to "Leninist grandfathers," but their contemporary. He was one of the "three who made a revolution."[17] More specifically, he was only nine years younger than Lenin, two years younger than Trotsky, and eleven *older* than Bukharin! If Feuer insists on using familial terminology to describe simply and briefly the complex events of the Russian revolution and the Soviet regime, then fratricide would be more apt.

2.   Stalin took control of the Soviet Union at age forty-five. His extremism, if anything, increased with age.

3.   There was no Stalinist generation of bureaucrats who benefited from the purges. Both the victims and the beneficiaries of Stalin's excesses were drawn indiscriminately from all ages. Among his victims were many young opponents of the regime.

Various reasons may be advanced for Stalinism: Stalin's own personality, the nature of Russian society, the customary harshness in the early stages of many revolutions. All of these may have varying degrees of relevance for Stalin's excesses, but each must surely have more relevance than his unconscious parricidal tendencies.

In dealing with the control exercised by Stalin's regime, Feuer suggests that although Stalin was "outraged by the prying and spying of his teachers," he later "outdid his fathers by prying and spying on them tenfold."[18] Yet despite his awareness of the consequences that such prying and spying might have on those antagonistic to the regime, Feuer has disdain for any student groups that resort to secret organizational methods.

Throughout his analysis Feuer stresses the importance of secrecy in the organizational activities of the students. Ignoring completely the surveillance and control of an authoritarian regime, he compares the propensity of the students to set up secret societies with the similar propensity of young children to form secret groups:

> Student movements tend to choose a secret society form of organization not because of any political necessity but precisely because it marks the generational separation. Children have always revelled in secret groups with secret passwords precisely because these establish their mark of independence in conspiracy against the adults. . . . The student movement is almost like a secret society of sons and daughters banded against the father. The secret society is like a voluntary family, a new "primary group," in which one chooses anew one's brothers and sisters. Its confidences cannot yield to those of the natural family.[19]

The implication of the last sentence is that Sophia Perovskaya, for example, refrained from telling her father of her revolutionary activities not because he occupied a high-ranking position in the Czarist bureaucracy but merely because keeping a secret from her father gave her a feeling of independence and belonging within a new "voluntary family."

Feuer's lack of logic and consistency in this matter emerges clearly when he notes approvingly the secret groups existing in post-Stalinist Russia at the time of his visit there in 1963, under a much less oppressive regime. In the preface to his book, Feuer recounts the unusual experience he had, while an exchange scholar at the Soviet Institute of Philosophy,

> of getting to know well one of the circles of student dissenters at Moscow State University which met and discussed problems raised by their aspirations toward freedom in a dictatorial political system. Here one saw students reliving, in the same buildings, the secret experiences of courageous students during Czarist times a hundred years before.[20]

When dealing directly, in the body of the book, with the secret activities of Russian students during Czarist times, Feuer has only disdain for them; when linking them, in the preface, to similar activities in 1963, in which he himself had been a participant, he uses the epithet "courageous." One wonders how his new-found friends felt about his theory of why young people prefer secret activities to open expression of dissent or about his publicly divulging the existence of this particular group six years later. One can only hope that the identities of these modern-day dissenters and conspirators were not revealed through Feuer's announcement.

However, if the Soviet regime tries to repress dissent the blame would probably lie with the youth themselves. Just as the youth prevented the Czarist regime from moving toward gradual constitutionalism, so too the irrationality c f student activists in the 1930s deflected Stalin from his plan to moderate his regime and led to the harsh totalitarianism associated with his name. Once again, the students were responsible for the tragic course of history: "Strangely enough, in some ways the paranoid psychology of Stalinism, like its Czarist forerunner, was stimulated by the self-destructive terrorist tactics of student activists."[21] Feuer notes that, in 1934, several of his contemporaries had indicated that Stalin was becoming milder and more affable. Then, in that year, one of the Soviet leaders, Kirov, was assassinated by a young man. The following year there was a plot to kill Stalin and several similar cases in which students had been involved. "From them Stalin traced his thread of suspicion and involvement to the students' professors in political science and party history, and from the latter to the former leaders of the Opposition. The Nightmare of the Purges began."[22]

It is possible that the purges of politicians instituted by Stalin had their origins in the assassination of Kirov. Unfortunately for Feuer's thesis, it seems quite likely that Kirov's assassination was not the cause of the purges but their initial act. For there is evidence to indicate that Stalin knew of the assassin's plans; instead of having him arrested, he gave instructions to facilitate the plans—thereby ensuring that Kirov, his chief rival in the party, who was popular and had challenged him on a number of issues, would be removed. The day following Kirov's death, his bodyguard, who had become suspicious, was killed in an automobile accident. The facts will probably never be known.[23] But knowing today the full extent of the excesses committed by Stalin (against millions of Kulaks in an earlier purge even before Kirov's death), it requires a rather distorted view of history to believe that Stalin's actions were no more than a response to the provocative acts of student activists.

Feuer's stress on the role of the Russian student movement is not capricious; it is based on his perception of the importance of generations and generational conflict in understanding history. This is of particular significance for those student movements that do not exist on their own but as part of a larger social and political movement. Generational conflict is not a chance phenomenon. It must be counted as a "universal theme of history."[24] Feuer stresses that, in this respect, there are parallels between generational struggles and other social struggles, such as class or national movements. At the same time, he affirms the uniqueness of the youth movement. Unlike the struggles of classes, for instance, there is a large degree of inevitable irrationality in a student movement. In contrast to the rational struggles of classes for specific, pragmatic aims—better wages, hours, working conditions—student movments have no definite aims, but represent a vague, amorphous yearning for better society. "Student movements, unlike those of workingmen, are born of vague, undefined emotions which seek for some issue, some cause to which to attach themselves."[25] They do not, and cannot, exist in their own right and their own behalf.

Student movements, therefore, are obliged to link themselves to some other movement. "Every student movement tries to attach itself to a 'carrier' movement of more major proportions—such as a peasant, labor, nationalist, racial or anticolonial movement. . . ."[26] This concept of the "carrier" movement has far-reaching implications, for it is qualitatively affected by the infusion of the student movement:

> Emotions issuing from the students' unconscious, and deriving from the conflict of generations, impose or attach themselves to the underlying political carrier movement, and deflect it in irrational directions. Given a set of alternative paths—rational or irrational—for realizing a social goal, the influence of a student movement will be toward the use of the most irrational means to achieve the end. Student movements are thus what one would least expect—among the most irrationalist in history.[27]

This is a key paragraph for understanding the whole tenor of Feuer's thinking and his theoretical embellishments of widely disparate facts. Since the student movements cannot exist on their own but must attach themselves to "carrier" movements, since student movements tend to be irrational, since student movements will deflect the "carrier" movements in irrational directions, the rest follows logically. The students can be blamed for the failures of any of the "carrier" movements and even for many of the ills of the world.

Feuer develops his theme in order to explain the rise of Nazism. The background of Hitler's rise to power may be traced to German youth of the nineteenth century; his actual support, to their counterparts in the twentieth century; and the failure of the Western democracies to take adequate, prompt steps against him, to the youth of those countries.

Feuer pays special attention to the student Wartburg Festival, held on October 19, 1817 (*eighteen* seventeen) when two dozen books were burned and anti-Semitic remarks were made. One of the students boasted that this would be the pattern of the future. This is all that Feuer needs in order to conclude: "Adolf Hitler was the executor of the students' will."[28]

In dealing with the immediate post-World War II years in Germany, Feuer notes that no student movement arose in reaction to the humiliating defeat to which Hitler had led them. Here was a ready-made situation in which there should surely have been a deauthoritization of the elder generation. But no student movement arose. For this Feuer has a simple explanation: it was not the elders but the youth who were responsible for Hitler. "It was the student movement which was deauthoritized, because it had given itself to the Nazis lock, stock and barrel. This was a studentry discredited by its failure of character and betrayal of intellect; it could claim no mission to redeem others."[29] The fact that the students of the postwar years were children during the key years of Hitler's rise to power is of no account for Feuer. Unlike in Russia, where he assigned Lenin and Stalin to different generations, Feuer here shows no interest in differentiating between genuinely different generations. The previous generation of students is referred to as "elder brothers." And what of the elder generation, the fathers of the children of the 1930s? For them and their predicament, Feuer shows understanding and even partial exoneration: "The elders of the previous generation, social democrats, liberals, conservatives, shared much less of the national guilt than the Nazi students, for the elders had been largely displaced and spiritually emasculated by the Nazis."[30]

Thus, faithful to his theme, Feuer shows how the perversions of one of the most irrational political movements in history—led for the most part by middle-aged men (Hitler was in his forties when he took political power), most of whom were not and had never been students, allowed into power, to a large extent, because of the vacillations and weaknesses of middle-aged and older men—is to be blamed on the student movement.

Even though German youth must bear major responsibility for Nazism, other youth, according to Feuer, cannot be completely absolved for sins of omission. Thus, for instance, the American student movement of the 1930s, for all its acknowledged idealism and self-sacrifice, nevertheless allowed its actions to be warped by irrationality stemming from generational conflict. Feuer moves inexorably to the climax:

> Precisely at a time when the shadow of Hitlerism was rising, precisely during those early years when collective action could have halted the rearmament of Germany, the militarization of the Rhineland, precisely during those years was the American student movement enacting its rebellion against a previous generation which had followed Woodrow Wilson into war, and disarming itself intellectually and physically before the Nazi advance.[31]

Although many students were economically hard-pressed at that time, the movement ignored these material issues and became involved in campus struggles:

> . . . it erupted in campus riots and disturbances, and ridiculed the naivete of the Roosevelt administration and the weakness of the liberals. Meanwhile it was weakening the resistance which should have been made to Hitler. Generational struggle, its slogans and antics, carried the day.[32]

A full answer to such a narrow appraisal of the 1930s would require a long dissertation on American politics, including the strong isolationist movement led by members of the parent generation. But such a dissertation is unnecessary. The answer to Feuer's far-reaching claim is in his own book. For this strong criticism of the American students' movement appears in a chapter entitled "Generational Equilibrium in the United States," devoted to expanding on the opening sentence: "The United States has never had a massive student movement of the national proportions of those which existed in Russia and Japan."[33] In numerical terms Feuer notes that, "At the height of its strength in 1939, the American Student Union, claiming twenty thousand members, represented a small minority on most campuses; the American university never knew anything like the turmoil of the Russian schools."[34] As Feuer notes, even the figure of twenty thousand was probably deliberately inflated by the leaders.

So, a minor group of students on American campuses, many of them drawn to radical doctrines precisely because of the danger of Nazism (as Feuer himself notes), are blamed for America's sin of failing to stifle early Nazism. It is, of course, true that a small group of dedicated activists might have an impact far beyond their actual numerical strength. Not so in this particular case—again according to Feuer's own evidence. In his preface, he writes. "During the thirties I observed at first hand the formation of a student movement. It was never large or really politically consequential in the United States. . . ."[35]

If student movements were to blame for the rise of Nazism, their responsibility for World War I is even more direct. The irrational act of a young Bosnian nationalist, Gavrilo Princip, in assassinating the Archduke Ferdinand at Sarajevo, plunged the world into war. Once again, this came at a particularly unfortunate time, as, just by chance, the elder generation had been making good progress toward a stable European society:

> . . . for two generations a tradition of peace had been taking root in Europe. Peaceful social democratic movements were gaining in influence; great figures, men of peace such as Jean Jaurès, were gaining renown and influence in Europe. It was likely indeed that Russia, if it were spared the stress of war, would continue rapidly to evolve in a liberal capitalist direction. There was hope in Europe that a rational society would emerge.

Feuer sums up:

> The equilibrium of Europe was shaky, but the roots of a growing stability were there too.[36]

This idyll was destroyed by the irrational act of a young activist. According to Feuer, while the political fact is well known, "What is less well known is the extent to which this incident was the outcome of generational conflict and of the superimposing of the psychological traits of the student movement on the processes of political change."[37] Feuer sees this at two levels, Princip's own "intense, unresolved Oedipal feelings," which were "evidently salient traits of the student activists,"[38] and the overall generational conflict existing in Bosnia ("the Bosnian student activists . . . were in thoroughgoing revolt against their fathers' ways"[39]). Because of the specific cultural traits in Bosnia, the "terrorist propensity of the Bosnian student movement was a compulsive pattern which issued from the intensity of its generational revolt."[40] For several pages Feuer discusses the irrational and destructive acts of the young Bosnians, and then observes: "Thirty years later the same emotions of conflict with the older generation which nurtured Gavrilo Princip and his terrorist friends issued in the heroism of the Yugoslav Partisans."[41] Use of the word "heroism" usually connotes approval. If the Partisans' fight was motivated not by love of their fatherland, nor by hatred of Nazism, nor by positive belief in Communism (for Tito's followers) or social democracy (for some of the other groups), but, according to Feuer, by their "conflict with the older generation," then surely the "heroic" aspects of their struggle in this instance deserve further analysis, even if only as the exception that proves the rule. Feuer remains silent.

Also not commented upon is the irrational response of world leaders to the assassination. If, indeed, "peace was taking root," why was there such an extreme reaction to the killing? Feuer finds no need apparently to deal with the world leaders; the blame rests entirely on poor young Princip, who "enacted his heroic politics of generational struggle and unknowingly imposed its pattern of self-destruction on all Europe and most of the world. Millions of men moved to their death, and over civilization drifted a nightmare which has not yet lifted."[42]

While Feuer does remark twice that it would be erroneous "to say that Gavrilo Princip's deed was *the* cause of the First World War,"[43] he makes sure that the reader is left in little doubt as to its major contributory effect.

Feuer fails to appreciate the significance of his analysis. If the irrational act of assassination was a major cause of World War I, then the real question is: which was the more irrational act—the assassination by a young activist or the response to it by world leaders? If, conversely, the world leaders acted rationally, then the causes for the war must have been far deeper, and Princip's act cannot be seen as more than a trigger action, of the kind that would sooner or later have led to the same denouement. Barbara Tuchman's detailed analysis of the events leading up to World War I presents a completely different picture, one of leaders on all sides caught up in the rush of events, afraid of losing face, irrationally leading their nations into a war nobody wanted.[44]

The essence of Feuer's analysis of these three major student movements—the Russian, German and Bosnian—is this:

1. student movements are a direct consequence of generational conflict, with oedipal overtones, within the family;

2. student movements are generally not independent but work in liaison with other movements of a class, national, or peasant nature, these serving as "carrier" movements for the nebulous student movement searching for issues;

3. student activists have an inevitable tendency to act irrationally, imposing their irrationality on the "carrier" movements, and swaying the course of human history in an irrational direction.

In discussing Feuer's case I have tried to point out the errors in his presentation—factual, methodological, logical, and theoretical. Even when his facts are correct, or his insights logical and relevant, they often lend themselves to alternative conclusions. S. N. Eisenstadt, for example, has also noticed that youth radicalism is associated with a certain degree of conflict with parents and that youth movements are often allied to larger, more comprehensive social and political movements.[45] But his interpretation and explanation is diametrically opposed to that of Feuer.

Eisenstadt sees the connection between a youth movement and a larger social movement as a consequence not of the search by the former for a "carrier" movement to provide it with concrete issues but, conversely, as a consequence of a revolutionary social movement's need for a "special youth ideology. The essence of these ideologies . . . is that the changes which they advocate and struggle for are more or less synonymous with rebellion against the 'old' order and generation, a rebellion of youth, a manipulation of the *rejuvenation* of national and social spirit."[46]

Eisenstadt goes on to explain: "Almost every modern revolutionary movement has to develop such youth ideology and youth organization, and most processes of social and political change must, to some extent, be realized through such channels and with such an ideological basis."[47]

As for conflict within the family, whereas Feuer sees such conflict as motivating and precipitating the larger social involvement, Eisenstadt claims that it is the larger revolutionary movements, with their "universal tendency to form special youth organizations with those whose aid they might muster youthful energies against the old order," which attempt "to disconnect the young people from their families, to turn them against the latter and the order they represent, and to intensify the conflict between the generations."[48] Inasmuch as young revolutionaries oppose their families, it is not because of conflict with the parents as such but because the "family with its values and authority structure stands as a symbol of the general social order against which they rebel."[49]

The conflict with the parents is thus a *consequence,* not a *cause,* of the rebellion; the society is not the larger arena on which child-parent struggles are played out; the family is not the precipitating agent of revolutionary fervor. It is the evils of the society that first arouse the emotions of the youthful activists; only afterward do they see the family as reflecting many of these weaknesses.

Eisenstadt's theory fits in well with Kenneth Keniston's empirical study of radical youth in the United States in the 1960s.[50] He found that the students had not rebelled against their parents; on the contrary, many of them were motivated to their radical ideas by values they had originally absorbed in their home environments.

Eisenstadt's ideas are put forward tentatively, since his book deals basically not with conflict but with the factors making for continuity between the generations. His discussion of the youth movements is actually part of a short section at the end of his book in which he deals with what he terms "deviant age groups," ranging from delinquent gangs to youth organizations of revolutionary movements and parties.[51] He stresses that much work is still to be done in this area. Referring to "Mazzini's Young Europe, the Young Turks, the various nuclei of students in most social and national movements of the nineteenth and twentieth centuries in Europe and Africa," he notes that "a detailed analysis of all these movements is yet to be written; only when this is done will a fully systematic analysis within the framework of an hypothesis be possible."[52]

In many respects Feuer's book sets out to present such a detailed analysis. Interestingly, Feuer refers only in passing to two movements specifically mentioned by Eisenstadt and generally considered to have been among the most important and relatively successful: Mazzini's group and the Young Turks. Eisenstadt's book he neglects completely, despite the fact that the book, published in 1955, was accorded wide recognition.

Of the two opposing models, Feuer's is the more deeply researched, but it is riddled with inconsistencies and flawed by uncritical submission to a dubious Freudian theoretical model; Eisenstadt's model is more tentative, but it seems to be built on logical assumptions. Part of the difference in their choice of approach may very well stem from sociology of knowledge considerations. Eisenstadt is an Israeli, well aware, as he indicates in his book, of the positive role that youth movements played in the national struggle of the Zionist movement for an independent state and for unique social forms, such as the kibbutz.[53] Feuer is an American, and he stresses in his book the uniqueness of American society (shared only by Great Britain) in achieving what he calls "generational equilibrium, when no generation feels that its energies and intelligence are being frustrated by the others, when no generation feels that solely because of its years it is being deprived of its proper place in society. . . ."[54] The nation's major cataclysmic events—the American Revolution and the Civil War—took place according to Feuer without any accompanying youth or student movement. A sociology of knowledge analysis of Feuer's work, insofar as it deals with American society, reveals much of the author's underlying assumptions and biases. In any event the assumption that the American Revolution was led mainly by older people has been challenged by Stanley Elkins and Eric McKitrick, while Morton Keller has suggested that generational conflict was a frequent occurrence in colonial American life and that the Revolution was seen at the time as being an uprising of sons against fathers, with only 22 percent of executive office-holders from the years 1773–1774 still in power in 1776–1777.[55]

Feuer acknowledges in his preface that *The Conflict of Generations* was written in response to his own personal experience of student movements in the course of forty years, from his student days at City College of New York in the 1920s to his presence at Berkeley as a member of the faculty during the Berkeley Student Uprising (his capitals) in 1964.[56] Before the uprising Feuer had made a study of student movements and had published his findings. When the uprising began Feuer noted that many of the errors he had noticed in other student movements were being repeated. Thus,

> As a member of the university community, I did what I could to counteract the drives to irrationality which were exhibiting themselves with growing intensity. Copies of my studies circulated among student and nonstudent leaders as well as among some of the university's administrators. The Law of Generational Struggle was in full ascendency, however, confirming my generalizations even as it rebuffed one's hopes for a higher wisdom.[57]

Feuer expresses the hope that his book, by exposing the irrationalities and self-destructiveness of the student movements, might help to overcome them.

He goes on to argue that, while generational conflict has always existed on American college campuses, it never led to the creation of a full-blown student movement. American society is exceptional in that it succeeded in diverting the potential for ideological student movements into more constructive efforts.

From this perspective Feuer proceeds to describe a series of violent clashes in American history between students and their professors and university administrations, emphasizing that in almost every instance there was no ideological confrontation and no emergence of a student political movement.[58] This seems a fair assessment of the situation in the United States, which in its overall politics is much less ideologically oriented than Europe. It is the explanation that Feuer provides that seems questionable. True to his Freudian model, Feuer claims that the reason the conflicts never became political or ideological is that there was no deauthoritization of the older generation. For some thirty pages the reader is treated to a list of violent acts, yet nowhere is there a hint that the students might be acting irrationally or destructively; ritually repeated throughout the chapter is the assertion that the older generation was never rejected and that there were no ideological overtones to the protest. The essence of Feuer's analysis is that

> there was never that upsurge of revolt against the older generation in the name of a new ethic and a new philosophy which characterizes a student movement. The young and the old in America lived by the same dreams and shared the same values
>
> Generational unrest, when it did exist, spent itself in campus outbreaks; it never emerged with politico-ideological issues to constitute a student movement.[59]

This situation was undermined in the 1930s and again in the 1960s. Ideological and political issues now becoming prevalent, Feuer activates the full power of his theoretical model, introducing his concepts of rejection and deauthoritization of the older generation. It is not the actual issues raised by the students that are the essence of the conflict but their unconscious oedipal struggles against their parents.

One of the main issues that caused conflict on the campuses in the 1960s was the war in Vietnam. Feuer does not find the war itself worth discussing but provides a facile explanation as to why the students took up this particular cause: "In the first months of 1965, the student movement began to turn rapidly from the civil rights issue to that of Vietnam. It was not that the problem of civil rights had suddenly ceased to exist; rather the issue no longer offered as good an emotional opportunity for conducting a generational struggle."[60] Feuer notes that governmental actions, such as the Voter Registration Act, had diminished the generational implications of civil rights. He goes on: "An issue was most attractive to the degree that it could readily channelize generational resentment; involvement in an issue subsided when the issue failed to provide the occasion for a clear generational struggle. It is this motivation which primarily explains the curious movement from issue to issue on the part of the student movement."[61] One would never know from this simple explanation that:

• The civil-rights movement fulfilled one of its major goals in 1964 with the passing of the civil-rights legislation, thereby reducing the need, at least temporarily, for intense activities in this specific area.

• 1965 was the year in which the crucial escalation in the war took place, immediately following elections in which the successful candidate had campaigned on an antiwar platform.

- In the sixties, many young people found constructive expression for their civil rights aspirations by government-sponsored work in programs such as Vista and the War on Poverty.
- In 1965 the Vietnam war was one of the last issues that could be expected to "channelize generational resentment." As Feuer himself notes *only one paragraph before, on the very same page*: "The overwhelming majority of the American studentry, . . . unlike their classmates in the 'student movement,' continued to support American involvement in the Vietnam War." He cites a survey showing that in 1966 only 16 percent of students were opposed to the war.
- By the time Feuer's book was published in 1969 the Vietnam War had become a major issue of American politics, and growing sections of the American population *of all age groups* were turning against the war and adopting a critical attitude similar to that of a few student activists in 1965.

It would appear that Feuer himself was a supporter of the Vietnam War. This too he does not explicitly state, but it is implied in his critique of antiwar activists:

> The new student generation could not recall the experience with American appeasement and inaction before the Second World War; they had not known the cost of rethinking which had been involved in stopping Stalin and Soviet imperialism after the war. They were a generation which knew not Joseph because it knew not Pharaoh. For the terrible fact about sociological experience is that, difficult as it is to impart from generation to generation in normal times, it is abruptly dismissed when generational struggle grows intense. '[M]any of the younger critics could not or would not remember or accept the analogies of the nineteen-thirties and nineteen-fifties for the nineteen-sixties.' A generational equilibrium allows for a cumulative principle of sociological experience and wisdom. The conflict of generations negates it.[62]

Now, this just will not do. Much of the debate over the Vietnam War revolved specifically around the key question as to whether it held parallels with Hitler and Stalin. It was specifically the question of whether the two periods were in fact analogous that was at stake. Feuer is entitled to believe that there was a parallel and to support the American effort in Vietnam, but he is not entitled casually to imply that all those who differed with him on this issue were obviously wrong since they lacked the "cumulative principle of sociological experience and wisdom." Some of the most eloquent opponents of the war belonged to the older generation, people such as Senators Wayne Morse and William J. Fulbright. The issues in the Vietnam War were manifold and complicated, involving questions of legality (interpretation of the Gulf of Tonkin Resolution, subsequently proved to have been based on false evidence; the "incursion" into Cambodia in 1970), the nature of the original conflict (a civil war or a war between two separate countries); the manner in which the war was conducted (defoliation, destroying villages "in order to save them," My Lai); the ideological perspectives (South Vietnam as a bastion of democracy or a military dictatorship); the price being paid (the casualties, the destruction of traditional Vietnamese society, America's image in the world, the investment in arms and equipment); and the pragmatic aims of the war (the domino theory and the containment of China).

There is no hint in Feuer's work of the agonizing debate that raged in American society, no hint of any logic in the attitude of the antiwar protesters. In fourteen references to the war, Feuer stresses mainly the small numbers of students involved in antiwar demonstrations. (His book came out before the nationwide campus moratorium of November 1969, when one million people, mainly students, demonstrated peacefully against the war in Washington.)

Beyond his well-worn themes of generational revolt, Feuer introduces an additional variable of a kind that he never used in his discussion of other student movements: "anti-Americanism." Some references to the war are in a short section with the subtitle, "Emergence of Anti-Americanism as a Student Ideology";[63] we read: "Anti-Americanism thus became a recognized article of faith in the ideology of generational revolt."[64]

This use, in an academic analysis, of terminology reminiscent of political sloganizing of the cheapest type (what is the precise difference between Feuer's "anti-Americanism" and Senator Joseph McCarthy's "un-Americanism"?) provides a clue to the political and ideological underpinnings of the book. At intervals throughout the book, Feuer refers positively to certain values of liberalism, capitalism, and business. At various points we read of the president of a university approvingly described as a "confirmed advocate of capitalism"; of American students wishing to emulate the leaders of business, not their professors; of the importance of bourgeois values. In no other instance does Feuer refer to radical students as being anti-Russian, anti-German, or anti-Bosnian.

It becomes almost impossible to avoid the impression that Feuer's argument is not with youth as such but only with youth, in the United States or any other country, who challenge the values to which he adheres. Precisely what these values are, Feuer does not state, but an educated guess would suggest that they are somehow bound up with the mainstream values of American society—its liberal democracy and its capitalism. These are values that are in direct opposition to what is generally represented as radical values, more specifically, perhaps, those of Marxist ideology. What upsets Feuer is not the concept of a youth movement per se, but those youth movements that challenge or threaten his values. The issues involved in capitalism versus communism, in bourgeois versus radical values, in

Marxism versus other philosophies (Freudianism, for example) are all important issues that can, should, and have been analyzed. But they must be analyzed on their own merits and cannot be subsumed or insidiously introduced into the separate issue of generational conflict. It is possible that generational conflict will overlap with these issues, but that is a changing empirical fact, not a predetermined one.

Feuer himself has clearly recognized the importance of an intellectual confrontation with the meaning, in the modern world, of Marxist thought. In 1969, the year in which his work on the conflict of generations was published, he published a separate work called *Marx and the Intellectuals: A Set of Post-Ideological Essays.*[65] In neither work is there any reference to the other (except in the biographical account about the author in the front matter of the book on Marx, where there is a reference to *The Conflict of Generations*). The book on Marx consists mainly of eleven articles that had all, except one, been published separately in the course of the previous ten years; there are also several references to these single articles in a chapter in *The Conflict of Generations* devoted to an analysis of "Alienation: The Study of Student Movements."[66]

Given the almost simultaneous publications of these two books, it is of particular interest to note Feuer's eight-page introduction to the book on Marx where he describes the intellectuals in almost identical terms to those he had used to describe the students. Feuer explains some of the personal background to the book, noting that he had once, some thirty years earlier, written a "series of articles defending historical materialism and its philosophy against what I believed were superficial criticisms, [as] [t]he Marxist philosophy, I felt, possessed certain truths its critics tended too readily to overlook."[67] Eventually he came to recognize that there were even deeper flaws in Marxist philosophy and sociology than in the criticisms leveled against them. He took up the study of Marxism again in the 1960s, this time from a critical perspective:

> Around 1960 . . . a revival of interest in Marxism began to take place in the United States which was coeval with the beginnings of a student movement. As I watched the reviving Neo-Marxism, I was disquieted by what I considered the irrationalism and amorality of the new movement. The fallacies of an older generation were evidently going to have their counterparts among the younger. Was there no law whatsoever of cumulative historical experience? In this mood I wrote from time to time the essays that compose this book.[68]

The parallels between the intellectuals and the students continue. Feuer notices the intellectuals' "motives of altruism and self-sacrifice," their alienation, their "longing to merge themselves, in an alternating dominance and submission, with the physical power of the people—peasantry, proletariat, primitive people, colored [sic] races, or backward nations."[69]

From this perspective some of the inconsistencies and nonsequiturs in *The Conflict of Generations* can be better understood. Perhaps the key to putting the puzzle of Feuer's analysis of youth together is his concluding paragraph. After devoting a book to devastating criticism of student movements, he ends it thus:

> When all our analysis is done, however, what endures is the promise and hope of a purified idealism. I recall one evening in 1963 when I met with a secret circle of Russian students at Moscow University. There were twelve or thirteen of them drawn from various fields but moved by a common aspiration toward freedom. Among them were young physicists, philosophers, economists, students of languages. Their teachers had been apologists for the Stalinist repression, and the students were groping for truthful ideas, for an honest philosophy rather than an official ideology. Clandestine papers and books circulated among them—a copy of Boris Pasternak's *Dr. Zhivago*, of George Orwell's *1984*, reprints of Western articles on Soviet literature, a revelation of the poet Osip Mandelstamm. The social system had failed to "socialize" them, had failed to stifle their longing for freedom. The elder generation was de-authorized in their eyes for its pusillanimous involvement in the "cult of personality." Here on a cold March night in a Moscow academic office I was encountering what gave hope to the future of the Soviet Union. The conflict of generations, disenthralled of its demonry, becomes a drama of substance and renewal which remains the historical bearer of humanity's highest hopes.[70]

These students were in essence repeating all the inanities of the student movements that Feuer had taken such pains to condemn. They were meeting in secret (presumably like children, so that their elders would not know); they were an insignificant minority in a total studentry of hundreds of thousands; they were circulating clandestine books among themselves (Feuer earlier derides nineteenth-century Russian students for similar activity); they had no clear-cut plan and were only groping for an honest philosophy (one of the factors, according to Feuer, that makes for irrational actions); they had deauthorized the elder generation (and so were merely acting out their oedipal conflicts). They were, in fact, a typical example of all that Feuer had condemned throughout his book, yet he sees hope in what they were doing. Why? Might one suggest that they represented values closely identified with those that Feuer believes in? Their efforts were directed against a regime that he rejects; they in no way threatened Feuer's own values. Despite their parallels with the Russian students of the nineteenth century, Feuer was unable to show the latter any similar sympathy because, I suggest, we already know in retrospect the final outcome of their activities: the establishment of the oppressive Stalinist regime and the institution of communism in the Soviet Union.

And so forsaking his theme of generational conflict, and slipping neatly into his confrontation with Marxism, Feuer ends his book with the hope that a typical student movement in Russia will lead to changes in the regime there. Yet when he wrote that final paragraph he knew full well that even this sanguine hope was almost baseless, at least as far as the group he met with was concerned. For even this modest effort to subvert the regime had succumbed to the "prying and spying" of Stalin's successors. The full story is revealed elsewhere—in Feuer's book on Marxism. Here he devotes several pages to discussing his meetings with such a group (presumably the same one), even giving details of the contents of their discussion, despite the "tacit understanding within them that their discussions are sincere and private, and not to be repeated to the authorities."[71] He ends:

> Late in the spring this circle discontinued its meetings. Fears were beginning to arise, and some persons thought that perhaps they should wait to see what conditions would be imposed by the next ideological plenum. Toward the end of May I met several of them at the Lenin Library. They were much worried. They told me that agents of the State Security had apprehended fifteen persons of another circle which was more primarily devoted to freedom of art. They had been interrogated at length, and their cases were remanded to the university for action. The Moscow University Communist apparatus had decided to expel six of the students—four of whom were from the natural sciences. The students were charged, among other things, with having fallen under "foreign" influences. I was reassured that I had never met them. But we all felt it advisable not to see each other again.[72]

One would have thought that a personal experience of this nature would, at least, have sensitized Feuer to the terrible dilemma of young people such as those in Czarist Russia or oppressed Bosnia, repelled by an oppressive regime of whatever ideology, exposed to constant surveillance, groping for truths different from those of the regime. But Feuer's compassion is touched only by those antagonistic to the Soviet regime. This selectivity is the key to understanding his approach of when to activate the simplistic Freudian model and when not. The riddle of Feuer's book is resolved by this final quote. The simplistic, straightforward Freudian model of rejection and deauthoritization of the older generation is to be used to condemn out of hand any student movement whose ideology is inconsistent with Feuer's. This allows the specific issues, whatever they are—the war in Vietnam, civil rights, anticolonialism, educational reform—to be evaded. The older generation is under no obligation to deal with the content of student protest when it is no more than an expression of unresolved oedipal conflicts, leading inexorably to irrational and self-destructive actions.

I have dealt at length with Feuer's work because it exemplifies many of the flaws and potential perversions of Freudian modes of thinking. The book itself was not written in an academic cloister or a social vacuum but as a direct response to the student unrest of the 1960s; it was meant to provide a scientific explanation for what was happening. The book does not deal with esoteric or peripheral issues, as do the analyses of mythology, religion, and literature that were dealt with earlier, but with ongoing struggles for ideological influence, popular support, and political power.

For those, particularly in the United States, who were perturbed by the depth of the ideological cleavage during the 1960s, who were upset by the challenge that the young were posing to established authority, who were incapable of coping with the questions of youth in a whole range of areas, Feuer's book provided a reassuring answer. The protests were motivated by the unresolved, unconscious hostility of the young toward their parents; the violence was a familiar phenomenon, a repetition of similar historical experiences from other countries, the consequence of allowing ideological issues to be injected into American politics, the result of destructive and suicidal tendencies. Feuer's authority as a political scientist was matched even by his personal authenticity. He had been through similar experiences in his youth and therefore possessed the special knowledge gained by the bitter experiences of his own youthful errors. Furthermore, he was also apparently sympathetic to the youths, repeatedly expressing awareness of their altruism and idealism.

Feuer's book not only provided a troubled older generation with an explanation that it was more than willing to accept, but it probably confirmed what many older people had already felt. Their inchoate impressions were now given a scientific legitimacy through piles of data and a clear, theoretical presentation.

Today, a decade after the publication of Feuer's book, it would be interesting to apply some of his terminology and perceptions to some of the political happenings of the seventies. The Watergate affair has certainly led to the total deauthoritization of the generation that ruled when Feuer's book was written and published. Can there be a more significant deauthoritization than a recommendation to impeach a President, his resignation, the prior resignation of his Vice President under a cloud of suspicion, the resignation of most of the President's confidants and advisers, the trials and convictions of many of them, a prison sentence for his Attorney General? By Feuer's reasoning, surely this was just the occasion for a total onslaught by the young against the disgraced and discredited older generation. Surely this was the very issue for the students to turn their attention to in order to intensify generational hatreds. Yet at just this moment the student movement became quiescent. Its major antagonism against President Nixon was expressed when he was at the height of his power and his popularity. Once he had been deauthoritized, deprived of power, there was no need to deal with him and what he stood for; it was while he was implementing his policies that the student movement took action against him.

Even so, his final removal from office, his actual deauthoritization, had almost nothing to do with the youth. It was his own peers, in Congress and in the courts, who deprived him of power.

Watergate has illuminated certain other factors of Feuer's analysis. There was hardly a phenomenon that Feuer did not emphasize in relation to youth that was not an integral part of the affair: there was irrational and self-destructive behavior (even in as simple a matter of taking the most elementary safeguard of destroying the incriminating tapes, at an early stage before the intervention of the court); there were the conspiratorial activities (by people in power who had nothing to fear from a secret police); there was the secrecy of those who struggled to unravel the tangled threads of the story (the devious means by which the anonymous "Deep Throat" and the journalists of the *Washington Post* arranged and executed their post midnight meetings[73] surely must have reminded Feuer of his meeting in Moscow with a secret group of students); there was dishonesty (of a type much worse than that which so shocked Feuer in the case of the Berkeley student uprising).

I do not wish to probe the Watergate affair; nor have I presented it as an example because it happens to be the other side of the American youth protest. But Watergate is an example of an extreme aberration of a duly elected regime. Whether the actions were unique or typical is open to debate; perhaps they constitute an extreme instance of irrational, secretive, self-destructive, dishonest behavior that is more or less common in the political process. When these activities appear among frustrated youths in an oppressive regime, such as Czarist or Stalinist Russia, they are at least understandable. When they appear in the inner circles of a democratically elected government swept into power by a landslide vote, then certain questions cry out for analysis. In fact, a number of writers, both academic and popular, have used psychohistory to try to understand the unconscious motivations of President Nixon.[74]

Much of what Feuer describes and condemns in student movements exists in other social and political movements, including even nonideological ones. Irrationality, self-destruction, and secrecy apparently play some part in the political process; they are not within the exclusive province of student movements. As a *polemical critique of some* radical student movements, Feuer's book makes some telling and pertinent points; as a *scientific analysis of all* student movements, it is a caricature. Yet its academic pretensions provide an aura of respectability for the prejudices and hostilities that underlie so much adult reaction to student activity.

The answer to Feuer's model cannot be a mere catalogue of his flaws and foibles; a full study of generational conflict cannot be embraced by mutual accusations of irrationality and self-destruction. The nature of both generational contacts and the political process is far more complex, rich, and positive than to be limited to purely negative aspects.

The moment one foregoes the binding constraints of a Freudian theoretical model revolving round the rejection of the parents, the positive qualities of student movements may be noticed, appreciated, and acknowledged. I shall deal with two examples to show how easily this may be achieved. What is required is not a particular proyouth bias, only a modicum of open-mindedness and goodwill.

Although Feuer's book was published one year after the revolt in Czechoslovakia, in which students played a prominent part, he makes only one passing reference to this event—to point out that the student activist in that country "shares with his father the oppression of the same totalitarian regime"[75] and that, in contrast to the pseudogoals of Western student movements, "the Czech sons . . . are in quest for real freedom together with their fathers."[76] Here was obviously an ideal opportunity to analyze the nature of the student movement under circumstances of potentially fruitful cooperation between the generations against a communist regime, but Feuer failed to seize the opportunity. Had he done so he might have found how inapplicable his theory was.

Galia Golan in fact, has shown exactly how constructive this youth movement was and how any youth movement may work in harmony with the older generation, provided the latter shares its ideological commitments.[77] In this case the joint commitment was to a liberalization of the regime. Golan notes how, in the years preceding the revolt, the Czechoslovakian regime had been antagonistic to youth organizations, not because it feared their opposition to the regime as a separate movement but for precisely the opposite reason—that "the youth would join forces—were clearly doing so—with their elders among the liberals."[78]

The young had been "raised in an atmosphere of shame and even contempt for the capitulation of 1938" (the deauthoritization of the elder generation?),

> and it was little comfort that the students had heroically resisted the occupation of Czechoslovakia in 1939. In 1968 the young people were intent upon *not* repeating the shameful mistake of the past. Their open and courageous defiance in the days of the invasion may be seen in this light, and indeed many older Czechs felt that the young people's behaviour had restored their pride.[79]

Even though the revolt was crushed through Russian intervention, "it would not be true to say that the younger generation had been broken, for it continues to organize protest wherever and however it can. The alliance between young workers and students has held, as has the broader alliance of youth with the liberals of the older generation."[80]

Even a youth that was less heroic and positive may be seen in a perspective very different from that portrayed by Feuer. While Feuer assigns almost total responsibility for Hitler's success to the German youth movements, he discusses them only in perfunctory fashion, ignoring major books on the topic, such as those by Howard Becker[81] and Walter Laqueur.[82] Neither Becker nor Laqueur is sparing of the failings of German youth in general or, more specifically, of the fact that some elements of the youth supported Hitler in his rise to power. But the final overall assessment is more complicated. Laqueur specifically apportions the blame to the students for their share of the responsibility but adds that, with but very few exceptions, the blame is shared with all other German movements and parties. Since the youth did not have the decisive political power in the state, their sins were more those of omissions, of not having done more to block the Nazis in their rise to power.

Unlike Feuer, Laqueur remembers that there were young people who opposed Hitler to the end, and he cites the bravery of those who defied Nazism and the penalty paid by many of left-wing persuasion, who were sent to concentration camps or sentenced to death. Laqueur concludes that in Germany's darkest hours: "there were witnesses to the survival of a more human Germany, albeit submerged and none too numerous . . . and a good few of them came from the youth movement."[83]

In another work, taking issue specifically with Feuer, Laqueur argues that "peaceful change is not always possible in history, nor are patience and prudence invariably the best counsel."[84] Drawing on the examples of both the Munich students who revolted against Hitler in 1943 (an event ignored by Feuer) and the student rebels recently sentenced in the Soviet Union, Laqueur goes on to argue that, had they limited themselves to rational considerations, they might well have refused to act and chosen instead to acquiesce in tyranny:

> To their eternal credit such rational considerations did not enter the students' minds. The impetuosity, the impatience, and sometimes the madness of youth movements had been a liberating force in the struggle against tyranny and dictatorship. Tyranny cannot be overthrown unless at least some people are willing to sacrifice their lives, and those willing to do so usually do not come from the ranks of the senior citizens.[85]

This analysis does not prevent Laqueur from criticizing youth movements elsewhere, including those of the 1960s in the United States. But his criticisms relate to empirical evidence carefully examined, unlike Feuer, who tailored the wealth of data at his disposal to fit his particular theoretical mold.

But even Laqueur's criticism of Feuer's attitude to German youth may be based on only a partial assessment of youth opposition to Hitler. Daniel Horn argues very convincingly that a significant proportion of German youth was strongly opposed to the Nazi regime and was considered by the Nazi leaders to constitute a threat to the legions of the Hitler youth.[86] Horn not only documents the evidence of such opposition but also suggests that there has been an incorrect perception of how widespread this opposition was because both Nazi propaganda and Allied stereotyping led to the widespread assumption that all of Germany's youth had succumbed to the ideology of the Hitler Youth. Much of this opposition was in the form of "wild gangs," and most writers who have noted their activities have dismissed them as little more than delinquent groupings, since they lacked any clearly formulated ideology. Horn criticizes particularly the German writers who have minimized the youthful opposition. He sees their approach as being determined more by the needs of their ideological position than actual reality: "[T]hese writers, most of whom were former members of the pre-Hitler Jugendbewegung, have been so blinded by their own tradition and to a certain extent by a pronounced middle-class bias that they have been unable to conceive of a youth opposition existing without the traditions and ideology of the bundische Jugend."[87] In fact he notes that the only German author, Arno Klonne, "who acknowledged the importance of the wild clique phenomenon never published his real findings"; in a private communication Klonne specifically argues that the youthful opposition was probably more meaningful than that of the adults, and that, however subsequent writers have perceived it, the Nazis themselves clearly recognized it as a real threat to their system.

Richard Flacks, a participant in the youth revolt of the sixties but on the other side of the barrier from Feuer, also suggests that the possibility of intergenerational communication and cooperation is always present; when it breaks down, it may be the adult generation that is at fault.[88] Specifically rejecting the oedipal thesis, Flacks suggests that cooperation between the generations, as occurred in Czechoslovakia, is always a possibility, but it depends not only on the students but also on their elders:

> The history of the new left in the United States, and student movements elsewhere, suggests that hostility toward the older generation becomes fully manifest when substantial segments of the adult generation do not use available opportunities to oppose the existing regime and to promote social reform. When adult reform movements are vigorously active, youth are more likely to join them than to seek independent means of political expression.[89]

A similar approach is adopted by Robert Michels, who was also involved in the events of the sixties, not as a protagonist but as a psychoanalyst who worked with some of the student leaders.[90] He strongly attacks those who use facile oedipal explanations to describe student dissent, which leads only to "a onesided paternal view" and "is usually offered by those over 30 to explain the behavior of youth as irrational rebellion."[91] In contrast to those, such as Feuer, who see youth using the larger societal arena to express their oedipal hatred of their parents, Michels claims that "most of us who have studied specific student leaders of these revolts (real people, not myths) have been impressed by their warm and close relations with their parents and their tendency to resemble them in political philosophy."[92] Michels concludes: "Facile explanations which see student rebellions as reflecting failure to resolve oedipal complexes, without discussing adult response in similar terms, are biased and unscientific."[93]

Feuer's failure to deal with the positive facts adduced by Golan, Laqueur, Flacks, Michels, and others constitutes a serious lacuna in his work. It is indeed strange that his extensive collation of facts should, in the end, turn out to be so selective. No less than his theorizing, even Feuer's empirical research would seem to have been unduly affected by his basic Freudian model. The errors in his book can best be understood in terms of the ideological underpinning of his book, with its commitment to the status quo and, in generational terms, its identification with the older generation.

Feuer himself is insistent on the scientific and nonideological nature of his book. He is also ruthlessly critical of those who allow ideology to be imposed on scientific analysis. Feuer's own detailed views on ideology were stated in *Ideology and the Ideologists*,[94] wherein he condemns ideologists in terms that overlap with his earlier critique of student movements and of radical intellectuals.

In many respects, his book published in 1975, is a repetition of his earlier attack on the young. One chapter is devoted to an analysis of the "generational basis for ideological waves."[95] Feuer draws a sharp distinction between the intellectual activities of the different generations: The young are ideological, the old (or to be more precise, the middle-aged) are scientific. Most contributions to intellectual thought are made by those who have grown into the postideological phase of their lives. According to Feuer:

> An ideological wave always has its followers among the young. The doctrine itself is often formulated by an elder thinker who stands in relation of a "master-intellectual," or "youth master," or "father-figure" to the young. But it is young intellectuals who feel the need for ideology, for its assignment to them of a historical mission, for its charter of an opportunity to define themselves and their own ideas in rupture with the old ideological thinking arises primarily not from an economic unconscious but a generational unconscious. Its underlying aim is to provide the dramatic outline, the myth . . . for its dethronement of the elders (now Establishment figures) and for the coming to power of the new generation as an intellectual elite; the more reluctant the ideologists are to avow their latent goal—they stress their manifest goal, the historic mission of the class, race, or nation.[96]

Caught up in the excitement of an ideological cause, sharing ideas with their cogenerationists, young intellectuals forsake the scientific mode of thought. Thus there can never be an end of ideology, for "so long as there are new generations of young intellectuals, ideology, as a mode of thought, will be recurrent."[97]

In the course of time, as they grow older, the young intellectuals drop their ideology and are capable, in their postideological phase, of doing serious, constructive, realistic, and scientific work: "By middle age, most former ideologists have become de-ideologized. They have become scientific. . . ."[98]

To Feuer, the debate over the possibility of a value-free and neutral social science reflects the different generational approaches to intellectual endeavor, with the young, by arguing for a normative approach, seeking to discredit the scientific and objective work of their elders: Thus "in the sixties . . . the Utopian impulse revived strongly among the new generation of social scientists. . . . They were . . . in revolt against the classics in social science, which, written by men in their middle age, were largely de-ideologized works."[99] Feuer then notes that Marx, Pareto, Weber and Durkheim were in their forties and fifties when they wrote their major works. To this list he then adds a fifth name, Freud, who "was an old man when he wrote his sociological essays."[100]

Here is a further puzzle in Feuer's work. I have already mentioned the rather curious phenomenon that Feuer, despite having extensively used the Freudian framework, avoids any direct acknowledgment of his intellectual antecedents and of his undoubted indebtedness to Freud for providing the theoretical framework upon which his key concepts of rejection and of deauthoritization of the elders is based. Even more puzzling, however, is Feuer's discussion of ideology in terms of what he calls the "Mosaic myth."[101] Feuer claims that all ideologies have their roots in a Mosaic myth, which gives " 'meaning' to the lives of the younger generational intellectuals," in which they see themselves as reenacting the key aspects of the life of Moses, from the initial situation where "A people is oppressed; . . . [and] a young man, not himself of the oppressed, appears," through the liberation of that people, the declaration of a code of law for them, their reluctance to obey the new rules, and the struggle by a false prophet against the leader, to the ultimate success of the leader and his climactic death as a revered lawgiver, "as he glimpses from afar the new existence."[102]

Feuer notes that both Karl Marx and Ferdinand Lasalle used the story of Moses to draw attention to the nature of their political struggle, while Lincoln Steffens "wrote a whole book *Moses in Red* to show that *Exodus* was the classical model for all revolutions."[103]

Yet, interestingly, not one of these writers was as closely identified with the figure of Moses as was Freud. Not only did Freud devote his final published work to a full-length and controversial analysis of the life and death of Moses but, throughout his life, he showed an ongoing fascination at the deepest and most personal level with the biblical figure. As Paul Roazen writes: "It is well known that the figure of Moses had a special fascination

for Freud";[106] while David Bakan writes: "The primary key to the understanding of Freud is contained in his concern with Moses."[105] Freud's
correspondence with Arnold Zweig also contains several references to his
interest in Moses,[106] long before he actually published his book. Ernest
Jones, in his biography of Freud, concludes his discussion of *Moses and
Monotheism:*

> We cannot refrain from wondering how, when nearing his end, Freud came to
> be so engrossed in [these] topics . . . and to devote to them all his intellectual
> interest during the last five years of his life. To answer such questions we have
> to hark back to the earliest riddles of life that perplexed him . . . his personal
> identity and the problem of his birth, as with every child, but in more mature
> years this had taken the wider form of interest in the nature and origin of man
> in general.[107]

Gregory Zilboorg expresses similar sentiments:

> It does seem that in *Moses* Freud attained the completion of a deeply seated
> and greatly cherished idea that demanded expression in some sort of rational
> order. It does appear that he rounded out, so to speak, with one system of
> thought the origin of neuroses in man as an individual and the origin of belief
> in God in man as a race. The hypothesis of parricide seemed to be *the* missing
> link, and to Freud the clue to understanding man's yearning for a knowledge
> of God.[108]

There can be little doubt then that Freud, both in his early years and the
final stages of his life, had been intrigued by the story of Moses and had
sensed many personal parallels between his own life and that of the biblical
character. Far more than for any of the radical writers mentioned by Feuer,
Freud had been deeply and personally involved with what Feuer calls the
"Mosaic myth." Yet Feuer fails to mention Freud's book. Of course, it had
been written by Freud when he was already old and in his "post-ideological
phase," and so it was hardly compatible with Feuer's theory. But then why
mention Freud at all as an example of a person who, in his old age, "wrote
his sociological essays," of which one of the most important was ironically a
controversial presentation, based on dubious empirical evidence, of the
Moses myth?

Perhaps more than any other modern intellectual, Freud was deeply
gripped by the drama of the Mosaic myth. Is there an explanation for this
that would be compatible with the thesis of both *The Conflict of Generations*
and *Ideology and the Ideologists?*

I very much doubt it. For whatever the value of *Conflict of Generations* in
terms of its accumulation of data, the style of writing, the consistent pursuit
of a coherent theory, or the provocative thesis advanced, the book is a
typical example of an essentially ideological discussion of social phenomena.

There is nothing inherently wrong in this, since, as Karl Mannheim and others have remarked, social thinking cannot be completely value-free.

The danger of ideological writing arises only when the writer attempts to deny his ideological biases and to claim that his work is pure, objective science. Louis Wirth notes in his preface to Mannheim's *Ideology and Utopia* that thought

> becomes fully comprehensible only if it is viewed sociologically. This involves tracing the basis of social judgments to their specific interest-bound roots in society, through which the particularity, and hence the limitations, of each view will become apparent.[109]

Although I have not explored all the influences on Feuer's work, neither his views on the major political philosophies of the modern era nor his personal place in the social structure, it is clear that his theories of generational conflict reflect his membership in the adult world and are designed to defend the interests of that world against those, the young, who challenge it.

As an ideological tract, Feuer's book on the generations is important, stimulating, deserving of discussion. As science, it is an almost classic example of the use of a theoretical framework to mask the true intentions of the writer and his basic ideological position.

References

1. Lewis S. Feuer, *The Conflict of Generations: The Character and Significance of Student Movements* (New York: Basic Books, 1969).

2. Ibid., chapter 9, "The Berkeley Student Uprising: 1964–1966," pp. 436–500.

3. Ibid., p. ix. It might be noted that in referring to "Oedipal determinism," Feuer adds "as John Stuart Mill called it," thereby accentuating the determinism, since Mill dealt with determinism and not Oedipal ideas.

4. Most writers who have commented on the book have had little difficulty recognizing its Freudian base. Those writing from a Freudian base have given the book strong support. See Robert Endelman, "Oedipal Elements in Student Rebellion," *Psychoanalytic Review* 57 (1970): 442. He adds his own interpretation: "If we set side by side the evidence of parricidal rage shown in the burning or tearing to pieces of an effigy of the college president with the intention of the rebels to take over *alma mater* from the paternal authorities, one can certainly construct a picture of an at least symbolic revolt" (p. 459).

5. Feuer, *The Conflict of Generations*, p. 9. For an almost identical quote, see p. 162.

6. Ibid., pp. 89–90.

7. Ibid., p. 92.

8. Ibid., p. 9. For an almost identical statement, see pp. 161–162.

9. Ibid. See also p. 162.

10. Ibid., p. 93.

11. Ibid., p. 93.

12. Ibid. Feuer quotes from N. P. Arhesov, *Sophia Perovskaya* (St. Petersburg, 1920), Vera Figner, *Memoirs of a Revolutionist* (New York: Greenwood Press (reprint), 1968), David Footman, *Red Prelude* (New Haven: Yale University Press, 1945); Avrahm Yarmolinsky, *Road to Revolution* (New York: Macmillan, 1959).

13. Feuer, *The Conflict of Generations*, p. 93.

14. Ibid.

15. Ibid, p. 308.

16. Ibid.

17. See Bertram D. Wolfe, *Three Who Made a Revolution: A Biographical History* (New York: Dial Press, 1948).

18. Feuer, *The Conflict of Generations*, p. 96.

19. Ibid., p. 22.

20. Ibid., p. viii.

21. Ibid., p. 312.

22. Ibid.

23. For a discussion of Stalin's possible implication in the death of Kirov, see Malise Ruthven, *Torture: The Grand Conspiracy* (London: Weidenfeld & Nicolson, 1978), pp. 222–225.

24. Feuer, *The Conflict of Generations*, p. 10.

25. Ibid.

26. Ibid., p. 8.

27. Ibid.

28. Ibid., p. 57. For a fuller discussion of the Wartburg Festival, see Anthony Esler, *Bombs, Beards and Barricades: 150 Years of Youth in Revolt* (New York: Stein & Day, 1971), pp. 53–60. This book, by an historian, discusses many of the events dealt with by Feuer and stresses the role of social generations in furthering social change. In general, Esler provides a balanced picture of youth revolt, in both its positive and negative aspects.

29. Feuer, *The Conflict of Generations*, p. 290.

30. Ibid.

31. Ibid., p. 363.

32. Ibid., p. 318.

33. Ibid.

34. Ibid., p. 353.

35. Ibid., p. vii.

36. Ibid., p. 9. See an almost identical statement on p. 85.

37. Ibid., p. 76.

38. Ibid., p. 84.

39. Ibid., p. 81.

40. Ibid., p. 86.

41. Ibid., p. 85.

42. Ibid.

43. Ibid., and similar statement on p. 9.

44. See Barbara Tuchman, *The Guns of August* (New York: Macmillan, 1962).

45. S. N. Eisenstadt, *From Generation to Generation: Age Groups and Social Structure* (Glencoe: Free Press, 1956).

46. Ibid., p. 311.

47. Ibid., p. 312.

48. Ibid., p. 311.

49. Ibid., p. 314.

50. Kenneth Keniston, *Young Radicals* (New York: Harcourt Brace, 1968).

51. Eisenstadt, *From Generation to Generation,* pp. 306–323.

52. Ibid., p. 311.

53. Ibid., especially pp. 98–101. As a fellow Israeli and a former member of a Zionist youth movement, Habonim, I too have been affected by the positive contribution that youth movements can make to their society. This ideological belief has obviously influenced my own appraisal of the role of youth in political and social struggles.

54. Feuer, *The Conflict of Generations,* p. 318.

55. Stanley Elkins and Eric McKitrick, "The Founding Fathers: Young Men of the Revolution," *Political Science Quarterly* 76 (1961): 181–216; and Morton Keller, "Reflections on Politics and Generations in America," *Daedalus* 107 (Fall 1978): 126.

56. Feuer, *The Conflict of Generations,* pp. vii–viii.

57. Ibid., p. viii.

58. Ibid., chapter 7, "Generational Equilibrium in the United States," pp. 318–384.

59. Ibid., p. 327.

60. Ibid., p. 414.

61. Ibid.

62. Ibid., p. 413. Feuer does not tell us whom he is quoting on younger critics' refusing to see the analogies between the 1930s and the 1960s.

63. Ibid., pp. 414–416.

64. Ibid., p. 415.

65. Lewis S. Feuer, *Marx and the Intellectuals: A Set of Post-Ideological Essays* (Garden City, N.Y.: Anchor, 1969).

66. Feuer, *The Conflict of Generations,* chapter 10, pp. 501–534.

67. Feuer, *Marx and the Intellectuals,* p. 1.

68. Ibid. It should be noted that most of these articles were written before 1965, i.e., according to Feuer, when the student movement was still involved in its presumably commendable struggle for civil rights, before it turned to the issue of the Vietnam war.

69. Ibid., p. 2.

70. Feuer, *The Conflict of Generations,* p. 531.

71. Feuer, *Marx and the Intellectuals,* p. 252.

72. Ibid., p. 255. Feuer even notes that some of the Russian students sensed a kinship with the "anti-organizationism" of American beatniks.

73. Carl Bernstein and Bob Woodward, *All the President's Men* (New York: Simon & Schuster, 1974).

74. See, for instance, Bruce Mazlish, *In Search of Nixon: A Psychohistorical Inquiry* (New York: Basic Books, 1972), and Eli S. Chesen, *President Nixon's Psychiatric Profile: A Psycho-dynamic-Genetic Interpretation* (New York: Peter H. Wyden, 1973).

75. Feuer, *The Conflict of Generations,* p. 310.

76. Ibid., p. 311.

77. Galia Golan, "Youth and Politics in Czechoslovakia," *Journal of Contemporary History* 5 (1970): 3–22.

78. Ibid., p. 8.

79. Ibid., p. 19.

80. Ibid., p. 22.

81. Howard Becker, *German Youth—Bond or Free?* (London: Kegan Paul, Trench, Trubner, 1946).

82. Walter Z. Laqueur, *Young Germany: A History of the German Youth Movement* (New York: Basic Books, 1962). For a contemporary account of the Wandervögel, see Stanley High, *The Revolt of Youth* (New York: Abingdon Press, 1923), pp. 54–99.

83. Laqueur, *Young Germany,* p. 214.

84. Walter Laqueur, "Reflections on Youth Movements," in Peter K. Manning, ed., *Youth: Divergent Perspectives* (New York: John Wiley, 1973), p. 67; reprinted from *Commentary* 47 (June 1969): 33–41.

85. Ibid.

86. Daniel Horn, "Youth Resistance in the Third Reich: A Social Portrait," *Journal of Social History* 7 (1973): 28–43. For confirmation of Horn's contention that the youth opposed Hitler see Lawrence Walker, *Hitler Youth and Catholic Youth: 1933–1936* (Washington: Catholic University of America, 1970). In contrast to Horn, Walker deals with organized youth activity—in the Catholic youth movements. For a contrary view of German youth, see Peter Loewenberg's psychoanalytical study, where he argues that the youth were an important factor in the Nazis' rise

to power: "Psychohistorical Origins of the Nazi Youth Cohort," *American Historical Review,* 76 (1971): 1457.

87. Horn, "Youth Resistance in the Third Reich" p. 27.

88. Richard Flacks, *Youth and Social Change* (Chicago: Markham, 1971).

89. Ibid., pp. 89–90.

90. Robert Michels, "Student Dissent," *Journal of the American Psychoanalytic Association,* 19 (1971): 417.

91. Ibid., p. 425.

92. Ibid.

93. Ibid., p. 431. Although Michels does not refer to Feuer directly in the text he includes him in his bibliography.

94. Lewis S. Feuer, *Ideology and the Ideologists* (New York: Harper Torchbooks, 1975).

95. Ibid., chapter 3, pp. 69–95.

96. Ibid., p. 69.

97. Ibid.

98. Ibid.

99. Ibid., p. 115.

100. Ibid.

101. Ibid., pp. 1–16.

102. Ibid., p. 2.

103. Ibid., p. 4.

104. Paul Roazen, *Freud: Political and Social Thought* (New York: Knopf, 1970), p. 168.

105. David Bakan, *Sigmund Freud and the Jewish Mystical Tradition* (Princeton, N.J.: D. Van Nostrand, 1958), p. 121.

106. See Ernst L. Freud, ed., *The Letters of Sigmund Freud and Arnold Zweig* (New York: Harcourt Brace, 1970).

107. Ernest Jones, *The Life and Work of Sigmund Freud,* vol. 3 (New York: Basic Books, 1957), p. 367.

108. Gregory Zilboorg, *Psychoanalysis and Religion* (New York: Farrar, Straus and Cudahy, 1962), p. 223.

109. Louis Wirth, "Introduction" to Karl Mannheim, *Ideology and Utopia* (New York: Harvest n.d.) p. xxvi.

PART THREE
THE RUSTUM COMPLEX

CHAPTER SEVEN
CHILDREN OF
ALL AGES

The full story of parent-child or adult-youth relationships within an historical context will probably never be known. In many areas the data are incomplete and relate mainly to physical and material facts. It is not possible, even when dealing with modern times, to delve fully into the world of childhood in order to discover the manifold ways in which harm may be subtly caused to the child.

Below a certain age the evidence is locked deeply in the recesses of the unconscious. In other cases some of the evidence could be gleaned only after the development of the medical technology that has become available in recent years. Thus, in the past, not only were there no psychologists, sociologists, or social workers carrying out practical work and field research, but there was no machinery for revealing the broken bones and internal bleeding of battered and bullied children. The technological advances of modern medicine, especially X-rays, have enabled doctors to find the hidden clues of vicious physical attacks on infants and children too weak to defend themselves and too young or frightened to report the deeds. How many children in earlier times carried the secret knowledge of such beatings hidden in their unconscious—or to their early graves? We know much of the anguish of peoples, nations, and tribes with which history has dealt severely, for scribes often recorded, and historians later related, the events,[1] but not always is similar evidence available for children of different societies and different periods of time.

Even with their technology, modern pediatricians, radiologists, and surgeons have not always been cognizant of the real meaning of their medical diagnoses.[2] Often it was easier and more convenient to unquestioningly accept the explanation of the parents that an accident had taken place. It is only recently that there have developed an awareness of the battered-child syndrome and an openness to investigate in this direction. Yet, despite this awareness of the battered-child syndrome, despite the sophisticated technical means of revealing it, despite the legal sanctions obligating the reporting of such incidents, there is a general consensus that only a small percentage of the total number of cases are made known to the authorities.[3] And for the present the battered-child syndrome deals mainly with physical harm; it is generally not applied to the mental torments, the verbal humiliation, and the social indignities suffered through the abuse of absolute parental/adult power.

Where there is historical and sociological evidence about childhood, it is not always clear-cut. In modern times, such ostensibly progressive institutions and laws as juvenile courts, compulsory education, and the prohibition of child labor have come under attack.[4] It is even more difficult to evaluate institutions in other societies as recorded by historians and anthropologists. Where absolute legal powers were given to parents, including the right of life and death, were these powers merely the dead letter of the law, or were they rights regularly enforced? Are the ceremonial rites of passage to be seen as a positive educative means of absorbing the young into society, or a cruel, threatening means of enforcing conformity and ensuring compliance with the wishes of the elder generation?

As the interest in historical analyses of childhood has increased, and as the evidence has mounted, a supplementary issue has emerged: the overall historical trend of the phenomenon being examined. Briefly put, are things getting better or worse? Has modern civilization done away with the injustices imposed on children, or has its value system merely created the need for other means of control? Has the basic nature of parent-child or adult-youth relations remained constant, or has there been a change, a progression to a healthy interaction, or a retrogression into a more negative one? Are we merely repeating, in modern guise, harmful actions toward the young, or are we on the point of a major breakthrough in thought and practice that will provide additional protection and extended rights for the young?

The issue has been delineated in the debate between some of the leading modern scholars of the history of childhood. In one of the best known works in this area, Philippe Aries claims that the medieval family, by its benign indifference, actually provided more freedom, respect and equality for the child than the modern family, which, though outwardly concerned with the welfare of the child and committed to his independence, has, in fact, imposed far greater controls.[5] Aries suggests that children were better off in medieval times, since there was no age or class stratification, in contrast to modern society with its antagonistic social groupings. Since there was no clear-cut age differentiation of childhood, or for that matter of adolescence, children grew up as an integral accepted part of society. Since there was no differentiation there was also no discrimination.

Aries cites extensive evidence drawn from art, diaries, iconography, styles of clothing, use of language, and types of games to show how children were almost invariably treated as adults and incorporated directly into social life.

Centuries of Childhood has had a tremendous impact and has been approvingly cited by historians and sociologists impressed by the creative use of neglected data in order to form a reliable picture of social life within an historical perspective. It has also excited the imagination of some critics of modern society, who have drawn upon it in order to suggest the superiority of premodern patterns of social and family life and in order to stress the practicability and advantages of alternative approaches.

Shulamith Firestone, for example, in a study combining Marxist and feminist theory, quotes extensively from Aries's thesis in order to point out the exploitation of children in modern times, compared to the freedom and joy that characterized their lives in the medieval family.[6] According to her, it was the emergence of childhood as a separate life situation (akin to class) that led to the segregation of children and to their subsequent subjugation:

> The development of the modern family meant the breakdown of a large, integrated society into small, self-centered units. The child within these conjugal units now became important; for he was the product of that unit, the reason for its maintenance. It became desirable to keep one's children at home for as long as possible to bind them psychologically, financially and emotionally to the family unit until such time as they were ready to create a new family unit. For this purpose the Age of Childhood was created . . . the concept of childhood dictated that children were a species different not just in age, but in kind, from adults. An ideology was developed to prove this.[7]

Richard Farson, in a thought-provoking book that argues for children's rights, has also approvingly noted Aries's thesis.[8] Chapter 2 of his book, entitled "The Invention of Children," provides a concise precis of Aries's major arguments.[9]

Aries himself poses the family in conflict with society. "Sociability and the concept of the family were incompatible, and could develop only at each other's expense."[10] Further, "the modern family . . . cuts itself off from the world, and opposes to society the isolated group of parents and children."[11]

While this presumed accent on the children could certainly be given a positive interpretation, Aries deprecates it, claiming that the family and the educational institutions have deprived children of their innate spontaneity and imposed on them demands of discipline. While his critique of the modern situation has much validity, his enthusiasm for medieval society raises a number of questions.

Although Aries argues that the idea of childhood did not exist in medieval society, he assures his readers that

> this is not to suggest that children were neglected, forsaken or despised. The idea of childhood is not to be confused with affection for children: it corresponds to an awareness of the particular nature of childhood, that particular nature which distinguishes the child from the adult, even the young adult. In medieval society this awareness was lacking. That is why, as soon as the child

could live without the constant solicitude of his mother, his nanny or his cradle-rocker, he belonged to adult society.[12]

It is not always clear why Aries is so approving of the lack of childhood or of some of the practices in the medieval family that he recounts, nor, in fact, why the book has been so widely acclaimed. One sometimes senses that the impact of the book may be a consequence of the originality of the approach—the use of paintings and styles of clothing to reconstruct the past—and that the details themselves were not closely examined by those who praised the book. Later writers working specifically in Aries's chosen area have, in fact, been critical of his thesis.

A major criticism of the work was published by David Hunt, whose analysis of the psychology of family life in early modern France[13] contains an attempt to fuse Aries's historical methodology with Erik Erikson's psychological theory of the interlocking life cycles of parents and children.[14] While appreciative of much of Aries's work, Hunt is critical of many of the details and of the theoretical perspective.

Hunt claims that, inasmuch as there was indeed indifference to the very young in medieval society, and inasmuch as there was no accent on childhood as such, this did not necessarily lead to a healthy interaction between the generations nor to an easy absorption of the young into the society; on the contrary, it signified "a reluctance or an inability to analyze infantile needs, and a comparatively insensitive treatment of the very young."[15] Whereas Aries and Firestone are positive in their assessments of a society with no distinctions between young and old, they downplay the vital importance of a basic fact: the world of childhood is a different one from that of adults, with separate needs, sensations, and perceptions.

To recognize that distinction, and to create special institutions, is, of course, no guarantee of providing children with their necessary requirements. But to ignore it is almost certainly to ensure inequitable practices toward the young.

As Hunt notes, part of the unfortunate consequences of ignoring the special world of infants and children may be seen within the evidence provided by Aries himself. For instance, Aries deals at length with the childhood experiences of Louis XIII, whose childhood, in the first years of the seventeenth century, was recorded in minute detail by his doctor at the court, Jean Heroard.[16] Aries claims that this particular childhood may be seen as typical, even though it was that of a future king, and argues that "no other document can give us a better idea of the non-existence of the modern idea of childhood at the beginning of the seventeenth century."[17] Whether this contention is correct or not (and it has been challenged),[18] what is of particular interest is Aries's uncritical presentation of everything that was done to the young prince, whether positive (successfully teaching him to play the violin at seventeen months), neutral (many of the child's accomplishments that impress Aries would not seem extraordinary to the average preschool teacher), or negative (such as sexual abuse).[19]

In the latter case, Aries notes that, in contrast to contemporary morality, which requires "adults to avoid any reference . . . to sexual matters in the presence of children, [t]his notion was entirely foreign to the society of old."[20] Aries sees nothing wrong with this and argues that the attitude of the royal court to the young prince in sexual matters is proof positive of his overall theme of the nonexistence of childhood.

The data that he presents seem, on the contrary, to indicate not an open attitude that would give the child a positive approach to sex from an early age, but bawdiness and ribaldry that amount occasionally to downright sexual abuse. Here are a few examples quoted by Aries:

> During his first three years nobody showed any reluctance or saw any harm in jokingly touching the child's sexual parts.

> His nanny had told him, "Monsieur, never let anybody touch your nipples, or your cock, or they will cut it off.

> He was undressed and Madama too [his sister], and they were placed naked in bed with the king, where they kissed and twittered and gave great amusement to the king.

> His servants, who were sometimes married, slept in his bedroom, and do not seem to have allowed his presence to embarrass them.

> At the age of fourteen years two months . . . he was put almost by force into his wife's bed. After the [wedding] ceremony . . . a few young lords told him some broad stories to encourage him. He asked for his slippers and put on his robe and went to the Queen's bedchamber . . . where he was put to bed beside the Queen, his wife, in the presence of the Queen his mother.[21]

Recognizing the questionable nature of many of the examples, Aries notes: "This lack of reserve with regard to children surprises us: we raise our eyebrows at the outspoken talk but even more at the bold gestures, the physical contacts, about which it is easy to imagine what a modern psycho-analyst would say. The psycho-analyst would be wrong."[22] Aries is at pains to make clear that although he has presented the record of a prince, "there is no reason to believe that the moral climate was any different in other families, whether of nobles or commoners; the practice of associating children with the sexual ribaldries of adults formed part of contemporary manners."[23]

Aries is correct in pointing out that such behavior was not deviant since it was part of a cultural milieu sanctioning it. But that is merely to beg the question. What is at issue is that very milieu, the actual treatment accorded to the young. The more such behavior is seen as being part of the norm, and not a mere aberration, the more serious it is. One need not be a modern psychologist to appreciate that something is wrong in the behavior described. It was not an expression of openness and honesty about sex, nor the encouragement of legitimate infantile desires for tender, tactile contact advocated by neo-Freudians such as Reik, Suttie, Horney, Brown and Marcuse, but an exploitation of that sexuality for adult titillation.

In sum, Louis XIII's early years, far from being idyllic as Aries suggests, were full of harmful actions perpetrated against him by servants, most of them untrained and uncaring, including a governess "whom one observer characterized as a 'violent and unkind' woman,"[24] and with almost no proper surveillance or even regular contacts with his own parents.

The use of governesses, nurses, and servants was not limited to royalty; it was a common practice among all those with means, who also used wet nurses for infants and sometimes even transferred their children to the nurse's lodgings. The nurses themselves were untrained, often poor, motivated more by the financial remuneration than the challenge or joy of looking after young children. The parents saw in this custom a means of regaining their freedom; it especially released the mother "from the job of childrearing [which] tended to degrade the mother who undertook it."[25]

Hunt, however, believes that the real initiative for such arrangements probably came from the husband: "Putting a baby out to nurse had the effect of leaving the mother at the disposal of her mate. If the child remained on his mother's breast, the husband would then find himself in the position of competing for the attentions and loyalty of his wife. He had much to lose if his spouse became absorbed in the pleasure and duties of motherhood."[26]

The husband of the wet nurse came off worst in the arrangement. Unable to afford to send away his own child, he was forced by his poverty to accept temporarily an additional strange child into the home, in order to take pecuniary advantage of his wife's nursing capacities: "The psychological and social spheres interlock. The upper-class father buys a clear Oedipal victory, keeping the mother to himself. This victory is the more complete if the child is sent away into the nurse's home. The husband of the latter, unable to remove the first child who stood between him and his wife, is now doubly defeated by the coming of a second rival."[27]

Hunt sums up the social and psychological consequences of the practice of using wet nurses. The infant "was told that his mother's breasts were forbidden and that his father did not want him around. These were the first of the hard realities which . . . made up the curriculum of childhood in the old regime,"[28] a society in which "fathers and mothers were not always overjoyed by conception and the birth of children, and so abortions, infanticide and abandoned children were often resorted to."[29]

While critical of the child-rearing practices of seventeenth-century French society, Hunt is also sensitively aware of their problems. In expounding on them he touches at the root of generational tensions:

I hope that earlier discussion has made clear how hard pressed adults were by the various challenges of bringing up small children. Feeding and caring for them, as well as dealing with their aggressive and sexual impulses, severely taxed parental patience, understanding and physical ability. Cause and effect are of course difficult to separate, but I think that much of the repudiation of children, the refusal to see them as completely human, was prompted by the nagging awareness that they, the parents, were not able to fathom the secrets of this stage of life and were conspicuously unsuccessful in keeping children alive and well. The various ways in which adults categorized children as little animals amounted to an unconscious confession of failure. Finally, out of frustration, adults located the fault in infancy itself, dismissing it as a kind of disease.[30]

Whereas Aries stresses the positive benefits that arise out of the early incorporation of children into adult society, an earlier study, using a similar methodological approach, and coming to almost identical conclusions as to the lack of a clear-cut stage of childhood, sets out explicitly some of the difficulties and dangers arising out of such lack of differentiation between children and adults. In his study of "the place of children in the life and thought of New England churches,"[31] Sandford Fleming not only preceded Aries in the use of paintings to recapture earlier social life; he also examined the role of the child in church beliefs and practices, through references to children in books and sermons, and came to the identical conclusion that "children were regarded simply as miniature adults."[32]

Fleming sees the numerous references not as advantageous to children but as indicative of a failure to appreciate the child and his uniqueness. While "it would seem that children had a fairly large place in church life," this was only superficially so; "in reality the child as such had no recognition. There was an utter failure to appreciate the distinction between the child and the adult."[33] This conclusion accords with Aries's perception. Fleming, however, believes that such nondifferentiation led to children's being exposed to doctrines and ceremonies that were probably extremely harmful. Stressing the Puritan approach to religion, Fleming claims that the church's excessive emotionalism "could hardly fail to do permanent physical, mental and spiritual injury" to children: "It is particularly pathetic to think of children being exposed to the strong appeal to fear which was characteristic of the preaching, with the emphasis on the divine wrath at the violation of the law, and the inevitable punishment that must follow."[34]

Children "from earliest childhood, were terrified with the awful description of hell, and the declaration that they might be sent there."[35] In addition the stress was placed on the depravity of children born in sin, and they were classified with the unregenerate.

Whereas Hunt and Fleming seem to undermine many of the assumptions made by Aries in respect of the positive aspects of childhood in the historical period he investigated, Lloyd deMause has been critical also of Aries's view of the modern family as impinging on the freedom of children, specifically because of its emphasis on the concept of childhood.[36] DeMause states unequivocally that Aries's "argument that the modern family restricts the child's freedom and increases the severity of punishment, runs counter to all the evidence."[37] DeMause's critique rests on the larger theoretical premises that he has outlined, an ambitious attempt at using psychohistory to set out a sweeping developmental approach to parent-child relations, in which the nature of the relation is seen as improving from the "infanticidal mode" of antiquity through the "abandonment mode" (fourth to thirteenth centuries), the "ambivalent mode" (fourteenth to seventeenth centuries), the "intrusive mode" (eighteenth century), and the "socialization mode" (nineteenth to mid-twentieth centuries), to the present-day possibilities of a breakthrough into the "helping mode." In the latter, the child is allowed to develop according to his or her own needs, with the help of both parents.[38]

This is an interesting, extensively researched thesis, with important implications for understanding generational contact and child-rearing practices. DeMause's work, and that of his colleagues, has opened up new vistas for analyzing and understanding society and the role and place of children. The empirical data are impressive, the theoretical presentation stimulating, and the work has already earned deserved praise. Yet from the outset it has also drawn a number of critical responses, some of them challenging, in one way or another, the progressive evolutionary approach that is the essence of the theory.[39]

Although deMause's work is still in its formative stages, some of the critical empirical evidence he has already presented to support his thesis is problematical. Moreover, his methodology is questionable, based as it is on "parent-child relations . . . exhibited by the psychologically most advanced part of the population in the most advanced countries"[40] rather than on widespread practices current at most times in history. Yet deMause ignores the fact that, while child-rearing practices might change, the underlying problems might remain. Infanticide in its gross, primitive forms is no longer practiced; the gods no longer require propitiatory sacrifices; unwanted or deformed children are no longer destroyed. Yet, as we have already noted, several writers who are attuned to the hostile pressures of parents and adults have suggested that wars, in which the young are killed, may be seen as a symbolic continuation of sacrifice of the young. Modern methods of abortion and the ready availability of refined birth-control measures have severely curtailed the need for infanticide to get rid of unwanted children. Institutions often solve the problem of the survival of deformed and handicapped children, while not always providing the desired standards of care.

One doubts if deMause's reliance on a first-recorded instance is sufficient justification to mark the beginning of a new mode of child-raising. This may be particularly noticed in his analysis of the sixth and final stage, that in which the helping mode is dominant. DeMause himself acknowledges that "few parents have yet consistently attempted this kind of child care," then notes that there are only "four books which describe children brought up according to the helping mode" (one of these books being his own unpublished work).[41]

For all the extensive bibliography that deMause relies on, it is doubtful if one can categorically state that earlier periods did not have similar isolated examples of sensitive parents applying what deMause calls the "helping mode." Thus Xenophon in his *Memorabilia* describes Socrates's understanding attitude to his sons, an instance of parent-child relations very similar to what deMause considers "the helping mode." In the periods before the printing press many such parents probably never committed their philosophies and their practices to paper. On the other hand, in this age of mass communication, it is doubtful if four books are sufficient to constitute a true harbinger of a fundamental change in parent-child relations.

While building on a few isolated examples of positive approaches to children taken from modern times, deMause has largely avoided the accumulating data on widespread, hitherto little-recognized child abuse. Although referring to the phenomenon, he downplays its importance and uses the evidence mainly in order to argue for the validity of unrelated points that he is trying to make. His extensive research into earlier historical data is not at all matched by his casual treatment of readily available data on present-day instances of child abuse.

Thus he notes in passing: "since some people still kill, beat and sexually abuse children, any attempt to periodize modes of child rearing must first admit that psychogenic evolution proceeds at different rates in different family lines, and that many parents appear to be 'stuck' in earlier historical modes."[42] Even when dealing with the problem, he all but ignores the academic research; his first reference is to a newspaper article, which quoted an estimated figure of a little less than one million abused children in the United States, followed by a footnote citing two and one-half million as an estimate. Instead of relating to that fact as significant in and of itself, he argues that the figures show that in the past the abuse must have been greater and that "most children suffered from such abuse,"[43] though he provides no supporting data. Children were certainly beaten in the past, but it is not clear whether this practice is increasing or declining.

Later deMause does make reference to some of the pioneering academic research of Ray Helfer and Henry Kempe and of David Gil, but only to explain a secondary theoretical concept of "reversal reaction," in which the parent uses the "child as a substitute for an adult figure important in his own childhood."[44] For deMause present-day child abuse is not an issue to examine in and of itself but only a means of providing an example to help in studying childhood over many generations.

In a third reference, deMause uses research on present-day child abuse to again describe the reversal reaction, this time to show "how responsive little children are to the needs of their parents."[45] As for the past, deMause and his colleagues provide many examples of hostility, including infanticide in fairly recent times—certainly long after the infanticidal mode stage was presumed to have ended in the fourth century. DeMause's work contains also clear evidence that, in addition to residual traces of older forms, the disappearance of one form of abusive child-rearing practice is often accompanied by the substitution of another form of abuse. Thus the eighteenth century presumably saw a significant transformation with the inception of the fourth stage, the "intrusive mode." Since the child was now "so much less threatening . . . true empathy was possible."[46] DeMause notes that at this stage there was a sharp decrease in the incidence of the beating of children; he then goes on: "As beating began to decrease, substitutes had to be found. For instance, shutting children up in the dark room became quite popular in the eighteenth and nineteenth century."[47] One doubts if such behavior can be considered an example of "true empathy" or even indicative of any progress in child-rearing.

Similarly, diminution in the extent of sexual abuse of young children led to the opposite approach of severe punishment of children for their sexual desires. At that time, too, doctors began to warn against the many diseases—insanity, blindness, and even death—that could result from masturbation:

> By the nineteenth century this campaign reached an unbelievable frenzy. Doctors and parents sometimes appeared before the child armed with knives and scissors, threatening to cut off the child's genitals; circumcision, clitoridectomy, and infibulation were sometimes used as punishment; and all sorts of restraint devices, including plaster casts and cages with spikes, were prescribed.[48]

It would be difficult to determine which approach had the most harmful effects on the child: the actual abuse, or the threats and restrictions.

One hopes that the impact of deMause and the other writers cited by him will indeed prove to be harbingers of a new trend in child-rearing, but the issue is far from decided at this stage. Certainly there is little ground yet for claiming a new unique mode of parent-child relations.

Other writers, such as Erik Erikson[49] and Margaret Mead,[50] preceded deMause and his collegaues in stressing the interactive role of child-rearing practices and the larger cultural milieu, but without using an evolutionary model based on constant progress. If anything, their work throws some doubt on the evolutionary nature of approaches to child-rearing, for much of Mead's work centered on positive approaches to childhood among societies that, though chronologically in the twentieth century, have sociological and cultural forms that are more closely aligned to the societies and cultures of earlier times. She provides many examples of positive child-raising practices in which children are helped to develop according to their own needs. In fact, the very popularity of Mead's work has often conjured up idealized views of child-rearing practices in more simple society, where people live closer to nature. But this, too, would be a distortion based on selective data; there is plenty of contrary evidence in anthropological writing. At the same time, there is always the possibility that in those societies in which there were norms sanctioning cruel practices against the young there were those few parents who acted contrary to the norms and according to the "helping mode"; but such personal approaches might not have been recorded by anthropologists intent on studying the overall norms of the society.

One of the few books devoted specifically to the position and role of children in simple societies in modern times is replete with instances of cruelty toward children. Nathan Miller's work, *The Child in Primitive Society,* serves as a useful starting point for putting together the accumulated evidence, which seems in conflict with the optimistic approaches of Aries and Firestone for the Middle Ages, of deMause for modern times, of Mead for modern simple societies, or of those who may believe that early or ancient societies might provide the ideal approach.[51]

Miller's book was, admittedly, written before many of the major anthropological works of recent years, including the work of Mead, but also before many of these societies had been fully exposed to outer influence, so that the evidence may be closer to reality.

One of Miller's examples to represent the negative situation of the child is the derogatory meaning that the word "child" has in many of the societies examined: "The child . . . is identified with that which is immature, unfashioned, unripe, weak, negligible, pitiable, incomplete. Traces of this kind often remain the dominating abstract conception of the child in societies even more advanced. This notation may easily be discovered by examination of the vocabulary and linguistics of primitive man. . . ."[52] The languages of primitive peoples provide clues to the legal status of the child as a "nonentity," "less than a human being," "a thing," or "an incomplete being" until he is formally and ceremoniously accepted into the group upon reaching maturity. Such lack of legal status facilitates the practice of infanticide, "for there is nothing to hinder the primitive man from doing away with the child, since he has not yet acquired any measure or form of status or bonds in the group. It is a stranger from other parts, and it is wholly within the discretion of the parents to write 'Finis' upon its social career before it has acquired any 'rights' to its life in the tribe."[53]

Yet, despite the complete power of the parents and the many hardships of parenthood, the majority of parents in most tribal and other simple societies resist the temptation to rid themselves of their children. Surely, it might be argued, this is sufficient indication of the deep affection that the parent has for the child. Miller himself disagrees with such a conclusion. On the contrary, he is of the opinion that egoistic and utilitarian factors are more significant in promoting positive feelings on the part of the parents toward their progeny. Several clear benefits accrue to the parents as a result of having children, and it is the awareness of these that underlies the "tenderness and touching intimacy" of the parental attitudes. Children are an economic asset and serve to "enhance the dignity, respect, prestige, social dimensions and ego of the parents," particularly in those societies where social and class differentiations have already appeared. "Like the man who holds much cattle, the man with many children acquires renown and social prowess." Vanity, in addition to the desire for means, becomes the motive for having children. As a consequence, "the evolution of social prestige is based upon an abundant offspring as a major type of material wealth."[54]

The status of women is often even more directly related to their child-bearing capacity; the bride-price is really a payment for her child-producing capacities. "The barren woman is despised, hounded and calumniated. Sterility becomes a grievous fault and shortcoming, an unpardonable sin and a loathsome affliction."[55]

Miller concludes: "it is clear that children are man's most precious possession in the simpler society. The primitive man's heart is full of this desire. . . . The primitive man does not customarily wrap himself up in the child for the child's sake and the child's destiny. The parent's urge is first of all a utilitarian and selfish one."[56]

More recent research has substantiated much of Miller's argument. George M. Foster writes of the contribution that the possession of children in traditional societies makes to the social standing of their parents and the degree to which the relative lack of children serves as a source of envy.[57] High mortality rates cause children to become much desired, together with food and health, which are also in short supply.

Otto Klineberg also dwells on the ambivalence that parents in widely differing cultures show toward their children. He, too, stresses the fact that positive attitudes toward them are often a reflection of the material or other advantages that they bring.[58] Among the Eskimos, children are an investment for old age; in China they ensure the immortality of the father; in many simple societies they are seen as an economic asset. Klineberg gives examples of widespread practices indicative of a minimum tie between parent and child, ranging from the extreme example of infanticide to the prevalent practice of giving children up for adoption.

These factors have been probed recently in an interesting and unique comparative research project conducted in Hawaii and several Asian countries to study the specific question of the value of children and the reasons people give for having them.[59] Overall there seems to have been a mixture of emotional and psychological considerations with economic and utilitarian ones. The latter were, however, far more noticed among the lower-class and rural respondents. These findings would suggest that economic pressures in earlier times could have led to a similar emphasis on utilitarian factors. Where children were of utilitarian benefit they would be welcomed and used. Where no such benefits appeared likely, they might be resented, and in some cases even put to death.

Marvin Harris has noted that population factors mainly determined infanticidal practices, and he cites the fact that generally it was the female child who would be killed, this having a more direct impact on future population growth.[60] Even here, however, the considerations might have been more directly economic: a male was more likely to provide recompense for what was invested in him than a female, especially in patrilineal and patrilocal societies where, on marriage, the daughter would leave the home and no amount of bride-price could compensate for the investment in her or for the loss of her working potential. In any event there is contrary evidence, as James Frazer notes, that often it was the first-born who was sacrificed, while the later children were spared.[61] This undermines the argument that infanticide was intended mainly as a means of population control.

The pressures to be rid of children are, however, more than just economic and utilitarian, and they find their expression not just in filicide. The advent of a child, particularly of a first child, invariably causes tensions between husband and wife. Attention has already been drawn to the use of wet nurses, both to release the wife from the strains of nursing and to release the husband from the rivalry of seeking his wife's attention and affection. Similar convenient arrangements were not available for parents in simpler societies, but similar problems were undoubtedly encountered with an even greater intensity, given the primitive conditions of life and the confined space shared by all family members.

In this regard it is interesting to note Jean-François Saucier's analysis of the societal impact of the postpartum taboo, "requiring a lactating mother to refrain from sexual intercourse."[62] Saucier sees a connection between this familial policy and the larger political and social structure. He argues that societies with long postpartum taboos (often more than a year) are generally community gerontocracies, where the pressures and strains of a lengthy taboo would be lessened for the older men, who in polygamous societies would be the ones with more wives since most men acquire additional wives late in life at a stage when their sexual potency is, in any event, declining. Here can be seen a sort of replication of the situation described by Hunt in relation to the latent social history of the wet nurse where the upper-class males solved their own problems vis-à-vis the newborn child by farming it off to a wet nurse, thereby intensifying the tensions within the wet nurse's family and particularly increasing the frustrations of the husband. In the example given by Saucier, it is the older generation that has the political power to decide on a long-term postpartum taboo and the economic resources to evade its consequences by the simple expedient of taking extra wives. It is the wives and the young monogamous men who suffer most from the taboo. Thus the tensions within the family are intensified on a generational basis, with class overtones, the younger men bearing the brunt of the older men's decision.

A prolonged postpartum taboo, if rigidly enforced, could cause resentment on the part of the parents toward the infant who was the direct cause of the sexual taboo. Such resentment might well engender feelings of rivalry linked to sex on the part of the father-husband toward his child that would be exactly the opposite of the oedipal situation.

Despite increasing anthropological research on child-rearing methods in simple societies, little attention has been given to the relations between parent and child as affected by the tensions involved in having sexual relations under conditions of limited privacy, the possible harm caused to the child in witnessing such activity, the strain imposed on the family by the constant exposure to the infant's crying and his excrement in a confined space. Children were indeed welcome as economic assets, as insurance for old age, as guarantors of the parents' immortality, but these pragmatic and ideological factors would not always compensate for the sheer burdens of raising the children, who would be exposed to the wrath of the parents' frustration. William Sumner has argued much more directly that one of the main causes of abortion and infanticide was the sheer burden involved in bearing and rearing children; those who survived this selective process would not always gain the parents' affection.[63]

According to Miller, "the child's lot is not an enviable one. Childhood is grim and earnest."[64] Disciplinary control is strict (Miller provides examples of beatings, pepper thrown in the eyes) and cruel methods are often used to train children to be healthy, partly also as preparation for the initiation rites. In fact, the purposes and practices of initiation rites are in need of reassessment. Too often they are considered outstanding examples of the manner in which simple societies knew how to incorporate their young in an orderly and organized fashion into the ongoing life of the society. Thus, for instance, Herbert Bloch and Arthur Niederhoffer, in their discussion of the defects of modern society that facilitate juvenile delinquency, point to the lack of an accepted ceremony in which the passage of the child into adult status would be clearly acknowledged and announced.[65]

While rites of passage do remove much of the uncertainty of a young person's status, it seems clear that, in many societies, the ceremonies of ritual advancement are often manipulative in their intention and cruel in their implementation. Inasmuch as the cruelty is noticed, the explanation generally given is that these are legitimate tests of courage and endurance, successful performance providing indisputable proof of the young person's qualities. It was a Freudian writer who challenged this approach—Theodore Reik, in his analysis of ritual, writes that while such tests "may be a secondary motive . . . we prefer to take these defined acts of cruelty at their face value, i.e., as cruel and hostile acts of the men against the youths."[66] In truth, Reik does not really take them at face value. On the contrary, he looks for symbolic reasons for this hostility and cruelty and argues that the hostile feelings that the father once had against his own parents are the prime motivating factor for such cruelty with the father now determined to prevent the child from giving concrete expression to the similar evil wishes the child is presumably harboring against him. Thus, "the different tests of courage and fortitude which we have denoted as tortures will be punishment for wicked wishes against the father."[67]

According to Reik, the condition the fathers make for accepting the sons into their society is that they must renounce their incestuous and hostile wishes. If not, they face possible death. Through this process, actual killing is replaced by cruel rites of passage, through which some of the generational ambivalence finds its outlet. Puberty rites thus become an educative means of enforcing the two fundamental taboos of incest and parricide. However, if the oedipal framework is removed, then the parental cruelty may be seen more directly for what it likely is—both as an expression of hostility per se and as a subtle means of ensuring that acceptance into the adult community is made contingent on passive acquiescence in the status quo, symbolized by compliance with the humiliations and deprivations of ritual passage.

However difficult it is to accurately interpret symbolic rituals, the problems of knowing the intimate nature of parent-child relations become even more complex when dealing with ancient and historical societies. Neither anthropologists nor diarists recorded the details. Some of the nature of the relationship may be gleaned from myths and drama. Other details may be found in documents that have been preserved, particularly those of a legal nature; but these are not always trustworthy, since it is not always possible to know the extent to which legal obligations were performed and enforced, the legal rights actually claimed. Even within modern legal systems controversy rages as to where the essence of the law is to be found: in statutes and judicial decisions, or in the "living law" of daily social and economic interaction.

One of the most significant legal phenomena of the ancient world was the extensive powers given to the head of the household over all the members of that household—the wife, the children, the slaves, and servants. It was in the Roman legal system that these powers were given their most extensive expression in the institution of the *paterfamilias,* the "father of the family," who possessed absolute rights over his children, which were terminated only on his death:

> Even if the son reached the highest offices of state, he still remained under the power of his pater. The father had complete power of life and death over his children—though if he used his power arbitrarily he might be punished by the censors. He could sell them into slavery, his consent to their marriage was needed, and he could bring about their divorce if he wished. The children could own no property . . . anything they acquired belonged to the father. If the son made a contract, the father immediately acquired all the rights under it against the other party.[68]

Moreover a father was entitled to all the rights acquired under a contract entered into by his son while being absolved from any responsibilities flowing therefrom. As far as tort actions were concerned, a special form of noxal liability was created:

> It was felt to be wrong that a father . . . should suffer great loss if his son . . . committed a delict, hence from earliest times it was possible for the father . . . to restrict his loss to the worth of the son. . . . When a delictual action was brought against a paterfamilias for a wrong committed by a son . . . he had the choice either of paying the amount of that claim or handing over his dependent.[69]

Identical provisions were in force for slaves; in terms of noxal liability no distinction was drawn between sons and slaves. It was only in Justinian's time that noxal liability was limited to slaves.

The very word *pater,* according to Fustel de Coulanges,

> contained in itself not the idea of paternity, but that of power, authority, majestic dignity. . . . That such a word should have been applied to the father of a family until it became his most common appellation is assuredly a very significant fact, and one whose importance will appear to all who wish to understand ancient institutions. The history of this word suffices to give us an idea of the power which the father exercised for a long time in the family, and of the sentiment of veneration which was due him as a pontiff and a sovereign.[70]

While the Roman law is generally considered to have sanctioned the most extreme paternal powers, other early legal systems had similar approaches to the powers and rights of the father. In an analysis of the social and legal position of the family in Athens, Charles Savage recounts the power of the father, at birth, to decide whether or not to "acknowledge the infant . . . or, as occasionally happened, to repudiate the child . . . or even to condemn it to death outright."[71] Savage notes that the practice of exposing children was actually sanctioned by law. Contrary to the general explanations given for such practices—controlling population growth, or even of performing propitiatory acts for the gods—Savage offers a far more mundane reason: "It is probable that children were sometimes exposed in order that parents might escape the trouble of rearing them."[72]

In discussing the laws of Eshunna, one of the earliest known codes, Reuven Yaron claims that, though Oriental law never went as far as conferring the total powers of the Roman paterfamilias, it contained some of the same provisions, including the widespread practice of selling a son for debts: "The possibility—encountered in many sources—that a person be sold, given into servitude or seized as a pledge on account of the debts of his father, has to be explained in terms of paternal power and filial dependence."[73] Referring to biblical times, Arthur Diamond describes "a Hebrew looking around upon a familiar scene—the pawning of children in their father's debt, then seized on account of his debt after his demise, the retaliation visited upon the children for his wrongs."[74]

Ancient societies sought both homiletical and disciplinary means of ensuring obedience by children to their parents; in the Bible the Fifth Commandment injunction of honoring a father and a mother is linked to a threat of adverse consequences for failure to comply.[75] Separate rules provide for stern measures to be taken against a stubborn and recalcitrant son; he was to be given up to the elders, who were to have him put to death.[76] Biblical authorities claim that such provisions were probably never enforced, just as some commentators on Roman law argue that the full powers of the *paterfamilias* were rarely invoked.

While many of the arbitrary powers of parents were curtailed in the course of time, some of the modern aspects of the law in relation to children, praised for reflecting society's concern for the child, often had ulterior motives. Even many of the laws that were ostensibly designed to protect the young had more direct and utilitarian overtones. Francis Bohlen suggests that the duty of parents to look after their children may have arisen not from concern for the child but from the state's interest in seeing that the child did not become a public charge.[77]

Sir William Blackstone, in his classic presentation of eighteenth-century law, acknowledges that

> The power of parents over their children is derived from . . . their duty; this authority being given, partly to enable the parent more effectively to perform his duty, and partly as a recompense for his care and trouble in the faithful discharge of it.[78]

Thus the obligation of a father to care for his children was often linked directly to his concomitant right to their services, as well as the right to claim damages against anyone who interfered with that right. Peter Bromley notes that the common-law duty of "protecting and maintaining one's legitimate infant children" was linked to the creation of parental rights, including "to the services of his children in his custody and to correct them by administering reasonable corporal punishment."[79] Even though "his powers were never as wide as those of the *paterfamilias* in Roman law, the same fundamental approach is apparent."[80]

The right to the child's services gave rise to the right to sue against any interference with that right. Many of the legal rights of the father stemmed not just from kinship bonds but also from the monetary value of the labor relationship: "The legal basis of the action lies . . . not in the relationship of parent and child, but in that of master and servant, and the parent is alleged to be a master, that he has been wrongfully deprived of his child's services."[81] This economic approach to parent-child relations is also to be seen in the rationale behind the right to recover damages for the seduction of a daughter. As explained by a leading judge, the action is based "not upon the seduction itself, which is the wrongful act of the defendant, but upon the loss of service of the daughter, in which he is supposed to have a legal right or interest."[82]

In many instances the powers of the parents, particularly the father, related not only to economic power and control but also to the right to interfere in the most personal and intimate aspects of his children's life, including both the right to sexual favors and the right to choose a marriage partner.

One of the most extreme examples of such parental powers is the custom practiced in various periods of Russian history allowing the father to have sexual privileges over his daughter-in-law. Samuel Kucherov, in discussing the extensive power of the father, describes the practice of *snokhachestuo*, "a remnant of polyandry which existed at a low level of cultural development, was known to the Slavic tribes in the earliest period of Russian history, and lasted for centuries."[83] It allowed for sexual relations between the father of the groom and the daughter-in-law. Here was an obvious source of potential friction, confirmed by Kucherov, between father and son: sexual rivalry not on the oedipal basis of love for the father's wife and son's mother, but for the father's daughter-in-law and son's wife. "The situation," according to Kucherov, "was the cause of scuffles in the family and fights between father and son."[84] The daughter-in-law was humiliated by such treatment and forced to submit to the wishes of the father-in-law, in whose house she often lived and on whom she would generally be economically dependent. In some cases, the father would ensure access to the daughter-in-law and minimize the son's competitive influence by marrying "the son at a tender age to a much older girl."[85]

While this particular custom may not have had many parallels, the right of the father to choose a marriage for his child was certainly widespread and still exists in many places. The major consideration was usually pecuniary, with bride-price constituting a key factor in the bargaining process between the two families.

These arrangements were generally made without the consent of the bridegroom and the bride; in many instances the binding agreements would be entered into while the children were still of tender age, while in others a young girl would be given over into marriage by her parents. David and Vera Mace discuss the common practice of child wives in India till very recent times.[86] Basing themselves on Katherine Mayo's controversial *Mother India,* published in 1927, they claim that about 10 percent of all girls between the ages of five and ten were married, while one quarter were married by the age of fifteen. While in many cases these marriages were really only betrothals, they still show the large degree of control maintained by families over their children in the most intimate area of choice of marriage partner.[87]

Much of the evidence I have so far adduced is based on random facts gleaned from a variety of sources. Many more details can be gathered from the pages of the *History of Childhood Quarterly.*[88] As noted already, the evidence of childhood is not always easily available, much of it resting on chance preservation or selective choice of facts. Of all the works in this area there is, however, one that stands out by virtue of the depth and breadth of its coverage, the meticulous tracing of a host of diverse facts, and the reliability of the presentation. Ivy Pinchbeck and Margaret Hewitt have collected in two massive volumes data giving detailed factual pictures of the English child from Tudor to modern times.[89] Their study has almost no theoretical framework except that of concern for the young; it is an attempt to collate carefully the scattered fragments of evidence over a specified period of time in one society. While the aid and succor granted to children is discussed, the total picture, especially of the early Tudor period, reflects a great deal of negativism and actual harm inflicted on them.

In Tudor England children were assimilated into adulthood between the ages of seven and nine. Such assimilation made the norms of adult life applicable to the children. Child marriages, often carried out for the advantages they brought to parents or guardians were common; and apprenticeships at work, where great power was accorded the master, allowed for the exploitation of child labor even before its advent in factories.

Pinchbeck and Hewitt confirm Fleming's analysis of the fears instilled into children through their exposure to religious concepts of sin and death.[90] Even the still-limited institution of schools come in for criticism for their long hours of work, few holidays, harsh discipline, and lack of any understanding of the child at all.[91] Children's books were preoccupied with death and sin. Given the high rate of infant mortality, the death of children was not a cause of deep grief. Parents were not merely indifferent; they were often fatalistic, seeing in the death of their little ones the mysterious ways of God.[92]

Pinchbeck and Hewitt stress, however, that indifference and fatalism were only

> a partial . . . explanation of the many deaths occurring among children in the seventeenth and eighteenth century. An unknown proportion were undoubtedly the result of culpable neglect and cruelty. . . . Until the end of the eighteenth century and to a less extent even in the nineteenth century, it was a common practice to expose unwanted children. . . . Frequently, these children died before being discovered. Sometimes, they were discovered by beggars who would mutilate them to excite pity and hire them out to other beggars.[93]

Flogging and similar disciplinary measures were common practices. The authors give an example from a 1752 newspaper of a woman who used to stick pins in her child and stir up the fire with his feet. There was no legal protection for children against such abuse until the last quarter of the eighteenth century, when the first Act for the Prevention of Cruelty to Children was passed. This lacuna was "in large measure . . . a reflection of the continuing social acceptance of violence which, as far as children are concerned, was as much a feature of their treatment by their parents as it was of their treatment by their teachers."[94]

Stressing their theme of the prevalence and respectability of violence toward children, Pinchbeck and Hewitt use the letters of a certain William Blundell to describe some of the inner workings of a presumably normal family:

> William Blundell . . . was not an especially harsh father. Indeed, he seems to have had some genuine sympathy for children. Yet, for minor misdemeanors such as faulty deportment or boisterous behavior his little daughters of about seven or eight were often whipped and penanced and after failing to keep their promise of better behaviour were whipped again.[95]

While there was a great awareness of the exploitation of child labor in factories in the early years of the industrial age, similar exploitation was prevalent in the older domestic industries as well:

> Hidden away in cottages, where they attracted no attention, thousands of children in rural areas worked factory hours every day, under conditions

which were often no better than those which caused so much feeling in the industrial centers.[96]

In fact, harsh as these conditions were, condemned as they have been by posterity, it is often forgotten that parents themselves favored child labor in order to supplement their income. In addition, among the arguments used for its abolition, was its general economic inefficiency and harmful competition with adult wage-earners.

In the child-rearing practices, too, the eighteenth century saw an increase in "the growing fashion among fashionable and wealthy women of refusing to nurse their children lest their figure should suffer."[97]

Although Pinchbeck and Hewitt have no fixed theoretical framework, contenting themselves with the factual presentation of the data, toward the end of the book they do note the dilemma posed by the fact that the interests of the child are not always identical, or even consonant, with those of the parents.[98]

Ending on an optimistic note, the authors cite the Children's Act of 1948, designed to provide more comprehensive protection for the child. This act, and similar acts in England as well as in many other countries of the modern world, certainly extend to children a degree of protection that was formerly lacking and provide legal and institutional frameworks for societal intervention against cruel parents in the home, intolerant teachers at school, and exploitative employers in industry and commerce.

These developments undoubtedly justify some of the optimism of de Mause and others. Yet such developments, theoretically desirable as they are, must be treated with a due amount of caution. First, the mere existence of protective laws does not guarantee their enforcement; second, earlier attempts to protect the child did not always meet with long-lasting success; third, many protective institutions, though commendable in their avowed aims, have other, ulterior or hidden intents that benefit adults rather than children.

Beyond this, there is growing evidence that physical abuse of children at all periods of history is much more widespread than has been commonly considered. Pinchbeck and Hewitt make only passing reference to the subject. But in a book devoted especially to the topic, George Scott quotes examples of well-known historical figures who recorded having been flogged in their childhood.[99] They run the gamut from Homer and Horace in ancient Greece, through Frederick the Great ("Carlyle describes how the young prince was goaded almost to despair by his suffering at the hands of the old king"), the sons of George III, Samuel Johnson, Erasmus ("who was very nearly turned against his studies altogether through the severity of the whippings he received"), Milton, who was flogged at Cambridge, and Lady Anne Barnard, who was whipped by her governess.

James Boswell also makes several references to the prevalence of corporal punishment and to the belief in its advantages. He quotes Samuel Johnson as saying that "schoolmasters were worse than the Egyptian taskmasters of old."[100] Writing in 1938, Scott suggests that corporal punishment is less prevalent in modern times than it was formerly. Even so he does make note of occasional cases of unnecessary severity, quoting three examples from British newspapers that appeared in 1937, the year before the book was published.[101] Scott notes these cases as aberrant examples and does not inquire whether they may not be part of a more general norm, having attracted attention and occasioned publicity by mere chance.

Recent revelations concerning the battered-child syndrome should serve as both a warning against such complacency and as an indication of the failure of the authorities to divulge numerous hidden cases of battered children. Despite increased public awareness of the problem, improved technical means of checking it, and legal means to enforce reporting, most cases still go unreported and unrecorded. Most of the research on the battered-child syndrome centers on the home and family, but it is quite likely that there are similar practices within the schools. The research is still very much in its preliminary stages, particularly in terms of determining clear and acceptable criteria for what constitutes child abuse and of creating accurate and refined instruments for measuring the total number of instances of mistreatment. At the same time, efforts are being made to set up theoretical models for explaining the causative factors.

Earlier theories concentrated on the psychopathology of parents. This is particularly clear in the pioneering work of C. Henry Kempe and Ray Helfer who first helped create an awareness of the dimensions of a hitherto unrecognized social problem, and who suggested the concept of "battered-child syndrome."[102] At the same time there were hints in their work and in that of some of their co-workers that the parents examined by them did constitute a fair cross section of the population. Their work was limited by its concentration on only the most extreme cases—those brought to the attention of the authorities, generally because the children were in need of medical treatment—but it was clear that these were only a small proportion of the total cases.

David Gil's work, published in 1970, was the first major study to address itself to the methodological and theoretical issues of widespread, unreported child abuse and to attempt to go beyond the earlier psychological and clinical models.[103] His empirical research indicated that, whereas the official statistics of all the states in the United States showed a total of 6–7,000 incidents, an epidemiological study based on reporting of a national sample suggested that the actual rate might be as high as 2 to 4 million. Gil notes that these projections from his samples were the maximum figures and that the true number was probably less; however, it was clear that the 6–7,000 officially reported instances constituted only a small fraction of all the cases.[104] Similar research in other countries seems to bear this out, and there is agreement among workers in this area that the amount of abuse is far greater than was generally thought or than the official figures show.

Gil explains the prevalence of child abuse in terms of sociological and cultural factors, such as a propensity to violence among certain groups or in "cultural values, traditions, and customs, and in actual child-rearing practices throughout the United States," all of which uphold the discretional right of parents and other caretakers of children to use a "reasonable amount of physical force" in disciplining children.[105] Focusing his analysis specifically on the overall value system of American society, Gil adopts an approach in which any diminution in child abuse is predicated on deep-seated changes in the society aimed at minimizing its competitive philosophy and encouraging instead human cooperation as a preliminary step to changing its child-rearing practices.

Gil claims that "violence against children in rearing them may . . . be a functional aspect of socialization into a highly competitive and often violent society"[106] and argues for the need for new, healthier forms of interaction between children and those entrusted with their care. Whereas society has imposed clear-cut taboos on violence among adults and has regulated its use in order to ensure survival and orderly processes of social behavior, there is an ambivalence in regard to the legitimacy of violence against children. With only a few exceptions, "most societies have not developed absolute cultural taboos and legal sanctions against the use of physical force against children by adults."[107] Gil suggests that it is the very physical weakness of children that has enabled society to allow the violence to continue. Whereas uncontrolled violence among adults with "an approximate balance of physical force" could be disastrous for society, similar immediate dangers do not arise in allowing violence against the young; thus such violence, ranging from mutilation for economic gain or ritualistic objectives in some societies to corporal punishment in schools in our own, can be officially legitimized.[108]

While some of Gil's arguments are speculative and not always directly related to his data, they deserve serious consideration. He was the first researcher to perceive of child abuse in the overall patterns of societal and cultural norms instead of as the pathology of a deviant minority. Although he has concentrated mainly on the situation in the United States, his approach is applicable to many other contemporary societies.

Gil's ideas have been further developed by Richard J. Gelles.[109] Whereas Gil dealt mainly with the cultural milieu, Gelles has brought a broader sociological perspective to bear on some of the structural factors endemic in intrafamily relations. He is part of a larger emerging group of writers who have drawn attention to the degree of conflict and violence within the family as a result of the inevitable tensions that accompany the intimacy of family life.

Noting that of the most serious known cases there seems to be a concentration of child abuse at the earliest ages (up to about three years old), Gelles suggests three structural reasons for the young infant's great vulnerability: (a) The child is physically too weak to withstand much physical punishment or force. (b) The infant is not capable of much meaningful social interaction and this may create a great deal of frustration for the parent who is trying to interact with the child. Case studies reveal that abusing parents often complain that they hit their child because they could not toilet-train him, get him to stop crying, or get him to obey their commands. (c) The very fact of the child's birth may interfere with the parents' professional, occupational, educational, or other plans, and/or may create economic hardship for the family.[110]

Gelles argues that as long as the reaction to child abuse remains within a psychopathological model, which sees the parents as mentally ill and deals only with the symptoms, little progress can be made. What is needed is a multidimensional approach, an attempt to come to terms with the larger social and structural variables and to formulate an acceptable definition of the concept. The work of Gil and Gelles presents the possibility of a major breakthrough into an understanding of the phenomenon, which would no longer be seen merely or primarily as a problem of psychopathology or deviance but as part of deeper ongoing patterns of behavior. What is needed is not merely research into those specific families in which the parents have been officially stigmatized as "child abusers" but a more comprehensive knowledge of exactly what goes on inside families in their daily interaction.

In a unique research project, John and Elizabeth Newson analyzed the way more than 700 mothers handled their infant children in their first year of life.[111] Their evidence indicates a clear propensity to use some form of physical force in disciplining and socializing young children:

> By the time it reaches its first birthday . . . the baby is more likely than not to have experienced being smacked by its mother. Sometimes the smacking will be no more than a token expression of the mother's disapproval; sometimes it will be very definitely painful, and the baby will be left in no doubt of its mother's intentions.
>
> These were normal parents, concerned with the welfare of their children, frustrated at the complex problems of caring for them and disciplining them, shocked at the intensity of their reaction to the infant's misbehavior.[112]

Elizabeth Newson stresses how much the strains of interaction between parents and infant children can often bring out degrees of violence previously unknown or unimagined: "We found a lot of mothers who were shocked at themselves. They didn't know that they had these wells of violence until they had children."[113]

None of the parents in the study had been officially classified as abusive. Even unofficially it is doubtful if their behavior could be so considered. Newson herself notes the terrible dilemma of not knowing how to handle certain confrontation situations, given the natural incapacities of infant children.

In dealing with children of seventeenth-century France, Hunt remarked how "hard pressed adults were by the various challenges of bringing up small children."[114] Little has changed. Parents are still hard pressed; they are still liable to succumb to a temporary weakness or eagerly to accept and apply a cultural norm that sanctions physical force. The borderline between officially recorded child abuse and the far-greater number of instances of abuse noted in research is as narrow and unclear as is the line between the abusive parents in Gil's research and the parents who resorted to smacking as described by the Newsons.

Exactly how thin the line really is may best be gauged by a story related by Jean Renvoize in the course of her research on "children in danger."[115] She describes how she was once approached by a woman who, on hearing about her research on battered children, asked for an interview, stating simply; "I used to batter my children. Would you like me to tell you about it?"[116] At the interview several days later, the woman retracted somewhat: "I exaggerated the other night. I didn't really batter my kids, not what a court would call battering, anyway. But I came near enough. I've been thinking about it all since I spoke to you, and a lot of things have got clearer."[117]

The woman went on to describe her two daughters: the "crazy sleep pattern of the [elder] daughter"; her husband's desire not to have children at all, since both were musicians and he wished for them to be able to travel freely; the husband's refusal to help with the children, partly because of the tension that concert appearances caused; her own partial sacrifice of her singing career; the "shock and pain" of realizing that they had to care "for this small thing so dependent on you"; the even more significant awareness that "I was no longer a single person at all—I was living a dual life now and would for ever, totally. . . . The bashing had its origins right there, I suppose, because I couldn't be cool enough about being a mother. . . . . I was *overwhelmed* by the responsibility I'd taken on. I couldn't cut off from her."[118]

The interviewee goes on to describe her reactions on being awakened in the middle of the night by the baby's crying:

I'd stand there trembling, not able to take it any more. Shaking her was the first thing I did. I'd grip her . . . but in a way I wasn't so much holding her tight as holding myself. . . . At first I didn't hurt her at all. But later I'd shake her, shake her really hard, or pick her up and throw her down in the cot so violently she'd bounce up again. . . .

No, I never banged her head or anything. I always took great care not to really hurt her. I frequently cracked her head carrying her through doors, though, but that was unintentional, just me being clumsy. I never drew blood or bruised either of them through an action of mine or marked them in any way. The most I've done is to make them cry uncontrollably, and once they were doing that, I'd calm down. I used to throw them to the floor too, but only so they'd land on their nappy. They never got hurt.[119]

She then relates a specific incident with her second daughter, "who was much less trouble to me than the first." In the course of a confrontation with her, after having interrupted her play and argued with her over what clothes to wear:

I lost my temper and I belabored her. . . . I shoved her down on the floor and I hit her and hit her and hit her. I knew I wasn't hurting her very much because she was so thickly covered with clothes, it was like beating a cushion. . . . [Then] I picked her up by the neck, pulling her straight up as though she were a heavy puppy. Then, suddenly I was horrified with myself. I wanted to break her neck, because I felt so sorry for her. That's daft, isn't it, but I knew I was spoiling things for her, and I thought why should I have the right to interrupt her pleasure just because I'm bigger than she is. . . .

I've never hit either of them again like that. I scared myself, I suppose.[120]

Renvoize concludes that "no one reading her story can feel other than pity and sympathy for her"[121]—to which might be added respect for her honesty and forthrightness. Her actions were never reported in the official statistics of child abuse. Yet, if the total nature of parent-child interaction is to be understood, this woman's evidence is of major importance. How often has it been replicated by other parents? More than anything it draws attention to the inevitable stresses of intrafamily life, pointing out the problem of ordinary, everyday parent-child interaction. There is almost a Rashomon quality about the evidence,[122] the lingering doubt as to whether her description really constitutes an instance of the battered-child syndrome or not. Which was the correct appraisal—her original statement, "I used to batter my children," or the subsequent "I didn't really batter my kids?" Gelles warns against the complacency of condemning and stigmatizing the most extreme examples without recognizing the similarities in the behavior between those declared to be abusive parents and the rest of society.[123]

The difficulties in this area of defining behavior are further brought out in one of the examples given by Leontine Young in her work on child abuse.[124] In this instance the parent lacks the sensitivity and self-critical approach of Renvoize's interviewee; he fails to see his behavior as abusive at all and was brought to the attention of the social agency only "because a neighbor has reluctantly complained that he beats his children with excessive brutality."[125] He is well dressed, well spoken, comfortably situated, and educated; he claims that "he loves his children," adding that when they disobey him they are punished. He gives an example of such punishment:

> One evening recently he told his four-year-old son to go into the basement and stay there. The little boy went down the stairs and ran quickly back. It was very dark and he was frightened. "I spanked him and told him to go back," explains the smiling father. "He went down the stairs and again ran back to the light, frightened, so I spanked him again and sent him back. He returned four times and each time I spanked him harder. The last time he stayed down."
>
> "And what did the little boy do that you punished him so severely?" asked the caseworker.
>
> A look of blank surprise comes over [his] face. He stares at the caseworker, and when he speaks his voice is for the first time uncertain. "I don't remember. I can't think what he did." A weariness appears in his eyes, and he remembers that his time is short and he must leave shortly.[126]

These few cases accentuate some of the preliminary problems confronting researchers of child abuse; how to define the nature of the actions, how to interpret them, how to understand them. There seems to be no clear-cut line of distinction between physical violence inflicted on a child necessitating medical treatment and the more refined and subtle forms of child abuse.

It is good to know that the recent public awareness of the battered-child syndrome has led to a higher incidence of reporting and an increased provision of services to help the battered child and his family. But it would be advisable for this new awareness to induce also a sense of humility as to the enormity of the damages inflicted on children, not just today when we have the means of divulging it but also in ages past, down the centuries, when the cry of the abused child went unheeded.

References

1.   Samuel Dubnow, the Jewish historian, on his way to his death in a concentration camp, is quoted as beseeching those who were to survive to record all that was happening so that posterity would know of the tragedy. See Judah Pilch, ed., *The Jewish Catastrophe in Europe* (New York: American Association for Jewish Education, 1963).

2.   See especially the articles by John Caffey, a specialist in pediatric radiology, "Multiple Fractures in the Long Bones of Infants Suffering from Chronic Subdural Hematoma," *American Journal of Roentgenology* 42 (1946) and "Some Traumatic Lesions in Growing Bones other than Fractures and Dislocations: Clinical and

Radiological Features," *British Journal of Radiology* 30 (1957): 225–238. In the later article Caffey suggests that the fractures he had noted in 1946 may likely have been deliberately caused by parents, although he had then failed to recognize such a possibility.

3.   For one of the original surveys of the work on the battered-child syndrome, see Ray E. Helfer and C. Henry Kempe, eds., *The Battered Child* (Chicago: The University of Chicago Press, 1968). For an extensive bibliographical analysis, see J. Spinetta and D. Rigler, "The Child-Abusing Parent: A Psychological Review," *Psychological Bulletin,* 77 (1972): 296–304.

4.   The issue of paternalism and modern institutions for the young will be discussed in the next chapter.

5.   Philippe Aries, *Centuries of Childhood: A Social History of Family Life* (New York: Vintage, 1962).

6.   Shulamith Firestone, *The Dialectic of Sex: The Case for Feminist Revolution* (London: Paladin, 1972).

7.   Ibid., pp. 85–86.

8.   Richard Farson, *Birthrights* (New York: Macmillan, 1974).

9.   Ibid., pp. 11–25.

10.   Aries, *Centuries of Childhood,* p. 407.

11.   Ibid., p. 404.

12.   Ibid., p. 128.

13.   David Hunt, *Parents and Children in History: The Psychology of Family Life in Early Modern France* (New York: Harper Torchbooks, 1972).

14.   Erik Erikson, *Identity and the Life Cycle: Selected Papers* (New York: Psychological Issues, 1959).

15.   Hunt, *Parents and Children in History,* p. 189.

16.   Jean Heroard, *Journal de Jean Heroard sur l'enfance et la jeunesse de Louis XIII (1601–1628)* (Paris, 1868).

17.   Aries, *Centuries of Childhood,* p. 100.

18.   See the critical comments by Lloyd deMause, *The History of Childhood* (New York: Harper Torchbooks, 1975), p. 5.

19.   Aries, *Centuries of Childhood,* especially pp. 62–67.

20.   Ibid., p. 100.

21.   Ibid., pp. 100–101.

22.   Ibid., p. 103.

23.   Ibid.

24.   Hunt, *Parents and Children in History,* p. 95. Hunt quotes from Heroard's diary.

25.   Ibid., p. 102.

26.   Ibid., p. 106.

27. Ibid., p. 107.

28. Ibid., p. 108.

29. Ibid., p. 81.

30. Ibid., pp. 185–186.

31. Sandford Fleming, *Children and Puritanism: The Place of Children in the Life and Thought of the New England Churches, 1620–1847* (New Haven: Yale University Press, 1933).

32. Ibid., p. 60.

33. Ibid., pp. 59–60.

34. Ibid., p. 66.

35. Ibid.

36. DeMause, *The History of Childhood,* chapter 1, "The Evolution of Childhood," pp. 1–75.

37. Ibid., pp. 5–6.

38. Ibid., p. 52. DeMause discusses the key concepts of each of the modes: (a) infanticidal, in which the myth of Medea reflects reality and "parents routinely resolved their anxieties about taking care of children by killing them"; (b) abandonment, when "parents began to accept the child as having a soul. The only way they could escape the dangers of their own projections was by abandonment, whether to the wet nurse, to the monastery or nunnery, to foster families, to the homes of other nobles as servants or hostages, or by severe emotional abandonment at home"; (c) ambivalent, invoking the image of "the physical molding of children, who were seen as soft wax, plaster or clay to be beaten into shape," with child-instruction manuals making their appearance; (d) intrusive, a stage of great transition in the nineteenth century in which "the child was so much less threatening that true empathy was possible, and pediatrics was born, which along with the general improvement in level of care by parents reduced infant mortality. . . ."; (e) socialization, in which "the raising of a child became less a process of conquering its will than of training it, guiding it into proper paths, teaching it to conform, socializing it."

39. See comments on deMause's article in *The History of Childhood Quarterly* 1 (1973) by Rudolf Binion (pp. 576–577), Helm Stierlin (p. 583), John F. Benton (pp. 584–585), Herbert Moller (pp. 590–591), and Michael B. Kala (pp. 601–602).

40. DeMause, "The Evolution of Childhood," p. 51.

41. Ibid., pp. 53–54. In addition to his own published work, deMause refers to A. S. Neill, *The Free Child* (London: Jenkins Herbert, 1953); Paul Ritter and Joan Ritter, *The Free Family: A Creative Experiment in Self-Regulation for Children* (London: Gollancz, 1959); Michael Deakin, *The Children on the Hill* (London: Andre Deutsch, 1972).

42. DeMause, "The Evolution of Childhood," p. 51.

43. Ibid., p. 3. The newspaper article quoted is by Enid Nemy, "Child Abuse: Does It Stem from the Nation's Ills and Its Culture?" *New York Times,* Aug. 16, 1971, p. 16.

44. DeMause, "The Evolution of Childhood," p. 6.

45. Ibid., p. 20.

46. Ibid., p. 52.

47. Ibid., p. 43.

48. Ibid., p. 48.

49. See Erik Erikson, *Childhood and Society*, rev. ed. (New York: Norton, 1964).

50. See especially, Margaret Mead, *Growing up in New Guinea*, (New York: Morrow, 1962); *Coming of Age in Samoa* (New York: New American Library, 1949); and *Sex and Temperament in Three Primitive Societies* (New York: Morrow, 1963).

51. Nathan Miller, *The Child in Primitive Society* (London: Kegan Paul, Trench, Trubner, 1928).

52. Ibid., p. 10.

53. Ibid., pp. 36–37. Of course part of the reason for this approach was the vulnerability of young children, who might not expect to survive beyond their early years. Parents would thus be reluctant to get too involved emotionally. But these factors certainly facilitated harsh measures, including infanticide, being practiced against children.

54. Ibid., pp. 63–64.

55. Ibid., pp. 55–56.

56. Ibid., pp. 61–62.

57. George M. Foster, "The Anatomy of Envy: A Study in Symbolic Behavior," *Current Anthropology* 13 (1972): 169.

58. Otto Klineberg, *Social Psychology,* rev. ed. (New York: Holt, Rinehart & Winston, 1954), pp. 82–89.

59. Fred Arnold, Rodolfo A. Bulatao, Chalio Burupakdi, Betty Jamie Chung, James F. Fawcett, Tosho Iritani, Sung Jin Lee, and Tsong-shien Wu, *The Value of Children: A Cross-National Study* (Honolulu: East-West Population Institute, 1975). Vol. 1 is an introduction to the project and a comparative analysis. Vols. 2 to 7 deal with each of the countries in the project: the Republic of China (Taiwan), Japan, the Republic of Korea, the Philippines, Thailand, and the United States (Hawaii).

60. Marvin Harris, *Cannibals and Kings: The Origins of Cultures* (New York: Random House, 1977).

61. James G. Frazer, *The Golden Bough,* 3d ed. (New York: St. Martins, 1966). See the section on "The Dying God."

62. Jean-François Saucier, "Correlates of the Long Post-partum Taboo: A Cross-cultural Study," *Current Anthropology* 13 (1972): 238.

63. William G. Sumner, *Folkways* (Boston: Ginn, 1907).

64. Miller, *The Child in Primitive Society,* p. 121.

65. Herbert Bloch and Arthur Niederhoffer, *The Gang—A Study in Adolescent Behavior* (New York: Philosophical Library, 1958).

66. Theodore Reik, *Ritual: Psychoanalytic Studies* (London: Hogarth Press, 1931), p. 104.

67. Ibid., p. 106.

68. Alan Watson, *The Law of the Ancient Romans* (Dallas: Southern Methodist University Press, 1970), p. 38.

69. Ibid., p. 83.

70. Fustel de Coulanges, *The Ancient City: A Study of the Religion, Laws and Institutions of Greece and Rome* (Garden City, N.Y.: Doubleday Anchor, 1956), p. 90.

71. Charles A. Savage, *The Athenian Family: A Sociological and Legal Study* (Baltimore: 1967), p. 89.

72. Ibid., p. 91.

73. Reuven Yaron, *The Laws of Eshunna* (Jerusalem: Magnes Press, Hebrew University, 1969), p. 56.

74. Arthur S. Diamond, *The Evolution of Law and Order* (London: Watts, 1951), p. 295.

75. Exodus 20, Deuteronomy 5.

76. Deuteronomy 21, 18–21.

77. Francis H. Bohlen, *Studies in the Law of Torts* (Indianapolis: Bobbs-Merrill, 1926), p. 302.

78. William Blackstone, *Commentaries on the Laws of England,* Book 1, "Of Parent and Child."

79. Peter M. Bromley, *Family Law,* 5th ed. (London: Butterworths, 1976) p. 298.

80. Ibid.

81. See P. R. H. Webb and H. K. Bevan, *Source Book of Family Law* (London: Butterworths, 1964), p. 462.

82. See the judgment of Chief Justice Tindal in *Grinnell v. Wells* (1844) 7 Man and G, p. 1033.

83. Samuel Kucherov, "Indigenous and Foreign Influences on the Early Russian Heritage," *Slavic Review* 31 (1972): 265. For an account of the practice in Hungary of sexual intercourse between fathers-in-law and daughters-in-law see Bela Gunda, "Sex and Semiotics," *Journal of American Folklore* 86 (1973): 147.

84. Kucherov, "Indigenous and Foreign Influences," p. 266.

85. Ibid.

86. David Mace and Vera Mace, *Marriage: East and West* (New York: Doubleday Dolphin, 1959), chapter 8, pp. 190–202.

87. Katherine Mayo, *Mother India* (New York: Harcourt, Brace, 1927). The Maces provide a brief summary of other books both supporting and attacking Mayo's thesis.

88. Particularly useful articles with extensive accounts of cruel practices against children are: Richard C. Trexler, "Infanticide in Florence: New Sources and First

Results," 1(1973–1974): 98–116; William L. Langer, "Infanticide: A Historical Survey," 1(1973–1974): 353–367; Barbara A. Kellum, "Infanticide in England in the Psychodynamics of the Victorian Family," 1(1973–1974): 437–461; Bogna W. Lorence, "Parents and Children in Eighteenth-Century Europe," 2(1974–1975): 1–30; R. H. Helmholz, "Infanticide in the Province of Canterbury during the Fifteenth Century," 2(1974–1975): 379–390; N. Ray Hiner, "Adolescence in Eighteenth-Century America," 3(1975–1976): 253–280.

89. Ivy Pinchbeck and Margaret Hewitt, *Children in English Society* (London: Routledge & Kegan Paul), vol. 1, *From Tudor Times to the Eighteenth Century* (1970); vol. 2, *From the Eighteenth Century to the Children's Act (1948)* (1973).

90. Ibid., vol. 1, p. 259.

91. Ibid., p. 259.

92. Ibid., p. 303.

93. Ibid., p. 302.

94. Ibid., p. 303.

95. Ibid., p. 303.

96. Ibid., p. 311. See discussion in Tom Ireland, *Child Labor as a Relic of the Dark Ages* (New York: G.P. Putnam's Sons, 1937), p. 33. This book has a comprehensive discussion of the exploitative practices, and of the political debate in the United States over the abolition of child labor. See also the contemporary report by John Spargo, *The Bitter Cry of the Children* (New York: Macmillan, 1906) especially chapter 3, "The Working Child," pp. 125–217.

97. See discussion in Pinchbeck and Hewitt, *Children in English Society,* vol. 1, p. 302.

98. Ibid., vol. 2, p. 625.

99. George Ryley Scott, *The History of Corporal Punishment: A Survey of Flagellation in Its Historical, Anthropological and Sociological Aspects* (London: Werner, Loune, 1938); see especially chapter 8, "Flogging Children in the Home and the School," pp. 94–110.

100. James Boswell, *Life of Johnson* (Oxford: Oxford University Press, 1934), vol. 2, p. 146, footnote 4.

101. Scott, *The History of Corporal Punishment,* p. 106.

102. See Ray E. Helfer and C. Henry Kempe, eds., *The Battered Child* (Chicago: University of Chicago Press, 1968); C. Henry Kempe, Frederic N. Silverman, Brandt F. Steele, William Draegemuelle, and Henry K. Silver, "The Battered Child Syndrome," *Journal of the American Medical Association* 181 (1962): 17–24. For a listing of research, see Beatrice J. Kalisch, *Child Abuse and Neglect: An Annotated Bibliography* (Westport, Conn.: Greenwood Press, 1978).

103. David Gil, *Violence Against Children: Physical Child Abuse in the United States* (Cambridge: Harvard University Press, 1970).

104. For the research methods used by Gil see ibid., pp. 50–60.

105. Ibid., p. 10.

106.   Ibid., p. 142.

107.   Ibid., p. 8.

108.   Ibid., pp. 8–9.

109.   See especially Richard J. Gelles, "Child Abuse as Psychopathology: A Socio-logical Critique and Reformulation," *American Journal of Orthopsychiatry* 43 (1973): 611–621; "The Social Construction of Child Abuse," *American Journal of Ortho-psychiatry* 45 (1975): 363–371; "Demythologizing Child Abuse," *The Family Coor-dinator* 25 (1976): 130–141.

110.   Gelles, "Child Abuse as Psychopathology," p. 617.

111.   John and Elizabeth Newson, *Patterns of Infant Care in an Urban Community* (Harmondsworth, Middlesex: Penguin, 1965). See also their later book, *Four Years Old in an Urban Community* (Harmondsworth, Middlesex: Penguin, 1971).

112.   Newson and Newson, *Patterns of Infant Care,* p. 204.

113.   See quote of statement by Elizabeth Newson in Myrna Blumberg, "When Parents Hit Out," *20th Century* (1965): 40.

114.   Hunt, *Parents and Children in History,* p. 185.

115.   Jean Renvoize, *Children in Danger: The Causes and Prevention of Baby Batter-ing* (London: Routledge & Kegan Paul, 1974).

116.   Ibid., p. 196.

117.   Ibid.

118.   Ibid., p. 198.

119.   Ibid., p. 199.

120.   Ibid., p. 200.

121.   Ibid., p. 202.

122.   *Rashomon* is a classic Japanese film that presents four different versions of a rape and violent death, each narrator believing his story to be the true one. For an analysis, see Akira Kurosawa, *Rashomon* (New York: Grove, 1969).

123.   See Gelles, "Demythologizing Child Abuse," p. 139: ". . . the abuser be-comes a scapegoat for an inadequate social system which deprives many parents from having an opportunity to meet their children's and their families' basic needs."

124.   Leontine Young, *Wednesday's Children* (New York: McGraw-Hill, 1964).

125.   Ibid., p. 42.

126.   Ibid.

CHAPTER EIGHT
IN LOCO
PATERNALISM

It is a widely held assumption that the rights of the young are better safeguarded today than in the past because of the benevolent paternalism of the state, which is ever ready to provide young people with needed benefits and to protect them from abuses. Strict child labor laws have done away with the economic exploitation of the young; in its stead, free, compulsory education has become the norm. A separate juvenile court system has been tailored to the special needs of juveniles, seeking not to punish them for their misdeeds but to provide them with the necessary treatment that will rectify erroneous value systems and patterns of behavior. Instead of undergoing painful rites of passage, the young are accorded all the latest benefits of scientific and technological knowledge to ease them through each crucial stage of life, from birth onward. Through legislation and voluntary measures, an extensive network of facilities and agencies stands ready to intervene at the first hint of abuse against a child. Thus, the omnipotence and omniscience of the modern state are harnessed in service to its youthful citizens. Or are they?

More and more students of public programs to assist and protect young people are discovering that much of the framework is no more than a glossy veneer hiding many blemishes. According to some critics, the various institutions have failed to fulfill their initial promise; for others, more radical in their approach, these institutions were *ab initio* intended to serve not the interests of the young but, rather, those of the older generation. The latter group regards schools and juvenile courts as a convenient means of controlling the young and ensuring adherence to the norms and values of the older generation. This is particularly important for societies that lack traditional ritual ceremonies of passage as a means of enforcing conformity and obedience.

A third group takes the issue even deeper, questioning the very philosophical base of paternalism, which, rather than a source of support for the young, is actually an ideological justification for denying them rights. Behind this convenient facade of concern for the young the older generation can ensure its own interests.

The paternalistic denial of rights to children is based on two interrelated assumptions: the young are incompetent to handle their own affairs in most areas of social endeavor, and adults possess the required solicitous consideration for the young that entitles them to act on their behalf.

Victor Worsfold notes that control by parents and adults

> has been justified, in the paternalistic view, by the need to protect children from themselves and others. It is argued that children cannot be responsible for their own welfare because by their nature, they lack an adequate conception of their own present and future interests. They are said to want instant gratification and to be incapable of fully rational decisions.
>
> Well intentioned though this view may be, its implicit claim that adults *do* have an adequate conception of children's interests, and that they are always willing to act upon this conception, is open to serious question. In fact, parents often do not know what is best for their children, and children often can make sensible decisions for themselves about their own lives. In addition, the parents, however wise, may have interests and preferences which do not coincide with those of the child.[1]

Worsfold shows how deeply ingrained is the philosophical base of paternalistic thinking. The major seventeenth-century British philosophers, Thomas Hobbes and John Locke,[2] both argue for paternalistic control over children, Hobbes emphasizing children's indebtedness to their parents, Locke striving to keep parental controls to the minimum, compatible with safeguarding the natural rights of children.

The question of paternalism is most acutely brought out in the work of John Stuart Mill.[3] Few people have made such an eloquent and persuasive case for individual rights and personal freedom as Mill. Yet children are expressly excluded from his demands that every person have absolute control over his own well-being. Whereas Mill argues that the adults should not be protected even from causing harm to themselves, since society's assessment might be wrong or, alternatively, adults may be expected to learn from experience, children in contrast, must be saved from the consequences of their misjudgment.

Although Hobbes is more authoritarian in stressing the need for the young to serve the old, and Locke and Mill are more concerned about the benefit that the child will derive from the benevolence of the older generation, the final result is not so different. None of the three "would have considered seriously the perspective of children themselves in determining their own best interests. None accorded children rights of their own."[4]

Worsfold argues that, however incompetent children might be in certain areas, there is no reason to deny them all rights. While it may be permissible to deny children certain rights, just as it is possible to deny adults rights when they lack competence in explicitly defined areas (for instance, a license is needed to drive and to practice many professions), the burden of proof to justify such a denial should be on those who wish to deny the right. The overriding assumption should always be that children have legitimate claims and that adults must be responsive to those claims and, in the final analysis, accountable to the children on whose behalf they are acting. Worsfold uses John Rawls's theory of justice[5] to suggest that children could, as their capacities develop, be given increasing rights within society. Young children should be entitled to participate in society since even they "often *do* know what they want, and are capable of weighing alternatives and of acting on the decisions they make."[6] The major factor that emerges from such an approach is that "children are entitled to rights of their own" and that "the interests of the child are not synonymous with those of parents or protectors."[7] Acting in the best interests of the child cannot be based only on the adults' perception of what is good for the child or be grounded in the belief that, in the course of time, the child will be presumed to have retroactively confirmed the correctness of the decisions made on his behalf.

Exactly how crucial is the difference between child-based rights and wide-ranging trusteeship control by adults may be seen in the shortcomings of some of the most lauded of modern institutions: the juvenile court, the school, and medical facilities for childbirth.

In his study of the juvenile court system, Anthony Platt[8] shows that the humanitarian philosophy of providing a special jurisdictional body to deal with children and to serve their best interests was not the only motivating factor that led to the creation of these courts. No less important was the desire to provide an institutionalized, legal means of controlling the normative behavior patterns of the young. While the juvenile court system guaranteed that children who stole or mugged would be judged in a separate, special judicial system ostensibly oriented to their individual welfare, the selfsame system also provided new and extensive authority to intervene in the behavior of the young:

> [The] child savers went beyond mere humanitarian reforms of existing institutions. They brought attention to—and, in doing so, invented—new categories of youthful misbehavior which had hitherto been unapprehended . . . .
> Granted the benign motives of the child savers, the programs they enthusiastically supported diminished the civil liberties and privacy of youth. Adolescents were treated as though they were naturally dependent, requiring constant and pervasive supervision. Although the child savers were rhetorically concerned with protecting children from the physical and moral dangers of an increasingly industrialized and urban society, their remedies seemed to aggravate the problem.[9]

Platt sees in the development of an ideology that invented delinquency a direct response to the growing awareness that the new industrialized, urban society then emerging was undermining many of the traditional controls that had formerly existed within the narrower confines of the family. The modern family was becoming too loose and too weak to be able to continue to impose such controls, and so the larger, more extensive resources of the society were utilized to reaffirm some of these values. Platt sees the large role played by women in the child-saving movement as a response to their sense of the diminished role that they were called upon to play in the new society. The child-saving movement was able to serve the two major aims of providing women with "a vehicle for promoting acceptable 'public' roles and for restoring some of the authority and spiritual influence that women had seemingly lost through the urbanization of family life."[10] Child-saving had both "important symbolic functions for preserving the prestige of middle-class women in a rapidly changing society" and "considerable instrumental significance for legitimizing new career openings for women. . . . Social work and philanthropy were thus an affirmation of cherished values and an instrumentality for women's emancipation."[11]

Although Shulamith Firestone[12] has argued that the subjugated status of women made them natural allies of the young, it would seem that a contrary process also took place: taking out one's frustrations on the most convenient victims. Platt indicates that when their power within the family was threatened, women had the resilience to use their increasingly emancipated status both to shore up the crumbling framework of the old values and to seek out newer and larger roles for themselves in the society.

Under the banner of concern for the young, new sanctions were imposed on youth, increasing the restrictions placed on their behavior patterns:

> Many of the child-savers' reforms were aimed at imposing sanctions on conduct unbecoming youth and disqualifying youth from the benefit of adult privileges. The child-savers were more concerned with restriction than liberation, with the protection of youth from moral weaknesses as well as from physical dangers. . . . [They were not] especially interested in problems relating to "classical" crimes against persons and property. Their central interest was in the normative behavior of youth—their recreation, leisure, education, outlook on life, attitudes to authority, family relationships and personal morality.
>
> Although the child-savers were responsible for minor reforms in jails and reformatories, they were most active and successful in extending governmental control over a whole range of youthful activities that had been previously ignored or dealt with informally. Their reforms were aimed at defining and regulating the dependent status of youth.[13]

While the juvenile courts in the United States were originally established at the end of the nineteenth century, and while they have been the subject of controversy, almost from their inception, it was only in the 1960s that the full weight of judicial consideration at the highest level was given to their actual operation. In the landmark Kent and Gault cases,[14] the Supreme Court spelled out the various infringements of constitutional rights and the violation of equitable guarantees that the juvenile courts had committed in the course of their routine and normal operations.

In the Kent case, the court expressed "concern that the child receives the worst of both worlds; that he gets neither the protection accorded to adults nor the solicitous care and regenerative treatment postulated for children."

The justices did not go into any detail as to how to remedy the weaknesses of the juvenile court; their decision, however, presaged the even more significant Gault decision a year later, in which the specific defects of the juvenile court were spelled out and the constitutional rights of the young clearly stipulated.

The Gault case is a particularly glaring example of the manner in which the fate of young people could be determined without adequate safeguards for ensuring their basic constitutional rights. The juvenile court judge sentenced a fifteen-year-old boy to a closed institution for delinquent boys for an offense (using obscene language on the telephone) that, when performed by an adult, carried a maximum penalty of two months in prison or a fine. The decision of the judge was made without hearing the evidence directly from the complainant, without the assistance of defense counsel, without prior notification of the charge, without protection of the privilege against self-incrimination, without the right to appeal the decision, and in spite of the youth's denial that he had made the lewd remark (he admitted only to dialing the number and handing the receiver to a friend). Gault's case could have ended with his six-year incarceration had not his parents taken out a writ of *habeas corpus* to have him released. The Supreme Court of Arizona rejected the plea; later it was accepted by the U.S. Supreme Court, which sharply criticized the manner in which the supposedly beneficial paternalistic aspects of the juvenile court were misused by insensitive judges:

Ultimately we confront the reality. . . . A boy is charged with misconduct. The boy is committed to an institution where he may be restrained of liberty for years. It is of no constitutional consequence—and of limited practical meaning—that the institution to which he is committed is called an Industrial School. The fact of the matter is that, however euphemistic the title, a "receiving home" or an "industrial school" for juveniles is an institution of confinement in which the child is incarcerated. . . . Instead of mother and father and sisters and brothers and friends and classmates, his world is peopled by guards, custodians, state employees, and "delinquents" confined with him for anything from waywardness to rape and homicide. . . .

Under our constitution the condition of being a boy does not justify a Kangaroo court.

When measuring the meaning of these cases, one should bear in mind that the decisions were made during a particularly liberal period in the history of the U.S. Supreme Court, in the wake of decisions that had vastly extended the protection of the accused in adult criminal cases. In a sense, the aberrant juvenile was the fortunate and fortuitous beneficiary of the far-stronger protection that the court, in the immediate preceding years, had carved out for the most hardened criminals. Without such a climate of concern and a framework of clearly articulated constitutional rights for adults, it is not clear that juvenile delinquents would have been accorded these extra rights.

The Supreme Court has not yet gone beyond constitutional rights to examine the practical issue of the consequences of adjudication and what actually happens to the delinquent who is assigned for his own "benefit" to an institution of confinement. Lawrence Sidman has argued that aspects of the laws of juvenile delinquency constitute gross violations of the basic rights of the child, and he questions whether the effect is not "fostering the perpetuation of second class citizenship for children."[15] He sees an inequity in the fact that children may be declared delinquent for acts such as stubbornness or curfew violations that are really status crimes, not even applicable to adults. The inequity becomes compounded when it is seen that in many cases the child's antisocial behavior, which is defined as delinquency, may be a direct consequence of a faulty home environment and of the parents' failures. Sidman feels that growing disillusionment with the defects of the juvenile court may well lead to its eventual abolition, as has been hinted at in some courts,[16] as juvenile court issues are increasingly brought within the purview of the general courts.

In fact, often it is only through the general courts that full protection for the child can be assured, in the light of the failings not only of the juvenile court system but also of the juvenile corrections system. One of the most devastating critiques of the corrections phase of the juvenile court system is Patrick Murphy's account of his efforts as a lawyer in the juvenile office of the Legal Aid Society in Chicago to help many of those who had been sent to correctional institutions by the juvenile court.[17] Murphy used the general court system to circumvent the protective powers of the juvenile court, so that he could expose the blatant inequities perpetrated by some of the correctional institutions. These include instances of brutality, solitary confinement, extreme punitive measures for minor infractions of the rules, unconscionable use of tranquilizers to control behavior without concern for negative side effects, and manipulation of the indeterminate nature of the corrective period as a coercive threat for exacting obedience.

While much of Murphy's work focused on an institution that was probably worse than average, abuses of a lesser nature are prevalent elsewhere. Often the kind of institution a child ends up in is a consequence of luck or bureaucratic caprice. Murphy describes how he became aware of the fact that hundreds of children in Illinois were transported across state lines to institutions in Texas. The right of the state to absolve itself in this manner from direct responsibility for its own wards was challenged in the courts. In the course of the investigations of the institutions in Texas, the lawyers came across many instances of abuse, including the sterilization of a young girl without her consent or knowledge; the handcuffing of inmates to a tree or to each other as a punishment; confinement to a room without toilet facilities or, in the case of a wilderness camp, to a cage; and widespread use of corporal punishment.

True, penal institutions for adults sometimes have similarly depressing conditions—but juveniles, by definition, are *not* in penal institutions. They are not being punished, and some of them have not even committed any misdeeds but are in the institution only because they were neglected, the passive recipients of their parents' sins of omission.

Murphy concludes his survey of this one small aspect of the paternalistic juvenile justice system:

> Cases in which the courts are merely used as a club to enforce the views of middle-class social workers and inept regulations should be no part of a judicial system. . . . The juvenile court too often acts as a rubber stamp, giving its imprimatur to the switching of children and families from agency to agency. Yet, if we examine the lives of the people described in this book, I believe it is safe to say that probably 90 per cent of them should never have been brought within the ambit of the juvenile justice system in the first place.[18]

Formerly such decisions as to commitment, despite their often harsh implications, were treated as though they were civil decisions, for which a lower standard of proof is required than in criminal cases. However in the case of *in re Winship,* the Supreme Court decided that the degree of proof required in a juvenile court was to be equivalent to that in a criminal case—beyond a reasonable doubt—and not, as had been the practice, merely of the lower standard of the preponderance of evidence. By this decision the court made it more difficult to have adverse decisions against a juvenile, as had been the situation.[19]

In another area, however, the court decided that the constitutional provisions of the Eighth Amendment (dealing with cruel and unusual punishment) and the Fourteenth Amendment (dealing with due process of law) were not applicable in the case of corporal punishment administered in the schools. A student was held to have no rights to any notice or to a hearing, even of an informal nature, prior to being subjected to physical punishment. The court did, however, note that where such punishment was excessive the student could always seek a remedy in the civil court by suing. Such a remedy is also applicable, of course, to criminals but that has not led to their being denied due process of law. In fact, as the dissenting judgment pointed out, the adult criminal is entitled to the constitutional protections even when subject to disciplinary action while in prison.[20]

More recently the Supreme Court has addressed itself to the question of whether minors may be admitted to a mental institution at the behest of their parents without due process of law. The court held that in such circumstances, it was sufficient if a medical examination was held subsequent to the child's admission; there was no need for an adversary-type formal hearing, in which the child would be represented by legal counsel.[21]

Although by so doing the court was denying the use of a protective device that is made available to adults, it reasoned that the family could be presumed to be acting in the best interests of the child:

> Our jurisprudence historically has reflected Western civilization concepts of the family as a unit with broad parental authority over minor children. . . . The law's concept of the family rests on a presumption that parents possess what a child lacks in maturity, experience and capacity for judgment, required for making life's difficult decisions. Most importantly, historically it has recognized that natural bonds of affection lead parents to act in the best interests of their child.

While the court did note that caution should be exercised since some parents do, at times, act against the interests of their children, this fact "is hardly a reason to discard wholesale those pages of human experience that teach that parents generally do act in the child's best interests."

A dissenting judgment by Justice Brennan (concurred in by Justices Marshall and Stevens) took issue with this approach, comparing the differential treatment accorded to adults and children.

"Adults facing commitment to mental institutions are entitled to full and fair adversarial hearings in which the necessity for their commitment is established to the satisfaction of a neutral tribunal." The judgment spelled out that this meant the right to counsel, to be heard, to confront witnesses and to offer evidence. Not only should such rights be made available to children, but the dissenting judgment added: "Indeed, it may well be that children are entitled to more protection than are adults. The consequences of an erroneous commitment decision are more tragic where children are involved." In addition, "the chances of an erroneous judgment are particularly great where children are involved."

In support of this latter statement reference was made to a report of the National Institute of Mental Health, which had found that in one hospital it had investigated only 36 percent of the patients below the age of twenty actually required such hospitalization. In addition, in Georgia, the very state whose procedures were in dispute, a commission had found that more than half of the state's institutionalized children were not in need of confinement if other forms of care were to be made available. Often decisions to confine a child "are the results of dislocation in the family unrelated to the child's mental condition."

The minority judgment stressed the fact that once the child had been admitted to an institution, there was no longer any need to be oversolicitous in not intruding into the family framework, since this had already clearly been disrupted. Specifically, the child at this stage was "ousted from his family" and therefore had "need for an independent advocate."

In conclusion Justice Brennan argued:

> Children incarcerated in public mental institutions are constitutionally entitled to a fair opportunity to contest the legitimacy of their confinement. They are entitled to some champion who can speak on their behalf and who stands ready to oppose a wrongful commitment. . . .
>
> The risk of erroneous commitment is simply too great unless there is some form of adversial review. And fairness demands that children abandoned by their supposed protectors to the rigors of institutional confinement be given the help of some separate voice.

Modern educational institutions may also be seen not merely as a means of educating the young and preparing them for helpful, constructive roles in society, but also as a subtle means of control, often with harmful effects on the child's development or personality. Desirable as compulsory, state-supplied education may seem, it has many drawbacks.

Recent years have seen a spate of studies critical of the school system, ranging from those that wish to transform the system of teaching to those that wish to abolish the schools in their present form altogether. The common theme is not just the failure of the schools to accomplish their various educational tasks, but, beyond this, the actual harm done to the pupils. Jonathan Kozol has summed up the essence of his critique of the slum school in which he once taught in the title of his book, *Death at an Early Age*.[22] He describes the debilitating effect of school on the child, its destruction of innate talents the pupils might have, its suffocating of any natural tendencies toward study and discovery, its extinction of creative learning. He details the total lack of communication between teachers and pupils and the inability of the former to empathize with the latter, to reach out to them as unique persons.

Charles E. Silberman's comparative survey of education[23] suggests that many of the failures of the school system may be traced to its fundamental commitment to order and control. Discipline becomes a primary aim; the needs of the institution take precedence over the individual needs of pupils. Learning becomes an imposed transference of information instead of a joyous process of discovery.

Within the framework of compulsory education the young are exposed to a host of impositions, partially reminiscent of what they were subject to when their labor was being exploited: long hours (including extensive homework assignments), compulsory attendance, poor facilities, over-crowded classrooms, little consideration for the unique aspects of a child's view of the world and his needs.

Some criminologists and educators have seen the various faults of the school system as major contributing causes to delinquency. In their report to a presidential commission, Walter E. Schafer and Kenneth Polk argue that

> available evidence strongly suggests that delinquent commitments result in part from adverse or negative school experiences of some youth, and, further, that there are fundamental defects within the educational system, especially as it touches lower income youth, that actively contribute to these negative experiences. . . . Despite the fact that the schools are meant to be the major agency for promoting progress along legitimate avenues to adulthood, prevailing conditions in education deter such progress for some youth and make the delinquent alternative more attractive.[24]

Others have seen the accent on book and rote learning as artificially separating the pupil from meaningful life experiences. Paul Goodman[25] urges the incorporation of the young into productive, satisfying work from an early age. The fact that, in the past, children were exploited at work does not mean that, under the right conditions, the young may not be given positive work assignments within their capabilities, with adequate psychic and pecuniary rewards. What is needed are schools oriented to the needs of the young, juxtaposing challenging learning experiences with meaningful work assignments.

Just as in the case of the juvenile courts, the positive aspects of the educational system have blinded many to its basic defects and drawbacks. Free and compulsory education is often praised as one of the more advanced achievements of modern society, yet its long term effect has been to extend the imposition of controls on the young. Some of this is undoubtedly due to the mass nature of the system, making necessary the use of efficient methods of controlling large numbers of pupils. The schools have taken on more and more of the characteristics of what Erving Goffman calls "total institutions,"[26] serving their own ends, not necessarily those of the children.

According to Goodman, the schools fulfill two indispensable aims for society at large: relieving the home of the constant responsibility for the care of the children and rescuing the child from the home. But this baby-sitting experience does not lead to an enjoyable experience; it becomes either "spirit breaking or a road to defiance."[27]

Ted Clark is even more extreme, claiming that the schools are a major contributing force to the "oppression of youth." Adopting an approach similar to that of Platt vis-à-vis the juvenile court system, he argues that

> the beginning of compulsory education and the development of a public school system were deliberately instituted for the purposes of defending society against young people's zeal or imagined potential for disruption and social change and of molding the young people to fit the needs of the society.[28]

More measured in their statements, but for that very reason more disturbing in their impact, are the critical papers presented at an educational symposium in 1972.[29] The writers have diverse professional backgrounds, political philosophies, and suggested solutions, but they are united in a "series of mature and scholarly explorations of the possibility that the emperor of compulsory government-operated schooling is in fact riding his horse before the public in a state of absolute nakedness."[30]

This reexamination of an institution supposedly benefiting the young is not the work of sensation-seeking mavericks. The authors' arguments are thoughtful and based on historical research into the background of compulsory education in the nineteenth century, on a careful analysis of judicial decisions in this area, and on an assessment of the economic implications of seeking alternative means of ensuring positive learning experiences.

Whatever the value of the extreme critiques, it is often the more staid pronouncements of official bodies that pinpoint the full tragedy of the school system. Such a document is the report of the prestigious White House Conference on Children held in 1970:

> It is not possible to spend any prolonged period visiting public school classrooms without being appalled by the mutilitation visible everywhere— mutilation of spontaneity, of joy in learning, of pleasure in creating, of sense of self. Because adults take the schools so much for granted, they fail to appreciate what grim, joyless places most American schools are, how oppressive and petty are the rules by which they are governed, how intellectually sterile and aesthetically barren the atmosphere, what an appalling lack of civility obtains on the part of teachers and principals, what contempt they unconsciously display for children as children.
>
> We cannot underestimate the psychological brutality, dehumanization, and irrelevance of life in many of our nation's schools. The creative spirit in our children is being destroyed in the schools many are forced to attend. We must demand that the schools make good on their promises to be concerned about the child's development as a whole human being. . . .
>
> Public schooling has become an increasingly pervasive part of the process of a child's socialization. Its actual function has been transformed from one of learning/teaching to that of socialization, selection, and certification. This shift makes it difficult to establish or expand programs which might help develop the creative potential in children. Immediate joy, fun, and play, so important

for creative expression, all have difficulty existing in an institution which is called upon first of all to determine the vocational future of a child.[31]

In recent years some of the criticism of the school system has focused even more piercingly on harmful practices imposed upon children as a means of ensuring the smooth functioning of the school within a disciplined atmosphere. Peter Schrag and Diane Divoky describe how under the aegis of a spreading ideology of "early intervention" and "treatment," the language and often the techniques of medicine are being used to serve the purposes of social control.[32]

Children are tested at an early age, sometimes even in preschool, to determine if any deviant tendencies or potential problematic behavior exist; they are then labeled as being in need of special care and treatment and are treated for their presumed defects. "The most significant trend is the dramatic growth of an ideology which sees almost all nonconformity as sickness, and which . . . in the name of prevention, imposes increasingly narrow limits on what it will accept as tolerable behavior. . . . When the impositions come in the name of diagnosis and treatment ('for the benefit of the child'), not in the name of punishment and control, otherwise arbitrary institutional procedures begin to look reasonable and the power to manipulate is immeasurably enhanced."[33]

Tens of thousands, possibly more, children are on regular drugs "to make them more manageable";[34] others have been placed in special classes or groups after being classified as problem or predelinquent children, based on dubious judgments or disputed techniques; still others are being used as guinea pigs in test programs for new drugs or new psychosurgical techniques; for most, confidential information, not always accurate, is kept on file. Schrag and Divoky claim that many of the trends they describe are of fairly recent vintage and that there seems to be an increasing tendency to utilize scientific innovations in order to strengthen control of the young.

Other works have also pointed out the deleterious effects of injudicious application of scientific material. Robert Rosenthal and Lerose Jacobson, for example, have shown how routine and wholesale classification of children according to their I.Q.—intended to facilitate the ability of the teacher to gain a better and deeper appreciation of each child—may actually lead to a simplistic, stereotyped relationship that often works to the child's disadvantage.[35]

While attacks on the school system in the United States in recent years have tended to center on schools serving the lower classes, many of the most extreme abuses of the educational system have been those practices introduced into the most respectable educational institutions serving the elites. Thus the public schools of England (actually private schools for the upper classes) are known for their strict discipline and regular and indiscriminate resort to flogging. According to George Scott, "Eton, Rugby, Winchester, Shrewsbury, Merchant Taylor's and many other halls of learning were famous for their flagellations."[36] While some reforms may have been introduced in recent years, the basic hierarchical, authoritarian structures laid down in the previous century are still prevalent.

It is a matter of some significance for the thesis of this book that one of the leading educational figures in the nineteenth century who set the tone for many harsh disciplinary measures was Dr. Thomas Arnold, famous headmaster of Rugby School and father of the poet Matthew Arnold. Scott notes that "as recently as 1840 Thomas was birching with the best of them."[37]

Arnold's impact on British education was tremendous. Lytton Strachey chose Arnold as one of his four examples of eminent Victorians,[38] together with Florence Nightingale, General Gordon, and Cardinal Manning. He writes of a man who was chosen to be headmaster of Rugby School in order to "change the face of education all through the public schools of England,"[39] and who was the best known headmaster in nineteenth-century England, immortalized in *Tom Brown's School Days*.[40] At the time of Arnold's appointment there was general dissatisfaction with the school system: "The moment was ripe; there was a general desire for educational changes."[41] Dr. Arnold, with his great reputation, could have precipitated farreaching reforms.

Arnold did, indeed, introduce many reforms, but they had nothing to do with subject matter or teaching methods. Nearly all his efforts were oriented toward promoting conformity to conventional moral standards, using methods reminiscent of the harshest forms of rites of passage. Strachey stresses that Arnold's means of inculcating moral values in his students was "not by spreading around them an atmosphere of cultivation and intelligence [nor] by bringing them into close and friendly contact with civilized men . . . [nor] by introducing into the life of his school all that he could of the humane, enlightened and progressive elements in the life of the community,"[42] but by enforcing strict discipline based on a narrow interpretation of the biblical morality of a wrathful God.

Arnold himself "ruled remotely," with little personal contact with his pupils:

> The Rugby schoolboy walked in holy dread of some sudden manifestation of the sweeping gown, the majestic tone, the piercing glance of Dr. Arnold. Among the lower forms of the school his appearances were rare and transitory, and upon the young children "the chief impression," we are told, "was of extreme fear."[43]

Arnold maintained order by publicly expelling the worst boys, quietly removing other troublesome pupils, and, when necessary, personally administering floggings, though the latter he preferred to delegate to the prefects in the highest grades, who under Arnold's stratified system were "excused from chastisement," while themselves being "given the right to chastise."[44] Arnold's contribution, in the final analysis, led to the "ancient system" becoming "more firmly established than ever."[45]

Significantly, Arnold's own son, Matthew, devoted some of his own efforts to a search for a transformation of the educational system, arguing for a more open, liberal and humane form.[46] His theoretical framework was the antithesis of the system advocated and implemented by his father. These opposing approaches to education may also have found their echo in *Sohrab and Rustum*. Arnold may have been hinting not only at parental hostility in the home, but also adult hostility in society, exemplified by the schools that were modeled so closely on his father's methods.

The intervention of the state in the lives of the family, through the prohibition of child labor, the institution of compulsory education, and the provision of child-welfare services, raised the possibility of saving children from the abuses to which they had been subjected in the privacy of the family. In many cases, unfortunately, the worst abuses were not eradicated but merely transferred to more public arenas.

Indeed it is the compulsory mass nature of education today that has led to strong attacks being made on the *in loco parentis* doctrine that has been the legal basis for legitimizing most of the disciplinary measures that schools have traditionally imposed on their students from corporal punishment through determining style of clothes and hair, to political expression.

Legal scholars have challenged the idea that the education system can any longer be considered to have an implied authority to act on behalf of the parents, when there is no meaningful consensual agreement between state and parent.

Further, the rights, not only of the parents, but of the students themselves, should be regarded before disciplinary action is taken. Edward Bolmeier sums up his discussion of recent judicial decisions by arguing that "such tremendous changes have occurred in the size, administration and programs of our public schools that the applicability of the *in loco parentis* doctrine is indeed questionable today."[47] Similarly William Buss argues that "In the modern school setting, the teacher does not and perhaps cannot have an individual, parent-like concern for the child's welfare. A close home-school community that might bring the teacher within the orbit of family trust rarely develops."[48]

Daniel Pekarsky has also shown how an anachronistic concept of the school as a familial enterprise has been used to impose all sorts of paternalistic controls on schoolchildren.[49] He argues for clearly defined rights for them—for instance, redress through grievance boards. His argument is based on a careful appraisal of paternalistic ideas, in which he suggests that we would do well not to be oversanguine that all teachers will be as "noble, kind and wise as we would like," so that we will be able to anticipate and cope with unpleasant actualities. While the familial model of a school is desirable, for as long as it does not exist (and Pekarsky stresses that it does not exist) there is no alternative but to introduce as many formal controls as possible.

Pekarsky also answers the critics of the children's rights movement in the schools by arguing that it is not the advocates of children's rights who have introduced legal, political, and constitutional issues into the schools or who have

> upset a preexisting familial harmony in the school. Long before they came on the scene, educational technologists— . . . infected by the ethos of human engineering—had been progressing along a road that has gradually eroded the foundations of meaningful personal relationships between children and educators in the school; far from being a cause of this erosion, politicization is, at least to some extent, a response to the problems that it has brought.[50]

School represents a great potentiality for children not only to garner knowledge and absorb book-learning but also to develop creative expression and to undergo exciting and meaningful experiences. The ultimate tragedy of the modern school system may lie not in its cruelties and harsh disciplinary measures but in its omissions in denying to the young the rich and rewarding experience of the joy of discovery, self-learning, and constructive work.

The task of building a sound educational framework is by no means an easy one. It would seem that the desire to ensure a perpetuation of values from one generation to the next, the need to impart control mechanisms over the behavior of the young, and the technical problems involved in providing mass education for everyone within the framework of limited financial and personnel resources have often loomed larger than the personal interests of individual children.

Modern society acknowledges that it has an obligation to the young, but too often that obligation seems to be met by the mere fact of enforcing attendance in a formal school system that, at best, may provide each child with little more than the rudimentary knowledge of the three R's.

Paradoxically, it is often the fact of compulsory mass education that is at the heart of some of the weaknesses of the educational system.

The need to provide for the masses often leads to an inability to cater to the personal needs, interests, and abilities of the individual pupil; to provide sufficient alternative modes of education; to orient the learning process of the child around his natural curiosity. Instead there is an exaggerated reliance on the pressures of grades and other formalistic criteria to force the child to learn.[51]

Moreover, much of the school experience is based less on the present needs of the child and more on presumed needs at some future time. Each stage of the learning process is seen as a preparation for the next stage, rather than as an inherently valuable experience. Arguments as to the value of a particular form of education often question whether or not it will benefit students in their future lives. We must also ask whether it will benefit them in the here and now, whether it will enrich their lives at this particular moment.

It is time that we gave greater recognition to the talents possessed by children not only as indicators of possible success in a future career but also as present qualities to be appreciated, respected, and rewarded. There are certain areas in which the young are able to participate with their elders on equal terms. There are a richness and an originality in creative activities—music, art, movement, and gymnastics—that need to be given greater recognition; not as something cute relative to age, or promising prestige to the child and his mentor, but as something possessing intrinsic value. Sorence Boocock claims that the competence of children is often under-estimated and suggests that the work of Matilda Riley and her co-workers on the aging is applicable to the young as well.[52] Riley notes that the presumed skills of older people are often based not on their actual abilities but on the expectations of others. The waning of their powers is not always as drastic as anticipated. Conversely, for the young, their acquisition of skills may be more extensive than is expected or acknowledged.

Children should not be educated out of their natural propensities for learning, for original insights, and for creative activities. Research on al-truism indicates that children in the first few grades often show more empathetic understanding of the needs of their classmates than children in higher grades.[53] It is suggested that the older children become more sensi-tive to the demands of teachers and elders not to behave in an unusual manner and more aware of adult disapproval of children's initiative. How many other forms of growth are being stunted in children by adult intervention?

A well-known aphorism has it that the school years are the happiest years of one's life, but the dropouts, the underachievers, the subsequent regrets of the time wasted and the opportunities missed, the gnawing awareness of potential talents left dormant—all belie this thesis. We can no longer escape the notion that failure of children at school must be linked to a larger question of the inability of adults to meet some of children's paramount needs, while at the same time adults delude themselves as to the extensive attention and benefits they are lavishing on the young.

Similar considerations apply to other institutions. Modern medicine, for example, is hailed for its major advances that, while benefiting the entire population, have conferred special benefits on the young by reducing the infant mortality rate, conquering many children's diseases, and establishing children's hospitals.

Certainly we have much to be grateful for. But we must not let our gratitude blind us to the faults of medical practice. The medical profession has recently come under attack from many quarters for its accent on pathology and treatment and its neglect of health and prevention; for its reliance on pain-killing drugs, and its impersonal way of treating the body, as if it were separate from the mind and heart of the person being treated. The rallying cry has been sounded for a holistic, empathetic approach to patients.

While this appeal has been made to virtually every branch of medicine, a major campaign has been mounted particularly against childbirth practices regarded as insensitive and dehumanizing. Over the years childbirth has changed from an essentially family event to one dominated by the medical profession. The midwife has been supplanted by obstetricians, home confinement by the hospital ward, support of family members by professional nurses. Due to advances in pharmacology and technology, even normal pregnancy and labor are treated by many physicians as a pathology requiring their intervention.[54]

Concerned members of the allied health professions and young couples determined to take active part in the birth of their children have joined together to protest the abuses of aggressive obstetrical practice. As a result of their efforts, many hospitals have changed their policies and now offer childbirth preparation classes, allow couples to remain together throughout labor and delivery, and provide some form of rooming-in. Some hospitals have established alternative birth centers to simulate home birth conditions, while at the same time assuring both mother and infant immediate emergency care if necessary.

The drive to humanize childbirth grew out of women's desire to be conscious, active participants, and for fathers to be present and to assist in one of the most meaningful experiences of their lives. Sympathetic doctors who devised breathing and relaxation exercises to reduce and control the pain of labor contractions focused their attention on the women and their psychological well-being.[55] The advantages accruing from a shorter labor without drugs were primarily physical.[56] Yet, with all this desire for change, there seemed to be little concern with the emotional response of newborns to what was surely an event of crisis proportions for them.

It took an exceptionally sensitive adult to force us to acknowledge and project ourselves into the perspective of the newborn infant. Frederick Leboyer, an obstetrician, has insisted upon the basic right of the infant to be born into as humane and receptive environment as possible.[57] In a book remarkable for its photographic studies of newborns and for its lyrical prose, Leboyer denounces the "violence" attendant upon most modern births: glaring lights, loud voices, cold instruments, hands pawing and slapping and turning the baby upside down, premature cutting of the umbilical cord before the lungs are ready to breathe, and, finally, abrupt separation from the one person whose warm, familiar body could best be expected to ameliorate the shock of birth.

Although the first reaction to Leboyer was skepticism, and even scorn, his ideas are now being given more respect and there is a growing reassessment of the emotional needs of both parents and infant at birth. This reevaluation has been given even greater impetus by the work of Marshall Klaus and John Kennell,[58] who have postulated a critical period immediately following birth, through which bonding between infant and parents is facilitated in the first months and years if they are allowed to remain together in the first hours after birth.

We do not know how much of an effect the birth trauma has upon later psychosocial development. This question is at least as controversial as the Oedipus complex itself.[59] But in choosing among different modes of childbirth—as with any other event affecting the lives of children—we must ask not only how it will affect the child's subsequent development but also how the child feels about a particular treatment at the time he is receiving it. What does it feel like for an infant to embark upon its exciting, terrifying journey into the unknown? Can we as adults conceive in any way of what the emotions of the infant are?

The truth is we may never know just how a human being feels at the moment of birth, but we cannot, for that reason, ignore the persuasive logic and warm empathy of Leboyer and his supporters. Instead, we should be asking ourselves: if Leboyer is right, if he is even partially correct, how could we—how can we—allow our children to enter the world to such a sterile, cold, and violent welcome, when what they need is warmth, affection, and tranquility?

Leboyer's thesis is exciting and challenging. He reminds us of the simple fact that the newborn infant is a human being with special needs, not just a nameless extension of ourselves. His work is also revealing in its very simplicity; for some of his insights, once reported, seem so obvious that one cannot help but wonder why we were so oblivious for so long.

We assumed that infants had no needs or demands of their own and that, even if they did, they had no way of telling us. Leboyer makes us see that there can be communication; only it "is we who do not listen."[60] Childbirth is an extreme example of the gap that separates old and young, of the difficulties that adults caring for the young must inevitably encounter in adapting their practices to the perspective of the child. It serves as a sobering reminder of the immensity of the problems of child care and of the early stage at which they confront us. Most particularly it is an indication that our modern technical advances may be circumscribed by the very limitations of age-old human needs; our technology may not always succeed in catering to these needs. This is true also of a wide range of activities such as children's television and toy gadgetry.[61] In all aspects of modern life, from childbirth methods through the education and judicial systems to the latest technology, we are in danger of creating an impressive edifice of paternalistic practices that will blunt our sensitivity to genuine needs.

Although we have, for the most part, moved beyond some of the more vicious aspects of earlier societies, we are confronted by other, sometimes newer, problems. Whatever advances have been made, we could do well to heed Orville Brim's warning that it may be precisely modern societies, where children are no longer a means of providing status and ego-satisfaction for women, that constitute the greatest problem for children. Referring to America, but in terms relevant to all modern societies, he writes that "we are . . . moving into an era which may be the most precarious for . . . children."[62]

The issue of paternalism versus children's rights looms larger than ever before. In earlier times, rights were sparingly allocated to privileged groups. As more and more minorities obtain rights formerly denied them, it becomes increasingly incongruous to continue denying the young their rights. If corporal punishment is no longer used in the penal system, it seems clearly inequitable to use it against the young alone. In certain areas, the young are even facing forms of discrimination that they did not encounter in the past, though they are familiar to other minority groups. Housing is a good example of this dual process. As legislation and judicial decision have, at least theoretically, assured nearly all minority groups of unfettered access to housing, a new phenomenon has arisen of discrimination against the young. "No children allowed" notices now greet families seeking accommodations, and the issue of housing discrimination is on the agenda of some legislative bodies and courts.

Constitutional guarantees make this issue a straightforward one in the United States: are juveniles to be the only group to be denied the protection of the Constitution? The answer, as far as their rights in the juvenile court system is concerned, has already been given in the Kent and Gault decisions; in the near future, the applicability of these rights in other areas, such as housing discrimination, and possibly job discrimination, will have to be tackled by the courts and civil-rights advocates.[63] In recent years an advocacy movement has developed to represent the specific legal and social interests of the young, seen as separate from, and perhaps in conflict with, that of their parents or other adults providing paternalistic services.[64] For instance, in the battle for custody of the children in a divorce case, the rights of the children are being increasingly recognized and their feelings are being given increasing consideration.[65] In contrast to the traditional paternalistic agencies, the work of these newer agencies is characterized by its militancy—not merely responding to harmful actions against children but actively and vigorously initiating actions to expand and guarantee the rights of children.

Important and effective as court action can be, the struggle also has political implications, having to do with the right of the young to a larger measure of control over their lives. It may no longer be possible to fight these deprivations and discriminations on an ad hoc basis. A clearly articulated and legally entrenched statement of the rights of the young is needed. Defining these rights in a manner compatible with the basically dependent status of the young for most of their early years is by no means an easy task. It entails divesting ourselves of many of the reassuring assumptions of the traditional doctrines of paternalism.

Both the League of Nations and the United Nations issued statements setting out the basic rights of children in a broad manner, as models for individual countries to formulate their own legislation, but the ideas are more protective from the worst abuses than assertive of the potential rights.[66] In fact, there are both national constitutions and international conventions declaring equality of all groups and prohibiting discrimination, yet they are careful to exclude age from the categories.

Recently a number of writers have argued strongly for the need for explicating the basic rights of children. After specifically rejecting the concept of paternalism, as being "thoroughly discredited," Henry Foster and Doris Freed[67] set out a ten-point Bill of Rights for Children, based on the fundamental premise that the child is a human being with dignity and worth. They hold that the stipulation of such a Bill of Rights would not diminish parents' legal and moral obligations but would, on the contrary, "enhance their sense of responsibility."[68]

Richard Farson and John Holt[69] have each delineated ten basic rights that they feel should be granted to children, including: the right to an environment tailored to their needs, thereby reducing their helplessness and dependency; the right to choose an alternative home; the right to work, earn money, and make independent commercial transactions; the right to design the kind of education that they want; and the right to take part in the political process.

Many of these ideas are clearly controversial; some of them seem problematical, especially when their advocates do not bother to differentiate among age groups. But however outlandish some of the ideas may appear, it should be remembered that ideas considered unfeasible when originally suggested in the not-so-distant past on behalf of various minority groups have been translated into reality.

If we are to contemplate seriously confronting the power of parents and adults over the young, and if we wish somehow to limit it, then we cannot shrink from reconsidering much of the present conventional wisdom as to limitations on the rights and power of the young. Social forms that have been developed are not inherently valid and immutable, whereas the problems caused by parent and adult hostility and power are relatively constant factors. To cope with the latter, we must be prepared to confront the former; to solve the problems, even partially, we must be prepared to change the forms, even radically.

Denial of rights to the young is often justified on the grounds of the immaturity and irresponsibility of the young. Yet little of the socialization of the young prepares them for assuming such responsibility, even though it is only through being given positions of responsibility that responsible behavior can be learned.

Many pre-modern societies that have no paternalistic ideologies or institutions entrust much more responsibility to their young. Anthropologists have recorded the way in which the young are gradually absorbed into positions of responsibility, such as looking after younger siblings, and how this contribution to the daily life of the community adds to their sense of worth and to a greater harmony between the generations. There is also some evidence that during wars and large-scale catastrophes, children suddenly orphaned and/or rendered homeless display remarkable qualities of independence and an ability to fend for themselves. Ashley Montagu provides an example of a group of young children who coped successfully, when forced to, on a deserted island in the Pacific. The half-a-dozen children, aged from two to twelve, spent several months on the island and "got along famously. . . . They knew how to dig for water . . . lived mainly on fish . . . had no difficulty fashioning shelters, and in general they flourished."[70]

One of the most radical examples of independence for the young exists among the Nyakyusa in East Africa.[71] Here the male adolescents, at the onset of puberty, build their own age-villages near the village of their parents. While pragmatic considerations of avoiding incestuous contacts and acquiring more land to cultivate underlie the system, it is also based on the awareness of the values of good fellowship among people of the same age. "Male contemporaries build together, and the company of, and good fellowship with, his age-mates is what creates a man of wisdom and character."[72] The actual working of the system described by Monica Wilson seems to have been breaking down even when she originally described it. Wilson notes that no other similar systems had been recorded in the anthropological literature. One wonders whether it was unique because it went so much against human nature, or because it displayed an unusual insight and sensitivity into the real needs of the young for independence—an independence that they seemed perfectly capable of exercising while retaining close contacts with their parents.

In modern times self-governing children's colonies and youth communes have been tried and pioneering attempts made to give the young control over their own lives, working and earning money, and laying down their own reasonable disciplinary rules.[73] On kibbutzim in Israel some of the best-known attempts have been made to develop children's societies not geographically separated from their parents but as part of the kibbutz life.[74] Children from the earliest age live with their own peer group, under the tutelage of trained personnel, themselves generally members of the kibbutz. Each age group has its own housing area, with furniture and facilities oriented to the specific needs of that group. Productive activities, mainly on their own farm but also on the general kibbutz farm, are part of the daily schedule of the children's activities. Contact with parents is close, since most of the activities of both adults and children take place on the kibbutz, and the children are able to visit their parents not only during the leisure hours in the afternoon but also at work.

The rationale behind the separate society for children was not so much to provide the children with greater autonomy as to release the women for work on an equal basis with the men. But its ramifications have been to give the young people on the kibbutz a degree of independence from their parents, in addition to the fact that the communal structure serves to break the economic nexus that is often a major factor in parental power. Yet the youth are not completely independent; often the diminished parental power is replaced by greater societal power through the collectivity of adults in the kibbutz, especially those with a strong commitment to political ideologies.

The kibbutz is a unique arrangement, much as is the Nyakyusa system. It may not serve as a model for more traditional family forms, and it is itself undergoing transition at present, with some kibbutzim choosing to have the children sleep in the parents' home until they reach their teens. Yet it is not the specifics of any utopian scheme that is the issue, but the larger idea of responsibility. It may well be argued that the more recognition and independence the young are accorded, commensurate with their capacities, the more likely they are to respond with respect and gratitude toward those who have granted them that recognition and independence.

The pragmatic question becomes: to what extent can the young be given a larger say in those aspects of life that have a direct impact on their lives, such as the educational system? Not until the youth revolt of the 1960s did many universities open up their committees and boards of trustees to student representation. Why were violent protests necessary before the legitimacy of such minimum access to the power structure of institutions directly affecting students (many long out of their teens) was recognized?

The denial of rights on the campus seems all the more strange when contrasted with the fact that in society at large the franchise has been extended downward, in many countries lowered to the age of eighteen. Yet the manner in which the vote is conferred is also indicative of a basic flaw in so much of arrangements made for the young. One of the main reasons for extending the vote to eighteen-year-olds was their conscription obligations. Anyone who was liable to be sent off to war, it was argued, should at least be entitled to vote. Yet there is a clear anomaly here, for while the biological age of eighteen allows participation in deciding on the most weighty national and international matters, the seventeen-year-old is denied the vote, even in limited local matters. I know of no voting system that makes allowance for the gradual entry of the young into the franchise. One might consider the possibility of instituting a partial vote equal to a fraction of the adult vote, but increasing at each birthday until a full franchise is attained, or a direct vote in certain limited areas of direct concern to the young (for instance, education and recreation), or even a special group of youth delegates for different age cohorts who would have advisory powers and would be consulted by their adult counterparts.[75]

The possibilities are varied and require serious consideration. It is not my intention to make specific suggestions, but rather to draw attention to the manner in which the young can be given increased control over their own lives and greater active participation in the decision-making processes of society. A wide range of ideas should be examined, involving education, living arrangements, franchise, employment, and other related areas. There are certainly no pat solutions, especially given the vulnerability and limited understanding of the very young. But limitations at early stages of life must not be used to deny rights at later stages.

Whatever course the movement for the rights of the young takes, it should be guided not by paternalistic concepts of what adults consider to be beneficial but by a more realistic appreciation of the legitimate aspirations of the young, of their growing capacities and maturity, of their proven responsibility, and of their willingness to exercise their rights with the prudence befitting those who have a stake in the present and the future of the society.

References

1. Victor L. Worsfold, "The Philosophical Justification for Children's Rights," *Harvard Educational Review* 44 (1974): 142.

2. See Thomas Hobbes, *Leviathan* (1651) and John Locke, *The Second Treatise of Government* (1690).

3. John Stuart Mill, *On Liberty* (New York: Washington Square Press, 1963).

4. Worsfold, "The Philosophical Justification," p. 146.

5. John Rawls, *A Theory of Justice* (Cambridge: Harvard University Press, 1972).

6. Worsfold, "The Philosophical Justification," pp. 153–154.

7.   Ibid., p. 155. See also Francis Schrag, "The Child in the Moral Order," *Philosophy* 52 (1977): 167–177; for a critique of Schrag's arguments against paternalism see Geoffrey Scarre, "Children and Paternalism," *Philosophy,* 55 (1980): 177–124.

8.   Anthony Platt, *The Child Savers: The Invention of Delinquency* (Chicago: University of Chicago Press, 1969). For a similar critical approach see Ellen Ryerson, *The Best-Laid Plans: America's Juvenile Court Experiment* (New York: Hill and Wang, 1977).

9.   Platt, *The Child Savers,* pp. 3–4.

10.   Ibid., p. 98.

11.   Ibid.

12.   Shulamith Firestone, *The Dialectic of Sex: The Case for Feminist Revolution* (London: Paladin, 1972), chapter 4, "Down with Childhood."

13.   Platt, *The Child Savers,* p. 99.

14.   *Kent v. United States,* 383 U.S. 541 (1966); *in re Gault,* 387 U.S. 1 (1967).

15.   Lawrence Sidman, "The Massachusetts Stubborn Child Law: Law and Order in the Home," *Family Law Quarterly* (1972): 35.

16.   See *McKeiver v. Pennsylvania,* 91 S.Ct. 1971 (1979).

17.   Patrick T. Murphy, *Our Kindly Parent—The State: The Juvenile System and How it Works* (New York: Viking, 1974). For a similar critical approach by a judge, see Lisa Aversa Richette, *The Throwaway Children* (Philadelphia: Lippincott, 1969).

18.   Murphy, *Our Kindly Parent,* p. 174. For further information on juvenile institutions, see Kenneth Wooden, *Weeping in the Playtime of Others: America's Incarcerated Children* (New York: McGraw-Hill, 1976).

19.   *In re Winship,* 397 U.S. 358 (1969).

20.   *Ingraham v. Wright,* 430 U.S. 651 (1977).

21.   *Parham v. J.R.,* 99 S.Ct. 2493 (1979). For a similar case decided at the same time, see *Secretary of Penn. v. Institutionalized Juveniles,* 99 S.Ct. 2523 (1979).

22.   Jonathan Kozol, *Death at an Early Age: The Destruction of the Hearts and Minds of Negro Children in the Boston Public Schools* (Boston: Houghton Mifflin, 1967).

23.   Charles E. Silberman, *Crisis in the Classroom: The Remaking of American Education* (New York: Vintage, 1971).

24.   Walter E. Schafer and Kenneth Polk, "Delinquency and the Schools," *The President's Commission on Law Enforcement and Administration of Justice: Juvenile Delinquency and Youth Crime* (Washington: U.S. Government Printing Office, 1967), p. 223.

25.   Paul Goodman, *Compulsory Mis-education* (New York: Vintage, 1964).

26.   Erving Goffman, *Asylums* (New York: Aldine, 1961).

27.   Goodman, *Compulsory Mis-education,* p. 148.

28.   Ted Clark, *The Oppression of Youth* (New York: Harper Colophon, 1975), p. 64.

29. William F. Rickenbacker, ed., *The Twelve-Year Sentence* (La Salle, Ill.: Open Court, 1974).

30. Benjamin A. Rogge, "Introduction" to Rickenbacker, ed., *The Twelve-Year Sentence*, p. 2.

31. *White House Conference on Children* (Washington: U.S. Government Printing Office, 1970), p. 94.

32. Peter Schrag and Diane Divoky, *The Myth of the Hyperactive Child and Other Forms of Child Control* (New York: Dell, 1975), p. 11.

33. Ibid., p. 12.

34. Ibid., p. 16.

35. Robert Rosenthal and Lerose Jacobson, *Pygmalion in the Classroom* (New York: Holt, Rinehart & Winston, 1968).

36. George Ryley Scott, *The History of Corporal Punishment: A Survey of Flagellation in Its Historical, Anthropological and Sociological Aspects* (London: Werner Lourie, 1938), p. 98.

37. Ibid., p. 96.

38. Lytton Strachey, *Eminent Victorians* (New York: The Modern Library, 1918).

39. Ibid., p. 201.

40. Thomas Hughes, *Tom Brown's Schooldays* (1857). A recent book on education in England uses the title of this book as its motif. See John R. de Symons Honey, *Tom Brown's Universe: The Development of the Victorian Public School* (London: Millington, 1977). The first chapter is devoted to an analysis of Thomas Arnold's work: "The Conception of the School in Arnold and in the first new Victorian Public Schools."

41. Strachey, *Eminent Victorians*, p. 207.

42. Ibid., p. 208.

43. Ibid., p. 211.

44. Ibid.

45. Ibid., p. 233.

46. See Matthew Arnold, *Schools and Universities on the Continent* (1868), especially the chapter on "School Studies."

47. Edward C. Bolmeier, *Legality of Student Disciplinary Practices* (Charlottesville, Va.: Michie Company, 1976), p. 29.

48. William G. Buss, "Procedural Due Process for School Discipline," *University of Pennsylvania Law Review* 119 (1971): 560.

49. Daniel Pekarsky, "Rights and Love in Education—An Essay on the Politicization of the School," *Educational Theory* 29 (1979): 11–20.

50. Ibid., p. 16. See also Daniel Pekarsky, "Education and Manipulation" in Ira Steinberg, ed., *Philosophy of Education* (Urbana, Ill.: Philosophy of Education Soci-

ety, 1977), pp. 354–362. For a critique of Pekarsky, see in same book Peter Goldstone, "Response to Pekarsky," p. 363.

51. For a suggestion of an evaluation system that would offer a student choice and motivation, while ensuring the maintenance of high academic standards, see my article, "A Credit Accumulation System: An Alternative to Grade-Point Average and Pass-Fail," *Educational Record* 53 (1972): 227–233.

52. S. Sorence Boocock, "The Social Context of Childhood," *Proceedings of the American Philosophical Society* 119 (1975): 423; Matilda White Riley, Marilyn Johnson, and Anne Foner, *Aging and Society* (New York: Russell Sage Foundation, 1972).

53. See, for instance, the work of Ervin Staub, "A Child in Distress: The Influence of Age and Number of Witnesses on Children's Attempts to Help," *Journal of Personality and Social Psychology* 14 (1970): 130–140.

54. For a critical analysis of present practices and a comparison with earlier practices, see Doris Haire, "The Cultural Warping of Childbirth," *Environmental Child Health* 19 (1973): 171–191 (also published separately by International Childbirth Association, Seattle); and Suzanne Arms, *Immaculate Deception* (Boston: Houghton Mifflin, 1975), especially chapter 6, "Birth's Machine Age," pp. 87–100.

55. For the best-known methods, see Grantly Dick-Read, *Childbirth Without Fear* (New York: Harper & Row, 1959); Fernand Lamaze, *Painless Childbirth* (Chicago: H. Regnery, 1970); and Robert A. Bradley, *Husband Coached Childbirth* (New York: Harper & Row, 1965).

56. M. A. Klinberg, A. Abramovici, and J. Chernke, eds., *Drugs and Fetal Development* (New York: Plenum Press, 1972); P. R. Lee and M. Silverman, *Pills, Profits and Politics* (Berkeley: University of California Press, 1974).

57. Frederick Leboyer, *Birth Without Violence* (New York: Knopf, 1975).

58. See Marshall H. Klaus and John H. Kennell, "Human Maternal and Paternal Behavior" in Klaus and Kennell, *Maternal-Infant Bonding* (St. Louis: C. V. Mosby, 1976), pp. 38–98.

59. See, for instance, Otto Rank, *The Trauma of Birth* (New York: R. Brunner, 1952); and Arthur Janov, *The Primal Scream* (New York: Putnam, 1970).

60. Leboyer, *Birth Without Violence*, p. 8.

61. For an account of the dangers of modern practices and gadgetry, and for unnecessary fatalities and accidents caused by facilities and toys for children, see Shirley Camper Somar, *Let's Stop Destroying Our Children* (New York: Hawthorn Books, 1974).

62. Orville G. Brim, "Childhood Social Indicators: Monitoring the Ecology of Development," *Proceedings of the American Philosophical Society* 119 (1975): 413.

63. There have been recent cases in the United States in which landlords have asked tenants to vacate apartments after the birth of a child. As yet, the Supreme Court has not pronounced on the issue as to whether such discrimination is unconstitutional.

64. Gilbert Y. Steiner, *The Children's Cause* (Washington: Brookings Institution,

1976); see also Sandford N. Katz, *When Parents Fail: The Law's Response to Family Breakdown* (Boston: Beacon Press, 1971) for a critical analysis of public intervention in parent-child relations.

65.   Joseph Goldstein, Anna Freud, and Albert J. Solnit, *Beyond the Best Interests of the Child* (New York: Free Press, 1973). They stress the need to give primary concern to the needs of the child during the divorce, pointing out the different time perspectives children have (and therefore they argue for faster procedures) and the importance of empathetic interaction (and therefore they argue for the precedence of psychological contacts over biological paternity). See also their more recent work, *Before the Best Interests of the Child* (New York: Free Press, 1979).

66.   See United Nations General Assembly Resolution 1386 (xiv), Nov. 20, 1959, Official Records of the General Assembly, 14th Session, Supp. no. 16, 1960, p. 19. Reprinted in Beatrice Gross and Ronald Gross, eds., *The Children's Rights Movement: Overcoming the Oppression of Young People* (Garden City, N.Y.: Doubleday Anchor, 1977), pp. 336–339. The declaration deals with special protection and needed opportunities and facilities for children, the right to "grow and develop in health," the right to healthy upbringing and education, with special treatment for handicapped children, the right to priority for protection and relief. The declaration also appears in Albert E. Wilkerson, ed., *The Rights of Children: Emergent Concepts in Law and Society* (Philadelphia: Temple University Press, 1973). Both books contain excellent selections of articles, statements, and extracts from books dealing with children's rights.

67.   Henry H. Foster and Doris Jonas Freed, "A Bill of Rights for Children," *Family Law Quarterly* 6 (1972): 343.

68.   Ibid., p. 344.

69.   Richard Farson, *Birthrights* (New York: Macmillan, 1974); John C. Holt, *Escape from Childhood* (New York: E. P. Dutton, 1974).

70.   Ashley Montagu, *The Nature of Human Aggression* (New York: Oxford University Press, 1976), p. 28.

71.   Monica Wilson, *Good Company: A Study of Nyakyusa Age-Villages* (Boston: Beacon Press, 1963).

72.   Ibid., p. 67.

73.   For a good discussion of several such colonies, see Leila Berg, "Moving towards Self-government," in Paul Adams, et al., *Children's Rights: Towards the Liberation of the Child* (London: Elek Books, 1971), pp. 9–50. There is a discussion of the work of famous educators such as Anton Makarenko, Homer Lane, and A. S. Neill.

74.   See Bruno Bettelheim, *Children of the Dream* (New York: Avon, 1971) and Melford A. Spiro and Audrey G. Spiro, *Children of the Kibbutz* (Cambridge: Harvard University Press, 1975).

75.   For a form of voting system that might be flexible enough to allow for such partial franchise rights to the young, see Leon S. Sheleff and Bernard Susser, "One Person, Several Votes: The Election-Referendum," *Parliamentary Affairs* 28 (1975): 299–311.

CHAPTER NINE
FAMILY
CARES

Nature has ordained that sexual intercourse between a man and a woman will, in a certain proportion of cases, lead to the creation of a new independent human being. The actual act of procreation may be an expression of deepest love and compatibility, or an act of passion, or merely a biological release of tension. The child born of such a union may, by the same token, express the ultimate peak of communion between a man and a woman or may be no more than the chance product of an isolated act, unplanned and unwanted, a constantly deplored reminder of a temporary moment of sexual excitement.

In either event the consequences are tremendous. The parent-child relation is one in which the wishes of one of the parties—the child—are of no import. Yet the bonds that are forged are physiologically permanent and psychologically of the greatest intimacy and intensity. Married couples, often joined through a voluntary choice based on love and prior experience of each other, are generally entitled to dissolve their union, but no such options are available to either parent or child, except in the unusual circumstance of adoption. Even then the psycho-physiological nexus remains, leading many adopted children to embark on a quest to discover their "true" identity.

Yet there is an aspect to the links beyond the immediate physiological connection and the subsequent psychological interaction. Temporally, the parent and child represent an historical link between the accumulated memories and achievements of the past—family and larger social groupings (race, nation, class, religion)—and the hopes and plans for the future. Both parties are in a symbiotic relationship: the younger generation dependent on their progenitors as the link providing them with an entree into the past and an identity formed thereby; the older generation dependent on their progeny for some chance to perpetuate their memory and influence.

This symbiosis is asymmetrical. The past is capable of being assimilated; it has its composite identity; it is recorded; it has its permanent relics. But the future is indefinite and uncertain; there can never be any guarantee that plans will be fulfilled, hopes realized. In this sense the parental generation remains forever dependent on the children. The young may share in much of the parents' life and their memories of the past; the parents, however, are denied full access to the children's life experiences.

To them, to the children, the future belongs; they alone dwell in what Kahlil Gibran called the "House of Tomorrow."[1] Their very birth, their very presence, is the most poignant reminder of the parents' own vulnerability. Donald Hall expresses this ambivalent feeling in his poem, "My Son, My Executioner,"[2] where he writes poignantly of sensing his own bodily decay while gazing on his newborn son.

James Joyce felt that the birth of a child may well be "the most important thing that can happen to a man."[3] Kafka considered parenthood the most difficult and meaningful challenge that a person could undertake;[4] Aristotle saw in it the desire for immortality.[5] This climactic achievement in a person's life signals also the beginning of decline, of eventual mortality.

Herein is the essential starting point for an understanding or analysis of generational contact. It constitutes a dilemma from which there is no escape, a dilemma for which there is no solution. It is a structural factor inherent in the very nature of generational contact, irrespective of any cultural overtones that might either exacerbate or mitigate this fundamental fact.

The birth of a child, the presumed outward expression of love, focuses the parental generation's feelings on two of the major driving forces in a person's makeup: the fear of death and the yearning for immortality, inextricably connected yet diametrically opposed to each other. Several writers, especially those in the neo-Freudian tradition, have related to these factors. Robert Jay Lifton's work on death in extreme situations has led him to claim that, in the wake of the Holocaust and of nuclear destruction, the modern world confronts novel themes of "unlimited technological violence and absurd death,"[6] yet his development of the theme and its implications show that it is not limited to this society. For within a "psychoformative perspective . . . of death and continuity of life,"[7] Lifton discusses a theory of "symbolic immortality" in which he makes reference to examples of several different cultures. He claims that there are five general modes of the sense of immortality, of which "the first and most obvious is the biological mode, the sense of living on *through* and *in* one's sons and daughters and their sons and daughters. At some level of consciousness we imagine an endless chain of biological attachments."[8] He stresses that the most typical example of such a mode was in East Asian culture, "with its extraordinary emphasis on the family line. In Confucian ethics, the greatest of all unfilial acts is lack of posterity."[9]

The impact of such a biological mode would naturally give rise to pressures and the desire for children. The drive for some measure of biological continuity may have been as relevant a factor in ensuring the continuity of the human race as the sexual impulse. Historically it may have been a factor in minimizing the practice of infanticide.

However, whatever the direct consequences in terms of encouraging birth and an acceptance of one's progeny, this does not resolve the deeper sociopsychological problems of relating to those who are charged with the task of ensuring that continuity, of bearing the memories, of guaranteeing the immortality. The normal processes of socialization and education are designed to ensure the perpetuation of the values, knowledge, and behavior patterns of the older generation. But there can be no ultimate certainty that all such values, knowledge, and behavior patterns will be fully assimilated. This is what lies at the heart of the ambivalence of parents toward their children, and it is accentuated in those societies with cultural imperatives oriented toward social change and progress, where the very hopes for one's children's development lead to their deviating from the old patterns, thereby diminishing the prospects of maintaining their parents' way of life.

The religions based upon familial piety—the Confucian principles, or the Athenian religion described by Fustel de Coulanges,[10] or the ancestor worship of many preliterate tribes—are typical examples of efforts to ensure immortality. Even nonfamilial religions use much of the terminology of family structures: God the father, Christ the son. The cultural norms of Judaism stress the need for a male heir so that, upon the death of the parents, there will be a son to say the *Kaddish*, the mourner's prayer. The widespread phenomenon of levirate marriage, in which a childless widow is obliged to marry a brother of the deceased husband in order to ensure the continuance of his family name, is a further indication of the importance of perpetuating the cycle of the generations.

A further mechanism for ensuring perpetuity is the legal concept of inheritance as practiced in certain legal systems. In his classic book on ancient law, Sir Henry Maine asks: "How came it that the dead were allowed to control the posthumous disposition of their property?"[11] and answers that the notion of universal succession was such that, "though the physical person of the deceased had perished, his legal personality survived and descended unimpaired on his heir or co-heirs, in whom his identity (so far as the law was concerned) was continued."[12] After describing how the basis for such universal succession lay in a view of the family as an ongoing corporation, without undue emphasis on individual personality, Maine concludes: "It is certain that, in the old Roman law of inheritance, the notion of a will or testament is inextricably mixed up, I might almost say confounded, with the theory of man's posthumous existence in the person of his heir."[13]

Whatever the positive effects of these pressures for immortality, they must also have affected the father's perception of his children as part of his property. Beyond this, there is the awareness that in the final analysis, however helpless and dependent the child is in his formative years, the ultimate dependence—the deep need for an expression of immortality after death—is bound up with the child's willingness to remember and respect. Psychologically, this is far more important than the legal provisions of rights and duties devolving upon the heirs. Deep down in the heart and mind of the parent there is the gnawing doubt that the one tenuous link with the future may be snuffed out by a rebellious, vengeful, indifferent, or forgetful child.

The anxiety of death must inevitably cause ambivalence toward one's children, for the final success in achieving immortality can never be known. It must remain a disquieting source of uncertainty. Parents may find some means of ensuring control over their children after death by conditions written into wills, but, for the most part, their dependence and helplessness in controlling the future is almost as great as the dependence and helplessness of the infant child. This is the real "reversal of generations."

Erik Erikson has stressed that the desire for parenthood, the wish of a man and a woman to "combine their personalities and energies in the production and care of common offspring,"[14] is one of the developmental crises confronting every person, the seventh of the eight stages in the development of a healthy human being. Erikson suggests a special term, "generativity," to connote not merely the wish to have children or the fact of having them but the desire and ability to interact positively with them. Generativity "concerns the establishment . . . of the next generation. . . . It is primarily the interest in establishing and guiding the next generation."[15] Erikson claims that the concept of generativity goes beyond such terms as creativity or productivity, or even of parenthood itself. While he makes several references to "generativity" and has elaborated on the idea in subsequent works,[16] he has not yet made a full-scale analysis of the concept and of all its implications.

Don Browning has tried to develop some of the possibilities inherent in the concept of generativity.[17] Like Brown and Becker,[18] Browning sees the possibility of extending the Oedipus complex beyond its sexual connotation to the larger existential concern with the meaning of life and the relations between the generations. Thus the basic human drive is not for sexuality but for generativity.

Browning notes that this aspect of Erikson's work has not always been recognized, and that

> most readers . . . fail to grasp the subtle but all-important shift from sexuality to generativity in Erikson's thought. Erikson himself has only gradually become aware of the true implications of this shift . . . . The crucial theory of the Oedipal complex receives a radically new meaning when generativity rather than sexual economics is given the seat of central theoretical importance.[19]

He then quotes Erikson's own attempt, in his biography of Mahatma Ghandi, to see the Oedipus complex as

> only the infantile and often only the neurotic core of an existential dilemma which . . . may be called the *generational complex,* for it derives from the fact that man experiences life and death—and past and future—as a matter of the turnover of the generations.[20]

The suggestion of a generational complex, while also not fully developed as a theoretical concept, seems to touch on the essence of the contacts between old and young. It may well be linked to, or stem from, the Oedipus complex, inasmuch as the individual ponders over contacts with preceding generations. But so far as the issue concerns the relations with succeeding generations, the existential dilemma must also be understood in terms of the Rustum complex, which deals primarily with the dilemma of the parent toward his children. Erikson himself acknowledges that there is a need for a "new *ethical orientation of adult man's relationship to childhood*; to his own childhood, now behind and within him; to his own child before him; and to every man's child around him."[21]

Browning notes that this insight of Erikson's is developed out of Freud's work, specifically that dealing with the psychotherapeutic relationship and the interaction between therapist and patient that causes transference and countertransference; but Erikson's insight was more than that of psychotherapeutic relationships. It opened, in effect, an entirely new area upon which to center ethical behavior. In so doing, Erikson, as Browning notes, "probably goes beyond anything Freud had in mind."[22] He does indeed go beyond Freud's intention, not only in terms of psychotherapeutic ideas but also with respect to the Oedipus complex. In raising the issue of the adult's relationship to children and childhood, Erikson touches upon the problematic aspects of generational contact from the perspective of the dilemmas and problems of the parental generation, which Freud, given his total commitment to the Oedipus complex, ignored.

It is, however, not clear that Erikson sees the depths of the dilemma, for he optimistically describes an ethical psychology of mutuality, in which both parties recognize themselves in each other. In the process of this positive interaction, done within the "context of everyone's internalization of the cycle of the generations in which he stands," the basis is laid for the "validation and the preservation of the individual in the context of the cycle of generations."[23] This leads Erikson to the important idea of the "interlocking of the human life stages," in which "adult man is so constituted as to *need to be needed* . . . and man *needs* to teach, not only for the sake of those who need to be taught . . . but because facts are kept alive by being told . . . . Every mature adult knows the satisfaction of explaining what is dear to him and of being understood by a groping mind."[24] For Erikson this is the peak of generativity—humanity's unique and innate capacity to respond to the needs of other generations: "Only man . . . can and must extend his solicitude over the long, parallel and overlapping childhoods of numerous offspring united in households and communities."[25] Erikson describes the attitude of the adult to the child as one of mutuality, understanding, a desire to teach and impart. Only casually does he mention that some adults fail to achieve the degree of mutuality that he writes of; instead of achieving generativity, they lapse into the alternative of stagnation. These are for him aberrant cases, suffering from bad experiences in their childhood backgrounds or from a lack of basic faith in the species: "The majority of young parents seen in child-guidance work suffer, it seems, from the retardation of or inability to develop this stage."[26]

Here we are back to the main dilemma of generational contacts. Are these few clinical cases examined by Erikson deviants from a norm, or extreme examples of a far larger failure on the part of many adults to fit into the neat pattern of interlocking cycles of generations? Is the desire for generativity a widespread, nigh-inevitable impulse, or is it an attitude that must be actively worked at?

Browning provides part of the answer: "it is irresponsible creativity devoid of a quality of enduring care that is man's greatest temptation and greatest fault."[27] This is particularly a problem of modern man, who has a

> nongenerative mentality—his inability to care for what he creates, what he generates. We see it in the way he treats his children, builds his buildings, conducts his science, experiments with his technology, and ravishes his environment . . . . For modern man his generativity has degenerated into mere creativeness, experimentation and inventiveness; it has become torn apart from that deeper capacity for care which completes and limits the truly generative impulse. Modern man appears to be generative because he creates so much; in reality his problem is his nongenerative mentality which is seen in the fact that he cares so poorly for that which he creates.[28]

This unnecessary creativity extends to the

> reckless tendency to produce more children than he can either educate or provide for; his unwitting habit of building cities that are uninhabitable for families and children . . . ; his knack for constructing societies so specialized and differentiated as virtually to segregate all children and young people from adult life; and . . . his heartless capacity to conduct wars that call for no sacrifice to himself but that end in the sacrifice of his sons and daughters . . . . In the modern situation we are witnessing a distortion of abilities and potentials that are in themselves human and natural. But this distortion is in itself enough to corrupt the integrity of the evolutionary pilgrimage, the cycle of the generations, the strength of the young and the very life of us all.[29]

Browning then goes on to cite specific aspects of American society that might have led to these distortions.[30] Yet, in many respects, the modern situation may actually be better than that of former times. What Browning and Erikson are really describing is not "modern man's nongenerative mentality" but the nongenerative mentality of people throughout history. There is probably less recklessness in producing children today in modern industrial society than in previous times, when the means of birth control were less reliable. And sacrifice of the young in wars as a common universal theme takes on a different perspective in the modern world, where missiles and nuclear warheads expose all sections of the population to the dangers of war. In addition, abandonment and filicide in previous ages clearly point to that same "inability to care for what he creates, what he generates." Basically what is described is not the dilemma of modern man but the dilemma of Everyman and Everywoman at all times.

The model of generative man is a warm, attractive one, but it is more a desirable model to strive toward than a representation of reality. It fails to take into account the universal dilemma of being responsible for what has, through a sexual act, been created. Both Erikson and Browning acknowledge that the act of conception does not guarantee a subsequent process of generativity. Their error lies in presuming that the failure to achieve generativity is a marginal problem, or at the most a generalized problem specific to modern man, instead of realizing that it goes to the heart of generational interaction. The question is: are the parents and the other adults in the community willing and capable of activating the potential for generativity?

However desirable Erikson's model, it does not sufficiently take into account the obstacles standing in the way of generativity: it ignores underlying parental hostilities; it ignores the fact that the "interlocking of human life stages" may lead to a parallel competitive interaction—more specifically, that the young child, far from fitting easily into the parents' life pattern, may upset it, undermining their plans and challenging their aspirations.

Both Therese Benedek and Alice Rossi, in perceptive and sensitive articles, tell us that the life cycles of mother and child are not always in harmony.[31] In most modern families, "new mothers shoulder total responsibility for the infant precisely at that stage of the child's life when his need for mothering is far in excess of the mother's need for the child."[32]

The mother is required to assume responsibility for the life and welfare of a helpless infant at the very stage when many of her other interests—career, relationship with husband, search for a variety of life experiences—are oriented in other directions. One manifestation of the tensions induced may be the postpartum depression, which probably signifies factors deeper than the normal psychobiological explanations of hormonal change will allow. It may be likened to a cry for help—at the enormity of the responsibility suddenly thrust on the mother, at her feelings of inadequacy and unpreparedness to discharge the trust reposed in her, at the sacrifices that she is called upon to shoulder in terms of her own life aspirations, and, perhaps, at a sense of failure in not responding with the exuberance that cultural norms dictate. I would suggest here that a greater awareness of the prevalence of these feelings, and a greater appreciation of their sociological (and not just biological) causes, would be of great help in coping with the problem.[33]

David Hunt is one of the few writers to have directly challenged Erikson's model. He suggests that Erikson "overestimates the degree to which life cycles interlock. The 'fit' between parents and children is not at all inevitable. We must keep in mind the qualitative differences between the child's needs and the parents' willingness to be caring."[34] While not wishing to reject completely Erikson's concept of generativity, particularly since it is so much more attractive than Freud's model of parent-child relations, Hunt stresses that his own historical research "sharply challenges such a notion."

> Inasfar as seventeenth-century culture was a unit with a set of goals and priorities, the welfare of children was not a matter of particular concern . . . . [B]eing a good parent did not add to a person's standing, and being a bad one brought no discredit. Adults had scant respect for children and neither the ability nor the inclination to make any sacrifices on their behalf. Parents understood little of infantile experience and did not especially care to know more.[35]

The major barrier preventing a proper fit of the generations is a result of the special paradox of parent-child relations:

> In all of childrearing there is a special paradox: parents must nurture and train the infants who will some day grow up and replace them, rendering them obsolete. The truth underlying psychoanalytic discussion of the Oedipus complex is that two generations cannot occupy the same space at the same time. As one advances, the other must get out of the way, give up its prerogatives, prepare for senescence and eventually for death.[36]

A contrary model to that of Erikson could readily be presented, in which each stage of the interlocking life cycle of parents and children could be shown to lead to conflict and tensions.

The burdens of parenthood begin with pregnancy itself, which some people consider distorts the natural form and beauty of the woman's body. Both pregnancy and birth involve certain risks for the health of the woman; the infant is an egocentric, demanding, and insensitive creature, aware only of his own physical needs, to which the parents, particularly the mother, are obliged to respond; the first child, particularly, brings a new structural element into the family, wherein the dyad becomes a triad,[37] introducing many new tensions for which the couple are unprepared. The birth of a child involves sundry extra expenses; the infant may be prone to crying and may cause his parents many sleepless nights; much of the routine of the family may revolve around the infant's physical needs of food and excretion. Assuming the correctness of the Oedipus theme, the child, at an early age, constitutes a source of sexual rivalry for the parent of the same sex and a cause of embarrassment for the parent of the opposite sex. Within the specific framework of Erikson's interlocking cycles, the child is born just at the stage when the parent is setting out on a life career and is liable to be disturbed by the presence of a child.

As the child grows older, the sources of tension persist, taking on different forms. Assuming an average age differential of twenty-five years, the child will reach puberty as the sexual potency of the parents begins to wane; the child reaches the peak of physical and intellectual power as the parents become aware that their own powers are beginning to dwindle; the child embellishes his own dreams of the future at the time that his parents have to consider, in middle age, the extent to which their own dreams of youth have been fulfilled, and perhaps to face up to a reality of frustrated ambitions; the separation problems as the youth moves into independence are greater for many parents than for the adolescent himself; and sexual rivalry may take on a new form as the youth forms permanent emotional and sexual attachments with members of his own generation. Finally, casting its shadow over all is the haunting specter of death and the longing for immortality, both of which become more intense as the parents grow older.

All these are structural factors, directly related to the inexorable biological processes of development; they pose problems for both generations, but, in most instances, more so for the parents. The structural factors themselves may, of course, be exacerbated or mitigated by cultural factors and even personal factors, such as whether the child is wanted or not, or whether the parents are happily married or not.

In the light of such factors it becomes a little easier to understand the widespread instances of child abuse, ranging from indifference to infanticide. It may also be easier to understand why an idyllic conception of parental life has been incorporated into so much of the common and popular culture. The pressures for rearing and bearing children are real and many, and the myth of the innocence of infancy and childhood has combined with the myth of the pleasures of parenthood. An ideology exists to counteract an ambiguous reality. This may have been necessary to assure propagation of the race. In a moment of rare candor, a respectable middle-class couple once confided to sociologist Barrington Moore that the problems of parenthood are so tremendous that if people were honest about them the future of the human race would be placed in jeopardy.[38]

Yet awareness of the problems of parenthood need not lead to an escape from parenthood; it can provoke a more realistic appraisal of what parenthood entails. As Mia Pringle suggests:

> A more realistic and perhaps even more daunting awareness needs to be created of the arduous demands which child rearing makes on the emotions, energy, time and finances, as well as the inevitable constraints on personal independence, freedom of movement and indeed, one's whole way of life .... Deglamourizing parenthood in this way will not deter those who truly want to care for children but it may act as a brake on those with unrealistic expectations.[39]

Recent years have seen an interesting transformation. As a growing awareness has spread of several new social problems—overpopulation, environmental dangers, the inequality of women—so too an ideology has been found for counteracting the trend of bearing and rearing children. The case against having children has now become viable because the concerns for the environment and for the rights of women have made it more palatable.

This extreme position has made it easier to speak more openly about the problems faced by people who do decide to have children: a new approach toward children is developing, some of it based on an awareness and admission of the ongoing problems and responsibilities of caring for children, others based on a barely concealed hostility toward them, camouflaged by presumably larger social concerns such as of a healthy environment and a fuller life. It is instructive to examine a number of books written in this genre and to note both the sincere grappling with a serious problem and the questionable attempt to utilize larger issues to justify negation of the positive aspects of childhood and parenthood. Three popular books, all written from intense personal perspectives, provide good examples of both approaches.

Ellen Peck's *The Baby Trap* is, in many respects, a courageous and pioneering work; it is an attempt made by a married woman without children to put the case for a childless marriage.[40] It is a hard-hitting book, full of factual examples of the problems of raising children, full of insights as to the consequences of such problems (contrary to popular belief, children break more marriages than they make), full of examples of the advantages that accrue to childless couples by not being weighed down by the cares of parenthood. The book appears to be a frank and forthright attempt to put a case that seems to go against the prevailing norms, arguing that married couples should seriously consider not having children. Much of the argument is persuasive—yet, and this is significant, the argument is not put in terms only of the problems of parenthood but is overladen with constant references to the contribution that childless couples make toward a healthy environment. The final impression is not one of sympathetic understanding of the parents' position but much personal rationalization.

Peck herself almost concedes this. She states that the "two usual reasons for voluntary childlessness are: (1) an awareness of ecology and the problem of the population explosion; (2) a desire for wider personal experience."[41] She acknowledges that "couples usually make their decision for one of these reasons, then use the other as a rationalization."[42] Peck states that in her own case it was the latter that influenced her; only later she "began to draw on the frightening state of the world and the facts about population explosion in order to justify my decision to people."[43]

On the one hand, Peck correctly points out many of the problems involved in raising children and the tensions that are thereby caused in the family. She does well to warn young couples against being pressured by the cultural values of the society, the mass media, or well-meaning friends and relatives to have children they do not necessarily want.

But her arguments do not stand up when linked to ecological concerns. For she seeks, practices, and espouses a way of life geared to materialistic consumption potentially harmful to the environment. After approvingly citing a statement by Isaac Asimov that "Babies are the enemies of the human race," she assures us that Asimov "doesn't hate children; it's just that there are too many of them. And they grow to pollute, despoil, defoliate and crowd the earth."[44]

Ecology is certainly a problem, as is overpopulation; they are connected, but not inextricably so. It is possible to control birth rates and yet seriously harm the environment; it is possible to have several children and yet not pollute or even crowd the earth. It is not, after all, the babies who pollute or even crowd the earth—it is what those babies do when they grow up that counts. Peck herself notes that because of high patterns of consumption, "one American child consumes (i.e., destroys) as much of the stuff of the world as *fifty* (!) children born in India."[45] The logical conclusion from such a state of affairs seems to be not to stop having children completely but rather to undertake a concerted effort to cut down on unnecessary consumption.

What is most disturbing in this book is the attempt to justify an accurate critique of the problems and burdens of child rearing by exploiting, to a large extent illogically, the complex problems of ecology. Peck's real attitude to ecology may be gauged by her concern for ecology as a "legitimate value system" superior to that which encourages babies who "interfere with valid value systems."[46] According to Peck, the money invested in babies and raising children could be much better employed in allowing people to develop a real appreciation for nature by having holidays at nature resorts. The desire to be close to nature is so strong that modern man "fills his foyer with plants and must have, if possible, a small replica of a natural lake: a swimming pool."[47] Finally, though some men might be prepared to make sacrifices for having a baby, "there are other men who find great satisfaction in the sense of personal power that comes from being able to buy whatever they want. They want their good Scotch, stereo, vacations. They want a bright young thing on their arm (that's you)."[48] In this vein Peck fights her valiant battle on behalf of a healthy environment and against bearing pollutant babies; against those wicked advertisers and a decadent culture that "expects you to trade the swimming pool for the car pool, the bikini for maternity garb."[49]

The Baby Trap is a personal statement containing many examples from Peck's own life, her husband's, and the lives of her friends. What emerges is a clear discrepancy between the altruistic aims of the ecology movement and the egocentric desires for a life unburdened by parental responsibilities. While it is true that Peck has made a contribution to limiting the population explosion, this in itself is no guarantee of preserving the environment, for her personal life style, the manner in which she seeks to express her "desire for wider personal experiences," is often detrimental to true ecological needs.

One cannot help sensing that Peck's rationalizations about ecology are a cover for a diatribe against children. Her book shows how easy it is to clothe negative attitudes toward the young in terms of positive concerns for society. There is a clear danger that hostility to the young, instead of being acknowledged (which at least would be healthy and would allow for dealing with the problem), will find an ideological outlet of feigned concern for the environment as a camouflage for presenting such views in a palatable fashion. Such a combination would be to the detriment of those who are working to resolve two difficult problems—that of raising children in a healthy manner and that of promoting a viable environment. There may well be connections between them, but to link them together in the manner that Peck has done is to do both issues a serious disservice—exploiting ecological concerns in order to evade the problem of parental hostility.

The problems of parenthood require not an attack on the concept but an honest attempt to acknowledge them and an effort to cope. Shirley Radl and Angela McBride have written books that constitute an attempt by mothers to confront their roles, not in terms of myth or theory or research, but in terms of the problems and tensions of everyday life.[50]

Both books confirm many of Peck's facts. The authors provide a host of examples of the harassments and frustrations, of the humdrum routine, of the tremendous and ever-present responsibility, of failures and consequent guilt, of aggressive tendencies aroused and of desperate efforts to maintain self-control, of resentment at not being adequately prepared, warned, and trained, of interference with previous life-patterns, of an undermining of prior marital harmony. Like Peck, Radl and McBride oppose casual assumption of the role of parenthood, particularly motherhood, in the facile belief that people are naturally endowed with the qualities necessary to perform such a challenging role. Like Peck, they write from very personal perspectives. They state that, though they love their respective children, they can no longer deny the ambivalence they feel toward them. Their books are outpourings of the anger and agony that they have known and that they have recorded in others who have been prodded into talking honestly and openly by the honesty and openness of the authors themselves.

Radl shares with the reader some of her doubts about the wisdom of even committing some of her pain to print, not merely because of the danger of hurting her children but because "it has been difficult to admit to myself that my beautiful, wanted, and planned children have been capable of arousing within me resentment, hostility and rage—and that they could be a source of profound frustration and a cause of serious disturbance in my once ideal marriage."[51] Much as she loves her children, she detests much of the work involved in being a mother: "I'm not really very well cut out for my role, and my kids deserve better than they got."[52]

However, where Peck's book concentrates on the sacrifice in time and money demanded by children, Radl states that the "drudgery, financial privation, or loss of glamour that accompanies motherhood" is not the core issue; it goes much deeper and can be known only through personal experience. "What cannot be deeply known ahead of time is the never-ending responsibility, the constant demands, and the nerve-shattering crises that characterize the role at least as much as the joys."[53]

Radl sees herself and her interviewees as normal parents who have at times been driven to the verge of physical violence. She notes that in most cases when she lost her temper, "my rage was almost never in proportion to the seriousness of what my child had done; and, more significant, I have always wondered what stopped me dead in my tracks in the middle of trembling anger—from beating."[54]

Radl writes that not only had she had doubts about writing the book, but that she also had been apprehensive of raising the issues at all in conversations with friends and acquaintances. It was only after she realized that "honesty begets honesty," and that her personal problem was actually shared with so many others, that she finally went ahead with her project.[55] Most important of all, she claims that the mothers with whom she talked "derived comfort from learning that many women shared their unhappy plight of feeling guilty for not adoring motherhood." It is through honesty and getting "everything out in the open where it can be dealt with" that "perhaps fuller relationships can develop between all members of . . . any family."[56]

This mode of thinking has been thoughtfully developed by McBride. In her view, parenthood must be assessed in terms of growth and development. "I am convinced that parenthood is a role you *grow into* by understanding your own behavior and by learning how to handle your own needs."[57] For mothers the possibility of growth and development are stifled because of the common view that "a baby is woman's ultimate fulfillment" and because of "sex-determined functional roles in child rearing."[58] In an attempt to move "beyond the motherhood mystique," whereby the woman achieves all she is ever going to achieve in bearing and raising children, McBride turns to Erikson's concept of generativity. To be a parent

> assumes that humans of both sexes have an interest in establishing and guiding the next generation .... "Parenting" doesn't conjure up romantic images of complete self-sacrifice; it does imply sensitivity to the needs of the next generation, kindliness, protectiveness, continuity of care, and respect for the dignity of children.[59]

McBride is well aware of how difficult it is to achieve these aims. What often arises out of parenthood is the opposite of generativity—stagnation. The constant pressures of feeding, clothing, sheltering, socializing, educating, and protecting children are so demanding that growth and development in the parent often cease altogether. Far from being an inspiration, the challenge of children presents the ever-present danger of lapsing into a slough, if not of stagnation, then of frustration and despair. In my discussion of the battered child, I quoted parents who discovered the latent violence in themselves only after becoming parents. McBride tells of similar experiences. She found that much of her behavior was at variance with the expected norms of society or the exhortations of parental guidance books:

> However I have come to realize that my feelings are normal. They must be normal, or else we have a nation of crazy mothers. No, I think my feelings belong in the category of "normal crazy." "Normal crazy" describes emotions and thoughts that deviate from what the literature and popular opinion hold up as ideal or good behavior. Yet I know everybody feels them, too, for I have spent countless hours collecting anecdotes and prevalence statistics. ... We must stop being ashamed of our real emotions; we must start getting out into the open some of the worries child-rearing books completely ignore.[60]

Both Radl and McBride have focused on the role of mothers, who are particularly pressured because of the traditional roles assigned to them. They claim that many of these pressures would be minimized if the roles of parenthood were more equitably shared by both parents. Indeed, some of the arguments by Peck against having children could be overcome if child-rearing involved fathers more and if more extensive provisions were made for child-care facilities to reduce the pressures on parents. Much of the discussion by Peck, Radl, and McBride is in fact culture-bound, premised on American middle-class norms. For example, day-care centers are very much part of many European countries.

But even if allowance is made for these facts, even if technical changes were to be made, the essence of the argument remains: the raising of children is a difficult task for which many parents are not prepared or competent. The authors' focus on motherhood as such is a consequence of the cultural patterns of their society; what they are really dealing with is the structural problem of parenthood, which fathers have shirked—or, more accurately, have used their economic and political power to evade. Indeed, foisting the bulk of the care of raising children onto the mother may have been one of the most significant victories of the male sex over the female sex. But it is a Pyrrhic victory in which all have suffered: the mother for having too many of the burdens placed on her; the father for being denied the opportunity to grow and develop as a fully involved parent and to find creative expression for his generativity; the children for being deprived of the paternal care they are entitled to and for being smothered with too much maternal care. Erikson and McBride are basically correct: true generativity must come from full involvement. McBride states that the growth and development of mothers is, to a large extent, dependent upon the mutual growth and development of both parents, actively and jointly sharing the burdensome and challenging task of parenthood.

Perhaps we have known so little about parental hostility because the bulk of research and theorizing about child development has been done by men. One wonders whether Freud would have been so concerned about his relationship with his lately deceased father if he had been more involved in the daily grind of raising his six children and coping with the complex problems confronting child-raisers.

The thrust of McBride's work stems from the overall theme of the feminist movement, which has called for a reappraisal of parenthood and of the respective roles of mothers and fathers. In McBride's words, "once you think of parenting, rather than mothering or fathering, you are free to . . . think about how to divide the task of parenting in new ways that might develop the growth potential of all concerned."[61] It also becomes permissible to raise questions about the nuclear family and the economic underpinnings of present life styles.

Even so, sharing the task is not in itself sufficient. The suppressed violence of mothers arises not merely because they alone are burdened with the major responsibility of caring for the children but also because they are the parent whose hostility is more likely to be revealed and activated as a result of the constant exposure to, and contact with, the younger generation. Increasing the father's involvement may lessen the pressures on the mother, but it may also increase the number of people more directly threatened with having their hidden hostilities exposed. In triadic relationships, there is always the danger of two ganging up against the one, and each parent might reinforce the other's hostility. Bringing the father into the care-taking situation must be predicated on a prior awareness of the problems of child-rearing, of the tensions within the family, of latent parental hostility.

Although these feminist approaches have shown how societal factors influence women's roles, other writers who have encountered instances of maternal hostility have claimed that it arises from the basic makeup of a woman and is transmitted from mother to daughter.

Joseph Rheingold's work is a noteworthy example of such an approach.[62] Drawing upon extensive experience as a psychoanalyst and a broad range of research findings, he has developed a theory of maternal destructiveness. Rheingold's work is a *tour de force*: a courageous attempt to cope with the existence of parental hostility; a rare accumulation of data taken from over 2,500 cases during some twenty years of clinical practice; an extensive compilation of references to the literature of hostility toward children; a fund of insights into familial interaction and human nature; a critical analysis of several writers, researchers, and clinicians (including Freud) for refusing to recognize the hostility to children that their empirical evidence contained.

But Rheingold's thesis is marred by a fatal flaw. Having discovered hostility on the part of both parents toward children of both sexes in both his clinical practice and the general professional literature, he opts not for a theory of parental hostility, not even for an exposition of the intrapsychic dynamics caused by the assumption of motherhood or fatherhood, but for a highly restrictive and questionable notion of innate *maternal* destructiveness born of women's fear of being women.

Rheingold is at great pains to assure the reader of his own initial reluctance to accept the gradually accumulating evidence of maternal destructiveness (reminiscent of Freud's reluctance to accept his own emerging ideas of the Oedipus complex), of his own objectivity in the analysis, and of his respect for women and their role and importance in society. Such protestations have not prevented a number of feminist writers from attacking him for his biases, though none of them has delved deeply into this issue.[63]

In discussing Rheingold's work I plan to draw a clear distinction between the very real value of his empirical evidence and the fallacy of his theoretical model, with its unfortunate consequences. For if efforts to solve parental hostility are limited to the mother—however important her role in the child-rearing process—then a significant aspect of that hostility—namely, that of the father—will be left unheeded and unresolved. To stress maternal hostility is not even to posit half the problem; it is to miss its essence completely. For it is the mother *as parent*, in conjunction with the father *as parent*, who must be understood and helped. The problems outlined by Radl and McBride do not spring from an innate maternal destructiveness but from the inescapable dilemma of being a parent—a dilemma that, because of societal arrangements, has devolved primarily on women.

The disparity between Rheingold's data and his theory is, I submit, a consequence of a bias against women, which prevented him from recognizing the real issue of parental hostility. The evidence for this bias may be found within the works themselves. Interestingly enough, Rheingold claims that several writers were on the threshold of discovering maternal destructiveness, but avoided "assigning responsibility to the mother or to the parents."[64] (This quote, citing "the parents," should not mislead the reader, as Rheingold earlier dissociates himself from such a generalization: "It will not do to speak of parents. The use of . . . 'parents' . . . in discussing the infantile experience strikes me as an evasion of assigning sole or preponderant responsibility to the mother."[65])

Rheingold claims that Freud provides a "prime example" of orienting an interpretation in a particular way. Alluding to maternal destructiveness, Freud wrote that the germ of paranoia in a woman is "the surprising, yet regular fear of being killed (devoured) by the mother"[66] and that "it is impossible to say how often this fear of the mother is supported by an unconscious hostility on the mother's part which is sensed by the girl."[67] Rheingold comments:

> Having arrived at the brink of the correlation, [Freud] then looked the other way: the child's fear and hatred of the mother are manifestations of one of the universal characteristics of infantile sexuality (ambivalence) and of the immaturity of the child's mind, as well as reactions to restrictions imposed by the mother in the process of training. He rejected the idea of parental seduction in the genesis of the Oedipus complex.

Rheingold suggests that Freud was influenced by a

> twofold orientation: toward instinct theory and away from parental responsibility. . . . [H]e ascribed his own conflicts with his parents to a biological factor, his instinctual impulses. His biological orientation had one root in his desire to exonerate his parents, particularly his mother. . . .
>
> The conclusion follows that a great structure of theory may rest on one man's defense against recognizing his own mother's destructiveness.[68]

Ironically, Rheingold, "having arrived at the brink" of parental hostility, fails, just as he accuses Freud of doing, to draw the correct conclusion because of his own "twofold orientation" toward maternal destructiveness and away from parental hostility. Even his reference to Freud is incomplete, for while he makes much of Freud's allusion to a child's fear of being devoured by the mother, he ignores references to the child's fear of being devoured by the father.

Despite Rheingold's attempt to focus on maternal hostility, the sheer weight of his evidence sometimes leads him to use the term "parental." Thus the first three chapters of his book, *The Fear of Being a Woman,* in which he sets out his evidence, have titles of subheadings referring to both parents (e.g., "parental cruelty," "parental seduction," "nonviolent parental abuse").[69] The section on "nonviolent parental abuse" provides an excellent example of Rheingold's confusion in trying to unite his data and his theory. Here we find the anomaly of a detailed account of the violent actions of a father presented under the heading "nonviolent parental abuse," since in this case the mother happens to be nonviolent. According to Rheingold, the mother of his patient "never punished her except once when [the patient] first wore lipstick in adolescence."[70] The mother's nonviolent abuse involved a series of acts reminiscent of the Cinderella story, such as forcing the patient at age nine to do most of the housework and cooking; not allowing her anything for breakfast except coffee; not allowing her to have any friends, to associate with boys, or to participate in extracurricular school activities; reproaching her constantly; and leaving her undernourished. All this, of course, constitutes fairly extreme examples of nonviolent maternal abuse, but it almost pales into insignificance in comparison with the violent *paternal* abuse:

> Her father was alcoholic and violent . . . . [A] former pugilist, [he] became abusive as soon as he was intoxicated. He "pounded" and kicked Elizabeth . . . . The father made repeated unprovoked assaults upon the patient. He ripped her crocheting to shreds. He dragged her by the hair and struck her in the face. He stabbed her in the hand with a knife . . . . On a number of occasions her father pulled her out of bed while asleep, ripped off her night clothes, and beat her maniacally . . . . Rarely the father was contrite and said he did not know what made him so cruel to her, but on the next day he beat her again . . . . The most frightening experience of all occurred when the father shot at her and barely missed her. With a crazed look on his face, he pulled her into the parlor by the hair, said he would "fix it right now," and shot her, the bullet clipping the patient's hair.[71]

All this, I repeat, is described immediately under a heading "*nonviolent parental abuse*" (my italics)! The nonviolent refers, of course, to the mother, who remained indifferent to the father's violence, but surely any objective appraisal would tend toward "parental destructiveness" and not "maternal destructiveness." At the very least, an unprejudiced mind would not include such a story in a section dealing with "nonviolent parental" abuse.

Rheingold's explanation is simple: "This case illustrates how destructive a mother's attitudes may be and yet not entail physical abuse on her part, for it would seem that the mother's annihilative impulses were communicated to the father and executed by him."[72] What is one to make of such a statement? Rheingold does not offer a shred of evidence to suggest that the father was acting as the mother's agent; the disclaimer "it would seem" is merely wishful thinking on his part to satisfy the demands of his theoretical framework. What this case undoubtedly shows is cruelty by *both* parents, the father's physical (and far more serious), the mother's nonviolent. To put it under the heading of "parental nonviolence" requires a misogynist prejudice of immense proportions.

Of course, Rheingold could claim that this is only an isolated case—but *he* chose it out of the 2,500 at his disposal. It occupies three out of the thirty pages in the chapter on *parental* cruelty and is an integral part of the empirical evidence that he offers before expounding his theme of *maternal* destructiveness. Yet Rheingold himself admits that, "while the insidious modes of destructiveness are more characteristic of the woman, there is *little difference between the parents in the frequency and severity* of explicit maltreatment [my italics]."[73] Rheingold does note, however, "an important temporal difference. Because of her almost constant association with the child in its infancy, the mother is more likely to be the perpetrator of violence, while the father tends to enter later as a destructive influence in the role of disciplinarian."[74]

Of course, this greater "constant association" is not an inviolable consequence of being a mother, at least apart from nursing; it is a consequence of social arrangements. Yet even given her greater contact with the child, there is still little difference in the explicit maltreatment, which, of course, means that, proportional to the time spent with his children, the father is actually more abusive. But, according to Rheingold, the child knows who is really to blame: "Regardless of the relative severity, the child usually hates the mother more than he hates the father,"[75] as

> the child knows, or later comes to know, that the father's abusiveness is not spontaneous but is forced upon him . . . . The child may perceive that the father is venting rage at his own frustration and that he beats the child because he dare not beat his wife. Many children also know that the father is "trained" to be the agent of the mother's hostile impulses . . . . Some men punish their children solely to appease their wives.[76]

To suggest that the husband does not dare to beat his wife becomes absurd, given the available data on battered wives.[77] Of course, much of the profuse data has been published only since the appearance of Rheingold's books, but his misconception of the plight of many women only bears out his obtuseness to the reality of women's lives.

What seems to emerge from Rheingold's work, then, is a nonsequitur between the facts that he had gathered of parental hostility by both sexes and the biased theory he set out of maternal destructiveness. I have dealt extensively with Rheingold's work because it contains many examples of parental hostility of all types—violent and nonviolent, overt and covert—and it could have been a major work on the empirical proof of child abuse, but its theoretical bias deprives it of much of its potential value and impact.

Rheingold asserts that his theory offers an opportunity to cope with much that is wrong with our society. Given the immense influence of women, any attempt to cope with and overcome their maternal destructiveness would have far-reaching consequences: "It is a deterrent to enlightened action not to recognize her pervasive influence in shaping personal destiny and human history."[78] Yet enlightened action may only be frustrated by a theory that attributes to mothers qualities stemming from their womanhood when they are more likely to be a consequence of parenthood.

The sort of model that might help to minimize maternal and paternal destructiveness would be one that acknowledged the manifestations of hostility in both parents and perceived this hostility in terms of structural factors directly connected with the status of parenthood. Such a model has been attempted by Ted Clark, who, like Rheingold, has drawn upon his clinical experience to extrapolate to the human experience.[79] Clark's patients are young people, and he claims that many of their problems are caused by adults,

> the result of oppressive relationships with authority . . . . [T]he responses of youth, while often problematic, are justifiable in the sense that behavior and attitudes are attempts to cope with the abuse of power by adults who attempt to control and shape children and youth. The responsibility for young people's difficulties does not lie with the fact that they are young but with adults who are terrified of children.
>
> Adults hate and fear young people or what young people might do or become; this is an inference I made from the way many adults deal with young people.[80]

In discussing the different forms of oppression imposed on youth, Clark concentrates particularly on the family, seeing it as "a social system and social institution which is invariably oppressive—oppression understood as the frustration of growth, of learning, and of development of a person's capabilities."[81] Clark sees the dynamics of the family as animated by power, with the parents exploiting the dependence of their child. Often they are driven not by evil desires of destructiveness but by misguided concern for the child. They wish to control and mold the child in his best interests without realizing that these interests are contingent upon permission for the child to seek "the fullest possible realization of his or her potential and individuality."[82]

Clark sets out a paradigm of the oppressive family in five categories:
(1) the development of fear and anxiety;
(2) the inculcation of dependency on authority figures;
(3) the modeling of authority for the child;
(4) the transmission of values as rules and limits;
(5) the internalization of the model in the child's consciousness.[83]

A number of dangers arise as a result of roles of power and dependency in the family. The family is, for the most part, an isolated and all-embracing system, "a private corner of the world where even the most deprived and weakest of people can exercise some power, express some frustrations, and escape from some tensions and pressures."[84] I have already suggested that the dark side of motherhood is often just such a manifestation of mothers' exploitation of children to find compensation for what they lack in authority, status, and power in the larger society. This is the essence of the "Momism" that Erikson,[85] Philip Wylie,[86] and others have discussed. But frustrations of this type are not limited to women and mothers; they are encountered by all adults. People dissatisfied in their work, denied in their ambitions, lacking in hope for the future, caught up in the endless struggle for economic survival, alienated from their surrounding society, powerless to influence the larger social issues, and frustrated in much of their daily interaction—all are liable to seek outlets for the accumulation of life's failures in the outside world by compensatory exploitation in the confines of their home.

Alfred Adler related the problems of the young to their sense of powerlessness and inferiority.[87] This was one of his major differences with Freud, eventually leading to the break between them. The overwhelming sense of lack of control over one's own life makes an impact on the mind of the infant and the child. The complete helplessness of the infant only gradually gives way as he becomes more and more capable of fending for himself. But this assumption of power is a two-way interactive process: the extent to which a child will be allowed to develop his potentialities depends, to a large degree, on the manner in which the parents relinquish their hold on him. From the severing of the umbilical cord and the weaning of the infant, through the first hesitant, exploratory steps of the child in a myriad of novel activities, to the final assumption of an independent role in life as an adult, parent-child relationships become a reflection of the manner in which, on the one hand, the child is prepared to assume the extra responsibilities and, on the other, the parents are prepared to surrender their control.

It is at the age of adolescence that the problem of separation reaches its peak. Many primitive societies partially resolve the tensions by instituting rites of passage[88] that formalize not only the transition from childhood to adulthood but also the separation of the child from his parents. Since the separation is abrupt, the ritual of passage is judiciously utilized to ensure the continuing subservience of the young to the cultural standards and societal demands of the older generation.

In modern societies there is little or no ritual, but the stage of adolescence itself has been given added prominence as a bridge between childhood and adulthood. In the absence of ritual guidance, the tensions surrounding adolescence increase. While most research looks at the problems of the adolescent searching for a clear, defined identity, there is growing evidence that the separation also causes anxiety and problems for the parents.

Bruno Bettelheim sees the so-called revival of the oedipal conflict in adolescence, as being attributable to "a parent's wish to remain as important to his child in adolescence as he was in infancy."[89] Leon Rongell has also noted the various jealousies that are liable to be felt by parents as their children move into adolescence and early adulthood. More particularly, "the starting point of a train of neurotic symptoms in an older adult is not infrequently discovered to be the actual or impending marriage of an offspring."[90] For Rongell, too, this phenomenon is part of a continuous and dynamic development of the Oedipus complex, which accompanies the individual throughout his life.

Therese Benedek confirms the existence of a "reversed Oedipus complex," relating it to the sexual competition of "middle-aged fathers who are not infrequently jealous of the virility of their adult sons," and to competition in work, where "the success of the son does not always . . . lead to harmony between the generations."[91]

These insights into the problems of parents of adolescents and young adults are valuable; the feelings of the parents may well be related to the residual effects of childhood experiences (whether oedipal or otherwise). Watching one's children grow up and pass through the tensions and challenges of each succeeding stage in life may well revive memories of one's own childhood and trigger off emotional and behavioral patterns developed early in life, not only of oedipal hostility, but also of childhood deprivations and suffering. One's children, especially of the same sex, may present a mirror of one's own past—and many of the ambitions for a child, or warnings to a child, may reflect these concerns. This is understandable, but oedipal concepts alone seem too narrow to totally encompass the wealth of such past experiences. For, after all, it is not the adult's childhood and adolescence that are at stake, but those of the children.

For the parents, in fact, the issue is different. It is their role as parents that is being tested. If they do have residual ambivalences and anxieties, they will cope with them not by wallowing in their childhood memories but by confronting the newer challenges of adulthood and parenthood. Indeed, it is these challenges that may act as a powerful catalytic agent for growth and maturity—but their potential may well be missed if it is incorrectly perceived purely in terms of past problems.

To constantly look back to the past, to constantly see parental tensions vis-à-vis children as a reemergence of the oedipal conflict alone, is to ignore the factors that lead to ambivalence as parents witness the growing powers of their children and their reaching out for independence and for the excitement of building dreams for a future in which the parents cannot share. The "empty nest syndrome"—the mother bereft of dependent children around whom she can weave her dreams and plan her days, left alone without a career and life of her own—is only one aspect of this condition.[92] The father, too, has to come to terms with the crisis of separation. Both parents are forced into soul-searching, wondering whether their efforts and sacrifices on behalf of their children will be rewarded, their hopes and aspirations realized.

It is at this stage that a generally ignored factor of parenthood assumes major significance—namely, that there can rarely be full recompense for the parents. The tasks of parenthood, whether properly performed or not, are manifold, all-consuming, never-ending. It is difficult for the child to provide full return for the gratitude he owes his parents, from whom he gained life itself, then sustenance, then the knowledge and values that have made his acceptance into normal social life possible.

Most research into family life ignores this aspect of the family drama. In fact, one of the few writers to give due cognizance to this factor is Lawrence Berns in his analysis of Shakespeare's *King Lear*.[93] Berns stresses that the debts owed to those who are the "very source of one's being" are inestimable. "Since one is always in their debt, the command 'Honor thy father and thy mother' can be invoked almost without any reservations."[94]

The debt a child owes his parents is almost impossible to repay, although Edgar comes as close to discharging it as is possible. The tragedy of his concern for his father in the play "seems to have been designed to show what would be required for such a debt to be paid in full."[95] On the other hand, Mia Pringle's advice on child care shows the other aspect of this crucial factor in parent-child relations: "Don't expect gratitude; your child did not ask to be born—the choice was yours."[96]

It is of course at adolescence that the demands for gratitude will be most persistent. Generational conflict may well become more intense in adolescence because it is then that the real nature of the relationship between parents and children is fully tested. Unlike the child, the adolescent is not completely dependent upon his parents, and he is less susceptible to control by the usual methods of reward and punishment, especially physical punishment: "An adolescent does not rebel against his *parents*. He rebels against their power."[97]

Helm Stierlin and his co-workers have looked at the problem from the perspective of the parents.[98] Stressing the interlocking crises of the generations, they suggest that it is not only the young person's search for an Eriksonian "identity" that is crucial to the tensions of this age, but also the problems of the parents in coming to terms with the child's new identity. They note that many parents, especially fathers, undergo severe emotional crises at about the time that their children—especially their sons—enter young adulthood. This is borne out by an interesting study of the personal and social factors causing heart attacks, which points to a child's leaving home or disappointing the father's expectations in some way as a common precipitating factor.[99]

Stierlin subsequently expanded upon the theme of separation of parents and their adolescent children.[100] Using the parable of the prodigal son as the theoretical paradigm for his book, he describes the process of separation between parents and children as

> a drama played for the highest stakes. Death and re-birth, loving and leaving what one holds dearest, deepest distress and joy, and conflict and reconciliation, and its elements. These elements hide questions concerning the nature of love, of obedience, and of mutual growth and liberation in families.[101]

Stierlin postulates three modes of separation: binding (the parents keep the child locked in the parental orbit); expelling (the parents neglect and reject their children, consider them a nuisance and a hindrance to their own goals, and the result is often premature separation); and delegation (the child is allowed to move out of the family unit but remains tied to his parents by a long leash of loyalty).

Focusing on the problems that the child's adolescence constitutes for the parents, Stierlin notices their own last-ditch efforts to capture (or recapture) fading youth and their feeling that they are stuck in marital and professional dead-ends. Not just their children, but they themselves have identity crises, and many of them, sparked by their children's efforts, may "desperately wish to make new starts in life."[102]

Stierlin finds that the basic crisis of a child's adolescence is related to the parents' reaction, and that the child's own tension (exemplified in extreme cases by running away from home) is often a response to the parents' prior tensions. The problems of both parents and children can be resolved only by an awareness of the total picture and a search for mutual liberation.

Stierlin's pioneering work investigates a phase of the life cycle that is generally ignored, as research commonly focuses on infancy, childhood, adolescence, youth, and then, at the other end of the life scale, old age. Only an infinitesimal amount of consideration has been devoted to the crisis of the middle-aged, although recently academic work by Daniel Levinson and others has opened up new possibilities.[103] However, much of this work still revolves around oedipal considerations. A good example of that approach is found in a thoughtful analysis of "middlescence" by Barbara Fried:

> . . . it seems logical to hypothesize that individuals going through a developmental crisis even at forty might be apt to experience yet another revival of oedipal conflicts, however attenuated, which would probably be associated with adolescent-like attempts to handle the threats they pose.[104]

To substantiate her premise, Fried quotes Edmund Bergler's contention that many middle-aged men go through an emotional second adolescence in which oedipal fantasies are revived.[105]

Fried also quotes Jones's work on the reversal of generations in which he claims that the parents become jealous of the children's powers as they were once jealous of their own parents' powers.[106] Like Jones, Fried does not consider the possibility that this jealousy may have no connection with presumed residual feelings but may be based on parental jealousy per se. The very description that Fried presents has little connection with residual oedipal feelings but is linked almost directly to actual, existential problems that a parent has with his children. Describing the "conflicting impulses" of a forty-year-old parent toward adolescent children, she writes:

> Consciously he (or she) is pleased and delighted that all the hard work involved in bringing up the children is finally paying off in their maturity; unconsciously he's jealous and resentful of them because they possess a youthful potential that he wishes he still had . . . . When [he] compares himself to teenagers, he sees that they are able to do things that he now cannot, and he realizes that they can expect to reach goals that he might once have attained but that now are beyond him. Even a very loving parent cannot help traces of ambivalence.[107]

So, although the crisis relates to the very real jealousies of the present, Fried, like so many other writers, turns to the popular, well-worn oedipal theme for an explanation of her otherwise perceptive analysis of the crisis of the middle-aged.

Fried uses the Oedipus complex with far greater relevance when she attempts to understand the middle-age crisis in terms of three generations. Here she stresses the feeling of the middle-aged that they are replacing their parents. Thus, for the first time since the idea entered a person's head that it would be nice to replace his parent, he realizes that he is finally able to consummate this wish. He will inherit the power, position, and seniority of his parents, but only "at the expense of the generation preceding his." As a result, he is liable

> on the unconscious level . . . to be confusing real life with the ancient history of the oedipal situation. Conscious comprehension that he is entitled to authority doesn't . . . affect his unconscious tendency to equate his grownup wish for power with the infantile oedipal desire to replace or kill the parent of the same sex.

This confusion "arouses guilt, expectation of punishment and loss of love, and anxiety about death."[108]

Logically this argument makes much sense. If one accepts the oedipal premises, then the Oedipus complex should indeed have some impact on the middle-aged when they are about to consummate the parricidal aspect of the complex: the replacement of the father's generation as the new dominant generation in the onward sweep of history. However, a full analysis of the middle-age crisis, like that of the crisis of adolescence, probably involves the interlocking problems of both the younger and the older generation. One would wish to know more about the feelings of the parents of the middle-aged: their resentment at having to be replaced, their fear of obsolescence and approaching death, their apprehension about the fidelity with which their children will preserve their values and memory now that they are on the threshold of power, and the means at their disposal to either encourage or hinder their children's takeover.

Just as it is not possible to understand adolescence without being aware of the crisis of the middle-aged, so too it is not possible to understand the middle-age crisis without being aware of the parallel crisis of the elderly. In fact, it is quite possible that a complete understanding of generational contact and conflict may be gained only by analyzing the interaction among three generations—not only parents and children but also grandparents and grandchildren.

One of the few attempts to examine this interrelationship is an interesting work by Ivan Boszormenyi-Nagy and Geraldine Spark, who, working in the tradition of family therapy, have built a model of intrafamilial conflict resolution by incorporating the three generations in order to minimize the tensions emanating from two-generational contact. Their book is an important attempt at understanding the nature of interrelationships within a family.[109] Based on years of clinical experience, the book elaborates major concepts involving reciprocity and interaction in human and family relations, the continuity of the generations, and the role of justice in social life. Specifically, the authors conceive of an "invisible ledger" that keeps an account of past and present obligations among family members. They stress that, in the long run, "Perhaps nothing is as significant in determining the relationship between parent and child as the degree of fairness of expected filial gratitude."[110]

Interaction between different members of the family enters into a constant, partly unconscious system of assigning merit and demerit, of determining how much benefit has been derived from other family members and how much accorded, of how many obligations are owed and how many owing. For the authors, the "supreme cohesive value of a group is justice .... [I]f need for equitable balancing of benefits is a major regulatory and motivational force of any social group it is our task to understand what are the social arrangements which monitor justice." Specifically they ask: "What is every man's due in his family? What does a child deserve? What do his parents owe him? How do parent and child evaluate the justness of their *quid pro quo*? How much gratitude will any child owe his parents?"[111]

The writers are well aware of the fact that total equilibrium is virtually unattainable and that, consequently, tensions within the family are liable to result. Of particular importance is the fact that dyadic relations, for instance between parent and child, cannot be fully encompassed without taking into account the larger field of family relationships. No specific relationship can develop within a vacuum; what determines its ultimate quality is the nature of the family group as a total ongoing entity and the degree to which a climate of trust has been created among its members.

The key to understanding the family group is to see it within an historical perspective, existing across the generations—those who have been and those who are to come. The concept of justice

> views the individual in a multidirectional ethical and existential balance with others. He "inherits" transgenerational commitments. He is obligated to those who raised him and is in a field of reciprocal exchange of give and take with his contemporaries. He also faces his essentially unilateral obligations towards his dependent, young children.
>
> Justice has a particular relevance for family life. Reciprocal equity, the traditional framework for assessing justice among adults, fails as a guideline when it comes to the balance of the parent-child relationship. Every parent finds himself in an asymmetrically obligated position towards his newborn. The child has a source of unearned rights. Society does not expect him to repay the parent in equivalent benefits.[112]

In many cases, the imbalance between parent and child can never be resolved. It is this imbalance that may, deep down, lie at the root of much parental hostility, stemming from resentment caused by the constant demands that a child inevitably makes upon the parents and sustained by the inability of the parents easily to forget the sacrifices they have made on behalf of their children.

This is an aspect of parent-child relations that is very much stressed in Arnold Green's classical sociological analysis of the neuroses of the middle-class child that flow from tensions in the home.[113] Green notes the manifold sacrifices that are demanded of the parents: the time, energy, money, and resources that must be invested in caring for the children, the inroads made upon the parents' career ambitions, and the ensuing ambivalence of the parents. In return the parents demand filial loyalty as a recompense and employ excessive control over their children by threats of love withdrawal.

Green's evidence on the middle class is significant for understanding the manner in which parents may express their resentment at the sacrifices demanded of them. The details may be peculiar to the middle class; the principle is more universal.

In fact Green's analysis may not go far enough. The demands made upon children may involve not only loyalty and obedience, but even love, sometimes as a substitute for the love that is lacking in their parents' marital relations, sometimes as a substitute for the love their parents were themselves denied as children.[114]

Thus it seems as long as the relationship is dyadic, it will tend to be asymmetrical. It is only when previous and subsequent generations are taken into account that the pressures for total equilibrium may be diminished. In these circumstances, the parents may realize that, even if their own child is unable to repay them, this is true of their own relations, in turn, with their parents. Children, for their part, may realize that there is no need to feel guilty for not being able to repay their parents, since they in turn will offer similar services and benefits to their own children. Further, the issues of immortality are likely to become absorbed within a larger historical perspective, which sees the continuity of the generations over time.

True harmony within a family setting becomes predicated then upon the capacity to accept with equanimity the inevitable asymmetry inherent in purely dyadic relations. In most cases the parents might have given more—birth, sustenance, socialization—but, in some cases, these benefits may have been outweighed by parental hostility and the harm inflicted on the children. Either way, the possibility of coping with the accumulation of merits and demerits in the family ledger is enhanced the moment it is realized that the two generations directly involved are part of a larger ongoing, neverending process, that there is no pressing need for them to "balance the ledger" precisely or to seek an equilibrium between their respective demands on each other.

Instead of Jones's "reversal of generations," in which hatred in one dyadic relation gets transferred to other dyadic generational relations; instead of Erikson's overly optimistic "interlocking cycle of generations," in which both generations are presumed to complement each other, Boszormenyi-Nagy and Spark offer a different model of an "ongoing cycle of the generations"—a positive way of looking at the connections between the generations as a transference of reciprocal interaction, in which benefits received need not be repaid directly but may be held in abeyance for the benefit of later generations; in which obligations owed to the parents need not cause guilt feelings in the "debtor" child and resentment in the "creditor" parent but may be "written off" by taking into account the interaction of earlier and later generations. Long before the modern family therapists William Sumner and Albert Keller had also argued similarly that "one generation pays for the next, it does not pay back to the last. In this way the society keeps up an advancing fight, as a corporate body, against the limitations of its existence."[115] Huntington Cairns adds that the implications for such an approach are that, "the child owes neither unquestioning allegiance to the political, religious or other social concepts of its parents, nor is it obligated to pay in kind the material advancements made on its behalf."[116]

It is on this basis that true trust within a large family framework and between the generations may be built, and on the basis of such trust that the needs for immortality may be assured. When the parental generation ceases to attempt to impose itself on the future, cordial relations in the present can be worked at and achieved and this, in turn, provides the best basis for preserving the memory of the parents into the future.

Thomas Cottle has aptly expressed the nature of the continuing and inevitable interaction between the generations:

> Sadly perhaps, gratefully perhaps, we find that the motion of young people everywhere is in a sense the motion of ourselves. It is a reminder of the passing of our own private and unshared years, as well as a conclusion to the public and social years we spend with children or as children. The motion of youth and the passage of years imprint time upon all of us, or at least upon those of us belonging to that generation now feeling its age. Children, certainly the very youngest people . . . are time itself . . . . The future seems to them, or ought to seem, so open and endless, complicated, to be sure, but ultimately possible.[117]

Cottle goes on perceptively and lyrically to suggest that:

> By their hopes for the young and in their prayers that the young may liberate the world if only because they are young, the old seek a liberation of their own lives of increasing constraint and incapacities. On these prayers and the efforts they initiate glistens the love being transferred between the generations. But often, too, the old wish for the obliteration of the young, and in this curse they covet a paradoxical liberation, a liberation turned on its head with time running backward, for we just cannot be young again like the young. We must instead be young like the middle-aged, or young like the old. When care for and trust in the young are entertained, succeeding futures, also paradoxically, are preserved and the histories of prior generations finally safeguarded. But when enduring antipathies toward the young dominate the transactions be-

tween generations, a false freedom is born, a freedom conceived in the belief that if one liquidates another's future, one's own past is cured and one's own future is rendered limitless. Among so many inherited rights, aging confers the power of potential rejector on all who survive. Soon the son will become the father who leaves. . . . It's funny and sad to think what we teach children in the name of "preparing" them for adulthood and for the time when we are no longer here.

It's also funny and sad to think of false liberation movements attempted each day as parents and children wrestle with and among themselves in the hopes of "getting together" and moving apart all at the same time.[118]

How to leave gracefully, how to let go willingly, how to separate with understanding, love, and respect at all stages—these are among the key issues of generational contact. Cognizance of this fact will make it possible to try to cope with generational conflict, the hostility of *both* generations, the Oedipus *and* Rustum complexes. But the problem is primarily that of the parental generation. There is no instinctive built-in propensity or preparation for the role of parent, one of the most important roles that a person can assume. It is a transition deserving of its own ritual no less than birth, adolescence, marriage. It is a role that too many undertake with casual indifference, that others shirk for its frightening obligations. It is a role that should be undertaken with humble awe, both in its initial assumption and in the course of continued transference of growing independence to the child, commensurate with his powers to cope with the added responsibility.

It should be undertaken with a willingness neither to exploit nor to resent the helpless dependence of the children in their early years; neither to restrict nor to abandon them as they seek out their independence, their privacy, their own way of life; and finally, to accept an inevitable reversal of the generations when old age sometimes creates a partial physical dependence on one's children, and always a total dependence for the continuity of one's name, memory, and values.

For these stages in the growth of the individual, there is an added relevance to the Oedipus story. It was these stages that formed the riddle of the Sphinx: "What creature goes on four feet in the morning, on two at noonday, on three in the evening?" And Oedipus's answer was: a human being, who in childhood crawls, in adulthood walks erect, and in old age is in need of a stick.[119] Here we have the total dependence of the infant and the partial dependence of the aged. The riddle of the Sphinx embraces the essence of a person's life cycle and hints clearly at the stages and degrees of dependence. This, too, is the message of the Oedipus story. It interlocks aptly with the oracular message of the story warning that children supplant their parents, a warning that is given, not so that the parents will try to evade the consequences but so that they will be well prepared to accept them.

References

1. Kahlil Gibran, *The Prophet* (New York: Knopf, 1951), pp. 21–33.

2. Donald Hall, "My Son, My Executioner," *The Alligator Bride* (New York: Harper & Row, 1969), p. 12.

3. As quoted by Richard Ellman, *James Joyce* (New York: Oxford University Press, 1959), p. 212.

4. Franz Kafka, *Letter to his Father* (New York: Schocken, 1953), p. 99.

5. See Aristotle, *De Anima* 2.4.415a 25–32.

6. Robert Jay Lifton, *Death in Life* (New York: Random House, 1968), pp. 540–541. See also R. J. Lifton and Eric Olson, *Living and Dying* (New York, Praeger, 1974).

7. Robert Jay Lifton, "The Sense of Immortality: On Death and the Continuity of Life," *American Journal of Psychoanalysis* 33 (1973): 4.

8. Ibid., p. 6.

9. Ibid.

10. For a discussion of Athenian religion, see Fustel de Coulanges, *The Ancient City* (Garden City, N.Y.: Doubleday Anchor, 1956; original French edition, 1864). For a good discussion of a Freudian approach to familial concepts in religion, see J. C. Flugel, *The Psycho-Analytic Study of the Family* (London: Hogarth Press, 1921), chapter 13, "Family Influences in Religion."

11. Sir Henry Maine, *Ancient Law* (London, 1919), p. 157.

12. Ibid., p. 161.

13. Ibid., p. 168.

14. Erik H. Erikson, *Identity and the Life Cycle* (New York, International Universities Press, 1959), p. 97. For a good analysis of each stage of the life cycle, particularly as it affects generational contacts within the family, see Frances H. Scherz, "Maturational Crises and Parent-Child Interaction," *Social Casework* 52 (1971): 362. See also his "The Crisis of Adolescence in Family Life," *Social Casework* 48 (1967): 209.

15. Erikson, *Identity and the Life Cycle*, p. 97.

16. See, for example, Erik H. Erikson, *Insight and Responsibility: Lectures on the Ethical Implication of Psychoanalytic Insights* (New York: W. W. Norton, 1964).

17. Don S. Browning, *Generative Man: Psychoanalytic Perspectives* (New York: Delta, 1975).

18. See my discussion in chapter 11 of Norman O. Brown, *Life Against Death* (New York: Vintage, 1959) and Ernest Becker, *The Denial of Death* (New York: Free Press, 1975).

19. Browning, *Generative Man*, p. 147.

20. Erik H. Erikson, *Ghandi's Truth: On the Origins of Militant Non-violence* (New York: W. W. Norton, 1969), p. 132.

21.   Erikson, *Insight and Responsibility*, p. 44.

22.   Browning, *Generative Man*, p. 152. The quotation from Erikson in footnote 21 comes from a chapter entitled "The First Psychoanalyst" dealing with Freud. Erikson had been discussing the ethical and methodological problems of social scientists studying social phenomena, psychotherapists examining their patients, and the need for the observer to "develop the ability to include in his observational field his human obligations, his methodological responsibilities, and his own motivations. In doing so, he will, in his own way, repeat that step in scientific conscience which Freud dares to make." It is at that point that Erikson adds that "that shift in self-awareness, however, cannot remain confined to professional partnerships such as the observer's with the observed, or the doctor's with his patient," and he then argues for the "new ethical orientation of an adult man's relationship to childhood" and so on, as just noted (p. 44).

23.   Ibid., p. 153.

24.   Erikson, *Insight and Responsibility*, pp. 130–131.

25.   Ibid., p. 130.

26.   Erikson, *Identity and The Life Cycle*, p. 97.

27.   Browning, *Generative Man*, p. 164.

28.   Ibid., p. 164.

29.   Ibid., pp. 164–165.

30.   Browning suggests that a close reading of Erikson's thought shows three main factors in American life causing a nongenerative mentality: (a) the Protestant ethic; (b) the inexhaustible and never-ending frontier; (c) the highly differentiated character of advanced industrial societies (p. 168).

31.   Therese Benedek, "The Family as a Psychologic Field," in E. James Anthony and Therese Benedek, eds., *Parenthood: Its Psychology and Psychopathology* (Boston: Little Brown, 1970), p. 124; Alice S. Rossi, "Transition to Parenthood," *Journal of Marriage and the Family* 30 (1968): 26–39. For an interesting debate, based on empirical research, as to whether parenthood causes crisis, see the series of articles, "Parenthood as Crisis," *Journal of Marriage and the Family*, by E. E. LeMasters (19 (1957): 352–355), Everett Dyer (25 (1963): 196–201), and Daniel F. Hobbs Jr. (27 (1965): 365–372). See also Dana Breen, *The Birth of a First Child: Towards an Understanding of Femininity* (London: Tavistock, 1975).

32.   Rossi, "Transition to Parenthood," p. 27.

33.   Gregory Zilboorg notes that the postpartum period affects husbands as well, and disguises death wishes against children. See "Repressive Reactions Related to Parenthood," *American Journal of Psychiatry* 87 (1931): 936.

34.   David Hunt, *Parents and Children in History: The Psychology of Family Life in Early Modern France* (New York: Harper Torchbooks, 1972), p. 25. See also book review basically supportive of Hunt's position and critical of Erikson: John Demos, "Reflections on the History of the Family," *Comparative Studies in Society and History* 15 (1973): 498.

35.   Hunt, *Parents and Children in History*, p. 26. Thus Hunt notes that he reserves

judgment on the question of generativity. In trying to modify Freud's "tragic picture" of child-rearing, where conflict between parents and children is "inevitable," Erikson has, according to Hunt, "stressed too much the reciprocal quality of the relationship between adults and their offspring."

36.   Ibid., p. 175.

37.   For a classic analysis of the structural differences between a dyadic and a triadic situation, see George Simmel, *The Sociology of George Simmel*, trans. and ed. by K. Wolff, (New York: Free Press, 1964), pp. 135–169.

38.   Barrington Moore, Jr., "Thoughts on the Future of the Family," in Frank Lindefeld, ed., *Radical Perspectives on Social Problems* (London: Macmillan, 1968), p. 106.

39.   Mia Kellmer Pringle, *The Needs of Children* (New York: Schocken Books, 1975), p. 175.

40.   Ellen Peck, *The Baby Trap* (New York: Pinnacle, 1971).

41.   Ibid., p. 16.

42.   Ibid.

43.   Ibid., pp. 16–17.

44.   Ibid., p. 17. It should be noted that, in a later book, under joint authorship, Peck displays a far more sensitive approach to the problems of parenthood and provides much good advice. See Ellen Peck and William Granzig, *The Parent Test: How to Measure and Develop Your Talent for Parenthood* (New York: G. P. Putnam, 1978).

45.   Peck, *The Baby Trap,* p. 185.

46.   Ibid., p. 44.

47.   Ibid., p. 69.

48.   Ibid., p. 113.

49.   Ibid., p. 170.

50.   Shirley L. Radl, *Mother's Day Is Over* (New York: Warner, 1974) and Angela Barron McBride, *The Growth and Development of Mothers* (New York: Perennial, 1974). I shall devote several pages to a discussion of these two books as I feel that their straightforward personal accounts reveal far more of the real structural effects of parenthood (not just motherhood, which is what their books relate to) than most research projects and academic approaches. They contain insights into the reality of the burdens of parenthood that research often fails to divulge. There are several other similar books that have appeared in recent years; see especially Virginia Barber and Merrill Maguire Skaggs, *The Mother Person* (Indianapolis: Bobbs-Merrill, 1975).

51.   Radl, *Mother's Day Is Over,* p. 9.

52.   Ibid., p. 37.

53.   Ibid., p. 53.

54.   Ibid., p. 147.

55. In the course of my own work I have come across a similar phenomenon, where discussion of my basic thesis—with friends or in lectures—has often evoked a surprising number of personal responses—of memories of unhappy childhoods and of admissions of the anger, frustrations, and fears often associated with parenthood.

56. Radl, *Mother's Day Is Over*, p. 229.

57. McBride, *The Growth and Development of Mothers*, p. xiv.

58. Ibid., p. 4.

59. Ibid., pp. 129–130.

60. Ibid., pp. 38–39.

61. Ibid., p. 130.

62. Joseph C. Rheingold, *The Fear of Being a Woman: A Theory of Maternal Destructiveness* (New York: Grune and Stratton, 1964) and *The Mother, Anxiety and Death: The Catastrophic Death Complex* (Boston: Little, Brown, 1967).

63. See, for example, McBride, *The Growth and Development of Mothers*; she refers to Rheingold briefly in a footnote, "Dr. Rheingold's important insights into maternal ambivalence (with its destructive components) are completely obscured by his own love affair with mother as omnipotent" (p. 120).

64. Rheingold, *The Mother, Anxiety and Death*, p. 109.

65. Ibid., p. 89. Rheingold also objects to more generally assigning responsibility to "caretakers" or to the "human environment." He refers to the father as "an auxiliary parent."

66. Sigmund Freud, *Female Sexuality* (1931), in *The Standard Edition of the Complete Psychological Works*, edited by James Strachey, 24 vols. (London: Hogarth Press, 1953–66), 21: p. 227.

67. Ibid., p. 237.

68. Rheingold, *The Mother, Anxiety and Death*, pp. 110–111.

69. Rheingold, *The Fear of Being a Woman*, pp. 1–130.

70. Ibid., p. 21.

71. Ibid., pp. 21–22.

72. Ibid., p. 23.

73. Ibid., p. 19.

74. Ibid.

75. Ibid.

76. Ibid., p. 20.

77. See Richard Gelles, *The Violent Home: A Study of Physical Aggression Between Husbands and Wives* (Beverly Hills: Sage, 1972); Del Martin, *Battered Wives* (San Francisco: New Glide Publications, 1976).

78. Rheingold, *The Fear of Being a Woman*, p. 714.

79. Ted Clark, *The Oppression of Youth* (New York: Harper Colophon, 1975).

80. Ibid., "Preface," pp. ix–x.

81. Ibid., p. 30.

82. Ibid., p. 32.

83. See ibid., p. 33.

84. Ibid., p. 48. For a similar approach stressing power in the family as a resource see William J. Goode, "Force and Violence in the Family," in S. K. Steinmetz and M. A. Straus, *Violence in the Family* (New York: Dodd Mead, 1975), pp. 25–44.

85. Erik H. Erikson, *Childhood and Society* (New York: W. W. Norton, 1950), pp. 247–255.

86. Philip Wylie, *Generation of Vipers* (New York: Fervis, 1942), pp. 184–204.

87. See, for instance, Alfred Adler, *Understanding Human Nature* (New York: Greenberg, 1927) and *The Education of Children* (London: George Allen & Unwin, 1930).

88. See A. van Gennep, *Rites of Passage* (Paris: 1904).

89. Bruno Bettelheim, "The Problem of Generations," *Daedalus* (Winter 1962): 74.

90. Leon Rangell, "The Return of the Repressed 'Oedipus,' " in Anthony and Benedek, eds., *Parenthood,* p. 332.

91. Therese Benedek, "Parenthood During the Life Cycle," in Anthony and Benedek, eds., *Parenthood,* p. 332.

92. See especially Betty Friedan, *The Feminine Mystique* (New York: W. W. Norton, 1963).

93. Lawrence Berns, "Gratitude, Nature and Piety in *King Lear,*" *Interpretation: Journal of Political Philosophy* 2 (1972): 27–51.

94. Ibid., p. 27.

95. Ibid., p. 28.

96. Pringle, *The Needs of Children,* p. 159.

97. Thomas Gordon, *Parent Effectiveness Training* (New York: Peter Wyden, 1970), pp. 170–171.

98. Helm Stierlin, J. David Levi, and Robert J. Savard, "Parental Perception of Separating Children," *Family Process* 10 (1971): 411; J. David Levi, Helm Stierlin, and Robert J. Savard, "Fathers and Sons: The Interlocking Crises of Integrity and Identity," *Psychiatry* 35 (1972): 48.

99. William A. Greene, Sidney Goldstein and Arthur J. Moss, "Psychosocial Aspects of Sudden Death," *Archives of Internal Medicine* 129 (1972): 729.

100. Helm Stierlin, *Separating Parents and Adolescents* (New York: Quadrangle, 1974). For some similar interesting ideas on separation of adolescents from their parents, see S. Giora Shoham, "The Isaac Syndrome," *American Imago* 33 (1976): 329–349.

101. Stierlin, *Separating Parents and Adolescents,* p. ix.

102. Ibid., p. 30.

103. Daniel Levinson, *The Seasons of a Man's Life* (New York: Knopf, 1978).

104.   Barbara Fried, *The Middle-Age Crisis* (New York: Harper & Row, 1976) rev. ed., p. 39.

105.   Edmund Bergler, *The Revolt of the Middle-Aged* (New York: Hill & Wang, 1954).

106.   Ernest Jones, "The Fantasy of the Reversal of Generations," *Papers on Psychoanalysis* (New York: Beacon Press, 1961), pp. 407–412.

107.   Fried, *The Middle-Age Crisis,* p. 47.

108.   Ibid., p. 50–51.

109.   Ivan Boszormenyi-Nagy and Geraldine M. Spark, *Invisible Loyalties: Reciprocity in Inter-generational Family Therapy* (New York: Harper & Row, 1973).

110.   Ibid., p. 54.

111.   Ibid., p. 68.

112.   Ibid., p. 55.

113.   Arnold W. Green, "The Middle Class Male Child and Neurosis," *American Sociological Review* 11 (1946): 31–41.

114.   See, for example, Blair Justice and Rita Justice, *The Abusing Family* (New York: Human Sciences Press, 1976).

115.   William Graham Sumner and Albert G. Keller, *The Science of Society* (New Haven: Yale University Press, 1927), vol. 3, p. 1933.

116.   Huntington Cairns, "The Child and the Law," in Victor F. Calverton and Samuel D. Schmalhausen, eds., *The New Generation: The Intimate Problems of Modern Parents and Children* (New York: Macaulay, 1930), p. 217.

117.   Thomas J. Cottle, *Time's Children: Impressions of Youth* (Boston: Little, Brown, 1967), p. 312.

118.   Ibid., pp. 343–344.

119.   See Edith Hamilton, *Mythology* (New York: Mentor, 1971), p. 257. Sophocles's drama of the Oedipus story surprisingly contains only a passing allusion to the story of the Sphinx: Hamilton states that her own account of the story of Oedipus is taken "entirely from Sophocles' play of that name except for the riddle of the Sphinx which Sophocles merely alludes to." However, the story is recounted "by many writers, always in substantially the same form" (p. 256). One may even speculate further as to whether Freud had read a version of the Oedipus story with the full account of the Sphinx, or if he had been completely bound by Sophocles's truncated version. On one occasion he does refer to the riddle of the Sphinx, suggesting that it deals with the question of "where babies come from." ("An Autobiographical Study" [1925], in *The Standard Edition,* 20: 37.)

CHAPTER TEN
FAITHFUL TO
OUR YOUTH

Many of the factors that influence generational tensions within the family are also present at the societal level.

The flow of time favoring the young; the fear of being replaced, ignored, or forgotten; the investment the old make in the young, their desire to inculcate values and ideals so as to ensure their perpetuation; the interrelated crises of interlocking life cycles—all of these factors certainly apply to generational contacts at the societal as well as the familial level. And, while the absence of intimacy may make conflicts when they occur less personally intense, that very lack also means the absence of other moderating influences that might soften confrontations.

In specific sociological terms, the conflict revolves around the degree to which the older generation is able to maintain the status quo, as against the pressures for change emanating from the younger generation. The energies of the adult generation must, in some part, be devoted to ensuring the means of transmitting their cultural and social heritage to succeeding generations. Rites of passage in primitive societies, and educational systems in modern societies, are oriented to this end. But success can be only partial.

The very progress of the human race is dependent on the capacity of people to modify their values and institutions and to mold them to meet changing needs and/or external pressures. The close interconnection between the concept of generations and the concept of social change has been discussed by a number of writers, but only a few of them have made large-scale, comprehensive analyses of the theme.

In a major treatise on generations, Julian Marías notes that while the concept of generations is an old one, it has only recently been submitted to scientific analysis, and then only by a small number of people, most of whom seem to be unaware of each other's work.[1] He draws attention to the work of such leading sociologists and philosophers of the nineteenth century as Auguste Comte ("Our social progress is essentially dependent on death; that is, the successive steps of humanity suppose necessarily the continual and sufficiently rapid renewal of the agents of general change"), John Stuart Mill ("The fundamental problem . . . of the social sciences is to find the laws according to which any state of society produces the state which succeeds it and takes its place"), and Emile Durkheim ("Change takes place in large cities where the population is made up of young mature men who have come there from other places and been separated from their immediate traditions").[2] None of these thinkers focused on the interrelationship of the generations, nor did they attempt to define and categorize the concept of generation.

Subsequent writers did attempt to provide a definite framework for relating to generations as a sociological category, for the most part trying to encompass the idea of generation within a stipulated life-span. Perhaps the most significant work of this nature was that of José Ortega y Gasset,[3] in Marías's opinion, "the first theory of generations worthy of the name."[4] Ortega's work is based on the concept of fifteen-year cycles. Each individual has five periods of life—childhood, youth, initiation, dominance, and old age—each of which lasts fifteen years.

In viewing generational conflict as a struggle over differing ways of life, the two important periods are initiation (years 30 to 45) and dominance (years 45 to 60). Those in the period of initiation begin seeking out innovations, in the course of which they find themselves engaged in a struggle with the preceding generation, whom they attempt to remove from power. The dominant generation, on the other hand, tries to assert its power and defend its world from the onslaughts of the younger generation.

Ortega's originality lies in the fact that, in his view, the concept of generation is not marginal but is incorporated as an integral concept into his total theoretical formula. He fully recognizes the importance of the concept of generations as a key to understanding history. Nevertheless, although it paved the way for a recognition of the concept of generation, Ortega's work does not fully come to terms with what is generally considered the chief generational issue: the conflict that exists between adolescents and youth, on the one hand, and the middle-aged, on the other. For Ortega, the key generational struggle is between those moving into middle-age and those moving out of middle-age. His work also concentrates so much on fifteen-year periods that it leads to a rather forced search for cyclical patterns in history.

Karl Mannheim rejects both Ortega's simplistic ascription of generational affiliation to year of birth and an alternative approach based upon the unique experiences of each generation.[5] Instead, he shows how similar class and generation are as sociological concepts and stresses the need to take account of social forces. For Mannheim, the "problem of generations"

> is one of the indispensable guides to an understanding of the structure of social and intellectual movements. Its practical importance becomes clear as soon as one tries to obtain a more exact understanding of the accelerated pace of social change characteristic of our time.[6]

Arguing that a generation is neither like familial structures such as family, tribe, or sect, nor like officially constituted associations, Mannheim finds that the concept of class comes closest to demonstrating the sociological properties of generations, since there is a certain structural resemblance between them. "Both endow the individuals sharing in them with a common location in the social and historical process."[7]

Interestingly, while both Lewis Feuer and Mannheim see structural connections between class and generation, the actual content of their analysis is in direct opposition.[8] Feuer, as noted, sees class movements as being pragmatic and rational, in contrast to youth movements, which are naive and irrational; Mannheim, on the other hand, has no such reservations. In his view, the younger generation serve as essential catalysts for change and new ideas: "our culture is developed by individuals who come into contact anew with the accumulated heritage."[9]

Since the individual, limited in the extent to which he can absorb new experiences, lacks the flexibility for constantly instituting change, only "fresh contacts" will allow for necessary change. Thus "the continuous emergence of new human beings in our own society acts as compensation for the restricted and partial nature of the individual consciousness."[10] Simultaneously, this process of continuous transformation is facilitated by "the continuous withdrawal of previous participants in the process of culture," which serves "the necessary social purpose of enabling us to forget."[11] Nevertheless, Mannheim does not see any automatic inclination for youth to be progressive and the older generation to be conservative; their response will depend on their attitude toward social change. However, the significance of the social structure of adolescence ("round about the age of 17") is that this is the stage when "personal experimentation with life begins," allowing for the "possibility of really questioning and reflecting on things."[12]

The potential for friction between the generations, says Mannheim, is generally offset because both generations can learn from each other and because the old and the young do not always meet in extreme confrontation, since there are "intermediary" generations.

Having presented the overall structural and formal nature of generations, Mannheim notes that, as in the case of class, the final impact of these factors is dependent on the consciousness aroused; just as people from the same economic background do not always coalesce in concerted political endeavor, so for a generation to become an actuality there must be participation in a common destiny. Hence, beyond the passive, biological belonging, the crucial factor in the creation of a "generation-unit" is the active way in which people respond to their affiliation. A generation-unit need not comprise all the biological members of the generation. Pinpointing the differences between the two, Mannheim writes:

Whereas mere common "location" in a generation is of only potential significance, a generation as an actuality is constituted when similarly "located" contemporaries participate in a common destiny and in the ideas and concepts which are in some way bound up with its unfolding. Within this community of people with a common destiny there can then arise particular *generation-units*. These are characterized by the fact that they . . . involve . . . an identity of responses, a certain affinity in the way in which all move with and are formed by their common experiences.

Thus, within any generation there can exist a number of differentiated, antagonistic generation-units.[13]

Generations, then, cannot be analyzed in automatic terms of cyclic variations, but must be studied and understood within a given historical and social setting. Biology erects only the framework of a generation; sociological factors determine the actual content of that generation, the degree of consciousness of its members, their awareness of a common destiny, their formulation of an actual ideology, their participation in a joint struggle.

A key factor as to whether or not a consciousness of generation arises is the existence of some major event—a war, a revolution, an economic crisis—that indelibly makes its imprint on all those who are at an impressionable age at this time.

This is the essence of Mannheim's thesis. Unfortunately, it has not been given sufficient attention. Of the many books and articles posing explanations for the intensity of generational conflict in the 1960s, only an occasional attempt was made to apply Mannheim's approach to an understanding of the phenomenon. Most writers, both those who condemned the young and those who praised them, seemed to relate the events of the 1960s as if they were unique and, therefore, not relevant for a general theoretical framework.

Occasionally sociologists would refer to two articles that appeared in the early 1940s—one by a leading sociologist, Talcott Parsons, and the other by a leading anthropologist, Ralph Linton.[14] Perusal of these articles, however, shows that they were no more than preliminary speculations of a generalized nature, which had been given originally in a sociological symposium. Neither article contains any reference to Ortega, Mannheim, or other sociologists who do deal with the variable of age. These articles, and the references to them, only emphasize the paucity of material on, and the superficiality of the knowledge of, age stratification.

In contrast to the superficial manner of many sociologists in dealing with age category is the work of Allen Lambert, who has tried to expand on Mannheim's ideas within the context of unique aspects of the modern world.[15] Lambert asserts that the mere succession of generations, in and of itself, inevitably produces pressures for change, "death and resultant forgetting, birth and resultant fresh contact with the sociocultural system."[16] He stresses particularly the various ways different generations react to "new history" and how "significant change in fundamental aspects of society will produce a different consciousness among the different generations."[17] Change generally has more meaning for the younger generation, since they are the new members of society. Lambert also suggests that modern youth has certain unique features because of the impact of the atomic age and the mass media.

While each generation certainly possesses unique properties in keeping with societal and cultural circumstances, one of the most controversial issues raised by the turbulence of the 1960s in most parts of the Western world was whether or not a qualitative transformation had been attained, one that substantively altered the whole nature of generational contact between youth and the older generation as well as the nature of Western society.

Some writers have been adamant in proclaiming the unique qualities of the youth of the 1960s and of their revolt. Since my own thesis speaks of constant structural features, existing at the core of generational conflict, differing merely in form, it is necessary to examine some selected aspects of this debate, in particular those theories arguing for the uniqueness of modern-day youth.

One of the best known analyses of radical youth is Kenneth Keniston's *Young Radicals,* in which the author not only asserts the uniqueness and healthy qualities of the present young generation of activists but also contends that the modern age has witnessed the appearance of a new stage in the life cycle—youth, between adolescence and adulthood.[18] This stage, previously unrecognized, is now shared "by millions of young people in the advanced nations of the world"; it is characterized by tension between self and society. The activists themselves tended to have good relations with their parents.

Stanley Rothman and Robert Lichter have been very critical of Keniston's work, suggesting that his evidence is unconvincing and that his data are open to totally different interpretations.[19] According to them, his subjects and their families are less positive than he describes them. They argue that Keniston himself was partly manipulated by his subjects, who gave him answers he wanted to hear, and partly swayed by his own ideological propensities.

Herbert Hendin confirms this assessment and criticizes Keniston for ignoring the depth of pain and rage that many of the young, radicals and nonradicals alike, sense—the pain stemming from the rage directed at their parents.[20]

Hendin analyzes a far larger sample than Keniston, including youth of all backgrounds and beliefs. What is most significant in his study is the fact that many of his subjects were themselves unaware of how much of their pain and rage they had pushed into the subconscious. His women subjects would often not be aware of how troubled they were, having succeeded only in creating "a distance from the sources of their own unhappiness,"[21] while the men were characterized by "the degree to which they are irresistibly drawn to killing feeling as a means of survival."[22]

Even more definite about the uniqueness of the modern young is Theodore Roszak, who sees the age-old process of generational disaffiliation being "transformed from a peripheral experience in the life of the individual and the family into a major lever of radical social change." This change, says Roszak, is a welcome one, for "the alienated young are giving shape to something that looks like the saving vision our endangered civilization requires."[23]

Roszak's book, vastly superior to many others that merely echo paeans of praise for youth, is a serious attempt to understand the philosophical and ideological roots of the counterculture, but it is flawed by its lack of historical perspective. For example, Roszak ignores similar manifestations of the counterculture ethic in earlier periods in history, notably the German Wandervögel movement at the beginning of the century, with its rejection of technological, urbanized, bourgeois society.[24]

Moreover, Roszak's claim that the counterculture encompassed a large proportion of youth, especially at the universities, has been challenged in a little-known but important book by Clifford Adelman, who tries to probe beyond the facade without discounting the movement in its entirety.[25] On the basis of a research project in which large numbers of students failed to identify various features of the counterculture, Adelman shows that, even at its peak, the counterculture was much less prevalent than was commonly believed. Adelman is particularly ruthless with those whom he sees as being mere apologists for the student culture, with their uncritical praise for it.

Annie Kriegel's analysis also suggests that the unique nature of the sixties has been exaggerated.[26] In fact, in terms of the significance that Mannheim attaches to the impact of an important event on a generation, it may be specifically the lack of such a momentous happening that characterizes all those born after the end of World War II. She notes that it is quite possibly the "absence of a universal event likely to unify the memory of the whole of humanity that has given the search for generational identity its almost desperate character."[27]

Hendin's study of youth comes to similar conclusions. He is critical of the "romantic idealization of youth" that is found in the work of writers such as Keniston and Charles Reich and suggests that their description of the "freedom and joy" of youth "says more about the dissatisfaction with life of the older generation than it does of the joy of the younger."[28]

Henry Malcolm has attempted to draw a balanced picture of the youth movement of the 1960s.[29] His work, too, failed to attract much attention, though it is a fascinating analysis of youth, much of it deriving from Malcolm's experience as a counselor to university students in the 1960s. His theoretical approach also raises some interesting issues, as it is based on an attempt to apply oedipal principles to youth protest, while at the same time showing a sympathy for the youth position. Malcolm's book is a rare display of empathy for both generations as they face up to the new forms of society being forged in the wake of World War II. This, in fact, is Malcolm's starting point: the post-war years saw a dual trend of loss of paternal authority within the family and the son's increased practical powers outside of it; these phenomena were important catalysts in the youth protest movement of the 1960s.

Remarking on the traditional tendency of adults to blame the young for society's failures, Malcolm claims that nowadays "the argument is made precisely at a time when it no longer applies," since in the home there has been a "moral abdication of fathers,"[30] while simultaneously there are fewer parental surrogates against whom the young can struggle. The implication is that, in the past, oedipal principles were applicable but now are no longer valid.[31]

However, in the present weakened position of the father Malcolm sees the kernel of positive possibilities unique in history. While he accepts all the traditional interpretations of the Oedipus complex, its intensity is diminished at present specifically because the parents, particularly the father, are no longer as dominant as they were in the past; conversely the young are far more independent and autonomous. It is these latter qualities that often account for the anger and criticisms that the young direct at the society. But in youth's attacks on the society, Malcolm sees hope for society.

The parents should not be blamed for their children's critical faculties, says Malcolm, but commended for having raised children so perceptive of the faults of the society. It is not the youth who are at fault but society. In mounting a protest the young are using the only power at their command—their youth. Their protest takes the form of organized activities on campuses, where there is a natural congregation of the young, in order to combat the errors and the evils they see about them. Since the young are basically denied access to the real sources of power—in government and industry—they see organized student groupings as being a means of influencing the elders far more effectively than the nebulous power of exercising a vote at the elections.

Malcolm has put forward a novel and interesting thesis, but, in explaining youth protest, he seems to be caught between his broad acceptance of the basic principles of the Oedipus complex and his supportive stance on youth. Ultimately he tries to resolve some of the conflicts and confusions by claiming that society is moving from a stage where oedipal concepts were valid to what he calls a "post oedipal state,"[32] where a rethinking of the oedipal process is necessary. Many of the problems of youth in modern society are caused by the fact that the changes have taken place within the family but not as yet within the whole society. What is most needed to resolve the problems is a new approach to the question of authority and new ways of exercising authority.

Malcolm's attempt to explain why oedipal explanations are no longer applicable has much logical force. According to his thesis, it is possible that Freud was right in his description of oedipal processes, but these processes are no longer at work in the modern world. However, it is not at all clear that his historical perspective is a correct one, even from a Freudian perspective. Other writers have, in fact, described very similar changes in society—a diminution of the father's authority within the family and an increase in the son's role outside of the family—as having occurred in other periods of history. Fred Weinstein and Gerald Platt[33] argue that these twin phenomena were actually important factors in enabling Freud to have the insights that he had; it was the social climate of his time that had made the father susceptible to critical scrutiny.

According to Weinstein and Platt, by the end of the nineteenth century a marked transformation had come about in the father's position. His occupational role in emerging industrial society had removed him from active participation in the nurturant activities in the home. His importance to the family was most noticed as a connecting link between the members of the family and surrounding society, but there was a marked decline in the moral legitimacy of the paternal role. No longer fulfilling any nurturant function, the father tried, nevertheless, to extract the "same demands as before for authority, respect, submission and loyalty." Under these circumstances, the father's "demands could no longer be morally justified"[34] and were rejected by the children who now found themselves able to give freer expression to hostile sentiments without any overly acute sense of guilt.

More important, outside of the family the sons (but not yet the daughters) were able to find an independence that had been denied them in earlier periods. Prestige and status were now determined by one's personal qualities, and the son could move beyond idle fantasies of replacing and supplanting the father and directly challenge him on a realistic, competitive basis in the public arena, where the father had very little natural advantage.

Interesting and important as the work of Platt and Weinstein undoubtedly is, it is not clear that their historical presentation is any more accurate than that of Malcolm, for other writers have drawn similar pictures at even earlier periods in history. Frank Musgrove, for example, minimizes the importance of the end of the nineteenth century and points to a link between youth today and "in the early days of the classical Industrial Revolution."[35] Both of these periods saw a significant increase in the collective power of youth, occasioned by demographic and technological changes that gave youth "a strategic position in the nation's economic life." Moving the period of initial youth independence back even further than Weinstein and Platt, Musgrove claims that the young had "a large measure of control over their own lives . . . and their parents were often more dependent on them than they on their parents."[36]

Only a few years have passed since the student turbulence of the 1960s. For most of the 1970s quiet reigned on American campuses and those of most other Western societies. In some respects, this was because many of the ideas of the counterculture had been either accepted or co-opted. Charles Reich's vision of a "greening of America"[37] was clearly exaggerated, but certain lasting changes have been effected by virtue of youth protest and the impact of the counterculture. This fact in itself does not, of course, prove the uniqueness of the 1960s—for much of social change has historically been a consequence of the activities of the young. It is difficult to determine exactly how deep and substantial this impact is, for generally the particular contribution of youth has not been investigated by researchers.[38] Yet age must be seen as a major social variable. It seems to be of particular significance in respect of social and cultural change, for this is the arena where conflicts between the generations are most likely to arise.

In point of fact, it is not the banding together of young people into organizations or their creation of separate norms and cultural standards that should occasion surprise and precipitate research projects and theoretical analyses, but the failure of youth to do so. Some of the writers who are most conscious of the reasons why youth should be organized as a separate entity or class have tried to suggest why this does not always happen.

After noting that most groups of people tend to band together for the furtherance of their common interests and goals, and after enumerating a long list of particular groupings (from industrial workers, independent professionals and employers' organizations to animal lovers, war veterans and consumers), Frank Parkin expresses surprise that "no political or social organization has ever developed to represent the claims of the young, adolescents forming one of the few major social categories in modern society which lack formal representation."[39]

Parkin argues that there "are many features about young people's position in the social order which could give rise, potentially at least, to some kind of political movement."[40] For instance, youth in general suffer from handicaps in the realm of wages, higher contribution to the social services proportional to their benefit from them (e.g., health), war sacrifices, a whole series of legal prohibitions, and constant exposure to adult authority. What prevents the arousal of consciousness and organizational effectiveness is the temporary and transitory nature of adolescence; the success of the socialization process, particularly the role of parents "in socializing the young into the same political, as well as religious and other beliefs, as they themselves hold";[41] and the sheer personal pressures of coping with life's everyday problems.

While Parkin focuses mainly on the modern period, historians studying youth from an historical perspective see parallels with the stresses that already existed in the preindustrial age and in the early stages of industrialization. Says Herbert Moller:

> Throughout the centuries, spontaneous youth organizations have had a continuous existence, but a ferment among the young with its subsequent departure from cultural or political tradition can be observed only at certain times and in certain geographical areas.[42]

Moller's search for a principal causative factor underlying such ferment led him to suggest the variable of rapid demographic growth:

> Irrespective of social and economic conditions, an increase in the number of youth in any society involves an increase in social turbulence. Young people are conspicuously inclined to take risks, to expose themselves and others to danger, and thus to engage in socially disruptive behavior.[43]

In his well-documented survey of youth in history John Gillis, too, adduces evidence of generational tensions in the preindustrial age and in the early stages of industrial society.[44] According to his study, youth was a clearly recognized stage of life, the young sensed an identity with each other, and there were even a number of organizational frameworks that were concerned with the occupational interests of the young.

After describing the special status of the young, the folk traditions and festivals revolving around age-grading, the abundance and consequent superfluity of the young, the fact that so many of the young were living away from home (in schools, apprenticeships, as novitiates in the church, and in the large cities), Gillis notes that "it is remarkable that . . . there was not more generational conflict."[45] The difficult position of the young in schools and in apprenticeships should, he feels, have led to far more youth unrest than was actually recorded, and he suggests that the obedience of youth was ensured by the strong measures that society took against them: "The obedience of youth was due, in part, to the society's strict enforcement of the Fifth Commandment, which was interpreted to include not only natural parents but all such masters to whom youth was entrusted."[46]

Gillis describes the way the vested interests of the older generation were served by prolonging the semidependence of the young. In fact, his work suggests that the analyses of modern youth that stress the uniqueness of a prolonged stage of adolescence in the modern world are lacking in historical perspective. Many young people would spend time away from home, but this did not always lead to greater independence, as they would be organized into groupings that fell under the authority of the older generation. The ultimate effect of spending time away from home was to postpone their marriage, thereby prolonging the state of semidependence.

Often the potentials for criticism and revolt against existing institutions were deflected into traditional rituals, in which youth would be allowed to find outlets for their frustrations, their criticism of society, and their sense of powerlessness. Natalie Davis has described the institutions of misrule and charivaris, in which youth would, during special festive times, make mockery of traditional institutions. She notes the ambivalence in this amusement, where the "carnival form . . . can act both to re-enforce order and suggest alternatives for the existing order."[47]

Misrule probably fulfilled the functions of integrating youth into society, paralleled in other societies by more formal and ritualistic rites of passage. S. N. Eisenstadt's discussion of the roles of rites of passage follows these lines;[48] he sees them as dramatizing the conflict between the generations in the form of a fight or competition, the final aim being to stress the complementariness of the two generations. In modern societies, Eisenstadt cites the role of youth movements as one of the means used to ensure continuity between the generations. This is more blatant in the case where youth movements are set up as adjuncts to ideological parties, but even the formally neutral youth movements are often designed for similar adult control over youth. Eisenstadt's thesis is supported by a study of British youth movements, in particular that of the Boy Scouts, which concludes that the movements were

> carefully designed attempts . . . to harness their energies for great causes approved by their adult leaders—imperial defense, national defense, international cooperation, national efficiency, and so on. As educational movements they had no need to challenge the status quo. . . . Tactically, they were restricted to the pace permitted by their patrons among the political, ecclesiastical and military elite.[49]

For most generational historians and sociologists, youth is the most important generation. It is in a formative state; it has a more recognizable age framework; it is a force for change in the world. Youth has the ability, lacking for the most part in the older generation, to bring a new perspective to bear on social and political affairs, even in the absence of social and technological change or demographic pressures. Less committed to the existing system, less submerged in its ways, more recently exposed to its values and customs, more capable of discerning processes pointing to the future, youth is not afraid to criticize the faults and the flaws of a society not of its own making.

The capacity to think critically, often beyond the capacity or rather the desire of the older generation, is a structural fact of major proportions for understanding social change. No less important, however, in understanding the process of social change is the manner in which the older generation responds to the challenge precipitated by the young. The key issue is not rejection by the young or the extent of change demanded by them, but the degree to which the older generation is prepared to allow their cultural and political institutions to be subjected to criticism and the degree to which they are prepared to acquiesce in change, to forego and modify some of their values, and to adopt new ones.

Such openness and flexibility are not automatic concomitants of social life, nor are they characteristic of most older generations. Their aim is generally to preserve the values and customs and practices of the past and to seek means of transmitting them. They are not concerned with activating, sponsoring, or facilitating the changing patterns of the future.

Just as in the case of the family, where the period of adolescence may have an even greater effect on the parents, so, too, in the political area and at the societal level, conflict between the generations may be more related to the unwillingness of the dominant generation to incorporate the younger generation fully into the power and status structure and to accept with open minds the special insights of the young than to any banding together of sons to destroy their father, or even to a desperate attempt to usurp power.

Thus a full understanding of generational conflict in the political and social sphere is dependent on some perception of who and what the elder generation is. The mere pressures for change by the young need not necessarily lead to conflict unless there is resistance to these pressures. Most societies in human history have been past-oriented, while even in the active, changing societies of the modern world—future-oriented and attuned to change and progress as they are—the older generation often demands that change take place at a pace it sets and can cope with.

In his study of race conflict, Ronald Segal[50] comments that no privileged group voluntarily or willingly gives up its privileged position. This fact has particular pertinence for the generations. For whereas all other socially differentiated groups—race, religion, ethnicity, sex, ideology—are capable of preserving their status and power over time, age groups must inevitably make way for those that will succeed them. Often attempts will be made to defer, or even avert, the inevitable handing over of power: in extreme forms through filicide, in more subtle forms through co-optation. Eisenstadt, despite his model of generational contact based on continuity, notes that there is often an undercurrent of hostility connected with the strong emphasis on the differences between various age grades that becomes more acute when the time comes for one generation to succeed another.[51]

In the 1960s most of the generational tensions centered around the universities. Feuer notes that campus unrest may arise because so many

young people—including nonstudents—live in close proximity without acquiring "habits of work and discipline."[52] Other writers, however, feel it is
essential for society to have an intellectual youth with the leisure time to
allow the development of new ideas.

Paradoxically, as Parkin points out, those in radical student movements
"for whom a place in the sun has been more or less guaranteed, express
greater discontent with society than those for whom life appears to hold far
less promise."[53] Whereas the socialization of working youth, from the
standpoint of formal learning, is completed at secondary school, the socialization of university students continues, but at a qualitatively different level,

> a level of critical awareness and social concern that renders students highly
> suggestible to political appeals based on the activation of these values. To
> protest at discrimination against racial minorities, or at the government's
> prosecution of a seemingly unjust war, or at university autocracy, are perfectly
> rational responses on the part of those taught to revere the notions of
> equality, justice and democracy.[54]

The universities are a significant factor in the conflict of generations in
today's setting. They constitute a concentration of young people, forced
into close proximity with each other and partially isolated from the older
generation that makes "the collective consciousness and mass mobilization
of youth possible."[55] Furthermore, the universities have themselves become major agents of change—in the scientific and technological experiments that they undertake, in the new ideas that they sponsor. The university is no longer an ivory tower; in many respects it is where change starts; in
testing present reality and charting the future, it has become the "real
world."

Whether change is imparted and diffused in a spirit of willingness and
cooperation depends not only on how its sponsors act but also on how its
recipients react.

Often change may develop out of a dialogue between the young and
some of those in older and intermediary generations, such as the intellectual
precursors who precipitated the counterculture.[56] In the final analysis, the
interaction between the generations and the manner in which change is
consummated depends upon the willingness of the older generation to
display tolerance and flexibility toward the major carriers of that change.
Earlier we noted Mannheim's belief that continuity between the generations
is helped by a two-way process of learning. Margaret Mead[57] has gone even
further, suggesting that in the modern world learning must take place from
the young to the old, since only the former are capable of keeping up and
coping with the constant flow of change.

It may be that our analysis of generations should focus less on what makes youth reject the status quo and more on what makes the old reject the potentialities for change. Some fruitful areas to explore may be related to the same structural factors making for adult hostility in the family, only on a collective, societal level: the envy of youth, to whom the future belongs; the fact of approaching death, signaling the disappearance of a generation.

Richard Flacks concludes his book on youth and social change by noting:

> The idea of youth is a dangerous one for a social order, but it is also a very promising one. Youth revolt is a sign that a new culture and a new social order have been placed on the agenda of history. The promise of youth can only be fulfilled, however, if youth is transcended—if the young and the not-young who have a common interest in a new social order come together to make their collective mark and help each other realize their common dreams.[58]

But for some, the very innovations or idealism of youth may serve as an uncomfortable reminder of ideals discarded by many members of the older generation over the course of time. Having compromised with the visions and plans of their own formative years, they may resent being reminded of all that they once believed in or of the vigorous freshness of innovation and change that the younger generation is initiating.

Conversely, where the elders represent a generation of people who actually achieved the realization of their dreams of youth, they may also be reluctant to allow their hard-won gains to be undermined by a succeeding generation, itself revolutionary. Thus, it is often the most radical regimes that take the most care to ensure the preservation of all that they have wrought. Often such regimes impose the strictest control and conformity on the youth through strict school systems or ideological youth movements. The more radical the young revolutionaries were, the more rigid they are liable to be after taking power, for they are more keenly aware of the threat to the status quo (including a recently constituted status quo) that the youth represent.

Kingsley Davis describes the dilemma of the middle-aged, who

> notoriously forget the poetic ideals of a new social order which they cherished when young. . . . In their place they put simply the working ideals current in the society. There is, in short, a persistent tendency for the ideology of a person as he grows older to gravitate more and more toward the status quo ideology, unless other facts . . . intervene.[59]

Davis sees the variable of age as a "unique basis of social stratification," particularly in modern society, where "the time-interval between the generations, ordinarily but a mere moment in the life of a social system, becomes historically significant, thereby creating a hiatus between one generation and the next."[60] With each generation raised in a milieu different from the others, the young tend to be idealistic and utopian, the older conservative.

Although Davis's article is considered a classic, little attempt has been made to build on its basic premises of the special nature of age as a social factor or to expand its narrow focus on the family and make it applicable to generational contacts at the societal level. As recently as 1972, Matilda Riley and her colleagues were proclaiming the need for a "theory of age stratification" and bemoaning the fact that "no conceptual framework is at hand for interpreting age as a structural element in the society, for isolating the social components of the aging process from birth to death, or for assessing the impact of age upon societal stability and change."[61] Like Mannheim, Riley and her associates note that age categorization contains points of similarity with class but that it is also unique in being "universal, inevitable and irreversible."[62] They make no reference to Davis's article, perhaps because his point of departure was different from theirs. His analysis focuses on the young, particularly adolescents, while their perception of the sociological importance of age grew out of a six-year research project into the problems of the old.

Most of the articles in their collection also focus on the old as an age category; only one, by Talcott Parsons and Gerald Platt,[63] deals with the young, a new age group of "studentry," which the authors suggest should be recognized as an important period in the life cycle, differentiated from that of youth. The need for such a category arises out of the increase in mass higher education for an extended period of time, involving people in their late twenties and even thirties. Students are differentiated from others in their age category by virtue of the fact that they undergo a further process of socialization. Parsons and Platt rely heavily on basic Freudian concepts, seeing symbolic importance even in the use of the term "alma mater." Thus, "an outcome of student socialization should be emancipation from undue attachment to alma mater."[64] Further, where students realize that academe does not function in an isolated vacuum but is involved in "the evils of the larger society," then, "like the Oedipal Son," the student likes to feel that "Mother is really 'pure.' Discovery of her involvement outside the academic 'home' may then be taken as evidence that she is 'really' no better than a 'whore.' "[65]

The appeal that Freudian concepts hold for Talcott Parsons is of particular relevance for the question of social change. One of the dominant figures in American sociology, Parsons has sought a synthesis between psychoanalysis and sociology.[66] This involves almost a complete acceptance of the oedipal thesis and a quest to understand the process by which existing values may be transmitted to the younger generation, and how the young may be harmoniously assimilated into the society. Where differences between the generations are recorded they are seen not as conflicts between opposing groups, each seeking its own ends, but as stresses in the system.

Almost no attention is paid to the contribution that the young can play in fostering change.

It is of interest to note that although Weinstein and Platt in their joint works rely heavily on Parsons' work, they are, nevertheless, constrained to echo a frequently heard criticism: "Parsons has not devoted nearly so much attention to the dynamics of change as he has to those of stability."[67] They see similar deficiencies in Freud's work: "While social change obviously occurs and must be accounted for, no sound theory of change has ever emerged from psychoanalytic thought."[68] It may be that Parsons's attraction to Freud's ideas might have stemmed from their similar obliviousness to change. In any case, both of them seemed incapable of recognizing a major component of social life—the social change precipitated by youth.

Ironically, even in times of relative quiescence, which is Parsons's model of a desirable society, change may take place, and hostilities may exist. The recent analysis by Anne Foner and David Kertzer of twenty-one tribal societies bears this out clearly, pointing to the tensions associated with transitions through the life cycle and to the competition between the generations for rewarding roles.[69]

Similar considerations apply in quiescent periods in modern societies. Hendin, for instance, warns against present complacency, which finds satisfaction in the apparent termination of the generational tensions that had characterized the sixties. He argues that the aftermath in the United States of both Vietnam and Watergate and the economic anxiety have perhaps brought the generations together, but this is based not on a shared sense of common aspirations and endeavors but on mutual despair, a growing feeling of impotence in the face of forces that seem beyond human control, and a growing mistrust of those institutions in the society that possess power. Such "harmony in despair" is no more than a "sign of pure collective difficulty."[70]

Writing a short while before the outbursts of the 1960s at a time when there was little overt generational conflict, Frank Musgrove tried to discern the contrasting images that adults and adolescents have of each other. Adapting the Bogardus scale, which measures social distance between groups, to generations, Musgrove found that adults had a far greater dislike of adolescents than vice versa, and that adults also had an incorrect perception of adolescent capacities.[71] On the other hand, he found that "adolescents do not return in equal measure the hostility which adults direct towards them. They are on the whole kindly disposed to their seniors, value their approval and aim to be co-operative with them."[72]

Focusing on power relationships, Musgrove sees adult aversion to the young as a direct reflection of the threat that the latter pose to the economic and social hegemony of the adults. "The hatred with which the mature of western society regard the young is a testimony to the latter's importance, to their power potential and actual."[73] He sees adults employing any strategy to protect their own interests, while claiming ostensibly to be acting in the interests of the young. An example of this is the insistence on an unnecessarily long period of tutelage (apprenticeship, higher education) in preparation for occupational competency.

Generational conflict may best be seen then, even in modern times, as a consequence not of eroded moral authority of the father within the family and the consequent diminished control over his children, but of the very real challenge posed by youth to the economic and social power structure in the society at large. According to Musgrove, historical evidence would indicate that the more deprived the status of the young, the more likely their determination actively to seek change.

The search for various causative factors of social change by Weinstein and Platt, Malcolm, Musgrove, and others leads us inevitably back to the underlying theme that social change, precipitated by youth, is endemic in society. These prospects for change usually cause concern among those entrenched in comfortable positions of power and status, even though history teaches us that the overall well-being of society is best assured when such change is accepted with equanimity.

Anthony Esler concludes his historical study of modern youth movements by noting that, while they typically fail in the short run, their long-term impact "has generally been considerably greater than their contemporaries could well imagine." In fact, the historical function of disaffected youth seems to be to serve as "a crucial *first constituency* for radical new ideas whose time has *almost* come. . . . They serve as an essential *middle term* between yesterday's subversive notions and tomorrow's new majorities."[74] Whether the emergence of these new ideas will lead to bitter and divisive strife or be given sober consideration may well depend not so much on the way in which the young press their demands but on the way the older generation responds to these demands.

We have noted in the family that the older generation often suffers from the amnesia of not remembering what childhood is really like. Within society, between youth and middle-aged, the problem may be just the opposite. For the middle-aged do remember the dreams of their youth. Their problem may well be whether they can honestly say that they have been faithful to their youth.[75]

References

1. Julian Marías, *Generations: A Historical Method* (University, Ala.: University of Alabama Press, 1970).

2. Ibid., see chapter 2, "The Problem of Generations in the 19th Century," p. 21–67. The specific references are to Comte at p. 21 (from *Cours de philosophe*

positive); Mill at p. 25 (from *A System of Logic*); Durkheim at p. 28 (from *The Division of Labor in Society*).

3. José Ortega y Gasset, *Man and Crisis* (London: George Allen & Unwin, 1959).

4. Marías, *Generations*, p. 69. For a further analysis of the work of Ortega and Marías, see Nerina Jansen, *Generation Theory* (Johannesburg: McGraw-Hill, 1975).

5. Karl Mannheim, "The Problem of Generations," in *Essays on the Sociology of Knowledge* (London: Routledge & Kegan Paul, 1952). For a good summary of Mannheim's work, and for a survey of other writers who have used his concept of a generation-unit, see Richard G. Braungart, "Youth and Social Movements," in S. E. Dragostin and G. H. Elder, eds., *Adolescence in the Life Cycle: Psychological Change and Social Context* (New York: John Wiley & Sons, 1975).

6. Mannheim, "The Problem of Generations," pp. 286–287.

7. Ibid., p. 291.

8. Lewis S. Feuer, *The Conflict of Generations: The Character and Significance of Student Movements* (New York: Basic Books, 1969).

9. Mannheim, "The Problem of Generations," p. 293.

10. Ibid., p. 294.

11. Ibid.

12. Ibid., p. 300.

13. Ibid., p. 306.

14. Talcott Parsons, "Age and Sex in the Social Structure of the United States," *American Sociological Review* 7 (1942): 604–616; Ralph Linton, "Age and Sex Categories," *American Sociological Review* 7 (1942): 589–603. See also Linton's earlier article, "A Neglected Aspect of Social Organization," *American Journal of Sociology* 45 (1940): 870–886.

15. Allen Lambert, "Generations and Change: Toward a Theory of Generations as a Force in Historical Process," *Youth and Society* 4 (1972/3): 21–45. See other articles and presentations by Lambert as set out in his footnotes. For a similar approach to the link between age and social change (with the use of the term cohort), see Norman B. Ryder, "The Cohort as a Concept in the Study of Social Change," *American Sociological Review* 30 (1965): 843.

16. Lambert, "Generations and Change," p. 24.

17. Ibid., p. 37.

18. See Kenneth Keniston, *Young Radicals: Notes on Committed Youth* (New York: Harcourt, Brace, 1976). See also his collection of essays, *Youth and Dissent: The Rise of a New Opposition* (New York: Harcourt, Brace, 1971).

19. Stanley Rothman and S. Robert Lichter, "The Case of the Student Left," *Social Research* 45 (1978): 535–609.

20. Herbert Hendin, *The Age of Sensation: A Psychoanalytic Exploration of Youth in the 1970's* (New York: McGraw-Hill, 1975).

21. Ibid., p. 24.

22. Ibid., p. 103.

23. Theodore Roszak, *The Making of a Counter Culture: Reflections on the Techno-cratic Society and Its Youthful Opposition* (Garden City, N.Y.: Doubleday Anchor, 1969), p. 1.

24. See the important works by Howard Becker, *German Youth—Bond or Free* (New York: Oxford University Press, 1946), and Walter Z. Laqueur, *Young Germany: A History of the German Youth Movement* (New York: Basic Books, 1962).

25. Clifford Adelman, *Generations: A Collage on Youthcult* (New York: Praeger, 1972).

26. Annie Kriegel, "Generational Difference: The History of an Idea," *Daedalus* 107 (Fall, 1978): 23–38.

27. Ibid., p. 32.

28. Hendin, *The Age of Sensation,* p. 17.

29. Henry Malcolm, *Generation of Narcissus* (Boston: Little, Brown, 1971). Malcolm notes that the Czarists in Russia blamed the Communist revolt on the young, Hitler blamed the threat of communism on youth, and in America many adults "feel that the young people are trying to destroy their father-authority figures."

30. Ibid., p. 59.

31. Malcolm approvingly refers to Feuer's book as "most perceptive and useful" (p. 56), particularly for its explanation of how the oedipal structure in Europe and in Asian cultures had motivated student and youth unrest in those countries.

32. Ibid., p. 23.

33. Fred Weinstein and Gerald Platt, *The Wish to be Free: Society, Psyche and Value Change* (Berkeley: University of California Press, 1969).

34. Ibid., p. 146.

35. Frank Musgrove, *Youth and the Social Order* (Bloomington: Indiana University Press, 1964), p. 10.

36. Ibid., p. 10.

37. Charles Reich, *The Greening of America* (New York: Random House, 1970).

38. Thus, while George Rude does give the ages, where available, of people who took part in key social and political events associated with the French Revolution, no effort is made to relate to these people as an age category. See George Rude, *The Crowd in the French Revolution* (Oxford: Clarendon Press, 1959).

39. Frank Parkin, "Adolescent Status and Student Politics," *Journal of Contemporary History* 5 (1970): 144.

40. Ibid., p. 144.

41. Ibid., p. 146.

42. Herbert Moller, "Youth as a Force in the Modern World," *Comparative Studies in Society and History* 10 (1967): 237.

43. Ibid., pp. 256–257. Moller notes a number of recent historical studies on

revolutionary times that suggest that the role of youth is far more important in fomenting change than class antagonism. In modern times, Moller notes Smail's study of Indonesia where he claims that the main distinction between the radicals and the moderates of the Indonesian Revolution was one of generations (John R. W. Smail, *Bonding in the Early Revolution, 1945–46* [Ithaca: Cornell University Press, 1964]). Moller also refers to Eisenstadt's work, in which he asserts that most of the nationalistic movements in the Middle East, Asia, and Africa have consisted of young people, students, or officers who rebelled against their elders (S. N. Eisenstadt, "Archetypal Patterns of Youth," *Daedalus* 91 [1962]: 28–46.)

44. John R. Gillis, *Youth and History: Tradition and Change in European Age Relations, 1770–Present* (New York: Academic Press, 1974). See also his articles: "Conformity and Rebellion: Contrasting Styles of England and German Youth, 1900–1933," *History of Education Quarterly* 13 (1973): 249–260, and "Youth and History: Progress and Prospect," *Journal of Social History* 7 (1973), pp. 201–207.

45. Gillis, *Youth and History*, p. 21.

46. Ibid. Once again it is interesting to note that Gillis refers to the strict English school system, referring to the work of Thomas Arnold in this area.

47. Natalie Davis, "The Reasons of Misrule: Youth Groups and Charivaris in 16th Century France," *Past and Present* 50 (1971): 74.

48. See S. N. Eisenstadt, *From Generation to Generation* (New York: Free Press, 1956).

49. Paul Wilkinson, "English Youth Movements, 1908–1930," *Journal of Contemporary History* 4 (1969): 22. See also Norman McKenzie, "Scouting It Out with B–P," *New Statesman*, Oct. 15, 1965.

50. Ronald Segal, *The Race War* (New York: Viking, 1967), p. 3.

51. Eisenstadt, *From Generation to Generation*.

52. Feuer, *The Conflict of Generations*, p. 440.

53. Parkin, "Adolescent Status and Student Politics," p. 147.

54. Ibid., p. 152.

55. Richard Flacks, *Youth and Social Change* (Chicago: Markham Publishing, 1971), p. 99.

56. See for instance, Roszak, chapter 3, where he discusses the work of Marcuse and Brown. He notes that their "emergence . . . as major social theorists among the disaffiliated young . . . must be taken as one of the defining features of the counter culture," p. 84.

57. Margaret Mead, *Culture and Commitment* (Garden City, N.Y.: Doubleday, 1970).

58. Flacks, *Youth and Social Change*, p. 139.

59. Kingsley Davis, "The Sociology of Parent-Youth Conflict," *American Sociological Review* 5 (1960): 527.

60. Ibid., p. 523.

61. Matilda White Riley, Marilyn Johnson, and Anne Foner, *Aging and Society,* vol. 3: *A Sociology of Age Stratification* (New York: Russell Sage, 1972), p. xiv.

62. Ibid.

63. Talcott Parsons and Gerald Platt, "Higher Education and Changing Socialization," in Riley et al., *Aging and Society,* p. 236.

64. Ibid., p. 282.

65. Ibid., footnote 40.

66. See Talcott Parsons, *Social Structure and Personality* (New York: Free Press, 1964), especially the essays: "The Superego and the Theory of Social Systems" (pp. 17–33); "The Father Symbol: An Appraisal in the Light of Psychoanalytic and Sociological Theory" (pp. 34–56); "The Incest Taboo in Relation to Social Structure and the Socialization of the Child" (pp. 57–77); "Social Structure and the Development of Personality: Freud's Contribution to the Integration of Psychology and Sociology" (pp. 78–111); "Youth in the Context of American Society" (pp. 155–182). See also *Essays in Sociological Theory* (Glencoe, Ill.: Free Press, 1954), especially: "Psychoanalysis and the Social Structure," (pp. 336–347).

67. Fred Weinstein and Gerald Platt, *Psychoanalytic Sociology: An Essay on the Interpretation of Historical Data and the Phenomena of Collective Behavior* (Baltimore: Johns Hopkins University Press, 1973), p. 32.

68. Ibid., p. 57.

69. See, for instance, Anne Foner and David Kertzer, "Transitions over the Life-Course: Lessons from Age-Set Societies," *American Journal of Sociology* 83 (1978): 1081–1104.

70. Hendin, *The Age of Sensation,* p. 335.

71. See Musgrove, *Youth and the Social Order,* chapter 5, "Inter-Generation Attitudes," pp. 86–105.

72. Ibid., p. 11.

73. Ibid., p. 10.

74. Anthony Esler, *Bombs, Beards and Barricades: 150 Years of Youth in Revolt* (New York: Stein & Day, 1971), p. 304.

75. See Saul Alinsky's comment in his book, *Reveille for Radicals* (New York: Vintage, 1969), p. xvii.

PART FOUR
GENERATIONS TOGETHER

CHAPTER ELEVEN
THE RADICAL
ERROR

The total thrust of Freud's work on the Oedipus complex, as well as on such related aspects as sexuality and a repressed unconscious has been an ambiguous one. On the one hand he has been hailed for his liberating influence; his insights have provided the possibility of freeing human beings from the complications associated with the repression of instinctual sexual drives. By becoming aware of infantile sexuality and incestuous longings, persons become better equipped to control the negative consequences of these drives. Moreover in the course of resolving the Oedipus complex, the child develops a strong identity with the parent of the same sex while simultaneously forming a superego as the basis for a healthy personality.

On the other hand, however successful the individual may be in resolving the Oedipus complex, the total picture for humanity remains bleak, for ultimately the deeply embedded sexual drives affect the manner in which social and cultural progress can be attained. The energies, efforts, and perseverance required for civilization to arise and flourish become available only after control has been gained over libidinal urges.[1] Suppression and sublimation of the instinctual urges are an essential prerequisite for tapping the creative capacities of humanity. The reality principle must take precedence over the pleasure principle. For Freud, the greatest achievements of civilization were inextricably linked with control of the deepest biological needs. Humanity can fulfill its highest aspirations only by denying its most basic yearnings.

Around these two factors—partly contradictory—a group of radical neo-Freudians have attempted to go beyond Freud and to weave a sanguine picture of potential utopian social life, where sexuality will not be controlled but joyously embraced and expressed, and where social progress will proceed smoothly without those dire personal tensions that Freud saw as being inescapable. These theorists have sought to synthesize the work of the dominant figures of the past century, Freud and Karl Marx, trying to mold the role of sexuality and the unconscious in shaping human behavior, as set out by the former with the impact of the economic underpinnings determining social life, as set out by the latter.

Gad Horowitz provides a succinct statement of the issue: "Radical thought has for decades been faced with the challenge of taking fully into account the implications of Sigmund Freud's discovery that the 'Laws of slavery' are not only socioeconomic but also bio-psychological."[2]

While most orthodox Marxists shun any reconciliation between Marx and Freud and see psychoanalysis mainly as an ideological rationalization for capitalist society, other radicals, such as Wilhelm Reich and various members of the Critical School of Frankfurt, regard Freud's pessimistic appraisal of human nature as a consequence of the specific defects of capitalist, bourgeois society; therefore his ideas are amenable to incorporation into developing radical thought. Nevertheless, the inherent contradictions between Marx and Freud give rise to inevitable dilemmas.

Much of this effort has focused on the sexual elements of Freud's work, touching only minimally on the parricidal elements. Yet these works are of significance for understanding generational conflict, partly because the critics see the attempts to control the sexuality of the young as the first step toward a more general oppression. The impact of their work also calls into question the role that Freud's ideas, in their pure form, are presumed to have played in helping to liberate people in modern society from the constraints of the sexual urges.

Radical neo-Freudian writers, while agreeing that Freud did heighten our consciousness of the role of sexuality in the life of children, assert that his offered solution merely served to perpetuate the problem. Control of sexual drives can have only a detrimental and inhibitive effect on the individual, they say; what the young need is not diversion of the sexual impulses into other channels, but a chance to express themselves in sexual activities, and guidance toward this end.

In many respects Freud seems far removed from those radical and Marxist thinkers who see mankind's nature as primarily a product of socioeconomic forces. Freud appears to be irreconcilably in conflict with those who see society's evils as artificially constituted by historical circumstances and who envision a future society where all forms of repression will be eradicated. Why then have Marxist and other radical thinkers devoted so much effort to synthesizing the ideas of Freud and Marx?

These attempts stem not only from theoretical considerations but also from a disturbing political reality that involves both the rise of reactionary forces in Europe, particularly in the 1920s and 1930s, and the failure of revolutionary societies to implement many of the goals for human betterment that their ideologies proclaim. Although orthodox Marxism insists that economics is at the core of social life, the radical neo-Freudians have acknowledged also the power of psychological factors, particularly the ongoing influence of early socialization in the family. They have used Freud's ideas to explain the attraction of reactionary ideas for the masses and the refusal of the masses to embrace radical ideologies.

Freud is made relevant for Marxist theory by showing how life in the family and the process of socialization are materially affected by the historical circumstances of each society. What Freud regarded as the consequences of immutable human nature can be shown to be the product of human arrangements designed to serve the economic interests of dominant social classes.

Sexual repression is viewed not as an invariable concomitant of orderly social life but as only one more facet of the overall repressive qualities of bourgeois life. Any projection into a better future must, therefore, incorporate not only a resolution of the problems of economic exploitation and political power but also the psychological variables that affect the human condition, particularly the manner in which arrangements are made for family life and for the expression of sexual desires.

These ideas have distinct relevance for the issue of generational conflict, since some of the strictest controls imposed on the young are in the area of sexual behavior. Whereas Freud felt that without such controls there could be no social order, no civilization, and no proper socialization of the young, the radical neo-Freudians argue that as long as such controls exist, there can be no true human freedom and no spontaneous joy in social behavior. Whereas for Freud, civilization demands the price of these controls and their ensuing neurotic conflicts, for the radical neo-Freudians, a future ideal society promises the prospects of individual and social well-being without such controls.

One of the first attempts to probe the possibilities of using both Marxist and Freudian ideas was that of Wilhelm Reich,[3] who suggested that the political repression of modern society has its antecedents in sexual repression imposed on the young: "Man's authoritarian structure . . . is basically produced by the embedding of sexual inhibitions and fear in the living substance of sexual impulses."[4] For Freud and his followers, awareness of sexual impulses led to consideration as to how to keep these impulses in check or to sublimate them as part of therapeutic treatment. For Reich, the key issue became the need to remove the socially imposed restrictions and to allow healthy expression of sexual urges. Reich, like Freud, sees that sexual impulses and behavior have far-reaching social implications. But for Reich sexual repression does not further, but retards, social progress; far from residual oedipal feelings causing adolescent and adult nonconformist behavior, it is the obedience exacted by parents, particularly in the realm of sexual behavior, that is the precursor for the later blind obedience of adults to the state. In the final analysis, fascism emerges out of the prolonged denial of the most basic biological needs; the totalitarian state has its antecedents in the family:

> In the figure of the father the authoritarian state has its representative in every family, so that the family becomes its most important instrument of power. The authoritarian position of the father reflects his political role and discloses

the relation of the family to the authoritarian state. Within the family the father holds the same position that his boss holds toward him in the production process. And he reproduces his subservient attitude toward authority in his children, particularly in his sons. Lower-middle-class man's passive and servile attitude toward the Führer-figure issues from these conditions.[5]

Challenging traditional Freudian thought, Reich claims that there is no point in seeking therapeutic relief from the inevitable neuroses arising from restricted sexuality. Rather, the urgent need is to seek a means of allowing legitimate sexual expression, particularly for the young. Above all, children have to be allowed sexual expression without the inhibiting moralistic rules of their parents. The imposition of such rules is the underlying cause of oedipal complications, for sexual tendencies are not inherently incestuous. Free of parental controls, the child can develop a positive attitude to sex and lay the basis for a healthy personality. The best means of breaking away from the strict repression of parents is by facilitating as many activities as possible outside of the restrictive confines of the family and allowing as much interaction as possible with peers in children's societies and youth communes, as well as with an assortment of adults. The evils of the oedipal triangle will be broken only when the network of interaction is substantially altered.

In contrast to Reich, Francis Bartlett denies that Marxist and Freudian ideas can be reconciled.[6] Bartlett believes that parent-child relations are always determined by the overall social conditions and that the Oedipus complex, therefore, could not be universal. "The forms of the family and their corresponding sentiments are equally historical products and change as society changes. The jealousy of the Oedipus complex is no exception."[7]

For Bartlett, Freud's basic error was his failure to realize that human nature is forged in the crucible of society's rules and norms. Freud was unable to realize that his description of what ails mankind is really a description of the specific faults and deficiencies of bourgeois society. Human nature is not a static, a given, but changes in response to the onward sweep of society.

Yet, despite the fact that Freud's ahistoricity was a recognized fundamental weakness, other radical writers have also tried to combine Marxism and psychoanalysis. Some of the most noted work has been done by several members of the Critical School of Frankfurt, who developed their ideas first in Europe, then, after Hitler's rise to power, in the United States. Much of their work was motivated by a desire to understand the factors that had led to the rise of reactionary forces in Europe precisely at the time when capitalism was in a state of crisis and the conditions for the acceptance of radical ideas and the victory of the working class seemed to be ideal.

They saw oppression within the family as laying the basis for the oppressive conditions in society.[8] Nevertheless a basic inconsistency exists in these writings. At times it is the specific nature of bourgeois values that is seen to be the cause of the oppressive conditions within the family; at other times, the writers, often relying on Friedrich Engels's work on the origins of the family,[9] trace the oppression back to the rise of patriarchal domination in antiquity.

Herbert Marcuse,[10] one of the leading figures, vacillates in his emphasis between critical strictures of both patriarchal society and modern bourgeois society, although basically it is the latter that concerns him. In particular, he stresses that technological changes have led to a vastly transformed role for the father, whose power has declined and who no longer fits Freud's authoritarian model.[11] In generational terms, Marcuse notes that the "situation in which the ego and the superego were formed in the struggle with the father as the paradigmatic representative of the reality principle—this situation is historical; it came to an end with the changes in industrial society which took shape in the inter-war period."[12]

Although a major critic of modern society, Marcuse sees it as also having singular prospects for overcoming the repressive qualities that Freud had considered a constant of human life. One of Marcuse's major contributions to the synthesis of Freud and Marx is his explanation of repression. He differentiates between basic repression and surplus repression, the former being those restraints of the instincts that are necessary for the very survival of the human race and that are linked to a willingness to obey necessary authority, the latter being those restrictions imposed for the purpose of social domination.

This bifurcation of Freud's concept of repression enables Marcuse to reassess Freud's pessimistic appraisal of the human condition. For if repression can be limited only to basic aspects, then by total elimination of surplus repression it becomes possible to conceive of a nonrepressive civilization.

Many of the negative aspects of human nature that Freud saw as inevitable Marcuse sees as the result of historical factors, artificially induced because of stratified modes of living, and oriented to the benefit of the dominant groups in society. According to Marcuse, "All human needs, including sexuality, lie beyond the animal world. They are historically determined and historically mutable."[13] In this reinterpretation of a fundamental Freudian concept Marcuse found the means of linking the ideas of Marx and Freud—and of justifying hopes for a better future society.

For Marcuse the key issue is how to remove historically determined surplus repression, so that a nonrepressive civilization can emerge. While conceding that repression was once necessary to build modern civilization (just as for Marx, capitalism had a historic role to play as a precursor of communism), Marcuse believes that the very existence of a modern technological civilization provides the conditions for eliminating surplus repression, since work, instead of being a soulless task, imposed by a harsh natural environment, could for the first time be performed—through judicious use of technological achievements, through an equitable allocation of resources, and through a rejection of the pressures of artificially induced consumer desires—in a spirit of "sensuousness, play and song."[14]

Yet, despite the conviction with which Marcuse presents his concept of surplus repression and the eagerness with which he sees the conquest of this surplus repression as heralding a nonrepressive civilization, he fails to resolve a fundamental issue: the manner in which the underlying problem of *basic* repression is to be resolved.

Even if aspects of repression can be historicized and eliminated through the creation of desirable social conditions, the problem of basic repression would still remain. In fact, as Gad Horowitz argues, Marcuse's program for the abolition of surplus repression is open to criticism *not* for its "utopianism" but on the ground that basic, not surplus, repression is the primary source of renunciation and neurosis, of the "discontent" that pervades the human existence. "Even if all surplus repressions were abolished, the basic repressions, those required by the humanization process, by civilization per se, would remain . . . difficult and . . . painful."[15]

Robert Boocock, too, notes that Marcuse seems confused on this point. While Marcuse seems "to want a self-imposed repression which would be free from external domination [t]his seems confusing, for basic repression will be imposed on children by parents, or parental surrogates."[16] It is, of course, precisely basic repression that is so closely bound up with the early years of a child's existence and with the ahistorical fact of lengthy biological dependence of children on parents and adults.

On this score, Norman Brown has been more meticulous than Marcuse in spelling out the harsh implications of repression and the problematic role of childhood. In two chapters from *Life Against Death,* "Sexuality and Childhood" and "Death and Childhood," Brown thrusts at the heart of the generational issue, stressing that a full understanding of the Oedipus complex can be gained only when seen in relation to the impact of Thanatos, the death instinct.[17] Less Marxist and more Freudian than Marcuse, Brown's presentation is, in many respects, a far more radical reinterpretation of Freud's ideas.

Unwilling to accept the Marxist principle that specific historical factors alone are the root cause of human misery, Brown probes much deeper into the fundamental drives of human existence. According to him there can be no vision of a future nonrepressive society, as envisaged by radical thinkers, unless the psychological implications are considered. There is, he argues, "a vacuum in the Marxist utopia."[18] Unless one can conceive of a goal beyond economic necessity, there can be no relief from personal and social unhappiness. Freud's unique importance consists in his realization that the "essence of man lies not in the reality-principle but in repressed unconscious desires."[19]

Whereas Marcuse largely avoids detailed discussion of the relations between young and old, Brown is acutely conscious of the fact that prolonged parental responsibility and prolonged childhood dependence are the key to an understanding of the human condition. The attempts on the part of Marxists to historicize Freud break down partly on the simple fact that humanity's sexual organization and social organization

> are so deeply interconnected that we cannot say which came first, but can only assume a simultaneous evolution (whether sudden or gradual) of both.
>
> The critical institution in the transition from ape to man, the link between man's sexual and social organization, is parenthood, with the prolonged maintenance of children in a condition of helpless dependence. That parenthood implies family organization of some sort or another, and that family organization is the nucleus of all social organization, are anthropological axioms which Freud accepted and built into his structure. Freud's originality consists in drawing attention to the consequences of prolonged parenthood and prolonged infantile dependence on the sexual life of both parents and children.[20]

As a result, for the parents there is a close connection between the pleasure principle of the enjoyment of sex and the reality principle of the burdens of parenthood. For the child, in being released from concerns over the harshness of reality, free rein is given to seek out the "essential desires of the human being, without repression, and under the sign of the pleasure principle."[21] At the same time, the reliance on parental care leads to a need to be loved, which has an impact on later social interaction. "This psychological vulnerability is subsequently exploited to extract submission to social authority and to the reality principle in general."[22] But this control is not the essence of repression. Noting that Freud had in the course of time come to the conclusion that repression was basically caused by anxiety (and not the other way round, as he had originally thought), Brown seeks the cause of that anxiety—and finds it not in the outside world, with its reality principle, "but inside the child himself, making repression essentially self-repression."[23]

Claiming that Freud never fully developed some of his later writings on anxiety and its relation to infantile sexuality and instinctual ambivalence, Brown then proceeds to pursue these implications himself. He finds that the anxiety and ambivalence that are associated with infantile sexuality and that are the cause of repression must be "related to the death instinct."[24] Brown claims that "anxiety is the ego's incapacity to accept death" and he goes on to argue that "When Freud speaks of instinctual ambivalence in the infant, he has in mind love and hate; but . . . his death instinct must be taken more seriously than he took it, and systematically applied to the analysis of infancy."[25] The key to Brown's theory is that Eros and Thanatos, life and death, are closely bound up with each other. Freud, despite his preoccupation with both themes, failed to perceive the qualitative nature of the interconnection. Whereas Freud ignored the trauma of birth, Brown sees the biological birth of a baby as also signifying death. All organisms are destined to die; more directly and immediately, the birth of a baby marks the death of a fetus. The separation from the mother becomes the prototypical precedent of future separations, with the ensuing anxieties that they invariably engender:

> Freud's own analysis of anxiety shows, although Freud himself never said so, that there is a close and deep connection between anxiety and the death instinct. Anxiety is a response to experiences of separateness, individuality, and death. The human child, which at the mother's breast experiences a new and intense mode of union, of living, and of loving, must also experience a new and intense mode of separation, individuality, and death. . . . In the human family the expansion of Eros onto a new and higher level entails the expansion of death onto a new and higher level.[26]

Each separation from the mother is felt as though it were a death, and so, psychically, the infant is constantly experiencing death.

Brown analyzes the impact of the ambivalence—birth and death, loving and then leaving, bonding and separation—at the stages described by Freud as oral and anal. Then, within this new framework, he reinterprets the next stage, the oedipal stage, as the oedipal project that is basically "the quest to conquer death by becoming father of oneself,"[27] in essence a search for control of one's own fate. Brown argues that Freud showed changing positions and even confusion as to the precise nature of the Oedipus complex and as to whether it could ever be fully resolved. Brown suggests that the contradictions may be removed "if we think of the Oedipus project as the *causa-sui* (father-of-oneself) project, and therefore in essence a revolt against death generally, and specifically against the biological principle separating mother and child."[28]

Such an expansion and reinterpretation of Freud's concept of the Oedipus complex is so drastic that it inevitably raises questions as to whether the term "Oedipus" is at all applicable here or in any sense meaningful. Yet these ideas are of potentially crucial importance for a broader understanding of generational conflict. What must be emphasized is that the connection between life and death, Eros and Thanatos, bonding and separating, facilitates an understanding not only of the anxieties of the infant but also—and with no less pertinence—of the anxieties of the adult. For the awareness of death, and of its ever-increasing proximity, is one of the primary concerns of the adult and a causative factor in the Rustum complex. The close interrelation of Eros and Thanatos has relevance not only in the intrapsychical conflicts of the individual but also within the cyclical intersection of the generations.

"The birth of the son," Hegel once wrote, "is the death of the father." Inasmuch as the organism is destined for death, awareness of death is heightened precisely at the period when the organism is most likely to create a successor generation. The anxieties of separation and death are not those of the child alone, caught up in the ambiguous reality of bonding and separation, but also of the adult, caught up in the ambiguous reality of joy in procreation contrasted with the burden of its obligations, and of the prospects of perpetuating the family line contrasted with the certainty of demise.

Both child and adult experience ambivalence and ambiguity. But the adult's anxiety is liable to be the greater, not because of residual oedipal problems from childhood but because of the existential problems of adulthood and parenthood, because of the heightened awareness of the vulnerability of the body—not the infant's but the adult's. The child undoubtedly senses anxiety from each separation—the trauma of birth, the denial of the breast at weaning, the withdrawal of love—but is partly sheltered from the full consequences, precisely because he cannot fully comprehend the ultimate separation, that of death. It is the greater comprehension of the adult that may lead to the greater general anxiety.

Indeed, it may even be possible, from this perspective, to reinterpret the crisis that overtook Freud on the death of his father. His father died at the age of eighty when Freud was already forty years old. It is generally thought that Freud's strong reaction to his father's death was caused by the fact that Freud realized that his parricidal childhood wish had now, at last, been consummated. Could it not be, however, that the real impact of his father's death lay not just in reawakening repressed memories of his own long-forgotten childhood hostility but also in triggering an awareness of his own inevitable mortality? In addition, the recent birth of his own children (the four youngest were born between 1891 and 1895)[29] and the fact that, during the five years of his crisis, all were going through their own oedipal struggles may have added to his anxieties, for here Freud became the first person to be apprised of the awesome knowledge that his own children had incestuous yearnings and matricidal or parricidal wishes (depending on the sex of the child).[30] Surely this fact must have affected him. Surely the death of his own father at the very time that some of his own children were, according to his developing ideas, wishing also for his own death must have led to acute tensions. Yet Freud seems to have been oblivious to this issue. As Bruce Mazlish notes:

In the 1890's when Freud was struggling through to his concept [the Oedipus complex] he was also experiencing what it was to be a father. . . . Is it too much to assume that Freud's awareness was over-determined, in the sense that he stood between the generations, gradually becoming conscious of feelings toward him—and of his *own* reawakened feelings toward them? Or were the latter too painful and shocking to be acknowledged?[31]

Altogether Freud's work shows a continuing reluctance to submit himself as a father to the same searching probes that he showed toward himself as a son. Reuben Fine, in a book full of praise for Freud's overall achievements, has, on this point, expressed surprise at Freud's "failure to examine more critically his relationships to his own children. In his self-analysis he was interested in his functioning as a child; how he behaved as a parent was apparently of no concern to him."[32]

The evidence that we do have of Freud as a father is of basically smooth relations with his children.[33] But then, his relations with his father also seemed to be satisfactory. However, this did not prevent him from realizing that beneath the tranquil external relationship lay inner turmoil, the extent and nature of which was only fully revealed after the death of his father, in the course of his self-analysis. Could similar considerations not be applicable in respect of Freud as father toward his own children: that beneath the tranquil external framework lay hidden turmoil—not his alone but, just as he claimed in respect of the Oedipus theme, common to much of humanity? Yet, the insights that Freud utilized so creatively in so many areas he never applied to an attempt to understand the problems of parenthood, the possibility that there might be feelings of hostility, the underlying reasons for them, and the larger societal and historical implications.

The reasons for this lacuna in Freud's work may only be surmised; but those like Brown, Paul Roazen, Ernest Becker, and other writers who have written of Freud's constant concerns over death and immortality, raise the possibility of an explanation for Freud's selective approach in this respect. It would seem that Freud saw the prospects of gaining immortality not through his own children (which is a cause of much tension and ambivalence) but through the success of his psychoanalytic movement. In fact, several writers on Freud have shown the paternal nature of Freud's relations with some of his disciples,[34] while there are also generational overtones in the two fainting fits that Freud had while engaged in debates with Jung, who was destined, at first, to be his successor.[35]

When Freud fainted in the course of a discussion with Jung about Ikhnaton, the ancient Egyptian ruler, it may be presumed that the cause of Freud's tension was not the details of the historical data, but the personal nature of their implications. Ikhnaton had erased his father's name from all monuments; Freud—ever ready to identify with famous figures from the past, and ever sensitive to his status in the future—seems here to be inwardly apprehensive that Jung, already heir apparent to the psychoanalytic movement, might similarly symbolically erase Freud's name by minimizing Freud's contribution or by deviating from his principles (as did actually happen several years later).

In other words, Freud found an outlet for his concerns about immortality not through his natural children but through his disciples. For almost any other writer this fact would be no more than an interesting item. In Freud's case it takes on an added dimension because so much of Freud's work revolved around generational questions and, at the personal level, around his feelings toward his father and his own fears of death. Seeking immortality through his work, Freud was, psychologically at least, freed from too much concern over his relations with his children, not just superficially but even at the deepest emotional level.

Conversely, inasmuch as Freud's personal concerns about the generations affected his work, they centered constantly on the son's attitude to the father. For Freud these concerns may have been heightened over the years, as some writers suggest, because of his increasing awareness of the extent to which he was, through his success, surpassing his father.

There are larger implications to these aspects of Freud's work. In contrast to Freud, for most adults the main everyday and ongoing problems of generational conflict center not around their parents but around their children. Not sufficiently cognizant of the imbalance in Freud's work in this regard, many of his followers and readers have accepted his model of generational conflict in which the source of the conflict lies with the children, while ignoring Freud's failure to deal with the many problems that directly affect them as adults and parents. Of these, one of the most delicate and complicated issues is their concern for immortality, which, unlike Freud, they seek through their children.

These factors may well explain the dissatisfaction that Brown and other perceptive and sympathetic critics of Freud have sensed about his work on the death instinct.

Although critical of Freud's approach in this regard, Brown has nevertheless seen the death instinct as the basis for fertile extrapolations. Seeing it as the cause of anxiety in and of itself, he has not been bound by the narrower Freudian use of the death instinct mainly in terms of death wishes or aggressive drives. Thus he writes that the "adult flight from death—the immortality promised in all religions, the immortality of familial corporations, the immortality of cultural achievements—perpetuates the oedipal project of becoming father of oneself: adult sublimation continues the oedipal project."[36] Brown stresses that death holds a legitimate fear for the human being. It is by no means only a lamentable cause of aggression and destruction; it is a frightening reality that all human beings must confront, consider, and come to terms with. But can these ideas be properly examined within the oedipal framework?

However indebted thinkers are to Freud for the initial stimulation of their own later extrapolations, there are surely situations where the very development of a theme renders the original Freudian concept meaningless. The "adult flight from death" is so removed from the sexuality of the child as to necessitate a separate conceptualization. It is true that both link up with concerns about the body; it is also true that in many instances adults may be troubled by unresolved issues dating back to their childhood and linked to their relationship with their parents. But the crises of adulthood cannot always be encompassed purely within the oedipal framework, as Brown and others are trying to do, without distorting the oedipal meaning as intended by Freud and as used by most orthodox Freudians. It is not only the residual impact of unresolved childhood problems that agitates the parent and adult. It is also the very real and complex problems of parenthood and adulthood per se. The nature of these problems is not essentially oedipal except inasmuch as the popularity of the term provides a handy, readily recognized conceptual tool. However, the very use of such a tool is liable to obfuscate the nature of the problem being investigated.

Ernest Becker has been particularly adept in spelling out the confusion often caused by adhering too closely to the original oedipal concept.[37] Focusing specifically on the nature of the death instinct, he has shown how its ultimate implications have been obscured for several reasons—because of the desire of Freud to shape its meaning in a manner compatible with his other theoretical ideas, because of the inability of later writers such as Brown to break free from Freud's original framework, and because of the tendency by readers selectively to concentrate on those aspects of Freud's theory that hold out reassuring solutions for the human dilemma.

Becker argues that Freud's failure to treat the issue of death adequately was due to the fact that it posed a potential threat to other aspects of his theoretical framework that stressed the instinctual basis of human problems. While acknowledging that Freud "in his later work . . . moved away from narrow sexual formulations of the Oedipus complex and turned more to the nature of life itself, to the general problems of human existence," Becker argues that Freud was too bound to his instinct theory to appreciate fully the existential implications of human existence and so "as always, he hedged."[38] Becker finds Freud's work on the death instinct ("the most important idea that emerged in his later writings"[39]) particularly relevant and revealing, for it was largely an attempt to patch up the deficiencies of his ideas on sexuality, libido, and aggression, without having to abandon his emphasis on the instinctual basis of human behavior.

Unfortunately, the result was a "fusion of truthful insight with fallacious explanation,"[40] so that "Freud's tortuous formulations on the death instinct can now securely be relegated to the dust bin of history."[41] By incorporating the death instinct as a part of the instinctive makeup of human beings, Freud could avoid the real issues of human existence: the protest against death, the fear of death, the repression of death. In fact, the major error of Freud's work, according to Becker, is that, inasmuch as man's body was a "curse of fate," it was not because of the drive and the desire for sexuality, but because of the despairing hope to avoid death. *"Consciousness of death* is the primary repression, not sexuality. . . . This is the repression on which culture is built. . . ."[42]

Becker argues that Freud felt that he

did not need to rework his vision of man from that of primarily a pleasure seeker of sex to that of the terrified, death-avoiding animal. All he had to do was to say that man carried death within him unconsciously as part of his biology. The fiction of death as an "instinct" allowed Freud to keep the terror of death outside his formulations as a primary human problem of ego mastery.[43]

But this fiction has outlasted Freud, and it continues to deceive even some of his critics. Thus, according to Becker, Brown's work has won popularity for the wrong reasons; people have gladly accepted its message of an unrepressed life, with joyful bodily expression, while ignoring its sober analysis of death. Brown himself is partly responsible for this, as he suggests that it is in living the body to the full that the fear of death may be overcome. When Brown claims that the unrepressed person would become strong enough to die and to cope with the guilt of infantile fantasies, Becker retorts that "guilt is not a result of infantile fantasy but of self-conscious adult reality."[44]

The problem of death is a major aspect of this reality. It cannot be resolved by the varied suggestions of many neo-Freudians—by finding joy in life, by freely expressing the sensuous pleasures of the body, by a carefree childhood, by the acquisitions of property and its related patrimony, by happy, creative work, by medical breakthroughs increasing life expectancy. All the visions of a future idyllic society break down at this point.

These strictures apply particularly to writers such as Marcuse who are determined to conjure up the possibilities of revolutionary new societies achievable in the foreseeable future. So determined is Marcuse to offer such solace that, according to Becker, he, too, fails to see that "there is a demonism in human affairs that even the greatest and most sweeping revolution cannot undo" and that finally all these exciting ideas "come back to the same basic thing: the impossibility of living without repression."[45]

If fear of death is the enemy—and the long line of thinkers, mystics, theologians, poets, and now scientific researchers attest to its all-pervasive quality as a disturber of human tranquility[46]—then there can be no ultimate human triumph.

Yet, by deft use of surplus repression, Marcuse does manage to imply that there is a resolution for the problems of death. "The derivatives of the death instinct operate only in fusion with the sex instincts. . . . Consequently, a qualitative change in the development of sexuality must necessarily alter the manifestation of the death instinct."[47] In his article, "The Ideology of Death," Marcuse develops these ideas and reiterates that our perceptions of death, like all other facets of social life, are historically determined. Since the truly free life can be constituted only when all causes of anxiety are removed,

> there can be (or rather there should be) no life without anxiety as long as death has not been conquered—not in the sense of a conscious anticipation and acceptance when it comes anyway, but in the sense of depriving it of its horror and incalculable power as well as of its transcendental sanctity. This means that the concerted and systematic struggle against death in all its forms would be carried beyond the socially tabooed limits.[48]

Marcuse sees a reluctance to allow such confrontation with the concept of death, because it would undermine the control that society possesses over its members, and its power to ensure submission to the reality principle. The fear of death thus becomes not an inherent part of the dilemma of human life but an ideology manipulated for the purpose of ensuring social control—in legal penalties, in war, in the allocation of scarce resources. Marcuse concludes "Society's use of death and its attitude toward death seems to strengthen the hypothesis concerning the historical character of the death instinct."[49]

Theodore Roszak has also criticized Marcuse's position on the death instinct.[50] Arguing that Marcuse does not hold out any real hopes for "reintegrating the death instinct," Roszak maintains that far from offering any radical vision, Marcuse "finishes sounding like some very pedestrian homely philosophy" in which we are urged to protest and struggle against death with only the "prospect of marginal gains like greater longevity and consolations for the dying." Although not empty promises, these are "very traditional ideals that scarcely need repetition from Marcuse."[51]

These critiques by Becker and Roszak of Marcuse's work are of particular importance. Both have obvious respect for his creative thinking; Roszak, in particular, acknowledges Marcuse's major contribution to the formation of the counterculture. Yet both are uneasy with his handling of the death instinct.

Becker in particular is insistent that we reconcile ourselves to the fact that there is no solution to the primary problem of death. If that be so, then modern radical thought has been unable to take us much beyond the traditional attempts of religion—so despised by both Marx and Freud[52]—

to provide comfort and succor in the face of the inevitability and finality of death.

However, the implications of such a pessimistic outlook affect not only the difficulties of dealing with the specific question of death, or of assessing the possibility of creatively reinterpreting some of Freud's basic writings; they also affect the nature of generational contacts.

The search for immortality is a deep and recurrent concern of humanity. It is the uncertainty of that quest and the anxiety that it engenders that underlie much of adult behavior. Yet, there is one aspect of that quest that has been ignored in almost all of the writings—the impact that the fear of death and the yearning for immortality is liable to have on the adult's attitude toward the generation that will succeed him, the generation that can ensure whether immortality will be sustained on earth—in the preservation of memories of those no longer alive, in the maintenance of their values.

By ignoring this aspect, radical writers have been able to project their enticing models of future utopian societies. From a radical perspective it can, of course, be argued that in an ideal future society without oppression there will be at least a positive attitude to the young. Both Marcuse and Max Horkheimer hint at just such a solution. Marcuse suggests that the very existence of a utopian society raises the possibility of death "without anxiety," since people may know that "what they love is protected from misery and oblivion,"[53] ignoring the fact that often it is the creators of new societies who are most concerned that their achievements will not be dissipated by the succeeding generation and who are most intent on using their recently acquired political power to impose conformity on their children in the present so as to ensure the continuity of their achievements in the future.

Horkheimer focuses more specifically on the projected possibility of a lessening of the power of the family, claiming that this will lead to the cultivation of a sense of community: "Out of the suffering caused by the oppressive conditions that prevail under the sign of bourgeois authority," a new society will arise transcending constricting family bonds, in which "children will not be raised as future heirs and will, therefore, not be regarded, in the old way, as 'one's own.' "[54]

But is this a realistic appraisal? Even ignoring the complex questions of fear of death and hopes of immortality, the radical writers have been as remiss as mainstream sociologists in ignoring age as a differentiating factor. For the fact is that no future utopian society can cancel this differentiation. Utopian societies may be classless, may educate their citizens to be completely blind to skin color, may guarantee equality between the sexes, may educate for religious toleration—but they cannot ignore the fundamental fact of age difference.

Power will always be in the hands of the adults, and the wisdom and compassion with which they exercise and share that power will always be a factor to be examined empirically. The reluctance of most radicals to give this condition sufficient recognition is a fundamental flaw in their position. Only on rare occasions do radical writers pay attention to the oppression of the young, arising not from particular historical and economic conditions, nor from their membership in a larger deprived group—of class, race, ethnicity or sex—but from their very powerlessness and their dependence as young people.

An article by William Domhoff is a rare exception, when as a radical writer he acknowledges the relevance of age as a determining factor in social life and as being biologically based.[55] In place of a rigid commitment to historical materialism, Domhoff's "Archimedean point is man's long infancy and its inevitable concomitants. This must be the starting point, because it is man's starting point *qua* man."[56]

Even analyses based on the importance of changing historical conditions must take due account of fundamental psychological premises such as the Freudian concept of repression. Domhoff explains that, "oppression is the inevitable fate of humanity due to the anxiety of the helpless infant. Anxiety, the prototype of which is missing mother, causes repression and the cultural process (which attempts to both maintain and overcome repression)."[57]

Domhoff, while recognizing that this is different from the pure Marxist theoretical position, nevertheless insists that his own position could be seen as "a supplement to Marxism."[58] Thus he draws parallels between the infant's dependence and the dependence and passivity of the masses and depicts the ruling class as father symbols. As a supplement to radical thought, Domhoff's approach is important. But it remains a supplement, not a solution. The problem still remains that for the main part radical thinkers have failed to fully realize the unique nature of age differentiation. The young are the only deprived group in society whose position is not only a consequence of mutable historical and economic factors but also is bound up with the biological fact of dependence.

The solution to the deprived position of the young will not come automatically as a consequence of other major radical and progressive changes. Even if a classless society is established, even if all racial, ethnic, and religious prejudices and discriminations are removed, even if women achieve their liberation in the family and in society, we will still be left with the problem of the last deprived minority group: the minority of minors.

References

1. See Sigmund Freud, *Civilization and Its Discontents,* in *The Standard Edition of the Complete Psychological Works,* edited by James Strachey, 24 vols. (London: Hogarth Press, 1953–66), vol. 21.

2. Gad Horowitz, *Repression: Basic and Surplus Repression in Psychoanalytic Theory: Freud, Reich and Marcuse* (Toronto: University of Toronto Press, 1977), p. 2.

3. See especially Wilhelm Reich, *The Mass Psychology of Fascism* (New York: Farrar, Straus & Giroux, 1970); *Sex-Pol: Essays, 1929–1934* (New York: Random House, 1966); and *The Sexual Revolution: Toward a Self-Governing Character Structure*, 4th ed., rev. (New York: Farrar, Straus & Giroux, 1969).

4. Reich, *The Mass Psychology of Fascism*, p. 30.

5. Ibid., p. 53.

6. Francis H. Bartlett, *Sigmund Freud: A Marxian Essay* (London: Victor Gollancz, 1937). For a contrary view, see Reuben Osborn, *Freud and Marx: A Dialectical Study* (London: Victor Gollancz, 1938). For a good survey of the attempts to merge Freudianism and Marxism, see Russell Jacoby, *Social America: A Critique of Conformist Mythology from Adler to Laing* (Boston: Beacon Press, 1975).

7. Bartlett, *Sigmund Freud*, p. 67.

8. See, for instance, Max Horkheimer, "Authority and the Family," in *Critical Theory—Selected Essays* (New York: Herder & Herder, 1972), pp. 47–128. For a similar approach written after the war, see Horkheimer, "Authoritarianism and the Family," in Ruth Nanda Ansher, ed., *The Family: Its Function and Destiny* (New York: Harper & Row, 1959), pp. 381–398. See also Erich Fromm's book of essays, *The Crisis of Psychoanalysis* (New York: Holt, Rinehart & Winston, 1970), especially chapter 2, "Freud's Model of Man and Its Social Determinants," and chapter 3, "Marx's Contribution to the Knowledge of Man." For a personal account of the search for a synthesis between Freud and Marx, see Erich Fromm, *Beyond the Chains of Illusion: My Encounter with Marx and Freud* (New York: Simon & Schuster, 1962).

9. Friedrich Engels, *The Origin of the Family, Private Property and the State* (New York: International Publishers, 1971).

10. See especially Herbert Marcuse, *Eros and Civilization* (Boston: Beacon Press 1955) and *Five Lectures: Psychoanalysis, Politics, and Utopia* (Boston: Beacon Press, 1970). For critical analyses of Marcuse's work see Alasdair MacIntyre, *Herbert Marcuse: An Exposition and a Polemic* (New York: Viking, 1970), and Sidney Lipshires, *Herbert Marcuse: From Marx to Freud and Beyond* (Cambridge, Mass.: Schnekman, 1974).

11. As noted in the previous chapter, a number of other writers have similarly seen a critical change taking place in the authoritarian role of the father—except that they all assign it to different periods. In contrast to the interwar years espoused by Marcuse, Frank Musgrove claims it took place in the early days of the classical Industrial Revolution, Fred Weinstein and Gerald Platt at the time that Freud was working on the Oedipus complex, and Henry Malcolm in the post-World War II years. See also Alexander Miterscherlich, *Society Without the Father* (New York: Harcourt, Brace, 1969).

12. Marcuse, "Obsolescence of the Freudian Concept of Man," in *Five Lectures*, p. 46.

13. Marcuse, "End of Utopia," in *Five Lectures*, p. 65.

14. Marcuse, *Eros and Civilization*, p. 164.

15. Horowitz, *Repression,* p. 196.

16. Robert Boocock, *Freud and Modern Society: An Outline and Analysis of Freud's Sociology* (London: Nelson, 1976), p. 163.

17. Norman O. Brown, *Life Against Death: The Psychoanalytical Meaning of History* (Middletown, Conn.: Wesleyan University Press, 1959). Chapter 3, "Sexuality and Childhood," pp. 23–39, and chapter 9, "Death and Childhood," pp. 110–136.

18. Ibid., p. 17.

19. Ibid.

20. Ibid., p. 24.

21. Ibid., p. 25.

22. Ibid.

23. Ibid., p. 112.

24. Ibid.

25. Ibid., p. 113, and see chapter 8, "Death, Time, and Eternity," pp. 87–109.

26. Ibid., p. 115.

27. Ibid., p. 120.

28. Ibid., p. 127.

29. The birth dates of Freud's children were: Oct. 16, 1887; Dec. 6, 1889; Feb. 19, 1891; April 6, 1892; April 12, 1893; and Dec. 3, 1895. See Ernest Jones, *The Life and Work of Sigmund Freud* (New York: Basic Books, 1963), vol. 1, p. 152.

30. The issue of the gender of the child is an extremely important one. Freud's ideas underwent a gradual change and were affected particularly by the work of Ruth Mack Brunswick (see, for example, her article, "The Pre-Oedipal Phase of the Libido Development," in *The Psychoanalytic Reader* [London: Hogarth Press, 1950]). On several occasions in his earlier work, Freud had referred to possible differences in the sexual development of male and female infants, but for the most part he continued to see the process as symmetrical. It is only in 1925 that he has a longer analysis of the lack of symmetry in the Oedipus relations (see "Some Psychical Consequences of the Anatomical Distinction between the Sexes" [1925] in *The Standard Edition,* 19: 248–258). Even so, in a work published in the same year, Freud continues to refer to the analogies in the oedipal development of boys and girls (see "An Autobiographical Study," in *The Standard Edition,* 20: 36.) For further discussion by Freud see "Femininity" in *New Introductory Lectures on Psychoanalysis* (1933), in *The Standard Edition,* 19: 243–247. It should be noted that though some people use the term Electra complex to signify the girl's oedipal problems, this phrase was not used by Freud. For an overall discussion of this subject, see Humberta Nagera, *Female Sexuality and the Oedipus Complex* (New York: Jason Aronson, 1975).

31. Bruce Mazlish, *James and John Stuart Mill: Father and Son in the Nineteenth Century* (New York: Basic Books, 1975), p. 33.

32. Reuben Fine, *The Development of Freud's Thought* (New York: Jason Aronson,

1973), p. 30. See also comments by Frank J. Salloway, *Freud: Biologist of the Mind* (New York: Basic Books, 1979), p. 190.

33.   See, for instance, Martin Freud, *Glory Reflected—Sigmund Freud—Man and Father* (London: Angus and Robertson, n.d.); A. A. Brill, "Reflections, Reminiscences of Sigmund Freud," in Hendrik M. Ruitenbeek, ed., *Freud As We Knew Him* (Detroit: Wayne State University Press, 1973), p. 158 (originally published in *Medical Leaves* 3 [1940]: 18–29). On another occasion Brill refers to the "bright spot which shone resplendently throughout his life. He was an ideal husband and father. Those who had the pleasure of being admitted to his family circle were deeply impressed by the placid and genial home environment. His relation to his children was ideal." ("Reminiscences of Freud," in Ruitenbeek, ibid., p. 148, and *The Psychoanalytic Quarterly* 9 [1940]: 177–183). For further biographical information on Freud, see Helen Walker Pune, *Freud, His Life and His Mind* (New York: Bell, 1959); Henri F. Ellenberger, *The Discovery of the Unconscious: the History and Evolution of Dynamic Psychiatry* (New York: Basic Books, 1970), chapter 7, "Sigmund Freud and Psychoanalysis," pp. 418–570. For critical approaches, see Nat Morris, *A Man Possessed: The Case History of Sigmund Freud* (Los Angeles: Regent House, 1974); R. M. Jurjevich, *The Hoax of Freudism: A Study of Brainwashing the American Professionals and Laymen* (Philadelphia: Norrance, 1974); Andrew Slater, *The Case Against Psychoanalysis* (New York: Harper, 1972). For a good broad selection of views on Freud, see Jonathan Miller, ed., *Freud, The Man, His World, His Influence* (London: Weidenfeld & Nicholson, 1972).

34.   See especially Paul Roazen, *Freud and His Followers* (New York: Alfred Knopf, 1971). See also Roazen, *Freud: Political and Social Thought* (New York: Vintage Books, 1963), and Roazen, *Brother Animal: The Story of Freud and Tausk* (New York: Alfred Knopf, 1969). See also K. Eissler's reply to the latter book, *Talent and Genius: The Fictitious Case of Tausk Contra Freud* (New York: Quadrangle, 1971).

35.   See Jones, *The Life and Work of Sigmund Freud*, vol. 1, p. 317; vol. 2, p. 55. For Jung's account of the incident, see C. G. Jung, *Memories, Dreams, Reflections* (New York: Random House, 1963), p. 153.

36.   Brown, *Life Against Death*, p. 127.

37.   Ernest Becker, *The Denial of Death* (New York: Free Press, 1973).

38.   Ibid., p. 97.

39.   Ibid.

40.   Ibid., p. 98.

41.   Ibid., p. 99.

42.   Ibid., p. 96.

43.   Ibid., p. 99.

44.   Ibid., p. 261.

45.   Ibid., p. 265.

46.   See, for instance, Jacques Choran, *Death and Western Thought* (New York: Collier, 1963).

47.   Marcuse, *Eros and Civilization*, p. 139.

48.   Marcuse, "The Ideology of Death," in H. Feifel, ed., *The Meaning of Death* (New York: McGraw-Hill, 1959), p. 71.

49.   Ibid., p. 72.

50.   Theodore Roszak, *The Making of a Counter Culture: Reflections on the Technocratic Society and Its Youthful Opposition* (Garden City, N.Y.: Doubleday Anchor, 1969).

51.   Ibid., p. 113.

52.   See Sigmund Freud, *The Future of an Illusion,* in *The Standard Edition,* vol. 21; Saul K. Padover, ed., *Karl Marx on Religion* (New York: McGraw-Hill, 1974). See also Hans Küng, *Freud and the Problem of God* (New Haven: Yale University Press, 1979).

53.   Marcuse, *Eros and Civilization,* p. 216.

54.   Horkheimer, "Authority and the Family," p. 124.

55.   G. William Domhoff, "Historical Materialism, Cultural Determinism and the Origin of the Ruling Classes," *Psychoanalytic Review* 56 (1969): 271.

56.   Ibid., p. 274.

57.   Ibid., p. 278.

58.   Ibid.

CHAPTER TWELVE
THE UTOPIAN HOPE

I am well aware of the pessimistic tone of much of this book, of the deterministic implications of its thesis, of the apparent inevitability of endless generational conflict, of a possible future in which parents and adults seem foredoomed to repeat whatever wrongs and injustices were inflicted on them when they were young. I sense the need to balance this exposition of parental/adult hostility by holding out the prospects of a resolution of the Rustum complex.

It is, after all, an essential part of Freudian thought, particularly as it has developed over the years, to seek what Freud called a "dissolution of the Oedipus complex."[1] Confrontation with oedipal yearnings is seen as a key aspect of the normal socialization process, during which children learn to form a proper gender identification with their parents and to build a superego. Furthermore, at the societal level, in collectively coping with the challenge of oedipal tensions, human beings acquire the resources to create and develop their culture.

Can similar features be assigned to the Rustum complex? It would be pleasant to conclude this book with a definitive model of harmonious generational interaction, but it would perhaps be pretentious to do so.

It is easy, but rather banal, to point out the need to eliminate child abuse and economic exploitation of the young; to enact protective measures for their benefit; to foster an atmosphere of love and understanding, in which infants are provided with nurturance, children with education, adolescents with rights, youth with freedom. But how does one translate these amorphous goals into concrete and specific standards? Family forms are so diverse, and oppressive measures are often elusively subtle. The hostilities of the adult generation are endemic and run deep; the sacrifices demanded of adults immense, their jealousies, their fears, and their resentments understandable.

It is much easier to catalogue the manifestations of, and reasons for, hostility (though even this task is clearly not the easiest) than it is to specify the means by which the hostilities may be eliminated or minimized. This is true, of course, of all social problems. There is a world of difference between describing and explaining the causes of racial prejudice and fashioning a world where discrimination will not be practiced. It is one thing to recognize the concept of class, another to set up a truly classless society. One may talk of religious pluralism and ecumenical understanding and yet be unable to resolve the theological differences, however much the prayers are all directed to the same God. It is easy to advocate equality of the sexes, hard to agree on the areas in which it should be sought and the manner in which such equality should be attained.

So it is with generational conflict. The ennobling sentiments of the United Nations Declaration on the Rights of Children provide little guidance for the parent at home disturbed by a crying baby in the middle of the night. The benevolent intentions of the adult generation are of little value when confronted by the direct challenge of their younger protégés seeking an equal share in their power and resources.

Age relations also involve more than relations among class, race, religious groups; more even than just dealing with troublesome children, teenage gangs or rebellious students. Ultimately, they involve family relations, and in talking of the family we are not dealing with abstractions, with anonymous totalities. We are dealing with our own kith and kin, with our parents and with our children. *We are dealing with ourselves.* There is a qualitative difference between hostility expressed toward other races, classes, or religions and that expressed between the generations, for the simple fact is that, whatever the nature of the clash, it so often begins and ends at home. It is this that gives an added degree of tension to age differentiation—a tension that may be approached only by a similarly intimate struggle between the sexes.

In no other area of social concern are our own subjective and personal experiences so much a part of our perception as in the case of generations. In no other area are we so bombarded with a kaleidoscope of vague and distant memories of our own childhood; of youthful hopes and ambitions for ourselves, fulfilled or frustrated; of hopes and ambitions for our children, realistic or excessive; of our own passage through the life cycle, of our growing awareness of our diminishing capacities; of the changing perspectives of time; of our final physical frailty.

We can perhaps think about, write about, read about race, religion, class, or ethnicity with a certain amount of detachment, but we cannot dissociate ourselves from descriptions of parent-child relations.

Even as I write, I am conscious of how much my own position between the generations determines the flow of thoughts and ideas, and the manner in which memories and experiences have intruded: my own socialization and education, the home, family and friends of my youth, my activities at school and in youth movements. I am to a large degree the product of parents whose love and concern was deep and reciprocated but with whom there was at one stage a clash over ideological beliefs and life styles. A price was paid for that clash, but rewards were reaped, by both sides, in the resolution of the conflict over the years. My understanding of the very thesis of this book has grown immeasurably through sharing my life with my own two young children whose development is a delight to watch, whose presence is a constant source of joy—and yet also, sometimes of worry and challenge and conflict—and whose lives I am helping to shape, while myself being affected by the tasks of parenthood.

While writing this book there have been times when I have searched within myself and found instances of negative feelings sensed toward my children, of pent-up anger, of resentment at burdensome toils. I hope that I have coped adequately with these feelings. I sense that acknowledging them has helped. So has an awareness of how widespread these feelings are among others, an awareness made more clear when discussing my thesis with friends, colleagues, and students. Often I have seen them moved to recount memories of hostility felt by them as emanating from their parents or from themselves toward their own children. There is a moment of recognition that makes for honesty and enables them to speak of feelings they had never before admitted.

To be a parent is to be overwhelmed by conflicting emotions and changing moods. Rarely has this ambivalence been so poignantly described as in Adrienne Rich's sensitive description of motherhood:

> My children cause me the most exquisite suffering of which I have any experience. It is the suffering of ambivalence: the murderous alternation between bitter resentment and raw-edged nerves, and blissful gratification and tenderness. Sometimes I seem to myself, in my feelings toward these tiny guiltless beings, a monster of selfishness and intolerance. Their voices wear away at my nerves, their constant needs, above all their need for simplicity and patience, fill me with despair at my own failures, despair too at my fate, which is to serve a function for which I was not fitted. And I am weak sometimes from held-in rage. There are times when I feel only death will free us from one another. . . .
>
> And yet at other times I am melted with the sense of their helpless, charming, and quite irresistible beauty—their ability to go on loving and trusting—their staunchness and decency and unselfconsciousness. *I love them.* But it's in the enormity and inevitability of this love that the sufferings lie.[2]

What is true of parents is true also, to a lesser degree, at the societal level. The middle years are only now starting to be analyzed as significant milestones in the life cycle, with characteristic crises, problems, and challenges, as well as potentialities for growth. From Erik Erikson's original extension of Freud's work[3] to the recent research by Daniel Levinson[4] there has been increasing evidence that the middle years, presumed to be stable and settled, are, in fact, volatile. Some of the thinking, however, is still permeated by concerns for the lingering influences of childhood, instead of by direct confrontation with present problems (as was shown in the discussion on the family in chapter 9).

Reinterpretation of Freud's ideas with continued use of oedipal principles is not sufficient to allow us to fully comprehend the essence of the problems of the middle-aged as they face their replacing the older generation and resisting the pressures from the youth waiting to replace them.

It is time for more forthright revelations of the kind that Rich and others have made. It will not do to hide behind a facade where we glibly reiterate the instinctive love we sense for our own progeny, or the simultaneous concern we have for the younger generation as a whole; where we soberly declare the value-free, objective framework of our attempts to study scientifically the problem of generational conflict; where we self-righteously assign blame for breakdowns in communication to the willful spite of ungrateful children or the irrational excesses of impulsive youth; or where we indulge ourselves by confessing loudly our guilt and failure as parents, at the same time secretly believing that there was nothing we could or should have done differently.

There is need, above all, for a ruthless honesty through which parents and adults can acknowledge the difficulties of their role and the hostilities that often arise; for a humility combined with wisdom to appreciate the responsibility of the power over the young they have been given; for the emotional and intellectual maturity to let go graciously and to accord the young the extra degrees of independence their accumulating capacities entitle them to; for a sensitivity to the needs of those adults who falter in their task of caring for the young instead of conveniently using them as the scapegoats for our own weaknesses; and for irrevocable determination to seek out new patterns of contact and communication across the gap that separates those whose pasts and futures unavoidably intermingle in the present.

What are the prospects for such new patterns of behavior among the generations? In chapters 10 and 11, I pointed out the dangers of seeing in new social phenomena any deep, fundamental metamorphosis and, in particular, the dangers of facile assumptions that novel experiments in living will quickly lead to large-scale transformation of society. The prognosis of most of those writing in the late 1960s and early 1970s was clearly wrong. Much has certainly changed (society is never static) but not necessarily in the direction predicted by writers partial to the counterculture of the young. It is easy to fall into the trap of seeing some recent advance in social arrangement, in science, or in ideological concepts as a breakthrough portending fundamental and far-reaching change.

Yet, there are two factors of recent times that do require further consideration. Neither provides any guarantee of change, whether for good or ill, but both have the potentiality to affect directly the nature of generational contact. One is the possibility of controlling reproduction; the second is the potential impact of a changing relationship between male and female, husband and wife, upon the relationship between old and young, parents and children.

Modern society has the choice, denied earlier generations, of controlling the consequences of the sexual drives. We need no longer have children because we know not how to avoid having them. This choice allows for spacing births and limiting their number. It is a choice made possible because of the development of relatively inexpensive and efficient contraceptive devices and because a decline in infant and early child mortality, combined with social-welfare programs, has drastically reduced the pressures on parents to have more children so as to ensure support for themselves in old age.

But we must be wary of hasty conclusions. To a large extent the possibility of choice is still theoretical and potential, not always practical. Religious and ideological issues impinge upon the question of the morality of contraceptive measures, particularly the vexing question of abortion. Serious medical questions have been raised about the safety and desirability of certain contraceptive measures. There is emotional reluctance to use some methods, especially sterilization procedures. There are differing political reactions to the demographic realities of fluctuating population figures, and there is the frightening specter of population decimation owing to sudden atomic warfare, recurrent famine, or gradual ecological disaster.

Then again, the model of making a calculated choice with respect to children is hardly applicable to that part of the world's population—probably over half—that has yet to reach the minimum point of economic and physical security. Finally, even a rational choice of having or not having children may have unintended and unforeseen consequences.

So the basic question still remains: within the family and in society at large, how do two or more generations share the same space and time span, learning to live with each other in mutual tolerance, understanding, and cooperation? How can the hostilities be controlled; specifically for adults, how can the legitimate needs and demands of the young be met; how can adult fears of diminishing power, of disturbing social change, and of eventual mortality be mitigated?

Some of these concerns are closely allied with the other social variable that impinges directly on family life: sexual differentiation. Inevitably, a close connection exists between the manner in which male and female interact and the way in which old and young interact. This is a theme that recurs in the work of many writers dealing with one or the other of the two variables. It is most noted in the work of one of the leading feminists of the nineteenth century, Ellen Key,[5] and is strongly echoed in recent books by Jessie Bernard and Dorothy Dinnerstein.[6] There is, indeed, an eternal triangle—husband/father, mother/wife, son/daughter—and it is this interconnection that complicates the chances of resolving either the battle of the sexes or the conflict between the generations—just as the problems of race, class, ethnicity, religion, language are exacerbated when they overlap with each other. What makes both sex and age different from other variables is that they almost always overlap with each other and that they almost always are bound up with the family.

Recent developments making for changes in male-female interaction, more than any progress in the relationships among class, racial and religious groups, are likely to have the greatest impact on generational contacts. But the promise of progress mingles with the dangers of regression. In the resolution of the issues between male and female, the young may benefit— or alternatively, they may suffer as a result of the accommodations reached between the sexes. For the major factor affecting male-female relationships is not, and never really has been, physical strength, intellectual capacity, or emotional maturity, but one pragmatic question: *who will mind the children?*

Pregnancy and breast feeding clearly orient women to child-rearing tasks and have led many radical thinkers to talk regretfully of the "biological tragedy" of women, which prevents them—unfortunately—from taking their full place in the world. But neither pregnancy nor breast feeding is an automatic barrier to full female participation in political, economic, and social life (any more than compulsory conscription for young men is a bar to their subsequent advancement, despite their being removed temporarily from the normal social life). Nor, on the other hand, are they barriers to full male participation in nurturant child-rearing activities in the home. History records both female-dominated societies and male-oriented family arrangements. More than the biological factors of life, it is their ideological interpretation that determines the manner in which societies resolve the question of sexual differentiation. Modern society is at present in the throes of just such an ideological struggle.

Sorence Boocock sums up the interlocking nature of the confrontation between the sexes and the potential impact it has on the relationship between the generations:

> . . . parenthood may bring to the surface unresolved, and even unrecognized conflicts about the appropriate roles of men and women. However much in principle the couple may value sexual egalitarianism, the arrival of a child means that someone must be available twenty-four hours a day to care for it. It seems unlikely that current difficulties in the relationship between men and women in our society will be resolved until questions concerning both the value of children and the locus of responsibility for their routine care and supervision are acknowledged and resolved.[7]

It can be argued as a corollary that difficulties in the relationship between young and old are connected with the manner in which male and female, father and mother, will determine the nature of their respective responsibilities to the young. This is true both in society and in the family. On the one hand, increasing demands are being made for women to take their rightful place outside the home; on the other hand, increasing demands are being made on the father to take on a greater role inside the home. Linked with this is the prospect of using child-care centers to facilitate these changes.[8]

Patriarchal society has, over the centuries, decreed that woman's place is in the home, where she is charged with the difficult and sacred task of rearing the next generation. From Bachofen and Engels[9] to today's feminist writers,[10] the historical background and present consequences of patriarchy have been set out in academic and polemical forms. In the past decade women have made a concerted political effort to challenge the traditional structure. Women's struggles for the right to vote, to enjoy a full education, to earn equal pay, have all been preludes to the ultimate battle: the struggle to determine who should bear the responsibility for the care of children. Some writers, most notably Dinnerstein,[11] have claimed that there can be no real meaning to all these other issues until the issue of child-rearing is resolved; this is an issue that relates not merely to the private fancies of individual couples but also to the manner in which society facilitates the desire of couples to share in both the income-producing and child-rearing aspects of family life, in providing day-care centers, paternity leave as well as maternity leave, staggered working hours, and so on. Yet, while the life-style of men and women will be crucially affected by the outcome of this struggle (and the outcome is still far from clear), it is the noncombatant children who will reap the consequences.

How will their interests be affected by the new forms of child-rearing sought by women? How much consideration is even given to children's needs in the course of this battle? Are women insisting that fathers be brought into the home only in order to release themselves for more work outside the home, or because the child needs the additional nurturant experiences? Are there pressures being exerted for an extension of day-care centers only to allow women greater opportunities to work, or also because these may be important socializing experiences (meeting with peers and other adults) for the child?[12]

The concept of motherhood is undergoing a thorough reexamination as feminist writers challenge the impositions traditionally devolving upon that role. But, as some of them realize, the role of motherhood cannot be restructured unless related changes are instituted in the role of fatherhood; and a change in both these roles will materially affect the nature of childhood.

It is interesting to note that some of the most difficult problems plaguing utopian societies dedicated to egalitarianism have often centered on the question of child-rearing. It is this that most often threatens their ideology of equality and strains their social structure. For while it is relatively easy to allow women to take on "men's work" in the fields, factories, and offices, it is extremely difficult to persuade men to do "women's work," especially when such work confines them to the home with its many boring chores.

Despite the reluctance to perform such work, there are indications that men have the capacity and even the desire to be involved in child-rearing activities. Ian Suttie, as noted in chapter 3,[13] believes that the desire to participate in nurturant functions is so deep that much paternal hostility actually derives from the exclusion from such activities, and the ensuing envy that is engendered. Suttie's position contains an apparent contradiction that must be considered. If he is right, why do males not insist on greater involvement in child-rearing? While pregnancy and nursing are biological factors that clearly limit the nurturant capabilities of the father, it is the social interpretations and arrangements that determine the extent of these limitations. Yet the males who, according to Suttie, suffer the frustrations have used their political power to set up the present arrangements and seem to be largely satisfied with them, whereas it is mainly women who are seeking a change. Why is this so? I am not certain there is any clear answer. Three potential avenues of enquiry seem worthwhile pursuing. The first is that the deep-felt but repressed jealousy of the male for the nurturant capacities of the female gives rise to an ideological rationale that denigrates tasks that *ab initio* are not wholly attainable for males because of the women's biological capacity for nursing.

Second, the practice of father's mock childbirth (*couvade*) and other reactions at the time of childbirth suggests that occasionally male frustrations find symbolic expression. Till recently couvade was considered a quaint primitive practice—but in the last few years, a number of medical researchers have drawn attention to similar widespread manifestations in modern society of the fathers' abdominal pains, one project suggesting that over 10 percent of fathers have couvade-style symptoms at the time of childbirth, in some cases necessitating hospitalization.[14] Since these symptoms are generally ignored, the number may in fact be far higher.

A third hypothesis is that the tasks of child-rearing are so difficult that males have used their social power to resolve their ambivalence by adopting an ideological stance that clearly defines a sexual division of labor. In the long run, the burdens of parenthood seem to have repelled men more than the joys attracted them.

This paradox need not minimize the force of Suttie's insight about the frustrated desires of males to be more active in expressing tender emotions. If a transformation were to come about in gender roles, and if the daily burden of coping with children were to be more equally shared, then certain possibilities would arise. If greater involvement by both parents were to alleviate much of the pressures on the mother and activate the subdued nurturant inclinations of the father, certain positive benefits might result for the child.

Anthropologists, among them Ashley Montagu,[15] have shown how important and meaningful tactile sensations are to everyone, particularly since they are "our first means of communication,"[16] the first means by which a young infant can communicate with adults. Montagu stresses the vital importance of touching, holding, rocking, massaging, and caressing for the well-being for the child. These are experiences and gestures that speak of affection and acceptance. In our society, they come primarily from the mother, but they can also be given by other adults, including the father. Montagu devotes a chapter to "tender, loving care,"[17] quoting extensively from research among animals and humans to show its value to the young. In the same vein neuropsychologist James Prescott[18] even sees a correlation between denial of physical affection to children and the growth of violence, while a growing number of writers on infant and child care are stressing the importance of both maternal and paternal bonding with children, starting with childbirth, in order to provide the child with basic needs.[19] The importance of such change in child-rearing would have direct implications for the Oedipus complex.

Whereas Freud saw the child headed for an inevitable conflict with the parent of the opposite sex, in the course of which a key phase of socialization took place allowing for subsequent harmony only after the "dissolution of the Oedipus complex," there is the possibility of a totally different process taking place.

Seymour Fisher and Roger Greenberg, on the basis of their broad evaluation of research on the Oedipus complex, succinctly spell out an alternative approach to father-son relations:

> An area of major defect we have discerned in Freud's theories relates to his description of how male identification and superego formation evolve in the course of resolving the Oedipal dilemma. . . . After a detailed sifting of the empirical literature . . . we concluded that Freud was definitely incorrect in the emphasis he placed upon fear as a motivating force in the identification process and possibly wrong in the role he ascribed to fear in the formation of the superego. The scientific data suggest that it is the father's warmth and nurturance that are particularly important in persuading his son to be masculine like him and perhaps also to accept his moral norms. The evidence opposing Freud is sufficiently strong to justify doubting his formulations in these areas.[20]

However, Fisher and Greenberg do not ask where this fear comes from. According to Freudian theory, it is a result of the child's perception that the parent will be aware of the child's rivalry and ensuing hostility—basically, what he fears is the parent's vengeance for this rivalry and hostility.

Unfortunately, the extensive review of research by Fisher and Greenberg on all aspects of Freudian theory failed to examine fully the key question of the child's hostility. This is a serious flaw—for if there is no child hostility, then there would be no need for the subsequent fears of the child. Unless, of course, the fear was derived from another source. It is precisely this that another Freudian writer, Dorothy Bloch,[21] has suggested. In her radical reappraisal of pure Freudian thought, she suggests that the child's fears stem from his perception of the parents' prior hostility. In terms of the Fisher-Greenberg thesis, it may well be that it is the father's perceived harshness that causes the child's fear and that the father's warmth and nurturance, if freely and openly displayed, would remove many childhood problems that are regularly and probably incorrectly interpreted as being of an oedipal origin.

Although their review of the research ignores the question of child hostility, Fisher and Greenberg do suggest, in an aside, that it may be an unwarranted assumption in the normal process of socialization. They write:

> Freud's account of the male's relationship with his father is saturated with the language of antagonism. There now seems to be some reason to dispute the validity of such a schema as a context for exploring the history of a man's adventures with his father.[22]

But take away the son's antagonism, and the theoretical basis of the Oedipus complex is threatened. Fisher and Greenberg do not say as much, but their evidence seems to lead in this direction. In fact, they only partially appreciate the import of what they are saying. For a perception of the relationship with the father devoid of hostility would undermine the oedipal thesis and significantly affect the Freudian analysis of parent-child relations. Fisher and Greenberg do suggest a change in the oedipal perspective, but they consider it as no more than a minor amendment in one of what they call the several mini-theories of the total Oedipus theory. According to them: "The resolution of the Oedipus crisis would be based primarily on warmth and trust rather than fear."[23] And so, as they elucidate:

> If oedipal tension between father and son is actually dissipated as the result of a friendly rather than frightening transaction, this would give the oedipal phase a meaning quite different from that usually ascribed to it in psychoanalytic circles.[24]

It certainly would. And it would do more. It would provide an admission that often it is the harshness of parental behavior that is the source of the child's problems and that the child's fear of prior parental hostility is a relevant factor in child-parent relations.

It seems to me that two key factors emerge from these various attempts at reassessment of oedipal thinking, one involving the perceptions and problems of children, the other involving those of adults. For the former it seems that many innate and legitimate desires for affection by children are being both misinterpreted and denied.[25] On the other hand, many of the problems of adulthood and parenthood are being casually attributed to unresolved oedipal patterns. By failing to appreciate and to come to terms with the problems of the latter we are also failing to fully appreciate, understand, and at least partly resolve the problems of the former. I stress "partly," for here is the final paradox of generational conflict: if children are given the nurturance and the tenderness they want and need, it is indeed likely that the "oedipal" manifestations of hostility by the child may be avoided. But that is all.

We will still be left with the Rustum complex: with the burdens of parenthood that make nurturance a task of almost superhuman dimensions. And as we grow older we will still face the challenge of social change, the fear of death, the hopes of immortality. These elementary facts of life will continue to haunt us, just as they have haunted our ancestors. As our awareness increases of the problematic nature of the adult years, we would do well not to immerse ourselves in a study of residual oedipal problems but to directly confront the existential problems posed by adulthood and parenthood. If not, we will find ourselves permitting the very real, troublesome, and threatening problems of adulthood to be ignored. We will be trivializing our very maturity. We will be allowing the adult we now are to foist blame on the child we once were.

Childhood experiences are obviously important. But, whatever impact they have upon us, we cannot use them indiscriminately as an excuse to allow us to avoid confrontation with who we are and what we are today. Our childhood is important, and so is the impact of our parents—and if psychotherapy demands a return to the past, so be it. But equally important is the childhood of our children today and our own behavior as parents and as adults. Much contemporary psychotherapy is indeed focusing on the existential problems of the patient. My concern is, however, not with therapy but with social life as it is played out each day.

Let us concede: the problems of parenthood and adulthood are awesome. We need to confront them directly. We need also an overall perspective that will allow us to escape the confines of our own immediate experiences so that we can see beyond the fluctuating concerns that bog down in explanations limited to particular passing issues. Thus the torrent of writing on the generational gap of the 1960s gives way to an evaluation of what happened to the gap in the 1970s; or child abuse becomes an issue in the seventies as though some new epidemic has suddenly arrived on the scene. And so we find ourselves on a ceaseless treadmill, constantly shocked by the latest manifestation of generational conflict just when we were gratefully rejoicing in the solution of whatever problem it was that had only yesterday occupied our attention.

The truth is that there is an ebb and flow in generational conflict. The forms of its expression change, but the structural foundations for its existence remain. Both the youth revolt of the 1960s and child abuse in the 1970s are part of a larger problem of adult and parental hostility. The 1980s may bring some new issue to the fore. Class, religious, and national struggles also change in their expression—but their essence is seen to be the same. The women's struggle for equal pay today is not considered as separate from the struggle a generation ago for women's suffrage. They are inextricably connected, the former a logical development of the latter.

Nor is it relevant to state, as some people do, that most youth do not rebel, nor most children get beaten. Social struggles do not necessarily require majority participation. It is militant protest or, alternatively, extreme victimization, or both, even if borne by a minority, that determines the nature of social struggles. We would be better attuned to seeking rational responses and possible solutions to generational problems, as they emerge into our consciousness, if we could recognize the larger framework within which they are contained.

For what is needed above all is an awareness of tensions and hostilities that we are too often prone to ignore. What is needed is an appreciation of adult failings and errors instead of hasty denunciations of the young protagonists. Such awareness may produce the sensitivity that we need in order to minimize the hostilities and to rectify the faults.

But, in any event, we should have no illusions as to the enormity of the task, for there may in fact be no complete solution.

There may be no future utopia in which young and old will always harmoniously share their lives; in which the latter will be gracious in moving on, magnanimous in handing over power, and sagacious in controlling their frustrations, resentments, and fears. We may be doomed to a search that has no end. But that is no reason for abandoning the search and for evading the issue. On the contrary, the very difficulties obligate us to embark on this search with compassion, courage, and candor.

For the sake of our children.

And for our own sake.

References

1. Sigmund Freud, "The Dissolution of the Oedipus Complex" (1924), in *The Standard Edition of the Complete Psychological Works,* edited by James Strachey, 24 vols. (London: Hogarth Press, 1953–66), 19: 173–182. This is only a short exposition of how the process of the dissolution takes place, but it forms an ongoing part of

Freud's writing; see, for example, *The Ego and the Id* (1923), in *The Standard Edition,* 19: 12–68.

2. Adrienne Rich, *Of Woman Born: Motherhood as Experience and Institution* (New York: Bantam, 1977), pp. 1–2.

3. See, for example, Erik Erikson, "Identity and the Life Cycle," *Psychological Issues,* Monograph 1 (1959). For a personal description of the crises of middle age, see Arnold J. Mandell, *Coming of Middle Age: A Journey* (New York: Summit Books, 1977). For a good short survey, see Stanley H. Cath, "Some Dynamics of the Middle and Late Years," *Smith College Studies in Social Work* 33 (1963): 97–126.

4. Daniel J. Levinson, *The Seasons of a Man's Life* (New York: Knopf, 1978).

5. Ellen Key, *The Century of the Child* (New York: G. P. Putnam's Sons, 1912).

6. Jessie Bernard, *The Future of Marriage* (New York: Bantam Books, 1973); Dorothy Dinnerstein, *The Mermaid and the Minotaur: Sexual Arrangements and Human Malaise* (New York: Colophon, 1976).

7. S. Sorence Boocock, "The Social Context of Childhood," *Proceedings of the American Philosophical Society* 119 (1975): 423.

8. For an excellent analysis of child care, with its implications for society, see Urie Bronfenbrenner, "Ecology of Human Development," *Proceedings of the American Philosophical Society,* 119 (1975): 439, and "Toward an Experimental Ecology of Human Development," *American Psychologist* 32 (1977): 513; Orville G. Brim, "Childhood Social Indications: Monitoring the Ecology of Development," *Proceedings of the American Philosophical Society* 119 (1975): 413. These articles stress the need to maintain close contacts between child-care centers and the family.

9. Johann J. Bachofen, *Myth, Religion and Mother Right: Selected Writings,* trans. by Ralph Manheim (Princeton: Princeton University Press, 1967); and Friedrich Engels, *The Origin of the Family, Private Property and the State* (New York: International Publishers, 1971).

10. See especially Amaury de Riencourt, *Sex and Power in History* (New York: David McKay, 1974).

11. Dinnerstein, *The Mermaid and the Minotaur.*

12. In recent research Laurence Steinberg and Cindy Green point out that many women interviewed had placed their children in day-care centers for their own convenience. Not only were they unaware of the many potential benefits that their children might derive, but they also felt guilty about what they had done. See "Three Types of Day Care: Choices, Concerns and Consequences" (unpublished paper, 1978).

13. Ian Suttie, *The Origins of Love and Hate* (London: Kegan Paul, Trench, Trubner, 1935).

14. For a summary of the literature and for case-study examples, see Jesse O. Cavenar and William W. Weddington, "Abdominal Pain in Expectant Fathers," *Psychosomatics* 19 (December 1978): 761–768. See also W. Trethowan and M. Conlan, "The Couvade Syndrome," *British Journal of Psychiatry* 3 (1965): 57; W. Wainwright, "Fatherhood as a Precipitant of Mental Illness," *American Journal of Psychiatry* 123 (1966): 40. For an earlier article, see F. Boehm, "The Femininity

Complex in Man," *International Journal of Psychoanalysis* 11 (1930): 444. Boehm refers to parturition envy—man's wish to bear a child, which is similar to Suttie's Zeus jealousy. Suttie also discusses couvade as "an expression of unconscious desire on the part of the husband to share in the production of the child" (p. 108).

15.   Ashley Montagu, *Touching: The Human Significance of the Skin* (New York: Columbia University Press, 1971).

16.   Ibid., p. 1.

17.   Ibid., chapter 4, pp. 92–184.

18.   James W. Prescott, "Bodily Pleasure and the Origins of Violence," *The Futurist* 9 (April 1975): 64–74.

19.   See especially Marshall H. Klaus and John H. Kennell, *Maternal-Infant Bonding* (St. Louis: C. V. Mosby, 1976).

20.   Seymour Fisher and Roger P. Greenberg, *The Scientific Credibility of Freud's Theories and Therapy* (New York: Basic Books, 1977), p. 404.

21.   Dorothy Bloch, "Fantasy and the Fear of Infanticide," *Psychoanalytic Review* (1974): 5; *So the Witch Won't Eat Me* (Boston: Houghton Mifflin, 1978).

22.   Fisher and Greenberg, *The Scientific Credibility of Freud's Theories and Therapy,* p. 406.

23.   Ibid., p. 222.

24.   Ibid.

25.   For excellent descriptions of the lives of children, see Violet Oaklander, *Windows to Our Children: A Gestalt Therapy Approach to Children and Adolescents* (Moab, Utah: Real People Press, 1978). This book is valuable not only for therapy but also for its insights into the lives of all young people. For the early years of life, see Selma Fraiberg, *The Magic Years* (New York: Scribner, 1968). See also Mary Ellen Goodman, *The Culture of Childhood: Child's Eye View of Society and Culture* (New York: Teacher's College Press, 1970). For a broad analysis of the academic literature see Julius Segal, *A Child's Journey* (New York: McGraw-Hill, 1978).

AUTHOR INDEX

SUBJECT INDEX

About the author

Leon Sheleff, born in South Africa and today a citizen of Israel, earned his B.A. and LL.B. at the University of Cape Town, and his M.A. and Ph.D. at the Ohio State University. He is a member of both the Faculty of Law and the Department of Sociology at Tel Aviv University and has taught also at the University of Dayton, the University of Vermont, and the University of California at Irvine. He is the author of *The Bystander: Behavior, Law, Ethics* and is a frequent contributor to journals of sociology and of law.